PRAISE FOR
DEBUNKING HOWARD ZINN

"It's about time someone published a comprehensive answer to Howard Zinn's bestselling *A People's History of the United States,* which is the *Mein Kampf* of the Hate America Left. Zinn was a lifelong communist and sycophantic admirer of Stalin and Mao and the most murderous regimes in human history. But, for Zinn, the real source of evil in the world was his own country—tolerant, inclusive, and free. Mary Grabar has done Americans and the freedoms they have championed a great service by writing a definitive exposure of Zinn's treasonous life, along with a damning refutation of his dishonest, malignant, and ignorant work."

> —**DAVID HOROWITZ,** founder of Students for Academic Freedom and the David Horowitz Freedom Center and author of *Radical Son: A Generational Odyssey* and *The Black Book of the American Left*

"At long last we have a comprehensive critique of Howard Zinn's *A People's History of the United States,* an execrable work of pseudo-history, full of mistakes, lies, half-truths, and smears. Students and scholars alike are in Mary Grabar's debt for her incisive, powerful, and timely takedown of Zinn's highly popular, but utterly tendentious, 'study.' Reasonable people, regardless of their personal politics, should laud the publication of *Debunking Howard Zinn.*"

> —**PETER A. COCLANIS,** Albert R. Newsome Distinguished Professor of History and director of the Global Research Institute at the University of North Carolina at Chapel Hill

"Mary Grabar has produced a devastating analysis of the lies, plagiarism, violation of academic standards, and simple-minded platitudes that characterize Howard Zinn's bestselling *A People's History of the United States*. That Zinn is taken seriously as a historian is sad commentary on the teachers who rely on his fantasies and a terrible disservice to the students who are forced to read it. And, as Grabar demonstrates, it has contributed to a serious and potentially disastrous misunderstanding of American history and society."

> —**HARVEY KLEHR,** professor emeritus of politics and history at Emory University and author of *The Communist Experience in America*

"At last! Mary Grabar tells the truth about Howard Zinn's bestselling anti-American textbook, *A People's History of the United States*. Zinn's book has probably done more to poison the minds of high school students than any other work of history. Grabar provides an overdue anatomy of Zinn's many errors and tendentious interpretations of the United States as an evil, racist empire. Her book—which should be required reading—is a much-needed antidote to one of the chief intellectual frauds of our time."

> —**ROGER KIMBALL,** editor and publisher of the *New Criterion* and author of *Tenured Radicals: How Politics Has Corrupted Our Higher Education* and *The Long March: How the Cultural Revolution of the 1960s Changed America*

Debunking Howard Zinn

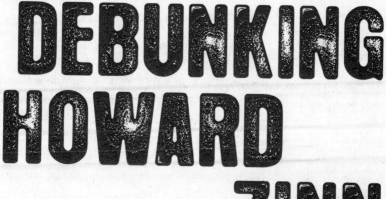

DEBUNKING HOWARD ZINN

**Exposing the
Fake History That
Turned a Generation
against America**

Mary Grabar

REGNERY
HISTORY
Washington, D.C.

Regnery History™ is a registered trademark of Salem Communications Holding Corporation
Regnery® is a registered trademark and its colophon is a trademark of Salem Communications Holding Corporation

Paperback ISBN: 978-1-68451-152-5

Library of Congress Control Number: 2020275314

Hardcover ISBN: 978-1-62157-773-7
ebook ISBN: 978-1-62157-894-9

Published in the United States by
Regnery History
An Imprint of Regnery Publishing
A Division of Salem Media Group
Washington, D.C.
www.RegneryHistory.com

Manufactured in the United States of America

10 9 8 7 6 5 4 3

Books are available in quantity for promotional or premium use.
For information on discounts and terms, please visit our website:
www.Regnery.com.

To Robert Paquette, fighter for truth in history

CONTENTS

A NOTE FROM THE AUTHOR

There is no historian like Howard Zinn. His cultish following continues to grow nearly forty years after the publication of his *A People's History of the United States*, the nation's bestselling American history survey book as both a trade book and textbook.[1]

A People's History is more than another left-wing interpretation of American history. Long before it appeared on bookstore shelves in 1980, historians were writing American history from a liberal, leftist, and even Marxist perspective. In fact, Zinn leans on these histories for much of his material. But their names have largely been forgotten, and Zinn's stature grows.

Certainly no other history book has taken the place of the Bible at the swearing-in of an elected official. But in April 2019, *A People's History* was the sacred object on which newly elected Oklahoma City council member JoBeth Hamon chose to place her hand for her oath of office.[2] Similarly, it is doubtful that a district attorney ever cited any other historian's autobiography in her maiden speech, as Natasha Irving of Waldoboro, Maine, did in January 2019 when she referred to Zinn's *You Can't Be Neutral on a Moving Train*. She said that she could not be "neutral in the face of mass incarceration.... in the face of prosecution of the sick for being sick, the poor, for being poor."[3]

Nearly a decade after Zinn's death, a new generation of readers is picking up his book and experiencing the feeling their parents felt in the 1980s and 1990s of having the wool pulled away from their eyes. These members of "Generation Z" seem undisturbed by Zinn's use of archaic 1960s lingo like "The Establishment" and "The System." They identify with the oft-mentioned "struggle," a staple of communist writing. In an age of racial hypersensitivity, no one seems bothered by Zinn's continual references to "Negroes," a term that has been considered offensive since the 1960s.

Zinn is often blamed for the decline in history writing, teaching, and knowledge. Conscientious historians seek to replicate the appeal of Zinn's book while presenting a more balanced and positive view of American history. Thus, a recent *Wall Street Journal* column about *Land of Hope*, a new book by Wilfred McClay, is titled, "Reclaiming History from Howard Zinn."[4] Previous attempts to provide an appealing corrective include William J. Bennett's three-volume *America, the Last Best Hope* in 2006, and in 2004 Larry Schweikart's and Michael Allen's *A Patriot's History of the United States*.

Historians on the Left, too, present their books as more respectable alternatives to Zinn. Harvard history professor Jill Lepore positioned her 2018 book *These Truths: A History of the United States* as a response not only to "the American triumphalism of popular history" but also to Zinn's "Marxist reckoning with American atrocity."[5] Before that was Eric Foner's *The Story of American Freedom*, published in 1996.

Neither such books nor the many critical assessments of *A People's History* seem to have decreased the book's popularity. In fact, controversies only increase sales for the "evergreen" title that sells "'incredibly well'" year after year.[6]

Stanford University education professor Sam Wineburg accounted for the book's "preternatural shelf life" by the fact that "Zinn shrewdly recognized that what might have been common knowledge among subscribers to the *Radical History Review* was largely invisible to the broader reading public.... It took Zinn's brilliance to draw a direct line from the rapier Columbus used to hack off the hands of the Arawaks, to the rifles aimed by Andrew Johnson to give the Creek Nation no quarter, and to the 9,000-pound 'Little Boy' that Paul Tibbets fatefully released over Hiroshima in August 1945." (Actually, as will be demonstrated in the following pages, Columbus did not "hack off the hands of the Arawaks" with a rapier.)

Wineburg noted that *A People's History* is "as radical in its rhetoric as in its politics." In fact, Zinn's rhetorical strategies are more than "radical." They are fundamentally and grossly dishonest. Wineburg pointed out the unusual way Zinn used questions—not as the rare "shoulder-shrugging admissions of the historian's epistemological quandary so much as devices that shock readers into considering the past anew." In one chapter, Wineburg counted twenty-nine "[b]ig in-your-face questions"—questions presenting two stark choices.

Such a "rhetorical turn" is "almost never encountered in professional historical writing," says Wineburg.[7] By presenting outrageous accusations against America as questions rather than assertions, Zinn attempts to evade responsibility for lying about American history. But he has in fact articulated these false claims and fixed them in his readers' minds.

Take one example highlighted by Wineburg. In the World War II chapter of *A People's History*, Zinn asks, "With the defeat of the Axis, were fascism's 'essential elements—militarism, racism, imperialism—now gone? Or were they absorbed into the already poisoned bones of the victors?'" Here Zinn is suggesting that the United States is the moral equivalent of Hitler's Germany. But by asking a question instead of stating a claim, Zinn has cleverly indemnified himself against the charge that he is making Americans out to be as bad as the Nazis. And no wonder. The proposition is as absurd as it is offensive.

And yet, with dozens of such outlandish suggestions and countless other grossly dishonest rhetorical tricks on nearly every page of *A People's History*, Howard Zinn has succeeded in convincing a generation of

Americans that the nation Abraham Lincoln truly called "the last best hope of Earth" is essentially a racist criminal enterprise built on murdering Indians, exploiting slaves, and oppressing the working man. It obviously needs to be replaced by something better. And of course, Zinn has the answer: a classless, egalitarian society. Yes, what Zinn is selling is the very same communist utopian fantasy that killed more than a hundred million human beings in the twentieth century.

The dream lives on, though, for the young and the uninformed. Zinn is particularly appealing to adolescents who are typically dissatisfied with their elders, believing themselves to be wiser. Many adults look back at this phase of their life as David Greenberg, writing in the March 19, 2013, *New Republic*, did as he reflected on his own "adolescent rebelliousness" as a sixteen-year-old when he "thrilled to Zinn's deflation of what he presented as the myths of standard-issue history." Zinn had "[m]ischievously" and "subversively . . . whispered that everything I had learned in school was a sugar-coated fairy tale, if not a deliberate lie."[8] Wineburg's diagnosis is along the same lines: "*A People's History* speaks directly to our inner Holden Caulfield. Our heroes are shameless frauds, our parents and teachers conniving liars, our textbooks propagandistic slop. . . . They're all phonies is a message that never goes out of style."[9]

Zinn whispers that the elders have lied about communism, as they have about everything else. And young people are buying it. In October 2018, the Victims of Communism Memorial Foundation reported that 52 percent of millennials surveyed would "prefer" to live in a socialist or communist country. Only 40 percent preferred a capitalist country.[10] A 2018 Gallup Poll revealed that only 45 percent of Americans aged 18 to 29 held a positive view of capitalism, marking a disturbing trend: as recently as 2010, 68 percent had "viewed [capitalism] positively."[11] Zinn's propaganda has been spectacularly effective. His dishonest American history is not the only factor in Americans' turn away from their heritage of freedom toward communist fantasies. But Howard Zinn has been instrumental in this destructive transformation. The task I undertake in this book is to expose Zinn's lies. The United States of America—still the last best hope—deserves better than slanders. She deserves our respect and gratitude—and the truth about her history.

Mary Grabar

June 16, 2019

INTRODUCTION

Howard Zinn: Icon, Rock Star

In *Good Will Hunting,* an emotionally scarred twenty-year-old working-class genius endorses *A People's History of the United States.* During his first visit to his therapist, Will Hunting looks over the books in the office and reads a title aloud, "*A History of the United States,* Volume 1," then comments, "If you want to read a real history book, read Howard Zinn's *A People's History of the United States.* That book will knock you on your ass."[1.]

The message is clear: Zinn's history stands superior to any multivolume history of America. A genius says so.

Will is a natural genius in both math and history. In a bar scene early on in the movie, he inserts himself into a conversation in which Clark, a Harvard graduate student, is challenging a friend who is trying to start a conversation with some young women by pretending to be a Harvard student. Clark challenges Will's friend by asking if he can provide some "insight into the evolution of the market economy in the early colonies." Will, observing Clark's mini-academic disquisition on the "economic modalities" of the Southern colonies, jumps into the conversation, saying, "Of course that's your contention. You're a first-year grad student. You just finished some Marxian historian, Pete Garrison prob'ly, and you're going to be convinced of that until next month when you get to James Lemon and you're goin' to be talkin' about how the economies of Virginia and Pennsylvania were strongly entrepreneurial and capitalist back in 1740. That's goin' to last until sometime next year, then you'll be in here regurgitating Gordon Wood about, you know, the pre-revolutionary utopia and the capital-forming effects of military mobilization."

When the grad student begins quoting from the monograph *Work in Essex County,* Will completes his sentence and gives the page number. As the bar patrons look on with awe, Will accuses the Harvard student of trying to impress the girls and predicts that in fifty years he may "start thinking" for himself and realize that he has spent $150,000 for an education he could have gotten for "a dollar-fifty" in library late fees.[2]

In this devastating exchange, Will has knocked down three historians in quick succession—leaving only the great Howard Zinn standing.

Matt Damon, who played the titular character in *Good Will Hunting*, was a young neighbor of the Zinns in Cambridge, Massachusetts. He and his brother lived with their divorced mother, an education professor, who "raised her boys with a deep social consciousness," according to Zinn. When Damon was ten, he took the family copy of the newly published *People's History* to school and read from it to his class for Columbus Day.[3]

And Matt Damon is far from the only American kid who has bought into Howard Zinn's take on our history. Zinn's version of our past—from the discovery of America (Columbus committed genocide), through slavery (worse here than anywhere in world history), the founding of the United States (white slave owners scheming to preserve the status quo), World War II (the Allies weren't any better than the Nazis), and Vietnam (yay! plucky Commies defeat the evil American war machine)—is widely taught and believed. In fact, it is becoming enshrined as an integral part of young Americans' beliefs. And no wonder—*A People's History* is taught throughout our schools and colleges. *A Young People's History of the United States*—Zinn's history adapted for middle schoolers with simplified sentences, but the same content—tells young readers that Zinn's "radically different" version of history was adapted for them because of parents' and teachers' demands. But some adults might object because they feel that young people are "not mature enough to look at their nation's policies honestly."[4]

If students aren't given Zinn's book, they may read passages from his work in other books—for example, if they check out young adult books by John M. Dunn from the library on such historical topics as the Vietnam War, the North American Indians, and the Civil Rights Movement. Each of those volumes contains extended passages from *A People's History of the United States*, which is listed in the "Works Consulted" and is described as "an unorthodox history told from the perspectives that are often overlooked by mainstream writers." Dunn presented Zinn as a respected historian.[5] And there's good evidence that the College Board, which "is becoming an unelected national school board, setting curricula—and just as important—largely replacing states and localities as the shaper of both textbooks and teacher training at the high school level" via their frameworks for the Advanced Placement (AP) U.S. History exam, promotes Zinn's version of history by including his books in AP teacher-training seminars.[6]

For years now, teachers have used a variety of editions of *A People's History* with discussion questions, exercises, lesson plans, and activities.[7] Many of these activities involve role-play, a favorite in-class activity of the decidedly non-intellectual Professor Zinn. Students at San Antonio College, to give just one example, learn history from an instructor who has adapted strategies from Zinn, her "mentor."[8] I have been to many teaching conferences through the years where Howard Zinn's materials were promoted.[9] One recently retired public high school history teacher in New York City, Jeffrey Ludwig, described how his fellow teachers would photocopy pages of Zinn's book (which was not on the officially approved list) for use in class. According to a college student who recently graduated from that school, teachers were still handing out excerpts from Zinn's book.[10] Many high school students are subjected to Zinn's book in class, along with the America-hating attitude that comes with it. Emily Rentz, now CEO of a clinical trials company she founded, described her horrific experience in Jim Buxton's Global Studies and International Relations classes at South Kingston High School in Rhode Island. Buxton made students read *A People's History* cover to cover and write papers regurgitating its points. He also bullied students who dared to express opinions that differed from Zinn's. The "grand finale" was a class visit from Zinn himself, who had been presented as a kind of "god," when Rentz was in eleventh grade in 2005. Zinn's book and visit at Rentz's high school enjoyed the blessing of many of the parents.[11] Sam Wineburg, a professor of education at Stanford University and the executive director of the Stanford History Education Group, notes that Zinn's book has become the "dominant narrative" in "many cases" and the "only history book on the syllabus" for future teachers.[12]

Zinn's pervasive influence is a national tragedy, especially considering just how distorted, manipulative, and plain dishonest *A People's History of the United States* is.

It's past time to take a closer look at Zinn's outrageous claims and outright lies and set the historical record straight. No other historian has gotten away with as much as Zinn has. Let's begin by putting *A People's History of the United States* in the context of some recent scandals.

It was around the turn of the twenty-first century that a number of American historians found themselves in the news. In 2000, Emory University professor Deborah Lipstadt was the defendant in a British courtroom for a lawsuit David Irving brought against her because she had called him a "Holocaust denier" in her 1993 book *Denying the Holocaust: The Growing Assault on Truth and Memory*. Well-known historians Stephen Ambrose and Doris Kearns Goodwin were shown to have plagiarized portions of their work. Award-winning author Joseph Ellis was revealed to have lied about his own history—about his service in Vietnam and during the Civil Rights Movement—to his students and to the media. And Michael Bellesiles—a history professor, founder of the Institute on the Study of Violence in America at Emory University, and former "rising star"—was found to have "misrepresented his findings" about the rate of gun ownership in early America in an effort to demonstrate the legitimacy of and need for gun control.[13]

Irving had never held an academic position or even finished college, yet he had established himself as a historian of "the German side of World War II," beginning in 1963 with his first book, *The Destruction of Dresden*. Although some of Irving's scholarship was respected, much was suspect. His books covered up Hitler's full role in the Jewish genocide and contained factual errors about leaders, events, and statistics. The overall effect was to minimize Hitler's culpability and the number of Jewish deaths. When Lipstadt's *Denying the Holocaust* was published in England in 1996, Irving sued for libel.[14] History professor Richard J. Evans, who served as an expert witness for the defense, and two graduate student assistants spent two years reviewing Irving's sources, a process described by Evans in his book *Lying About Hitler: History, Holocaust, and the David Irving Trial*. Irving lost the case.

Goodwin and Ambrose were exposed in the pages of the conservative magazine the *Weekly Standard*. Ambrose died in 2002, but Goodwin resigned from her post on the Pulitzer Prize review board and took a "leave" from *PBS NewsHour*.[15]

Ellis was suspended "without pay" from teaching for a year.[16]

Bellesiles was initially exposed by Clayton Cramer, who had questioned the Emory University professor while working on his master's degree in history. After much discussion in professional forums, Emory University finally undertook a three-month investigation. The "Emory committee of inquiry" uncovered "evidence of falsification" and "serious deviations from accepted practice in carrying out [and] reporting results from research." They found that Bellesiles had "violated Emory's regulations on research and the integrity code of the AHA [American Historical Association], 'the standard of professional historical scholarship.'" As a result, Bellesiles lost his contract with Knopf and the Bancroft Prize. He resigned his teaching position at Emory University in 2002.[17] Ten years later at the time of the publication of his *A People's History of the U.S.*

Military, Bellesiles was described as a "history buff" and reported to be bartending and working as an adjunct teacher at Central Connecticut State University.[18]

Meanwhile, another American historian, Howard Zinn, was enjoying increasing success with the book he wrote and published in 1980: *A People's History of the United States.* More than a decade after its initial publication, sales were so good that an updated and expanded version was released in 1995.

The book received a big boost when Matt Damon and fellow actor Ben Affleck incorporated it into key dramatic moments of *Good Will Hunting,* which won an Oscar.

As Irving, Ellis, Goodwin, Ambrose, and Bellesiles were disgraced and punished for their dishonesty, Zinn's sales marched steadily toward the million mark. In 2002, Zinn was negotiating with the Fox network for, as he said, "an option on the book for a miniseries." The deal fell through. But in 2008, a documentary titled *The People Speak,* featuring movie and rock stars, was recorded in Boston, California, Toronto, and at Bruce Springsteen's recording studio in New Jersey.[19] In 2003, a third revised and expanded edition of Zinn's book came out, and it passed a million in sales.[20]

To celebrate, Zinn was fêted at a celebrity-studded party in New York City where *A People's History* was given a dramatic reading by Danny Glover and James Earl Jones. Zinn, along with Damon and Affleck, was trying to get an HBO television series based on the book. Zinn's editor said that in his more than forty years of publishing experience, he had not known of another book "that sold more copies each year than it sold the year before."[21]

In 2012, Gilbert Sewall, director of the American Textbook Council—noting by then the sales of two million copies—called *A People's History of the United States* the nation's "best-known work of American history" and the "best-selling survey of American history."[22] As of this writing in 2018, it is estimated the book has sold more than 2.6 million copies.[23]

The enormous sales, though, do not mean that there is universal respect for Zinn's work. In fact, in the court of scholarly opinion, Zinn's book is closer to David Irving's frauds than to an esteemed work of history. Zinn has been slammed for distortions, omissions, and factual errors by reviewers and historians on both the left and right.

The late renowned historian Eugene Genovese was a declared Marxist in political agreement with Zinn at the time *A People's History* was published. But Genovese thought the book was so bad that he refused to review it. Years later, he told me it was nothing more than "incoherent left-wing sloganizing."[24]

Liberal historian Arthur Schlesinger called Zinn "a polemicist, not a historian."[25]

Cornell history professor Michael Kammen began his review of Zinn's history in the *Washington Post* by lauding Zinn as a "radical academic and social activist." But as much as he wanted to pronounce the attempt to write the "bottom-up" history a success, he said he could not. According to Kammen, the book was "a scissors-and-paste-pot job." Too much attention to "historians, historiography, and historical polemic" left "precious little space for the substance of history." Figures of social protest and political criticism crowded out influential religious figures, inventors, intellectuals, and authors. Kammen concluded, "We do deserve a people's history; but not singleminded, simpleminded history, too often of fools, knaves and Robin Hoods."[26]

History professor Eric Foner, who had met Zinn a few times and admired him,[27] gave *A People's History* a mixed review. Two paragraphs from the good part of the review have graced the covers of the book. Those excerpts include Foner's praise for writing that displays "enthusiasm rarely encountered in the leaden prose of academic history" with "vivid descriptions of events that are usually ignored" and "telling quotations from labor leaders, war resisters and fugitive slaves." *Not* appearing on the cover of the book are Foner's criticisms of Zinn's "deeply pessimistic vision of the American experience" in which "stirring protests, strikes and rebellions never seem to accomplish anything," and his portrayal of "anonymous Americans...strangely circumscribed" with targeted groups appearing "either as rebels or as victims." Foner suggested that the problem with

Zinn's book was "inherent in the method: history from the bottom up, though necessary as a corrective, is as limited in its own way as history from the top down." Zinn gives only a "partial view" of the history he purports to cover.[28]

Michael Kazin, a history professor at Georgetown University and an author or coauthor of several books on progressive and populist movements, as well as a well-known figure on the left from his days as a leader of the Harvard Students for a Democratic Society (and briefly a member of the Weatherman),[29] echoed Kammen's criticism in *Dissent Magazine*, a journal for social Democrats that he co-edits. Kazin described *A People's History* as "bad history, albeit gilded with virtuous intentions." That was the nice part of the review. According to Kazin, Zinn's book is "unworthy of [the] fame and influence" it has earned; he has reduced the past to a "Manichean fable" and failed to acknowledge the work and successes of progressives. Despite containing phrases "hint[ing] of Marxism," *A People's History* is really an insult to the memory of Karl Marx, who "never took so static or simplistic a view of history." Kazin charged that "Zinn's conception of American elites" such as George Washington, Thomas Jefferson, James Madison, and Alexander Hamilton "is akin to the medieval church's image of the Devil." Zinn's "failure," he said, was "grounded in a premise better suited to a conspiracy-monger's Web site than to a work of scholarship." Leftist Kazin deemed *A People's History* "polemic disguised as history."[30]

Stanford education professor Sam Wineburg, in an article in the Winter 2012–2013 *American Educator*, called Zinn's history "educationally dangerous." He homed in on points in the chapter about World War II, charging Zinn with using evidence selectively, conflating time periods, misrepresenting sources, using dishonest rhetorical strategies, and posing leading questions. Although Zinn drew together material that "blew apart the consensus school" of American history of the 1950s, he had substituted one "monolithic reading of the past for another." Zinn's history was written in a manner that spoke "directly" to students' "hearts," but his "power of persuasion" was dangerous because it "extinguishes students' ability to think." *A People's History* was a "history of certainty," and whether of the Left or the Right, such histories invite a slide into "intellectual fascism," according to Wineburg.[31]

From the Right, Harvard history professor Oscar Handlin attacked numerous claims of fact in Zinn's history in his 1980 review in the *American Scholar.* He called *A People's History* a "fairy tale" with "biased selections" that "falsify events"—from Zinn's claims of a widened "gap between rich and poor" in "the eighteenth century colonies" to his account of the Tet Offensive. Handlin charged that the book "conveniently omits whatever does not fit its overriding thesis."[32] In 2003, Daniel Flynn, then the executive director of Accuracy in Academia, called Zinn an "unreconstructed, anti-American Marxist" and his book a "cartoon anti-history."[33]

A 2012 survey of readers conducted by the History News Network (HNN), a site which trends left, revealed that *A People's History* was a close runner-up—after David Barton's *The Jefferson Lies*—for first place as the "least credible history book in print." While Barton's original publisher, Thomas Nelson, dropped his book after a groundswell of criticism by Christian historians, Zinn's book is in its fortieth year of continuous publication. The HNN editors also noted that Zinn received "the most intense discussion" on the discussion board with "some commentators on one end condemning the book as 'cheap propaganda' and 'the historians equivalent of medical malpractice.'"[34]

And yet, *A People's History* continues to be a phenomenal success. It started with an initial print run of only about four thousand copies and steadily picked up sales each year, going through twenty-four printings "in its first decade."[35] After retiring from Boston University in 1988, Zinn remained active in the promotion of the book until his death in 2010 at the age of eighty-seven. In fact, Zinn died of a heart attack while swimming in a hotel pool in Santa Monica, where he was giving a talk about using his materials in children's education. Throughout his retirement, Zinn continued to travel around the country and abroad for speaking engagements. In 1995, he enjoyed a Fulbright fellowship in Italy. He was sought out for radio and television interviews, including on *The Daily Show*. His book was featured on *The Sopranos* and *The Simpsons*. He starred in his own film, *The People Speak*, and the dramatization of his autobiography, *You Can't Be Neutral on a Moving Train*. Zinn participated in political activities, often as a speaker at protest rallies. With book royalties and earnings from multiple spin-off products—including films, curricula, and graphic adaptations—Zinn was much better off than the average retired professor. David Greenberg estimated that his "franchise was earning him some $200,000 annually."[36]

Howard Zinn's death in 2010 pushed his book to the number four position on the *New York Times* paperback nonfiction list [37] and inspired tributes from celebrities and rock bands on *Saturday Night Live* and MTV.[38] Plaudits also came from former students Alice Walker and Marian Wright Edelman; from Mumia Abu-Jamal, Bill Moyers, and Jane Fonda; from the *New York Times*, the *Boston Globe*, and the *Washington Post*; *The Daily Show*, the NAACP, NPR, and the *Nation*; several socialist publications, including *Socialist Review*; and the American Historical Association.[39] In the press, Zinn's book is routinely portrayed in just the way he promoted it: as a corrective "ground-up approach to history."[40]

Zinn's book has inspired a creative outpouring. The PEN Freedom to Write Award in 2015, in Zinn's honor, went to DeRay Mckesson and Johnetta Elzie, Black Lives Matter and Ferguson bloggers and activists. A 2011 movie, *Even the Rain*, about "Spanish imperialism" was inspired by Zinn's account of Christopher Columbus and was dedicated to Zinn.[41] Zinn's book has inspired songs for Columbus Day.[42] British actor Riz Ahmed was prompted by *A People's History* to write a nine-part BBC series titled *Englistan* about a British-Pakistani family in England (American oppression apparently translates to the British immigrant experience of the last four decades).[43] Zinn's memory lives on in loving performances, such as the dramatic reading "Voices of a People's History of the United States" by Marisa Tomei, Maggie Gyllenhaal, and others at the Brooklyn Academy of Music in March 2017.[44] Zinn's three plays are performed in major cities, especially on the anniversary of his death and on May Day.[45] Zinn's play, *Marx in Soho,* was a favorite in May 2018 on the two hundredth anniversary of Karl Marx's birth, enjoying performances in the United States and abroad.[46] The "political dance troupe" Grrrl Brigade's fifteenth anniversary show was based on *A People's History.*[47] "Monolinguist" Mike Daisey performed eighteen "stand-alone monologues that crib from Howard Zinn's...classic" at the Seattle Repertory Theatre in October and November 2018. Daisey's set was a classroom, and each performance focused on roughly a chapter of Zinn's book. A reviewer saw the lesson on the Mexican-American War.[48]

In the summer of 2018, New York City's Parks Foundation collaborated with VOICES, "a non-profit arts, education and social justice organization founded by Howard Zinn and Anthony Arnove" based on *Voices of a People's History of the United States,* for the Summer Stage series in Central Park. Zinn's tract "The Problem Is Civil Disobedience," from a debate in 1970 after he had been arrested in an anti-war protest, was read alongside works by such luminaries as Angela Davis, Malcolm X, Public Enemy, Martin Luther King Jr., and Maya Angelou. The final night, August 28, was a celebration of the 1963 March on Washington, with actor Viggo Mortensen reading from *A People's History* and from Bartolomé de Las Casas. The performance was part of Mortensen's effort to use American history to "understand the current political climate," including the "division and ideological rigidity" he believes is being "fomented'" by our current president.[49]

Zinn's book has provided inspiration for protestors from Occupy Wall Street to tree-sitters,[50] and even to sports figures. When former Patriots tight end Martellus Bennett tweeted a "scathing" message about Columbus Day, sportswriter Alex Reimer fact-checked with *A People's History* and declared Bennett's claims about Columbus "start[ing] the slave trade" to be "accurate."[51] In basketball, San Antonio Spurs' Rudy Gay was reported to have Zinn's book on his reading list as a result of the recommendation of Cam Hodges, the team's player development assistant.[52] One Arizona teacher read passages from Zinn's chapter on the Great Depression aloud to her seventh grade class before participating in a teacher walkout (she sees parallels between her condition and fruit-pickers of that era).[53]

When the successful *Hamilton* touring group in the spring of 2018 did a statewide student workshop in Utah on "rapping" history in the manner of the Broadway hit, the student playing King George recommended *A People's History*.[54] In November 2017, the fourth annual Howard Zinn Book Fair at City College in San Francisco featured such sessions as "Teaching Children About the Resistance," "Releasing Our Radical Imaginations: A Conversation on Movement Building in the Age of Trump" (featuring Weatherman cofounder Bill Ayers), "Teaching the Hidden History of Reconstruction in High School," and "100 Years of Struggle for Sex Workers' Rights in the Bay Area." They were held in rooms named after Howard Zinn and his heroes, including Emma Goldman and Fred Hampton.[55]

Clearly, Zinn's influence extends beyond history departments. At the University of Southern California, Viet Thanh Nguyen—the Aerol Arnold chair of English and professor of English, comparative literature, American studies, and ethnicity—claims that high school students should read *A People's History* as a "corrective" to the history of the "dominant and the powerful" (along with Harriet Jacobs's *Incidents in the Life of a Slave Girl* for insights on the #MeToo movement and "intersectional thinking").[56] Zinn's *Marx in Soho* was performed at Grand Valley State University in February 2018[57] and also at Carleton College, sponsored by Carleton's economics department.[58] In February 2017, a suburban Chicago school held an all-day attendance-mandatory seminar on "today's struggle for civil rights" that included a workshop titled "A People's History of Chicago" and described as "in the tradition of Howard Zinn."[59]

In September 2018, I attended a lecture on "A People's History of Utica" by Brandon Dunn, an adjunct faculty member of the history department at Mohawk Valley Community College. The room was packed with adults and teenagers. In the audience was Dunn's high school history teacher, Jeffrey Gressler, whom he credited with introducing him to Zinn and his "history from below." Dunn opened by projecting an image of Zinn and his now famous quotation: "Civil disobedience is not our problem. Our problem is civil obedience...." Dunn had given the same talk in January 2018.[60] Spin-off books—such as *A People's History of the Civil War, A People's History of Poverty in America,* and *A People's Art History of the United States*, to which Zinn lent his name as series editor for a percentage of the royalties—are published by the New Press. And a book by a former Zinn student, now a history and philosophy professor at Purdue University, claims that Zinn's detractors (including yours truly) are plagued by "Zinnophobia"![61]

By the turn of the twenty-first century, Zinn's book had become a status marker for radicals; it was featured as such in the 2017 movie *Lady Bird*, a "loosely autobiographical coming-of-age tale" set in the post-9/11 period. One of the heroine's "romantic interests," a seventeen-year-old boy named Kyle, "asserts his radical status by rolling his own cigarettes and toting Zinn's *A People's History of the United States*."[62] As Sam Wineburg has observed, Zinn "speaks directly to our inner Holden Caulfield," the cynical teenage protagonist of *The Catcher in the Rye*.[63] And just as J. D. Salinger's novel has earned a place as a favorite among adolescents since its publication in 1951, Zinn's "history" has appealed to adolescents since 1980.

Zinn's more than twenty books are ubiquitous on bookstore shelves—especially in college towns, where they are likely to be featured as staff picks. Zinn's history is guaranteed to be in stock at almost any bookstore, as it is at my local Barnes & Noble. There is even a *Zinn for Beginners*—as well as graphic adaptations, such as *A People's History of American Empire*.

Through the nonprofit Zinn Education Project (ZEP)—a collaborative effort with Rethinking Schools and Teaching for Change—Zinn's book and dozens of spin-off books, documentaries, role-playing activities, and lessons about Reconstruction, the 1921 Tulsa race riot, taking down "racist" statues, the "FBI's War on the Black Freedom Movement," the "Civil Rights Movement" (synonymous with the Black Panthers), the Black Panther Ten Point Program, "environmental racism," and other events that provide evidence of a corrupt U.S. regime are distributed in schools across the country. According to a September 2018 ZEP website post, "Close to 84,000 teachers have signed up to access" ZEP's history lessons and "at least 25 more sign up every day." Alison Kysia, a writer for ZEP who specializes in "A People's History of Muslims in the United States" and who taught at Northern Virginia Community College, used Zinn's book in her classes and defended it for its "consciousness-raising power."[64] ZEP sends organizers to give workshops to librarians and teachers on such topics as the labor movement, the environment and climate change, "Islamophobia," and "General Approaches to Teaching People's History" (with full or partial costs borne by the schools!). In 2017, workshops were given in six states, Washington, D.C., and Vancouver, Canada.[65]

In a particularly disturbing development, the Zinn lesson on Reconstruction is going to be taught throughout the state of South Carolina, partly in response to pressure from the Southern Poverty Law Center (SPLC). Victoria Smalls, a "veteran public historian who has worked for Charleston's planned International African American Museum and Saint Helena Island's Penn Center," became "the first state organizer" for the initiative.[66] Adam Sanchez's lead article gives some indication about how Reconstruction will be taught with the lesson plans: "Every day seems to bring new horrors as the U.S. president's racist rhetoric and policies have provided an increasingly encouraging environment for attacks on Black people and other communities of color."[67]

Teaching for Change operates the Busboys and Poets bookstore in Washington, D.C., where left-wing authors give readings, often recorded and featured on C-SPAN 2. In addition to providing curricular materials about Christopher Columbus, the Zinn Education Project offers materials for conducting political campaigns to abolish Columbus Day with sample resolutions for school districts, universities, and cities and specific instructions for engaging students in letter-writing campaigns and presentations to school boards. The Zinn Education Project also goes after funders of competing views, as they did when they attacked the Koch Foundation in 2014 for supporting the Bill of Rights Institute.[68]

There is *A Young People's History of the United States,* but Zinn is also quoted in other books for students, as I learned by checking out books by John M. Dunn from my rural Central New York public library system. Education professor Sam Wineburg writes, "for many students, *A People's History* will be the first full-length history book they read, and for some, it will be the only one." At the 2008 annual meeting of the National Council for the Social Studies ("the largest gathering of social studies teachers in the country"), Zinn received "raucous applause" from social studies and history teachers for his keynote speech. The president of that organization "hailed Zinn as 'an inspiration to many of us.'"[69] In 2013, the Philadelphia City Council went so far as to pass a non-binding resolution urging the school district to make *A People's History of the United States* required reading.[70]

A People's History has been translated into more than a dozen languages, including French, Spanish, Italian, German, Chinese, and Arabic.[71] The "People's" perspective on American history is now disseminated all over the world, including in a former people's republic—Russia—not by the Russians, but by the Bureau of Educational and Cultural Affairs of the American Embassy, which sponsored the 2006 Russian-language publication of *A People's History.*[72]

Zinn's name is invoked by college student editorialists at the *Daily Princetonian* and the *Yale Herald.*[73] A columnist at the *Detroit Daily News* found words of inspiration from Zinn as she wrote about the mass school shooting at Parkland High School in February 2018.[74] When Bill Cosby was convicted of drugging and sexually assaulting a woman, and his wife, Camille, issued a statement charging that "unproven accusations evolved into lynch mobs," she appealed to Zinn, "the renowned, honest historian" who had noted that the writers of the Constitution had excluded "women, Native Americans, poor white men, and…enslaved Africans."[75] My daily Google alerts tell me about references to his name by social justice warriors writing letters to the editor and articles in newsletters—as well as by those who use his name as shorthand for the decline of educational standards and the upsurge in America-hatred. Former President Barack Obama "had a special interest in the work" of Zinn, according to fellow community organizer Mike Kruglik.[76]

Conservative professors and education reformers fume about the "Zinnification" of history evidenced in new AP (Advanced Placement) standards.[77] Talk show host Rush Limbaugh routinely blames Zinn for "Mush Brains" on college campuses and in the voting booth.[78] Elected officials try to remove *A People's History* from classrooms.

In 2013, when it was revealed from emails sent during his tenure as governor that Purdue University president Mitch Daniels had sought to eliminate Zinn's book from classrooms, he was roundly excoriated. The Zinn Education Project conducted a fundraising campaign milking the controversy and sent free copies of *A People's History* to teachers across the country. In April 2018, the organization was bragging that "five years after former governor Mitch Daniels tried to ban" Zinn's *People's History* "from Indiana schools, the Zinn Education Project (ZEP) was able to offer three workshops to dozens of educators throughout the state."[79]

In 2017—when Arkansas state representative Kim Hendren introduced (ultimately unsuccessful) legislation to keep Zinn's materials out of "public schools and state-supported charter schools"—the Zinn Education Project sent Zinn's books for free to almost seven hundred teachers and librarians, claiming that donations for the book drive had "poured in from across the country" and visits to the website from Arkansas teachers increased "923 percent over the previous year."[80]

Zinn is widely touted as an innovator in writing history "from the bottom up." As he said, he did not want to focus on military, business, and political leaders, but on the common people. He explains early in *A People's History* that he is for the underdog: "I prefer to try to tell the story of the discovery of America from the viewpoint of the Arawaks, of the Constitution from the standpoint of the slaves, of Andrew Jackson as seen by the Cherokees, of the Civil War as seen by the New York Irish.... "[81]

Zinn's colleagues on the Left—like Kazin and Kammen—gave him credit for his good liberal intentions, but Bruce Kuklick, writing for the *Nation*—where Zinn frequently enjoyed a platform—pointed out that Zinn was far from the first historian to write a "bottom-up" history. "I don't mean to derogate *A People's History* by assessing it as a radical textbook," wrote Kuklick. "Zinn writes clearly and articulately; his narrative is coherent and thematically unified. On the assumption that textbooks are socializing agents I prefer this sort of text to the usual ones celebrating industrialists and Presidents, texts for which Zinn has an ill-concealed but justifiable contempt." Kuklick approved of the way *A People's History* covered "the oppression of the people" with "eloquent renditions of the destruction of Indian culture," "rich analyses of the torments of the slaves," and "long explorations of the misery of the working class." He liked how Zinn gave significant time "to the study of left and radical politics." But he complained that women were treated as if Zinn were "a relative newcomer to feminism" and that Zinn also neglected "the daily texture of the social life of the people" and "the people's religion." As Kuklick noted, a disproportionate number of pages in *A People's History* are devoted to *recent* history: one-third of the book was "on the last sixty years, one-quarter on the last thirty" (between 1950 and 1980), with fifteen percent "on Zinn's favorite decade in the history of humankind—the 1960s."

While Kuklick attributed part of the failures of *A People's History* to the "textbook genre," he preferred Carl Degler's *Out of Our Past*, published back in 1959: "Degler's biases are liberal, but he brought to his task a subtlety and sophistication that Zinn doesn't possess." According to Kuklick, Degler's book covers much of the same ground and should be read before Zinn's book.[82] *Out of Our Past* had been described on January 1, 1959, in the *New York Times* as a discussion of "the developments, forces and individuals that have made this country what it is" and of such subjects as "how racial discrimination began and what schools and churches have done about it."[83] Degler had the bona fides, as the headline to his obituary on January 14, 2015, in the *New York Times* attested: "Carl N. Degler, 93, a Scholarly Voice of the Oppressed." The Stanford University scholar had "delved into the corners of history" and "illuminated the role of women, the poor and ethnic minorities in the nation's evolution." His 1972 book about slavery, *Neither Black nor White,* won him the Pulitzer. And Degler's work did not suffer from Zinn's lack of familiarity with women's issues. As early as 1966, he had been invited by Betty Friedan "to be one of [the] two men among the founders of the National Organization for Women." Degler had the respect of colleagues, winning praise from Princeton professor Lawrence Stone for his 1980 book *At Odds: Women and the Family in America from the Revolution to the Present* and from C. Vann Woodward for *Southern Dissenters in the Nineteenth Century.*[84]

Out of Our Past—which is arranged pretty much like *A People's History*, though without a chapter on Columbus and the Indians, with which Zinn begins—had received a largely favorable review in the *American Historical Review* at the time of its publication.[85] Vincent Carosso, writing in the *Business History Review,* noted gaps such as in foreign affairs, but also said that "topics which are often neglected in standard one-volume histories receive detailed and penetrating analysis." These include "the part played by women, the importance of the changing status of the Negro, and the significance of urbanization in determining national character...." Carosso said that Degler's book "should appeal to the general reader who wants a one-volume survey which is sound in scholarship and well written" and recommended it as a supplementary college text.[86] *Out of Our Past* was updated and reprinted in 1970, but today few Americans recognize the name Carl Degler.

Or the name Oscar Handlin (1915–2011). Handlin, like Zinn, was a son of Russian-Jewish immigrants whose Wikipedia page begins by noting his fifty-year tenure at Harvard, where in the 1950s he "virtually invent[ed] the field of immigration history" and "helped promote social and ethnic history." Handlin won the 1951 Pulitzer for *The Uprooted.*

Stephan Thernstrom, writing for the American Historical Association, described the young Handlin pushing the grocery delivery cart for his family's business while reading, entering Brooklyn College at age fifteen, and proving himself at Harvard when few East European Jews of immigrant stock were admitted. Handlin's Ph.D. dissertation became the award-winning book *Boston's Immigrants: 1790–1865,* which "illuminated the experience of the common folks who crossed the ocean and settled in Boston" and marked him as "the nation's preeminent historian of American immigration." His many books "examined the American experience in its totality," covering not only immigration from Europe and beyond, but also African Americans, race, ethnicity, the biographies of Abraham Lincoln and Al Smith, war and diplomacy, and the discipline of history writing. He co-wrote a four-volume series, *Liberty in America,* and also advocated for reforming the immigration system—then based on the national origins quota system—and supervised more dissertations than any of his Harvard colleagues.[87]

Truth in History, which Handlin published a year before Zinn's *A People's History,* bemoaned the decay in history standards as New Left historians—including William Appleman Williams, Lloyd Gardner, Gabriel Kolko, Gerda Lerner, and Barton Bernstein—merged activism with scholarship, sacrificing historical accuracy. All those names would appear in the bibliography of *A People's History.*[88]

Why does Howard Zinn have name recognition—amounting to a status as the icon and rock star of historians—that more substantial scholars never achieved?

James Green, a professor of history and labor studies at the University of Massachusetts, wrote for the *Chronicle of Higher Education,* "While challenging official versions of historical truth, Zinn assumes a moral authority exceedingly rare in professional academic writing."[89] Unlike his New Left colleagues who got bogged down in quasi-Marxist theory, Zinn made dramatic emotional appeals. He forthrightly claimed to provide a corrective to previous histories, to bring long-suppressed facts to light, and to speak on behalf of the oppressed.

Zinn justified his methods in the first two pages of his afterword to the 2003 edition of *A People's History*. He began by describing how he came to write the book. The "circumstances" of his own life had inspired him to write "a new kind of history." When he sat down at his manual typewriter to type the first page, he had been teaching for twenty years and for as many years been involved in political activism with the Civil Rights Movement in the South and "activity against the war in Vietnam," experiences that were "hardly a recipe for neutrality in the teaching and writing of history." He had also been shaped by his upbringing in "a family of working-class immigrants in New York," years as a shipyard worker, and experiences as a bombardier in World War II.

Zinn claimed authority from his twenty-year tenure as a professor. But he did not tell the reader that after he wrote his book about Fiorello La Guardia while a graduate student, he wrote nothing else that could properly be called scholarly.

Zinn made no pretense of objectivity: "By the time I began teaching and writing, I had no illusions about 'objectivity,' if that meant avoiding a point of view. I knew that a historian (or a journalist, or anyone telling a story) was forced to choose, out of an infinite number of facts, what to present, what to omit. And that decision inevitably would reflect, whether consciously or not, the interests of the historian."[90]

He claimed that "there is no such thing as pure fact, innocent of interpretation. Behind every fact presented to the world—by a teacher, a writer, anyone—is a judgment. The judgment that has been made is that this fact is important, or that other facts, omitted, are not important."[91]

This is the defense that Zinn would regularly rely on when challenged about the errors of fact in *A People's History of the United States*, as he was by Handlin and other more scholarly—and honest—historians: there is no such thing as an objective fact. All that matters is Zinn's higher purpose: "There were themes of profound importance to me which I found missing in the orthodox histories that dominated American culture. The consequence of those omissions has been not simply to give a distorted view of the past but, more important, to mislead us all about the present."[92] And in any case, his critics were just ideologically motivated conservatives. Zinn claimed that Handlin was biased against his book because Handlin supported President Nixon and the Vietnam War.[93]

In fact, as we have seen, some of the most telling criticisms of *A People's History of the United States* have come from the Left. They're on board with the purpose of Zinn's history, but they fault his execution. Zinn's errors are those associated usually with an overabundance of enthusiasm. Sam Wineburg addressed a few egregious points of error, but he joined his colleagues on the Left in denouncing Mitch Daniels for attempting to keep Howard Zinn's writings out of classrooms and teachers' workshops.

Left-leaning historians have taken issue not so much with the nitty-gritty of Zinn's factual representations as with his perspective, tone, and balance. Yet these same historians would certainly condemn David Irving for history that misrepresents the facts about the Hitler regime. Why do the same scrupulous standards that Professor Evans and his research assistants applied to Irving's work not apply to Zinn's?

In their painstaking examination of German archival material, the Evans team found that Irving had misrepresented sources and data, used "insignificant and sometimes implausible pieces of evidence to dismiss more substantial evidence that did not support his thesis," and "ignored or deliberately suppressed material when it ran counter to his arguments." They also caught Irving "placing quotations in a false context, removing part of the record to a footnote, and mixing up two different conversations...."[94]

Such practices violate the principles set forth by the American Historical Association (AHA)—the standard that Peter Charles Hoffer, a history professor and member of the American Historical Association's professional division, calls an "integrity code." Hoffer does concede that "even the most honored historians are not always so willing to admit their own biases or so swift in 'disclosing...all significant qualifications' xxxviii **DEBUNKING HOWARD ZINN**

of their arguments. Errors of fact creep like sneak thieves into otherwise exemplary works of scholarship. Historians are only human...."[95] But Belesiles and Irving are guilty not just of the occasional lapse from the standards of the historians' profession, but of the deliberate attempt to deceive, as well.

And how do Zinn and *A People's History of the United States* measure up against those standards? These are from section three of the AHA's "Statement on Standards of Professional Conduct," updated in 2018. I have broken them into bullet points for ease in reading. The AHA begins by noting the need for "awareness of one's own biases and a readiness to follow sound method and analysis wherever they may lead." The rules read as follows:

- Historians should document their findings and be prepared to make available their sources, evidence, and data, including any documentation through interviews.
- Historians should not misrepresent their sources.
- They should report their findings as accurately as possible and not omit evidence that runs counter to their own interpretation.
- They should not commit plagiarism.
- They should oppose false or erroneous use of evidence, along with any efforts to ignore or conceal such false or erroneous use.

Another section is devoted to the topic of plagiarism, which is defined as "the expropriation of another's work, and the presentation of it as one's own." It takes such forms as "use of another's language without quotation marks and citation," "appropriation of concepts, data, or notes all disguised in newly crafted sentences, or reference to a borrowed work in an early note and then extensive further use without subsequent attribution," and "borrowing unexamined primary source references from a secondary work without citing that work."[96]

The AHA first published these standards in 1987,[97] but historians understood them long before then. In fact, the historian's aim to recreate the past in a narrative that is both enjoyable to read and accurate in its presentation of fact goes back to the ancient Greeks—Herodotus, born approximately in 484 B.C., who is considered to be the father of history, and Thucydides, born approximately in 460 B.C., who is considered to be the father of scientific history.

These are the standards by which *A People's History of the United States* will be judged in this book. The question is not, as Zinn liked to pretend, whether he chose the correct topics to investigate. We will not concern ourselves with whether presidents or slaves are more important. But we will also not assume that a purported concern with slaves, factory workers, and immigrants gives a historian a special dispensation to play fast and loose with the facts of history.

CHAPTER
ONE

Columbus Bad, Indians Good

oward Zinn rode to fame and fortune on the "untold story" of Christopher Columbus—a shocking tale of severed hands, raped women, and gentle, enslaved people worked to death to slake the white Europeans' lust for gold.[1] Today, that story is anything but untold. Zinn's narrative about the genocidal discoverer of America has captured our education system and popular culture.

Consider what Columbus Day had become by the fall of 2017 when the violent, Marxist-inspired group Antifa declared a nationwide "Deface Columbus Day."[2] The defacement of statues of Columbus with red paint had already become an annual ritual in many places. In the Pittsburgh area, it had been going on for twenty years.[3] In New York City, the large bronze statue in Columbus Circle at the corner of Central Park had had "hate will not be tolerated" scrawled on the base and Columbus's hands painted red.[4]

And the transformation in Americans' attitudes toward the man who discovered America wasn't limited to a few vandals. Besides the physical attacks, there were continual demands for the government to take down the statue. Zinn is the inspiration behind the current campaign to abolish

Columbus Day and replace it with "Indigenous Peoples' Day." High school teachers cite his book in making the case for the renaming to their local communities.[5]

In October 2018, San Francisco, Cincinnati, and Rochester, New York, joined at least sixty other cities in replacing Columbus Day with Indigenous Peoples' Day. Six states also do not recognize the holiday as Columbus Day.[6] In 2018, for the first time, Columbus, Ohio, did not observe the federal holiday, with officials claiming that the city could not afford to give its employees the day off. Many articles reporting on this trend cited Howard Zinn's role in the change in attitude.[7] *Courthouse News Service*, describing the overwhelming support in San Francisco for changing the holiday with a board vote of ten to one, explained, "Social activist and historian Howard Zinn dedicated the first chapter of his 1980 book, 'A People's History of the United States,' challenging the popular narrative of Christopher Columbus as a stoic hero who overcame adversity to become the first Western explorer to find the New World." The news report claimed that Zinn had "cited evidence that Columbus enslaved and killed the 'gentle' Native people he encountered in the Caribbean Islands, leading to the mass murder and taking of land from natives across the continent." The sponsor of the bill, San Francisco Supervisor Malia Cohen, had written in a Facebook post, "The indisputably horrific things that Christopher Columbus did to the established inhabitants of the Americas with whom he came in contact are #facts."

Stanford anthropology professor Carol Delaney, who was quoted in the *Courthouse News Service* article to provide a counter-narrative, informed reporters that Columbus acted on his Christian faith and instructed his crew to treat the native people with kindness.[8] But such inconvenient facts are inevitably drowned out by the Columbus-hate that Howard Zinn has succeeded in spreading. So it should not have been all that surprising when on Columbus Day in 2018, in a man-on-the-street interview at the Columbus Fountain near Union Station in Washington, D.C., a man who looked to be in his thirties explained in reply to a reporter's question about celebrating the holiday that "the guy [Columbus] killed a lot of Native Americans." He cited Zinn's "history."[9]

Zinn's work has "affected the teaching of history...even in cases where his own materials are not used," according to University of Massachusetts professor James Green, who noted in 2003 that "nearly every college textbook published during the last two decades now begins, as Zinn did, with the European destruction of the Indians."[10] Zinn was quite proud of that accomplishment. He lived to see the day when—on the five hundredth anniversary of Columbus's first landing in the New World—Americans were bitterly divided over whether Columbus Day should be a day of celebration or mourning, of pride or of shame.

Zinn's warped version of Columbus and the discovery of America was always intended to reverberate into American political life, as the 1995 edition's new chapter, "The Unreported Resistance," which dealt with protests against military efforts in Central America and Iraq under Presidents Ronald Reagan and George H. W. Bush, respectively, showed. Three-and-a-half pages were devoted to Native Americans who connected these "conquests" with the original one by Columbus and protested against the quincentennial celebration of the discovery of America. One promoter of Zinn's books, the co-sponsor of the Zinn Education Project, Rethinking Schools, sold two hundred thousand copies of a booklet called *Rethinking Columbus* in a few months. Protests of Columbus included workshops, meetings, multimedia shows, films, plays, art shows, and an opera at Lincoln Center.[11]

In that 1995 edition of *A People's History*, Zinn exulted, "For generations, exactly the same story had been told all American schoolchildren about Columbus, a romantic, admiring story. Now, thousands of teachers around the country were beginning to tell that story differently."[12] So what exactly was Zinn's new and different story about Columbus, and where did it come from?

In a 1998 interview, Zinn promoter David Barsamian asked his hero, "In the course of your investigations in writing *A People's History*, what facts came out that were startling to you?" Zinn replied:

I suppose just as the reader of my People's History were [sic] startled by my Story of Columbus, I was startled myself. I must confess that until I began looking into it, I did not know any more about Columbus than I had learned in school. By this time I had a Ph.D. in American history. Nothing that I learned on any level of education, from elementary school through Columbia University, changed the story of the heroic Columbus and his wonderful accomplishments. It wasn't until I began to look into it myself, read Columbus' journals, read Las Casas, the great eyewitness who produced many volumes on what happened to the Indians, not until I began to read did I suddenly realize with a kind of shock how ignorant I had been...led to be by the education I had gotten in our national education system.[13]

Presumably extrapolating from the "many volumes" he had read, Zinn found the inspiration for the dramatic opening sentences of *A People's History*: "Arawak men and women, naked, tawny, and full of wonder, emerged from their villages onto the island's beaches and swam out to get a closer look at the strange big boat. When Columbus and his sailors came ashore, carrying swords, speaking oddly, the Arawaks ran to greet them, brought them food, water, gifts. He later wrote of this in his log: 'They... brought us parrots and balls of cotton, and spears and many other things, which they exchanged for the glass beads and hawks' bells. They willingly traded everything they owned....'"

The quoted passage from Columbus's log continues with Columbus's description of the Arawaks. They are "well-built" and handsomely featured. Having never seen iron, they accidentally cut themselves on the Europeans' swords when they touch them. The passage ends with Columbus's now infamous words: "They have no iron. Their spears are made out of cane.... They would make fine servants.... With fifty men we could subjugate them all and make them do whatever we want."[14]

The ellipses in this passage are Zinn's, not mine. And as we shall see, those omissions are essential to Zinn's dishonest retelling of the Columbus story. By leaving crucial words out of the quotation, Zinn makes Columbus say something very different from what he actually said.

Zinn began and finished *A People's History of the United States* in less than a year, after he returned from a four-month professorship in Paris in 1978. This fact "surprises people and sometimes makes them think I obviously did it in a hurry and didn't spend much time on it," he explained. But he claimed, "I'd been accumulating the notes and material, the data, for twenty years as a result of teaching and writing about history." Once he sat down at his typewriter, "it came very fast."[15]

According to Zinn, he gave up on his original idea for organizing the book—by topics such as race, "from the first slaves brought to Jamestown down through the present, do the same thing with labor and so on"—and opted for the traditional rough chronological approach. "Then it would be more obvious that I was dealing with the same topics but from a different point of view, and also my book would be more useful to teachers."[16] Zinn told biographer Davis Joyce that he had started with a "fairly orthodox outline": for each chapter he would bring into his office the relevant books with slips of paper in the appropriate sections and files on periods like the American Revolution, the Civil War, and industrial development. Consulting these materials, he said he would "type out a first draft, go over it with pen and ink to make changes, and so on, and then type up the final copy. And that's it." Zinn considered himself "a pretty fast writer."[17]

But there is no evidence that Zinn ever actually made extensive notes in preparation for writing *A People's History*. On the contrary, there is telling proof that he did no such thing. It's unlikely that he even read as much of "Columbus's journals" or the works of "Las Casas, the great eyewitness" as he claimed. The truth is that Zinn's description of Columbus's first encounter with the American Indians is lifted from *Columbus: His Enterprise: Exploding the Myth,* a book for high school students that Zinn's friend and fellow anti-Vietnam War activist, Hans Koning, first published in 1976. In other words, though one of Zinn's radical

America-hating colleagues did the initial work of smearing Columbus, Zinn got the credit.

Koning's book is the source for Zinn's indictment of Columbus, which is the opening gambit of *A People's History*. The first five-and-a-half pages of *A People's History of the United States* are little more than slightly altered passages from *Columbus: His Enterprise*. The text on pages 1–3 of *A People's History*—Zinn's opening narrative about how Columbus cruelly exploited the generosity of the Arawaks—is paraphrased mostly from *Columbus* pages 51–58. From the middle of Zinn's page three to the middle of page four, he follows Koning's pages 59–70; then on the bottom half of page four and the top half of page five, he uses Koning's pages 82–84. Zinn lifts wholesale from Koning the very same quotations of Columbus. He also includes an attack on the historian Samuel Eliot Morison, just like Koning—complete with references to the Vietnam War. That's a rather odd coincidence, given that both Zinn and Koning were purportedly recounting the fifteenth-century discovery of America.

The material on Columbus with which Zinn begins *A People's History of the United States* is eerily similar to Koning's work. Zinn's introductory passage about the Arawaks bearing gifts quotes a passage from Bartolomé de Las Casas's transcription of Columbus's log that Koning quotes on page fifty-two of *Columbus*. Zinn even echoes Koning's bizarre attack on an aspect of Columbus's character that would hardly seem to be a weak point: the explorer's navigational expertise. To see how closely Zinn tracks Koning, compare the *People's History*'s description of Spain as a wicked European nation corrupted by the dual evils of Christianity and capitalism to Koning's description.

Zinn's description: "Spain was recently unified, one of the new modern nation-states, like France, England, and Portugal. Its population, mostly poor peasants, worked for the nobility, who were 2 percent of the population and owned 95 percent of the land. Spain had tied itself to the Catholic Church, expelled all the Jews, driven out the Moors. Like other states of the modern world, Spain sought gold, which was becoming the new mark of wealth, more useful than land because it could buy anything."[18]

Koning's description: "In 1492, Spain became autocratic, theocratic, and homogeneous. It became a 'modern' nation-state. After centuries of division (and religious tolerance), the last Moslem city had been conquered, and in that same year a royal decree was signed that expelled all Jews from the country. What this new state sorely lacked was gold...a means of payment universally acceptable.... The nobility, about 2 percent of the population, owned 95 percent of the land."[19]

(Of course, neither Koning nor Zinn acknowledges that Ferdinand and Isabella took Spain *back* from the Muslims, who had conquered the Christians there in 711.)

Here is Zinn's description of the Arawaks: "So, approaching land, they were met by the Arawak Indians.... The Arawaks lived in village communes, had developed agriculture of corn, yams, cassava. They could spin and weave, but they had no horses or work animals. They had no iron, but they wore tiny gold ornaments in their ears."[20]

Zinn's description is suspiciously like Koning's: "The population were Arawak Indians...a people who had a developed agriculture (corn, yams, cassava), who could spin and weave, but had no iron, no horses, no beasts of burden.... Their society seems to have been based on village communes where most property was jointly held.... Some of these people wore little gold ornaments in their ears or noses."[21]

When Koning's book, which called Columbus a "murderer," was republished in 1992 with a teaching guide in the back to capitalize on the quincentennial anniversary of Columbus's "landfall in the New World," the *New York Times* noted that it had been assigned to students in "several schools in the New York region" and to "students participating in the Native American Education Project, a federally financed agency that offers supplementary classes to American Indians attending the city's public schools."[22]

Koning's slim volume does not cite any sources. Koning was not a Columbus scholar any more than Zinn was. In fact, he was not even a historian, while Zinn was at least a college professor. But what the two men shared was an interesting history in politics. Koning had been a member of the Dutch Resistance under his original name, Hans Koningsberger, which he changed in 1970. He was a Socialist and a founder, along with Noam Chomsky and Zinn, of the anti-Vietnam War Resist organization. Koning's 2007 obituary in the *Guardian* described him as a novelist, a playwright, and a journalist who had traveled to Russia and China in the 1960s.[23]

Zinn mentions Koning only once in *A People's* History—on page seventeen, when he quotes a summary passage. He does include *Columbus: His Enterprise* in his bibliography. But Zinn completely glosses over how generously he borrowed from his friend's book. And Koning does not seem to have minded that Zinn filled up the first several pages of *A People's History of the United States* with slightly altered passages from his own *Columbus: His Enterprise*, and then marketed himself as having discovered this history. Commitment to the political agenda that they shared seems to have outweighed any authorial jealousy Koning might have felt about Zinn using his work, failing to give credit where credit was due, and becoming the rock star of leftist historians as a result.

And the two men absolutely did share a political agenda. The surprise bestseller *Columbus: His Enterprise* was described by the *Guardian* as "a highly polemical biography of the Genoese adventurer that countered the prevailing orthodoxy of heroic discovery in favour of a dark story of exploitation and fanaticism"; it "enraged traditionalists and attracted a politically conscious generation of 'third world' activists."[24]

The description of Koning's book as "highly polemical" says a lot coming from the left-wing *Guardian*—as does the fact that the *New York Times* obituary for Koning noted that he had created an "emotional firestorm" by portraying Columbus as "a deep-eyed [sic] villain, raping, pillaging and enslaving as he ruthlessly pursued profits."[25] The republication of Koning's book in 1992 was a strategic marketing ploy to capitalize on the attention on Columbus that year. But to begin the rain storm on the coming Columbus Day parade, Koning had already published a screed in the *New York Times* in August 1990 charging that Columbus "set into motion a sequence of greed, cruelty, slavery and genocide that, even in the bloody history of mankind has few parallels." He asserted that these claims were "substantiated in the logs of Columbus's son, in the writing of Bartolomé de las Casas... and other period documents."[26] In the *Monthly Review* in 1992, Koning argued, "We must tell our children that the industrial prosperity of the West was largely financed with the blood and tears of colonial and slave labor put in place by the Conquest."[27]

The polemics of *Columbus: His Enterprise* are crude. Koning claims, "The grade-school image of Columbus is not naïve, it is false."[28] Far from being "the dashing adventurer, the fearless knight with blazing blue eyes," Columbus was probably short, uneducated, intellectually unsophisticated, poor at navigation, and a thief of others' ideas.[29]

Koning's book was panned by commentators and historians who took notice of the change in tenor as the five hundredth anniversary of the discovery of America approached. On the day before Columbus Day in 1992, Harvey Morris, writing for the *Independent*, called Koning a "historical reductionist," someone who "refuse[s] to accept any nuances in the character or context of Columbus's life," instead resorting to "the cliché of comparing him to Hitler and the Nazis." Koning's work, he said, represented the "nadir" in the new "line of argument." An appalled Morris wrote, "Concluding a diatribe against the admiral as a 'typical man of the [white] West', Mr. Koning opines that at least the Nazis 'did the subject races of this world a favour. The great white-race civil war which we call World War II weakened Europe and broke its grip on Asia and Africa.'" Morris also noted that while Koning did not deny the cruelty of other races, he maintained that they were less "hypocritical." Koning had ignored the fact that Columbus, as primarily a discoverer who had "claimed the new lands of his patrons, King Ferdinand and Queen Isabella of Spain," could not be wholly blamed for the injustices of the "Spanish colonial enterprise."[30] Around the same time, *Time* magazine noted the "school of scandalized thought," represented by

Koning's book, which maintained that "Columbus's arrival instigated genocide." *Time* quoted Koning's claim that it was "almost obscene" to "celebrate a man who was really...worse than Attila the Hun."[31]

In the December 21, 1991, *Economist*, Professor Felipe Fernández-Armesto—a specialist in Latin American history and the author of *Columbus*, published that year by Oxford University Press—claimed that "the most damaging of the currently fashionable myths—damaging to the truth and damaging to race relations—is that Latin America was created by a crime of genocide initiated by Columbus...." He called it "a particularly wicked lie, because it makes real examples of genocide seem commonplace and unshocking." He titled Koning "the guru of Columbus-haters" who had "compounded the felony by claiming that 'the Nazis did the subject races of this world a favour.'" In reality, the "demographic catastrophe" that Koning blamed on Columbus was a "tragedy caused...by human failing and by a form of fate"—including the diseases that killed so many of the natives. As Fernández-Armesto pointed out, Columbus was actually "welcomed as a deliverer" by the Arawaks because they were "already doomed by the fierce imperialism of the neighboring Caribs."[32]

So, Zinn based his famous opening pages on a controversial book. And while Koning's work was treated dismissively, Zinn's transcriptions of Koning's material to his own book are taken as groundbreaking historical revelations. And few know that they are little more than transcriptions.

Zinn perpetuates Koning's smears. In Koning's telling and in Zinn's, Columbus set out to enslave a uniformly gentle people for the sole purpose of enriching himself with gold.

In fact, that is far from the truth. European efforts to find a sea route to Asia had been going on for hundreds of years. As William and Carla Phillips point out in *The Worlds of Christopher Columbus*, Columbus's voyages of discovery were a continuation of Europeans' ventures of sailing to Asia—at first, around Africa—that had begun in 1291. For centuries before Columbus, Portuguese and Spanish explorers had also ventured farther and farther out into the Atlantic Ocean.[33]

Spain had one particularly pressing reason—quite apart from greed for gold—for sailing to East Asia. As Andrew G. Bostom, quoting Louis Bertrand's 1934 book *The History of Spain,* pointed out in a Columbus Day 2018 post on PJ Media, "Columbus sought 'eastern (even far eastern) alliances' to end a millennium of Islam's jihad-imposed tyranny against Christendom.... When the Spanish Christian monarchs Ferdinand and Isabella recaptured Grenada on January 2, 1492, they ended almost eight centuries of jihad ravages...massacres, pillage, mass enslavement, and deportation" under Muslim rule. As Bertrand described it, the situation faced by the Spanish was "expel the foreigner or be expelled by him!" Thus, Columbus's mission was multi-faceted and inspired by several different motivations: "to reach the East Indies, so as to take Islam in the rear, and to effect an alliance with the Great Khan—a mythical personage who was believed to be the sovereign of all that region, and favorable to the Christian religion—and finally...to diffuse Christianity throughout that unknown continent and trade with the traditional sources of gold and spices."[34]

Desires to find new lands for more resources and to escape enemies and persecution are not impulses unique to Europeans. The natives of North America "in prehistoric times" themselves came from Asia and "crossed the land bridge across the Bering Strait to the lands of the Western Hemisphere."[35] When he encountered naked natives instead of the Asian merchants he was expecting, Columbus did not jump to thoughts of working them to death for gold as Zinn, following Koning, suggests. Koning introduces passages by leading sentences and then quotes, out of context, carefully selected passages from Columbus's log—which Zinn then quotes even more selectively, leaving out passages that flatly contradict the Columbus-as-greedy-for-gold-genocidaire narrative. For example, in his log entry for October 12, 1492, Columbus wrote, "I warned my men to take nothing from the people without giving something in exchange"[36]—a passage left out by both Koning and Zinn.

But Zinn's most crucial omissions are in the passage from Columbus's log that he quotes in the very first paragraph of his *People's History.*

There he uses ellipses to cover up the fact that he has left out enough of Columbus's words to deceive his readers about what the discoverer of America actually meant. The omission right before "They would make fine servants" is particularly dishonest. Here's the nub of what Zinn left out: "I saw some who bore marks of wounds on their bodies, and I made signs to them to ask how this came about, and they indicated to me that people came from other islands, which are near, and wished to capture them, and they defended themselves. And I believed and still believe that they come here from the mainland to take them for slaves."[37]

In his translation of Columbus's log, Robert Fuson discusses the context that Zinn deliberately left out: "The cultural unity of the Taino [the name for this particular tribe, which Zinn labels "Arawaks"] greatly impressed Columbus.... Those who see Columbus as the founder of slavery in the New World are grossly in error. This thought occurred to [Samuel Eliot] Morison (and many others), who misinterpreted a statement made by Columbus on the first day in America, when he said, 'They (the Indians) ought to be good servants.' In fact, Columbus offered this observation in explanation of an earlier comment he had made, theorizing that people from the mainland came to the islands to capture these Indians as slaves because they were so docile and obliging."[38]

Zinn's next ellipsis between "They would make fine servants" and "With fifty men we could subjugate them all and make them do whatever we want" covers for Zinn's dishonest pretense that the second statement has anything at all to do with the first. The sentences that Zinn joins here are not only not in the same paragraph—as he dishonestly pretends by printing them that way on the very first page of *A People's History*—but they're not even in the same entry of Columbus's log. In fact, they're from *two days* apart.[39]

Zinn's highly selective quotations from Columbus's log are designed to give the impression that Columbus had no concern for the Indians' spiritual or physical well-being—that the explorer was motivated only by a "frenzy for money" that drove him to enslave the natives for profit when he wasn't hunting them down with dogs because they couldn't supply him with large quantities of gold from supposed mines whose very existence was "part fiction" created by Columbus himself. Zinn wrote, "The Indians had been given an impossible task. The only gold around was bits of dust garnered from the streams. So they fled, were hunted down with dogs, and were killed."[40]

But literally the explorer's *first* concern—the hope that he expressed in the initial comment about the natives in his log—was for the Indians' freedom and their eternal salvation: "I want the natives to develop a friendly attitude toward us because I know that they are a people who can be made free and converted to our Holy Faith more by love than by force." Even Koning had quoted this passage—though only to make the discoverer of America out to be a shameless hypocrite. He immediately undercut what Columbus actually said by warning his readers about what he supposedly "said and did later."[41] According to Koning:

> Even in that religious and bigoted age, Columbus stood out as a very fierce Catholic. When he discussed his westward voyage, he always dwelt on its religious aspects....He must himself have believed that his Enterprise was Christian, if only to ensure God's help; and the priests who came west later were, with one or two glorious exceptions, as quick as he was in forgetting those pious intentions. (In a similar way, modern corporations used to capture oil fields and mines in underdeveloped nations while telling us and themselves that their main interest in these enterprises was to protect those unhappy countries from communism.)[42]

Zinn just entirely omits the passage in which Columbus expresses his respect and concern for the Indians.

In fact, even the quest for gold was related to the higher religious purpose that motivated Columbus and inspired him with a genuine concern for the Indians' well-being. As Carol Delaney explains, "Columbus wanted to launch a new Crusade to take back the Holy Land from the infidels (the Muslims). This desire was not merely to reclaim the land of the Bible and the place where Jesus had walked; it was part of the much larger and widespread, apocalyptic scenario in which Columbus and many of his contemporaries believed." Delaney notes Columbus's profound faith. Christopher Columbus, who was named after the patron saint of travelers, believed that he had been divinely ordained to carry out God's mission as discoverer. In reference to the October 12 log entry, Delaney comments, "In my first reading of the diary I could not understand why he seemed so driven to find gold.... But this understanding changes when one realizes that finding the gold was necessary not only to repay the people who had invested in the voyage (and to induce them to finance another), but also...essential if he was ever to finance another Crusade. Today, we might disapprove of that motive, but at the time it was felt to be a worthwhile and Christian duty."

The search for gold for Columbus was "less a commercial venture than 'a spiritual quest,' a medium not so much of exchange as 'a medium of redemption.'"[43]

And as William and Carla Phillips point out, "One prime motive for European expansion, reiterated by nearly all of the early explorers, was a desire to spread Christianity. To the current cynical age, religious motivation is difficult to understand; it is much easier to assume that missionary zeal merely served to justify a lust for gold and glory." Christian faith in early modern Europe touched "virtually every aspect of human life."[44]

Samuel Eliot Morison also commented on Columbus's ultimate goal of liberating Jerusalem in what Delaney calls his "superb, classic study, *Admiral of the Ocean Sea* (1942)."[45]

But Zinn, following Koning closely—where he doesn't outdo his source in the manipulation of the historical sources and the suppression of inconvenient facts—simply disregards all such historical context.

Leaning heavily on secondary sources was not that unusual for Zinn. In 1989, Yale University visiting associate professor Edward Countryman, checking a student's footnote that referenced *A People's History*, was, as he put it in a letter to Zinn, "perturbed...to find not only my ideas being borrowed ... but also my wording and then to find that you do not bother to list my piece in your bibliography...." Countryman laid out three passages from his essay "'Out of the Bounds of the Law': Northern Land Rioters in the Eighteenth Century," next to Zinn's very similarly worded ones.[46] Countryman's essay had appeared in the collection *The American Revolution: Explorations in the History of American Radicalism*, which was published in 1976 and upon which Zinn drew heavily for chapters four and five of *A People's History*. Zinn admitted to "roughly" paraphrasing Countryman's essay and promised to give him credit in a future edition,[47] which he did by inserting, "See Edward Countryman's pioneering work on rural rebellion" in parentheses[48] and including the Countryman essay in his bibliography. But the placement of Zinn's note about "Countryman's pioneering work" does not make clear how extensively Zinn relied on his work and his phraseology. There are other similar letters from colleagues among Zinn's papers.

Countryman told Zinn that he had "no intention of going public" on his charge because that "would be petty and uncomradely."[49] Koning apparently never complained either. As a fellow leftist, he was 100 percent on board with Zinn's project to destroy the reputation of Columbus in order to turn future generations of young Americans against Western civilization, capitalism, and America.

In pursuit of that agenda, Zinn reproduces three of Koning's quotations from Las Casas's *History of the Indies* and also selectively quotes from the edition of the *History* that Koning lists in his bibliography—omitting the many good things that Las Casas had to say about Columbus. But Zinn does approve of the Indians' primitive, communal way of life that Las Casas described:

> [The natives occupied] "large communal bell-shaped buildings, housing up to 600 people at one time...made of very strong wood and roofed with palm leaves....They prize bird feathers of various colors, beads made of fishbones, and green

and white stones with which they adorn their ears and lips, but they put no value on gold or other precious things. They lack all manner of commerce, neither buying nor selling, and rely exclusively on their natural environment for maintenance. They are extremely generous with their possessions and by the same token covet the possessions of their friends and expect the same degree of liberality...."[50]

Zinn's quotation from Las Casas is intended to contrast the communal and peaceful lifestyles of the natives to the acquisitive and militaristic lifestyles of the Europeans. So in language that follows Koning's closely, Zinn recounts how the first European fort in the Americas was built from the wood of the *Santa Maria* after that ship ran aground.

Zinn's version: "On Hispaniola, out of timbers from the Santa Maria, which had run aground, Columbus built a fort, the first European military base in the Western Hemisphere. He called it Navidad (Christmas) and left thirty-nine crewmembers there...."[51]

Or, in Koning's remarkably similar telling: "The Santa Maria had been run aground on Christmas day, and the fort that Columbus built from its timbers was named Puerto de Navidad, Spanish for Christmas Harbor. It was the first European foothold in the Western Hemisphere...."[52]

Columbus sailed back to Spain to report to Ferdinand and Isabella, leaving behind the thirty-nine men who couldn't fit on the return voyage now that the *Santa Maria* had been lost. And when he sailed back to the New World again, he found that the men he had left behind had been massacred by the Indians—to a man. Zinn essentially says the Spaniards were asking for it: "On Haiti [Hispaniola] they found that the sailors left behind at Fort Navidad had been killed in a battle with the Indians, after they had roamed the island in gangs looking for gold, taking women and children as slaves for sex and labor."[53]

But it is by no means certain that that's the reason they were killed. As William F. Keegan—professor of anthropology and Curator of Latin

American Studies at the University of Florida and the author of *The People Who Discovered Columbus: The Prehistory of the Bahamas*—pointed out in an article published in *Archaeology* magazine, the theory that the Spaniards were killed by the Indians because "they violated local behavioral rules—they stole looted and raped," is contradicted by the facts about which particular native chiefs the Spanish held responsible for killing their men. They blamed "primary caciques [chiefs]" who as "a matter of politics…could not permit a second-level cacique [chief] to harbor a garrison of well-armed Europeans. The Europeans had to be eliminated because they upset the established balance of power."

Yet another motivation for the killings of the Spaniards may have arisen out of the Indians' mythology. As Keegan also points out, Columbus recorded that the Indians "initially identified the Spaniards as Caribes. Caribes were mythical beings associated with the underworld who consumed human flesh. Rather than beings from heaven, then, the Spaniards were viewed as the incarnation of beings from hell. Thus, the Taino caciques [chiefs] may have justified the killing of 39 men who founded La Navidad as appropriate because the Spaniards had violated mythic proscriptions. After all, mythic beings were not supposed to remain on earth permanently."[54]

This information is hardly new or obscure. Keegan's *Archaeology* article was published in 1992—three years before Zinn brought out the second edition of *A People's History*—and it is cited in the Wikipedia article on the Arawak. At the very least, the reasons that the garrison at Fort Navidad was wiped out are complicated and difficult to be sure about. But Zinn does not hesitate to blame the Europeans for their fate. It's consistent with the rest of his chapter about Columbus, which is characterized by relentless bias against the explorer and his men and hopeless idealism about the Indians. The Europeans are always violent slavers and the Indians are always noble primitives—or budding Communists.

Not only were the Indians Communists ahead of their time—four hundred years before Karl Marx—but they were pro-choice feminists, too, who were comfortable with their bodies and advocates of free love. In support of which, Zinn gives us Bartolomé de Las Casas on "sex relations":

> Marriage laws are non-existent: men and women alike choose their mates and leave them as they please, without offense, jealousy or anger. They multiply in great abundance; pregnant women work to the last minute and give birth almost painlessly; up the next day, they bathe in the river and are as clean and healthy as before giving birth. If they tire of their men, they give themselves abortions with herbs that force stillbirths, covering their shameful parts with leaves or cotton cloth; although upon the whole, Indian men and women look upon total nakedness with as much casualness as we look upon a man's head or at his hands.

And in yet another eerie anticipation of Marx, the American natives weren't taken in by the opiate of the people: "The Indians, Las Casas says, have no religion, at least no temples."[55]

As is already obvious, Zinn relies heavily—both for his canards against Columbus and for his romantic idolization of the Indians—on Bartolomé de Las Casas, whose "many volumes on what happened to the Indians" Zinn implied he had read. But his quotations of Las Casas in *A People's History* (except the ones he cribbed from Koning!) are sourced to a single-volume edition of Las Casas's *History of the Indies* published by Harper & Row in 1971.

Bartolomé de Las Casas was consecrated Bishop of Chiapas in 1544. In 1552, he began writing his *History of the Indies* using Christopher Columbus's journals.[56] The first priest ordained in the Americas, he was known as the Apostle to the Indians. Zinn tells us, Las Casas "as a young priest, participated in the conquest of Cuba," and "owned a plantation on which Indian slaves were used, but he gave that up and became a vehement critic of Spanish cruelty."[57] Such a vehement critic, in fact, that even the introduction to the version of Las Casas's *History* that Zinn used admits his bias. As Andrée M. Collard, the translator of this particular version of the book, points out there, Las Casas's *Very Brief Relation of the Destruction of the Indies*, first translated into English in 1583, was one of two works that "supplied the main ammunition to the foreign detractors of Spain who instigated the so-called Black Legend."[58] According to Collard, the priest "intended his *History* to be a work of moral enlightenment and awakening, leading to political and social change."[59] Therefore, it "verge[s] on the polemical" and is marked by exaggerations. "The sweeping statements and prodigious numbers in the *History* must be taken with caution," warns Collard in her introduction, giving a telling example: "A Spaniard on horseback may not have killed '10,000 Indians in one hour's time'...."[60] Some of Las Casas's other numbers invite skepticism, as well—like, for example, when he concludes from the fact that there were "60,000 people living on this island [of Hispaniola], including the Indians" when he arrived there in 1508 "that from 1494 to 1508, over three million people had perished from war, slavery, and the mines."[61]

In fact, even Zinn, who quotes these incredible statistics, has to admit that they are in dispute.[62] But that doesn't stop him from building his argument on the work of the crusading priest: "Thus began the history, five hundred years ago, of the European invasion of the Indian settlements in the Americas. That beginning, when you read Las Casas—even if his figures are exaggerations (were there 3 million Indians to begin with, as he says, or less than a million, as some historians have calculated, or 8 million as others now believe?)—is conquest, slavery, death."[63]

As William and Carla Phillips observe, "One of the great ironies of Spanish history is that the work of...Las Casas and other Spanish reformers became a powerful weapon in the hands of Spain's enemies in sixteenth century and beyond." Besides being riddled with exaggeration, the priest's work is problematic in other ways. Las Casas ignored "evidence of peaceful contacts and intermarriage between Spanish colonists and the native population" and the enactment of laws to protect the

Indians in the colonies during the 1530s. Instead, he filled the *Brief History of the Destruction of the Indies* that he presented to Charles V in 1540 with the "horrendous cases" from the 1510s and 1520s, adding exaggerations. But Las Casas himself still accepted slavery as an institution and recommended that Spain buy "black African slaves," whom he saw as hardier, "to spare the Indians." It was not until late in life, and "not in print," that Las Casas recognized the wrongness of slavery—regardless of the race of the slaves.[64] As Collard explains, the priest saw America as "virgin territory, unspoiled by vitiated systems and corrupt men," with the Indians "possessing the innate goodness of man before the Fall."[65] Such a view, coupled with the fact that "the early years of conquest were marked by anarchy and license," went hand in hand with exaggerating the Indians' good qualities and the Europeans' bad ones. In Las Casas's work, "all Indians are disinterested and humble" and "all Spaniards are gold-hungry and power mad. Away from the battlefield, they are lazy, vain, arrogant....In short, they are materialistic beasts leading reckless lives of insubordination, adultery, rape and pillage."[66]

No wonder it was easy for Zinn to use Las Casas's book to make the Indians out to be noble savages, and the Europeans cartoon villains. But Zinn wanted to go beyond even Las Casas's exaggerations. To paint Columbus as a brutal genocidaire, Zinn had to suppress the distinctions that Las Casas made between Columbus and some Spaniards who truly were brutal and hide the genuine admiration that the priest expressed for the explorer. Here, for example, is an admiring Las Casas passage about Columbus, which Zinn deliberately did *not* quote: "Many is the time I have wished that God would again inspire me and that I had Cicero's gift of eloquence to extol the indescribable service to God and to the whole world which Christopher Columbus rendered at the cost of such pain and dangers, such skill and expertise, when he so courageously discovered the New World...."[67] This is not to say that Las Casas did not criticize Columbus. He blamed him for an "ignorance of the law" that led to abuses.[68] But even in his *Short Account of the Destruction of the Indies*, Las Casas described "the torture and genocidal practices of the Spanish colonialists who followed Columbus."[69] In the *History*, Las Casas blamed not Columbus, but "the men who turned Columbus's 'divine exploit' into a hellish performance and his own dream of Christianization into a nightmare."[70]

Zinn, however, gives the impression that Columbus personally and gleefully carried out the atrocities. He makes no distinction between Columbus and those who disobeyed his orders. In his wrap-up as he leads into a mid-chapter moralistic rant, Zinn indicts Columbus, proclaiming in high dudgeon, "The treatment of heroes (Columbus) and their victims (the Arawaks)—the quiet acceptance of conquest and murder in the name of progress, is only one aspect of a certain approach to history...." And Columbus is just one of many similar figures in the murderous Western tradition: "What Columbus did to the Arawaks of the Bahamas, Cortés did to the Aztecs of Mexico, Pizarro to the Incas of Peru, and the English settlers of Virginia and Massachusetts to the Powhatans and the Pequots." Thus, to "emphasize the heroism" of these men is "to deemphasize their genocide."[71]

Zinn also suppresses—and, where he doesn't suppress, downplays—the evidence from even the sympathetic Las Casas that the *Indians* could be violent and cruel. Zinn has to admit that they were "not completely peaceful, because they do battle from time to time with other tribes." But, like Koning, he is eager to explain *their* violent behavior away, arguing, "but their casualties seem small, and they fight when they are individually moved to do so because of some grievance, not on the orders of captains or kings."[72] Here he is following Las Casas: "They have no kings or captains but call on one another when they need to fight an enemy, who is usually an Indian of another language group who has killed one of them. In that case the aggrieved—the oldest member of the family—convokes his neighbors to help him against the enemy."[73] Where Zinn *doesn't* follow Las Casas is where the priest mentions the Indians' cannibalism—the priest reports, on the very next page after the passage Zinn has paraphrased, that the Indians eat very little meat "unless it be the flesh of their enemies."[74]

Zinn, busy painting the Europeans as uniquely violent and oppressive, naturally never gives credit to the feature of Western civilization that is actually responsible for Las Casas's indictment of the abuses to which many of the Spanish did subject the Indians: Christianity. It was after he heard anti-slavery sermons by Dominican monks that Las Casas gave up his own plantation and became "the Apostle to the Indians." Thus, the priest describes the perpetrators of atrocities against the Indians as "so-called Christians." Las Casas preaches, "Sin leads to sin, and for many years they lived unscrupulously, not observing Lent or other fasts" and eating meat on Fridays.[75] Zinn ignores such old-fashioned religious explanations for the Spaniards' descent into criminality against the natives and pretends that Las Casas, like himself, is a secular critic of imperialism. But in fact, as Collard explains: "Las Casas's criticism of slavery reflects the enlightened Spanish legal tradition, the main expression of which is found in the *Siete Partidas* (compiled in the thirteenth century), which under the code of slavery provides for slaves' civil rights. This liberal tradition is being reinforced by the strong influence of Erasmian humanism in Spain which stresses the Pauline view of humanity—*all* people are God's people. In dealing with the Indians, the Spaniards have failed to respect the God-given 'natural rights of man.'"[76]

All this—Christianity, enlightenment, human rights, the rule of law, humanism, equal dignity for all persons—is the very essence of the European civilization that Zinn was indicting in the person of Columbus. But all Zinn could see in Europe was "the religion of popes, the government of kings, the frenzy for money that marked Western civilization and its first messenger to the Americas, Christopher Columbus."[77]

Zinn claimed to be correcting for a massive coverup of Columbus's crimes. "When we read the history books given to children in the United States," Zinn asserts on page seven of *A People's History*, "it all starts with heroic adventure—there is no bloodshed—and Columbus Day is a celebration." According to Zinn, the pro-Columbus bias is not just about dumbing things down for little kids or protecting them from nightmares about rape and pillage: "Past the elementary and high schools, there are only hints of something else."[78] At this point, Zinn launches into his full-bore attack on historian Samuel Eliot Morison, the same man who was excoriated by Koning in *his* indictment of Columbus (to which Zinn's is so suspiciously similar).

Koning had called Morison a "Columbus fan."[79] Zinn takes it further and accuses Morison of spinning a "grand romance" and "bury[ing]" the facts about Columbus's genocide "in a mass of other information" so as "to say to the reader with a certain infectious calm: yes, mass murder took place, but it's not that important."[80]

Who was Zinn's scapegoat—the man he held up to represent the historians who had supposedly sold deluded generations of Americans on the Columbus myth? Samuel Eliot Morison was a Navy admiral, seaman, Harvard professor, and winner of the Pulitzer Prize (twice) and of numerous other prizes for dozens of books on history. His research on Columbus included retracing the discoverer's voyages to the New World. Writing in 2011, Laurence Bergreen, the author of *Columbus: The Four Voyages*, called Morison's 1942 *Admiral of the Ocean Sea*, based on his recreation of Columbus's journeys, "outstanding" and pointed out that it was still the "largest maritime database pertaining to Columbus."[81] Any historian writing about the discovery of America has to acknowledge the groundbreaking work of Morison. Unlike Zinn, whose purported scholarship was (as we shall see) just in pursuit of his radical politics by other means, Morison did real historical research. In 1939, while the teenaged Zinn was cavorting with the Communists (details will follow), Morison was recognizing the scarcity of objective reports about this period of history and writing an article, published in the *Hispanic American Historical Review*, about the "pitfalls into which English translators of [Columbus's] *Journal* have fallen"—for which he examined the French and English translations of Las Casas's *Abstract of the Journal of the First Voyage of Christopher Columbus*.[82]

And it is simply not the case that, as Zinn claims, Morison makes the story of Columbus a "grand romance" by discounting what Morison himself—as Zinn has to admit—calls "genocide." The fact is that what

Zinn actually hates about Morison is not his bias but his balance. As Fuson pointed out, Morison may have been too *hard* on Columbus. While Zinn accuses Morison of writing a "grand romance," the truth is that Zinn's book is the real "grand romance"—about himself. Zinn is the hero championing the approved downtrodden groups. Zinn is the swashbuckling historian rescuing the forgotten story—the one covered up by all previous historians who lack his compassion and moral vision. Here he is, the crusader-historian, the knight in shining armor rushing to the rescue of the oppressed:

> I prefer to try to tell the story of the discovery of America from the viewpoint of the Arawaks, of the Constitution from the standpoint of the slaves, of Andrew Jackson as seen by the Cherokees, of the Civil War as seen by the New York Irish, of the Mexican war as seen by the deserting soldiers of Scott's army, of the rise of industrialism as seen by the young women in the Lowell textile mills, of the Spanish-American war as seen by the Cubans, the conquest of the Philippines as seen by black soldiers on Luzon, the Gilded Age as seen by southern farmers, the First World War as seen by socialists, the Second World War by pacifists, the New Deal as seen by blacks in Harlem, the postwar American empire as seen by peons in Latin America. And so on, to the limited extent that any one person, however he or she strains, can "see" history from the standpoint of others.[83]

In Zinn's telling, the Arawaks—or black slaves, or Cherokees, or New York Irish, or whoever—must always be persecuted innocents and the condemnation of their sufferings must be absolute. The officially oppressed cannot be blamed even for any crimes they themselves commit, which are inevitably the fault of their oppressors: "The victims, themselves desperate and tainted with the culture that oppresses them, turn on other victims.... I will try not to overlook the cruelties that victims inflict on one another as they are jammed together in the boxcars of the system." (Here, Zinn is following Karl Marx's maxim that proletarian victims are "tainted with the culture that oppresses them" and so oppress others, in turn). To dilute the reader's indignation at the approved victims' injuries with balancing facts—any violence that the officially oppressed group might be legitimately held responsible for, for example, or any achievements of the oppressed group's enemies, or any benefits that the oppressors may have conferred on the world—is tantamount to saying that "mass murder" is "not that important."[84]

According to Zinn, there's no such thing as objective history, anyway: "the historian's distortion is more than technical, it is ideological; it is released into a world of contending interests, where any chosen emphasis supports (whether the historian means to or not) some kind of interest, whether economic or political or racial or national or sexual." Once ideology has become a moral virtue, Zinn can discount standards of scholarship—such as those of the American Historical Association—as having to do with nothing more important than "technical problems of excellence"—standards of no importance compared to his kind of history, which consists in forging "tools for contending social classes, races, nations."[85]

Thus it would seem that the noble political purpose behind Zinn's history justifies him in omitting facts that are inconvenient for his Columbus-bad-Indians-good narrative. The Edenic Arawaks were "remarkable (European observers were to say again and again) for their hospitality, their belief in sharing,"[86] but Zinn ignores the evidence Morison brings out of infighting among them and historical episodes in which the Spaniards were greeted with hostility, and even violence. For example, the tawny-skinned pacific "Arawaks" that Columbus first met turn out to be from the Taino branch of the Arawak language group, who "within the previous century…had wrested the Bahamas and most of Cuba from the more primitive Siboney."[87] One factor in the episode of Fort Navidad—not mentioned by Zinn, but covered in Morison's account—was a request from the cacique of Marien, the Indian chief of the northeastern part of Haiti, that Columbus establish a base there. The chief wanted the Spaniards to protect him from enemies on the island, as Fernández-Armesto also pointed out. And on their first return voyage to the New World, Columbus's men encountered "a branch of the Tainos called Ciguayos, who in self-defense against raiding Caribs from Puerto Rico had adopted their weapons." These Tainos, "not pleased to meet [Columbus's men]," were "appeased" with gifts of cloth and trinkets.[88] During an expedition to what is now St. Croix, twenty-five Spaniards returning to the ship were met by four Carib men and two women armed with bows and arrows who wounded two of the Spaniards, one mortally.[89]

Zinn ignores the historical context of slavery, which Morison brings out: "Slavery was so taken for granted in those days, both by Europeans and by the Moslems (who still practice it), that Columbus never gave a thought to the morality of this proposal. If he had, he would doubtless have reflected that the Indians enslaved each other, so why should we not enslave them, particularly if we convert them, too, and save their souls alive?"[90]

Zinn also ignores what Morison calls "one of Columbus's worst decisions" in delegating authority. He planned a "reconnaissance" of "four hundred men" to "relieve" a garrison under the command of Peter Margarit. Columbus "instructed [Alonso de] Hojeda [the delegated leader] to do the Indians no harm and reminded him that the Sovereigns desired their salvation even more than their gold, but the first thing Hojeda did was to cut off the ears of an Indian who stole some old Spanish clothes...." Unfortunately, Columbus did not learn of "these doings" before departing for Cuba. And his younger brother, whom he had left in charge, was incapable of controlling "egoists like Hojeda and Margarit."[91]

Columbus and his two brothers had little control on Hispaniola, in part because the Spaniards despised them for being Genoese.[92] Nonetheless, Columbus did prevent many abuses and crimes against the Indians. He instructed his men to treat the natives with kindness[93]—a fact that both Zinn and Koning somehow fail to mention. And on the return trip from Columbus's second voyage to the New World when the men were desperate for food, some of them proposed eating the captive Indians "starting with the Caribs, who were man-eaters themselves; thus it wouldn't be a sin to pay them in their own coin! Others proposed that all the natives be thrown overboard so that they would consume no more rations. Columbus, in one of his humanitarian moods, argued that after all Caribs were people and should be treated as such."[94]

Zinn painted the New World as a feminist paradise, but as Morison reports, when the Talamanca Indians wanted to trade with the Spaniards "to break down 'sales resistance,' the Indians sent on board two virgins, one about eight and the other about fourteen years old." Columbus had the girls fed and clothed and sent back, leaving the natives astonished at "the continence of the Spaniards."[95] The fact is—as a knowledgeable, careful, and balanced historian of Morison's caliber amply demonstrates—that relations between the Indians and the Europeans in the wake of Columbus's discovery of America were fraught with ambiguities that complicate Zinn's cartoon of Indian innocents enslaved and abused by European devils.

And Morison's balanced account of Columbus and the other European explorers was far from unique in the pre-Zinn period of history writing. College textbooks such as the 1961 edition of Thomas Bailey's popular *The American Pageant,* first published in 1956,[96] did not present Columbus as a larger-than-life hero that Zinn and Koning pretend dominated history before they set the record straight. Bailey described Columbus as a "skilled Italian seaman.... A man of vision, energy, resourcefulness, and courage," who, however, "failed to uncover the riches of the Indies" and died "a cruelly disappointed man."[97] The 1963 edition of *The Roots of American Civilization* by Curtis P. Nettels called Columbus "vain, boastful, arrogant, and deceitful," but also said he displayed "tenacity, courage, hardihood, and independence," and was "highly visionary" in his last years.[98] In fact, "the leading American history college textbook of the 1960s, *The Growth of the American Republic*"[99] by Morison and Henry Steele Commager, tells students that "Columbus expected to obtain the precious metal [gold] by trade," but after the Indians were satisfied, "the Spaniards began taking it by force. As elsewhere in America where Europeans came, the newcomers were first welcomed by the Indians as visitors, then resented as intruders, and finally resisted with fruitless desperation." Morison and Commager describe the complicated situation, explaining, "The Spaniards, who had come for gold and nothing else, resented their governor's orders to build houses, tend crops, and cut wood; the wine and food supplies from Spain gave out; and before long bands of men in armor were roving about the fertile interior of Hispaniola, living off the country, and torturing the natives to obtain gold." In the summer of 1494, while Columbus was off "exploring the southern coasts of Cuba and Hispaniola and discovering Jamaica, the colonists got completely out of hand." When Columbus tried to impose discipline, the "malcontents seiz[ed] vessels and return[ed] to Spain to complain of him...."[100]

Zinn, perhaps too lazy or too busy with political agitation to do even the most basic research, has to paint a false picture of those historians with whom he disagrees. He places straw men on pedestals and then knocks them down one by one until only he is standing. A result like that would be substandard coming from a high school student writing a research paper—much less a professional historian claiming to be blazing a new trail and leaving the existing Columbus scholarship behind in the dust. Zinn's pretense to break new ground on Columbus was nothing more than a clever marketing strategy, surpassing in chutzpah the most brazen of ad campaigns for quack tonics in our capitalistic system that he so vehemently condemns.

Morison's book *Christopher Columbus, Mariner* was published in 1955, but it is difficult to find today. Neither my public nor college library had a copy. I had to order one of the few remaining used copies to buy. Mine came from St. Mary's College in Leavenworth, Kansas. Most libraries carry multiple copies of *A People's History*.

Unfortunately, Zinn's attack on the historians who gave students a balanced picture of Columbus has been remarkably effective. Zinn successfully sold himself as a historian knocking down the giants who preceded him and championed the cause of the innocents oppressed by colonizers, capitalists, and Christians. Images of unspeakable cruelty against a gentle people remain in the minds of countless students who have read Zinn's propaganda, and they now color the public discussion about Columbus. As history education professor Sam Wineburg pointed out with no little amazement, Howard Zinn's readers *believe* him. Michael Kazin has noted that Zinn's *History* takes on "the force and authority of revelation."

An interlude Zinn throws into his Columbus chapter has a lot to do with the enormous impact of his take on the discovery of America. After throwing into question the historical method, he throws into question the legitimacy of the United States of America. He tars the Founding Fathers—and essentially every leading figure in American history—with the "conquest and murder" to which he reduced Columbus's discovery of America: "The treatment of heroes (Columbus) and their victims (the Arawaks)—the quiet acceptance of conquest and murder in the name of progress—is only one aspect of a certain approach to history, in which the past is told from the point of view of governments, conquerors, diplomats, leaders. It is as if they, like Columbus, deserve universal acceptance, as if they—the Founding Fathers, Jackson, Lincoln, Wilson, Roosevelt, Kennedy, the leading members of Congress, the famous Justices of the Supreme Court—represent the nation as a whole."[101]

It's tempting to point out that all these men—with the exception of the Supreme Court justices—were literally elected to "represent the nation as a whole," or at least one of its states.

Then Zinn goes for broke: "The pretense is that there really is such a thing as 'the United States,' subject to occasional conflicts and quarrels, but fundamentally a community of people with common interests. It is as if there really is a 'national interest' represented in the Constitution, in territorial expansion, in the laws passed by Congress, the decisions of the courts, the development of capitalism, the culture of education and the mass media."[102]

Those quotation marks around "United States" and "national inter-est" are doing a lot of heavy lifting. But the remarkable success of Zinn's anti-American history in persuading large swathes of the American people to despise their own country is evidence of the remarkable success of his rhetoric. In the absence of that evidence, who could have believed that an American history book denying "that there really is such a thing as 'the United States'" would be taken seriously by anyone?

One of Zinn's cleverest rhetorical tricks was to anticipate the doubts that his radical and deeply dishonest take on American history were bound to raise in the reader's mind and supply answers for them. Any reasonable reader, for example, is going to wonder whether Zinn's account of Columbus isn't just a bit biased. Thus, Zinn's defense of bias—and his attack on balance—in history writing. We have already seen how Zinn eschewed historical judgment and balance in favor of the partisan valorization of approved victim groups and the condemnation of their oppressors. For him, history is not about telling the story of what happened; it's about being on the right side, "not…on the side of the executioners."[103] But lest his readers be unmoved by this moral blackmail, lest they should fail to be carried away on the tide of piled-up atrocity stories and reiterated indictment of our former national heroes, Zinn also provides a theoretical defense of bias in history writing. We have already seen him arguing that to report genocide while also reporting "a mass of other information" is to bury the crimes of history and to tell the reader that mass murder is "not that important."[104] But it's worse than that. Historical balance also ensures that the heinous crimes of history will continue into the future: "One reason these atrocities are still with us is that we have learned to bury them in a mass of other facts, as radioactive wastes are buried in containers in earth."[105] And Zinn was on a mission to stop those atrocities with a new style of partisan history that likens "facts" to radioactive wastes.

In his opening chapter on Columbus, Zinn pretty much revealed himself as the leftist political activist that he was. But Zinn's success is also due in part to who he was and to the fact that he incessantly promoted himself. He was born at just the right time and cannily took advantage of political shifts. Unlike many of his colleagues, Zinn made the transition from Old Left to New Left quite easily, as Eugene Genovese told me.[106] In fact, Zinn was at the forefront leading the youth, adapting Old Left (Communist) goals to the times, and speaking the language of the 1960s Youth Movement. Zinn parlayed a comrade's work into his own, shunting aside the author of the work that fills up the first several pages of his radical magnum opus. The son of poor Russian-Jewish immigrants in Brooklyn, the professor who claimed that the United States has no right to exist became one of the most popular historians of the United States—and one of the most influential. In 2017, a Harvard Graduate School of Education post on teaching about Columbus listed *A People's History* as a resource for teachers.[107]

Other historians wrote more books and won more awards for scholarly achievement, but none has achieved the celebrity status of Howard Zinn, who is cited as an inspirational figure years after his death and as cool as Che Guevara to the radical youth. Few, if any, history professors have had their autobiographies made into movies. But Zinn has. Zinn was instrumental in the sea change that has transformed Columbus from the discoverer of America into the genocidal villain whose murder and enslavement of the Indians is the original sin that makes America a crime. And the facts of his life are crucial to explaining how he was able to do it. So, the next chapter will take a look at his autobiography.

TWO

The Life of Zinn

Howard Zinn's 1994 autobiography *You Can't Be Neutral on a Moving Train* begins with a scene in Kalamazoo, Michigan. It is the night of the final televised debate of the 1992 presidential campaign, but hundreds of people have chosen to hear Howard Zinn speak on "The Legacy of Columbus, 1492–1992." He writes:

> Ten years earlier, in the very first pages of my book *A People's History of the United States*, I had written about Columbus in a way that startled readers. They, like me, had learned in elementary school (an account never contradicted, however far their education continued) that Columbus was one of the great heroes of world history, to be admired for his daring feat of imagination and courage. In my account, I acknowledged that he was an intrepid sailor, but also pointed out (based on his own journal and the reports of many eyewitnesses) that he was vicious in his treatment of the gentle Arawak Indians who greeted his arrival in this hemisphere. He enslaved them, tortured them, murdered them—all in the pursuit of wealth....[1]

That night in Kalamazoo, Howard Zinn was doing his part to trans-form Americans' opinions about Christopher Columbus. As Zinn's friend and biographer Martin Duberman recounts, "in Howard's opinion, the truth about Columbus hadn't sufficiently sunk in" by 1994. "There *were* a number of anti-Columbus protests, and Howard delighted in them," but there were still a significant number of parades and celebrations.[2]

Looking back at the 1992 election from two years out, Zinn didn't see Clinton's victory as a harbinger of change for the better. As he explained in the 2003 edition of *A People's History*, Clinton's presidency was marred by "sensational scandals surrounding his personal life," capitulation to "caution and conservatism," and "futile shows of military braggadocio."[3] Clinton's presidency did not alter "The Establishment—that uneasy club of business executives, generals, and politicos" main-taining "a pretension of national unity"—which is really only a unity of the "highly privileged and slightly privileged." The elites see to it that "the 99 percent remain split in countless ways...."[4]

But is there any reason for optimism? Yes! The surprising "success of *A People's History*," which, "in its first decade...went through twenty-four printings, sold three hundred thousand copies, [and] was nominated for an American Book Award...." (The American Book Award, not to be confused with the prestigious National Book Award, is given by the Before Columbus Foundation for outstanding "contem-porary American multicultural literature."[5]) Zinn was getting letters "from all over the country...a large proportion of them...in excited reaction" to his chapter on Columbus. Most of these, he wrote, "thanked me for telling an untold story." But some, like "a mother in Califor-nia...became enraged" upon learning that it was being used in her daughter's class and demanded that the teacher be investigated.[6]

Zinn explained that people react to *A People's History* in such passionate—but divergent—ways because of his "irreverence": his radical approach to American history, which in the words of "one reviewer" involves "'a reversal of perspective, a reshuffling of heroes and villains.'"[7]

There's no doubt that Zinn reshuffled the good guys and the bad guys. As we shall see, *A People's History* recast World War II—the "good war" fought by the "Greatest Generation"—as a string of Allied atrocities matching those of our Nazi enemies. Zinn inspired young activists to embrace Marxism and see civil rights through its lens rather than as a fight for equal opportunity, as it was originally envisioned by the abolitionists, the NAACP, and even the early black nationalists. He celebrated the defeat of America by the Communists in Vietnam. And, as we have already seen, in the opening chapter of *A People's History of the United States* he called into doubt the legitimacy—even the reality—of the United States, itself. Indeed, on page nine of *A People's History,* Zinn called the idea that "there really is such a thing as 'the United States'...a community of people with common interests" a "pretense."[8]

Zinn presented himself as a path-breaking truth-teller. What he did in his *History*, as Zinn explained on page two of his autobiography, was to reveal the Founding Fathers to be not only "ingenious organizers" but also "rich white slaveholders, merchants, bondholders, fearful of lower-class rebellion, or, as James Madison put it, of 'an equal division of property.' Our military heroes—Andrew Jackson, Theodore Roosevelt—were racists, Indian-killers, war-lovers, imperialists. Our most liberal presidents—Jefferson, Lincoln, Wilson, Roosevelt, Kennedy—were more concerned with political power and national aggrandizement than with the rights of nonwhite people."[9]

A People's History certainly does attack revered and established ideas. Consider the opening paragraph of chapter four of Zinn's history, ostensibly about the American Revolution and the founding of the United States: "Around 1776, certain important people in the English colonies made a discovery that would prove enormously useful for the next two hundred years. They found that by creating a nation, a symbol, a legal unity called the United States, they could take over land, profits, and political power from favorites of the British Empire. In the process, they could hold back a number of potential rebellions and create a consensus of popular support for the rule of a new, privileged leadership."[10]

The idea that the Revolution "was on behalf of a united people" is a "myth," Zinn asserts. As evidence for this claim, Zinn tells us that John Locke, whose ideas influenced our government, "himself was a wealthy man, with investments in the silk trade and slave trade, income from loans and mortgages." Zinn criticizes The Declaration of Independence, which, "like Locke's *Second Treatise*, talked about government and political rights, but ignored the existing inequalities in property." He asks the loaded question, "And how could people truly have equal rights, with stark differences in wealth?"[11]

Even the universal franchise would not solve the inherent problems in such a government, Zinn says in the next chapter of *A People's History*: "The problem of democracy in the post-Revolutionary society was not...Constitutional limitations on voting. It lay deeper, beyond the Constitution, in the division of society into rich and poor. For if some people had great wealth and great influence; if they had the land, the money, the newspapers, the church, the educational system—how could voting, however broad, cut into such power?"[12]

According to Zinn, the Constitution was really written to maintain the privileges of the wealthy elite. It does just "enough for small property owners, for middle-income mechanics and farmers" to keep them invested in the status quo, just the right amount for "the slightly prosperous people who make up this base of support" for the existing regime, and serve as "buffers against the blacks, the Indians, the very poor whites."[13]

It is only for being the champion of "the blacks, the Indians, the very poor whites," and other victim groups that Zinn's history has made him enemies and critics—according to Zinn. But is Zinn's advocacy for the downtrodden really the sole reason that anyone might object to the radically jaundiced view of American history on display in *A People's History*? In his defense of his magnum opus, Zinn continually deflects attention away from criticism of the inaccuracies and distortions of the history he tells by suggesting that every critique of his work is really just a masked critique of his life and political activism.

For "some people," Zinn maintained in his autobiography, "not only was my book out of order, my whole life was out of order." Thus, Zinn attempted to move the battle to the venue where he clearly thought he had the best chance of victory: he was much more comfortable defending his political activism than defending his history.[14]

The last questioner at the event in Kalamazoo asked, "Given the depressing news of what is happening in the world, you seem surprisingly optimistic. What gives you hope?" Zinn's immediate answer was his activist creed: "I said I could understand being depressed by the state of the world, but the questioner had caught my mood accurately. To him and to others, mine seemed an absurdly cheerful approach to a violent and unjust world. But to me what is often disdained as romantic idealism, as wishful thinking, is justified if it prompts *action* to fulfill those wishes, to bring to life those ideals [emphasis in the original]."[15]

But in order to fully answer the questioner in Kalamazoo, Zinn wrote, "I would have had to go back over my life." Here ensues a catalogue of events from the life of Zinn that justify his hope. Here Zinn employs the literary device known as anaphora—note the repetition at the beginning of the lines:

> I would have to tell about going to work in a shipyard at the age of eighteen and spending three years working on the docks, in the cold and heat, amid deafening noise and poisonous fumes, building battleships and landing ships in the early years of the Second World War.
>
> I would have to tell about enlisting in the Air Force at twenty-one, being trained as a bombardier, flying combat missions in Europe, and later asking myself troubling questions about what I had done in the war.
>
> And about getting married, becoming a father, going to college under the G.I. Bill while loading trucks in a warehouse, with my wife working and our two children in a charity day-care center, and all of us living in a low-income housing project on the Lower East Side of Manhattan.

And about getting my Ph.D. from Columbia and my first real teaching job (I had a number of unreal teaching jobs), going to live and teach in a black community in the Deep South for seven years. And about the students at Spelman College who one day decided to climb over a symbolic and actual stone wall surrounding the campus to make history in the early years of the civil rights movement.

And about my experiences in that movement, in Atlanta, in Albany, Georgia, and Selma, Alabama, in Hattiesburg and Jackson and Greenwood, Mississippi.

I would have to tell about moving north to teach in Boston, and joining the protests against the war in Vietnam, and being arrested a half-dozen times....

I would have to recapture the scenes in a dozen courtrooms where I testified in the 1970s and 1980s. I would have to tell about the prisoners I have known....[16]

Like Walt Whitman, who employed anaphora to good effect as he swept the vast multitudes and diverse scenes of a young democratic republic in the mid-nineteenth century into his *Song of Myself,* Howard Zinn, too, "contains multitudes." He is the worker, the brave civil rights activist, the popular professor leading the young social justice warriors. It was an image that he cultivated through the decades. But what did Zinn leave out?

Let's start with one of the "unreal" teaching jobs that he doesn't give the details of. Zinn's first "real"—full-time—teaching position was at Spelman College, beginning in 1956, when he was appointed as "acting chairman of the department of history and social sciences."[17] Before then, while still working on his degree in the early 1950s, Zinn was a part-time instructor at Brooklyn College and Upsala College in New Jersey.[18] During those years, though, in 1951, Zinn also taught a class in Marxism at the Communist Party headquarters in Brooklyn. That's according to his FBI file. Zinn's Communist activities came to the attention of the FBI beginning in 1948 when an informant reported that Zinn had told him that he was a member of the Communist Party and attended meetings five nights a week. According to the file, Zinn was "a delegate to the New York State Communist Party Convention." The memo in Zinn's FBI file lists a number of Communist-affiliated groups with which Zinn was working, including the Henry Wallace for President campaign. A different informant told the FBI that Zinn had been a member of the CPUSA (Communist Party USA) from at least 1949 to mid-1953. While teaching at Spelman, Zinn picketed against the quarantine of Cuba with other known Communists. At the loading dock where he had worked, he had had a reputation as a Communist.[19]

Charges of Communist Party membership dogged Zinn throughout his life, but he continued to deny those charges from 1953 when FBI agents confronted him on that subject to the end of his life. He admitted only to tangential involvement with the party—activities such as attending the Paul Robeson concert in Peekskill in 1949 and being involved in the American Labor Party and the Veterans Committee Against the Mundt-Nixon Bill (later the McCarran Act), and to being a "leftist."[20]

In his autobiography, Zinn recounts how his youthful quest for justice—as he witnessed his parents' inability to reach the American dream—drew him in the direction of "radical" politics. The Zinns owned candy stores that failed, and Zinn worked alongside his father as a waiter, delivery boy, and caddy. He recalls the summer when he was seventeen. At that time, his family was living in a four-room apartment above a candy store on Bushwick Avenue when some "regular guys"—in fact, Communists—who were a few years older than he was came into the neighborhood distributing Marxist literature and discussing politics "with whoever was interested." Zinn argued with them about the Russian invasion of Finland, but found himself agreeing with them "on lots of things," such as the "contrasts of wealth and poverty in America." He admired their courage and their willingness to "defy the local policeman." So, the teenage Zinn went with them to "a demonstration" in Times Square. They strolled around until ten o'clock in the evening, when suddenly "banners were unfurled, and people, perhaps a thousand or more," formed up on sidewalks "chanting slogans about peace and justice" in "nonviolent lines."[21]

The scene quickly changed. There were sirens and screams and "hundreds of policemen, mounted on horses and on foot, charging into the lines of marchers, smashing people with their clubs." Zinn recalls waking up in a doorway with both a painful lump on his head and a "painful thought" inside it: "Those young Communists on the block were right! The state and its police were not neutral referees in a society of contending interests. They were on the side of the rich and powerful." From that moment on he was "no longer a liberal, a believer in the self-correcting character of American democracy," but "a radical, believing that something fundamental was wrong in this country.... the situation required...an uprooting of the old order, the introduction of a new kind of society—cooperative, peaceful, egalitarian."[22]

It's impossible to be sure what event Zinn was describing here, but on October 1, 1938, when Zinn was sixteen years old, "5,000 boys and girls of high school age, members of the Young Communist League," marching two and three abreast, "invaded Times Square" at about nine o'clock in the evening, according to the *New York Times*. After they snarled vehicular and pedestrian traffic for fifteen minutes, police broke up the "demonstration."[23]

Zinn denied that he was a Communist Party member, but he avowed his belief in the statement by Marx and Engels in the *Communist Manifesto*: "The history of all hitherto existing society is the history of class struggle." That principle was, for the young Zinn, "undeniably true, verifiable in any reading of history. Certainly true for the United States, despite all the promises of the Constitution...." He believed that what he called the "socialist vision" of Marx and Engels would lead to a "rational, just economic system [that] would allow a short work day and leave everyone freedom and time to do as they liked—to write poetry, to be in nature, to play sports, to be truly human. Nationalism would be a thing of the past. People all over the world, of whatever race, of whatever continent, would live in peace and cooperation."[24]

Howard Zinn's formative years were spent at the epicenter of the American Communist Movement at the time when the Communists were making their biggest inroads into Americans' hearts and minds: New York City in the 1930s, when the Depression seemed to show the failure of capitalism. "By 1938 the Party counted 38,000 members in New York State, about half its national membership, and most of those lived in New York City," according to Maurice Isserman in his *New York Times* article on the occasion of the one-hundred-year anniversary of the Bolshevik Revolution. Up to twenty thousand participants attended party-organized mass meetings in the old Madison Square Garden and tens of thousands went to annual May Day parades. Howard Zinn, whose family lived in Brooklyn, was close to the action. Neighborhoods in the Bronx, East Harlem, the Lower East Side, and Brooklyn formed a kind of "red belt," according to Isserman. Thousands of students at Brooklyn College, City College, and Columbia University, where Zinn earned his Ph.D., joined Communist front groups such as the American Youth Congress.[25] The Young Communist League had organized the October 1, 1938, "demonstration" in Times Square. In 1994, Zinn received a letter from Phil, a Young Communist League member who remembered seeing Zinn at a meeting "somewhat more than fifty years [previously]" and said that they had both probably "participated in Times Square demonstrations."[26]

According to John Earl Haynes, the CPUSA's "greatest success" was in "the labor movement where it dominated the leadership of unions with a quarter of the CIO's membership." But acting covertly through front groups and auxiliary organizations, the party also gained "toeholds among immigrant groups, in the civil rights movement, on college campuses, and in Hollywood." The years "just before and just after World War II" represented the party's "peak membership of 65,000 to 70,000."[27] Although the party failed in national politics, namely with the 1948 Henry Wallace presidential campaign, its support for campaigns "coat[ed] the party with a veneer of respectability and insinuate[d] Soviet themes into American political discourse." That was at least part of the reason for Communist support for the 1938 Illinois senatorial campaign of Morris Childs before he left the party, according to his biographer.[28]

Ron Radosh—who was a Communist for a year or two in college, and whose father was a fellow traveler—has stated categorically that Zinn was a Communist. In 1949, when Zinn's FBI file was opened, he was vice chairman of a Brooklyn branch of the American Labor Party (ALP), "by then a group run and dominated by Communists." In the 1948 presidential election, the ALP backed Henry Wallace, who had been dismissed by President Harry Truman as secretary of commerce; Wallace's campaign was run "entirely by the CPUSA." Radosh also explains, "Zinn's lifelong silence about his membership fits the profile of most American Communists of that era.... most members were covert and were told to infiltrate liberal groups, pretend to be regular Progressives, and try to get the gullible to adopt pro-Soviet positions." Radosh's experience in working with FBI dossiers (including his own, at five hundred pages) shows that informants who, like most of those who informed on Zinn, were former party members or had infiltrated Communist groups were usually accurate.

Besides the ALP, Communist front groups Zinn belonged to or worked with included the American Veterans Committee, the American Peace Mobilization, and the Joint Anti-Fascist Refugee Committee. His memberships, Radosh says, "appear to be a party assignment." By the time the New Left and the Civil Rights Movement came on the scene, Zinn had left the party's ranks, but he was toying with the Maoist Progressive Labor Party and the Trotskyist Socialist Workers party and "gave his support to young black militants" of the Student Nonviolent Coordinating Committee (SNCC) and the Black Panthers.[29] Actually, Zinn radicalized the students, turned them into militants, and helped found and guide the radical SNCC.

And how did Howard Zinn, a doctoral candidate from Brooklyn who was heavily involved in Communist activities, end up teaching at Spelman—a Christian college for black women in Atlanta, Georgia?

According to friendly biographer Duberman, Zinn was interviewed by Spelman College president Albert Manley, the first black and first male president of the college, after a placement bureau contacted Zinn, who was hired after negotiating for an additional five hundred dollars to the proffered "midrange" yearly salary of four thousand dollars. According to Duberman, "Howard hadn't given the slightest thought to teaching in a black college," even though his "sympathies were decisively with the black struggle."[30]

The year 1956, when Zinn began teaching at Spelman, was significant for the worldwide Communist Movement. Zygmund Dobbs, the anti-communist who had been raised in a Communist household and been a Trotskyite in his youth, warned about the encroachment of the Communists. In his 1958 pamphlet "Red Intrigue and Race Turmoil," Dobbs described how the Communist Party was infiltrating the NAACP and warned about "the left-wing white support that the NAACP has in the South."[31] The year 1956 marked a low point for the CPUSA. In February, Soviet leader Nikita Khrushchev's speech denouncing Stalin for his ideological deviance had encouraged uprisings in Poland and Hungary, and then brutal suppressions, especially in Hungary. As Maurice Isserman recounts, these events helped lead to a crisis in CPUSA leadership and a further decline in membership. Disillusioned with the party, but still adhering to socialist principles, former Communist Party members found a new outlet for their activism in the Civil Rights Movement. Tom Kahn, a white socialist, enrolled in 1960 at Howard University, where he radicalized black students "who would soon play leading roles in the Student Nonviolent Coordinating Committee."[32]

Zinn told biographer Davis Joyce in a December 3, 1996, email message that he had moved South when "McCarthyism was plaguing colleges and universities throughout the country...and it may be that black colleges were a kind of refuge (although I did not consciously seek out Spelman for that reason!) for white radicals." As Zinn explained, "radical whites (me, Staughton Lynd, others) were especially welcome, and since our radicalism was expressed mostly in our views on race relations, well, that fitted in with the black community quite well."[33]

In fact, Zinn's radicalism was not a good fit for Spelman College, where he must have stood out like a sore thumb. Spelman was a conservative Christian school that had been founded in 1881 by eleven ex-slaves who met in Friendship Baptist Church, wanting to read the Bible.[34] It became Atlanta Baptist Female Seminary and then, in 1924, Spelman College. Karen Vanlandingham in her 1985 master's thesis, "In Pursuit of a Changing Dream: Spelman College Students and the Civil Rights Movement, 1955–1962," explains that the "religious tradition inherent in Spelman's founding endured as a part of the school's educational philosophy." The 1958–1959 college catalogue asserted, "Spelman College is emphatically Christian. The attitude toward life exemplified by the life and teachings of Jesus is the ideal which governs the institution."[35] College life there included mandatory daily chapel attendance and adherence to a strict curfew and dress code.

Howard Zinn, however, felt it was his mission and his right to change the college. In the August 6, 1960, *Nation*, he observed: "'You can always tell a Spelman girl,' alumni and friends of the college have boasted for years. The 'Spelman girl' walked gracefully, talked properly, went to church every Sunday, poured tea elegantly and, in general, had all the attributes of the product of a fine finishing school. If intellect and talent and social consciousness happened to develop also, they were, to an alarming extent, by-products."[36]

Zinn set out to transform the "finishing school" into a "school for protest."

As if surprised, Zinn writes in his autobiography, "I learned that President Manley resented the article for its criticism of the college as it was."[37]

Manley, who had been born to parents of Jamaican descent in Honduras, had come to the United States for his education and been appalled by the segregation he encountered on the journey and after he arrived, as he describes in his memoir *A Legacy Continues: The Manley Years at Spelman College, 1953–1976*. Once he assumed the reins at Spelman in 1953, he began an effort to upgrade the college's academic standing by hiring more professors with Ph.D.'s.[38] Manley was a proponent of black civil rights, but also of maintaining high academic standards and an orderly atmosphere for learning.

Zinn must have appeared to be a good candidate. A World War II veteran holding a master's degree from Columbia University with a major in history and minor in economics, he was about to get a Ph.D. from the same institution. As Joyce points out in his biography, Zinn had "studied under some of the great names in the profession at the time, including Henry Steele Commager, David Donald, Richard B. Morris, Jacques Barzun, William Leuchtenburg, and Richard Hofstadter." His dissertation on the congressional career of Fiorello LaGuardia was submitted by his adviser, Leuchtenburg, to the Beveridge Award competition of the American Historical Association. It won second place and was published in 1959 by Cornell University Press as *LaGuardia in Congress*.[39]

Campus minister Norman Rates told Vanlandingham that Zinn "quickly became one of the most important white adults involved with the student movement in Atlanta. Fellow professors tended to label him a 'rabble rouser.'"[40] According to Rates, Manley was in a tricky position after Zinn started his direct-action civil rights campaigns. The college president "had to be sensitive to the demands of the leaders of the black and white communities who were upset with the student activists, but he did not want to alienate his students.'" He also "had to answer to angry or concerned parents who wanted to know why the school was allowing their daughters to be involved in such risky activities."[41]

While Zinn accused Manley of authoritarianism and worse, Vanlandingham explains, "Professors at public colleges often feared for their jobs, but at Spelman it appears that Manley did not pressure faculty members who supported or encouraged the students." In fact, according to student activist leader Herschelle Sullivan, when students came to Manley with plans for a sit-in with other Atlanta University schools, "Manley appreciated the trust in him which this action demonstrated and did not pressure her to cancel the proposed demonstration." Manley, along with the presidents of the other Atlanta University colleges, actually paid for the full-page "Appeal for Human Rights" advertisement that led to sit-ins.[42]

In *A Legacy Continues*, Manley describes these events and the advertisement, which motivated "two hundred students from the Atlanta University Center on March 15, 1960, to stage sit-ins in nine public, tax-supported buildings," as well as visits by students to several historically white churches that summer, and a conference.[43] He remarks favorably on negotiations with Mayor William Hartsfield and then his successor, Mayor Ivan Allen, which resulted in the desegregation of public and private places, as well as the addition of blacks to the ranks of policemen, firefighters, school board members, and candidates for the Atlanta Board of Aldermen. The Spelman president bragged about the city's progress in the ensuing years, as evidenced by an invigorated economy and two black mayors. But it appears that Zinn eventually went too far for even this tolerant college president who was on board for equal rights. Interestingly, Manley never mentions Howard Zinn by name but only writes, "These improvements were made despite efforts on the part of some small groups to hamper progress by destructive means."[44] And in 1963, Zinn was fired from Spelman.

Howard Zinn begins the chapter of his autobiography about his firing by quoting a student who commented that the Spelman administrators assumed "we're savages and that it's their job to civilize us." According to Zinn, she was complaining about "the antiquated restrictions, the finishing-school atmosphere, the paternalism and control." The students had been radicalized: "When 'the Spelman girls' emerged from jail and returned to campus, they were in no mood to accept what they had accepted before."[45] Zinn obviously was encouraging adolescent rebelliousness and stoking resentment against authority. When Zinn offered to play a tape of the students' grievances about campus rules at a faculty meeting, Manley refused. "It was becoming clear that he saw me as an instigator rather than simply a supporter of the protests," Zinn protested.[46]

Two months later as the Zinn family was in the car heading north for the summer in June 1963, Zinn found in his mailbox the letter informing him of his dismissal with a check for a full year's salary. It became clear to Zinn why "everyone's letters of reappointment for the next year had been held up for two months.... Manley was waiting until all students were off campus and this could be done without an uproar."[47] Zinn presents himself as a victim. But he had continually provoked the administration. One of his students, Marian Wright Edelman, recalled feeling "shock and confusion" when Zinn "announced in class that he did not believe in Jesus Christ."[48] William Nix, director of the personnel office at Morehouse, thought Zinn was fired because he had too much influence over the student body and because he opposed the administration "too vigorously." Spelman Dean Mercile Johnson Lee observed that the college "could not operate with two Presidents."[49]

Howard Zinn had strayed from traditional professorial duties in other ways. In 1962, after writing "Another Look at Chinese Communists" for the *Antioch Review* (the look was friendly), the Non-Western Program, which Zinn founded and directed, sponsored a talk on campus by Edgar Snow advocating that "Red China" be admitted to the United Nations. Snow reported favorably on conditions there—where he had traveled—and reported seeing "'no professional beggars.'"[50]

Zinn, with Ella Baker, had been one of the few adults at the founding meeting of SNCC. His role in that organization went beyond the scope of even a faculty advisor. Students in SNCC, according to the editor of Zinn's diary, "trusted, confided in, and accepted advice from" Zinn. Because he had "warm relationships with its activists," he was "elected to its executive boards" and was "invited to undertake important tasks for the movement."[51] After his firing from Spelman, Zinn continued his involvement with the group, returning to Atlanta in October 1963 to observe and write about its voter registration campaign. He also addressed the annual meeting in April 1964.[52]

Zinn presents his firing as another example of American injustice against the poor and powerless. While the American Association of

University Professors (AAUP) issued a statement citing Spelman for violating his academic freedom, Zinn did not have the money to fight for his job. This demonstrates one of his oft-repeated plaints: "By this time I was acutely conscious of the gap between law and justice. I knew that the letter of the law was not as important as who held the power in any real-life situation."[53]

Despite this insight, Zinn did all he could to provoke the people with the power to hire or fire him. Although his severance letter was accompanied by a year's pay, Zinn demanded more money—something he does not mention in his autobiography. Nor does he write about the thirty-five-page memo he sent to the Board of Trustees in which he not only disputed the terms of his hiring (insisting he had tenure), but also accused Spelman of not keeping pace with the "revolution of expectations." He also complained about the lack of democracy on campus and the low wages paid to staff and accused Manley of being "rigid and dogmatic" and acting "like a colonial administrator." Zinn also attacked "the air of piety, the ceremonial occasions, the compulsory chapel attendance" at Spelman, calling the Christian worship service a "pompous and empty ritual." According to Duberman, Zinn drew "a direct analogy" between the administration's "rigid attitudes and the arguments for maintaining segregation, linking Manley's authoritarianism and that of white segregationists." Zinn claimed that both justified themselves "by speaking of 'tradition' and 'our way of life.'" Duberman admits, "Howard's analogy would have infuriated the most composed and imperturbable of human beings.... it was about as politic as calling a Jew a minion of Hitler."[54]

But Zinn's incessant hostility to Spelman's administration and its traditions was not the only reason he lost his job. In the back and forth over his termination, college president Manley explained that he had not renewed Zinn's contract because he knew "of no outstanding book in history that [Zinn] has written or articles of great significance in the history journals."[55] And, in fact, there were none. The man who would become America's most influential historian was not engaged in historical scholarship. His publications—the new "Look" at Communist

China, for example, which was the fruit of a year-long postdoctoral fellowship at Harvard—were essentially political agitation for radical causes and leftist and Communist regimes.

After writing his dissertation on Fiorello LaGuardia and revising it into a book back in 1959, Zinn had written nothing that could properly be called scholarly. His subsequent publications are not the fruit of diligent historical research with footnotes and primary sources. His writings did not adorn the pages of the *American Historical Review* or the *Journal of History* in the stacks of periodicals in college libraries. Instead, Zinn was filling the pages of the *Nation* and other far-left publications with writing about the causes with which he was engaged: SNCC, radicalizing a Christian college, civil disobedience, the joys of jail, protests, demonstrations, and anti-war rallies. And he was the star, the speaker rousing thousands of young people at rallies. His books, too, were about the causes he was involved in, as is clear from their titles: *The Southern Mystique, SNNC: The New Abolitionists*, and *Vietnam: The Logic of Withdrawal*. Even the writing he was doing for book collections published by university presses focused on his activism. A 1980 biographical sheet lists his contribution of "Abolitionists, Freedom Riders, and the Tactics of Agitation" to the 1965 collection *The Anti-Slavery Vanguard,* and "Marxism and the New Left" to the 1968 collection *Dissent: Explorations in the History of American Radicalism.*[56] Aside from book reviews, his shorter publications appeared in popular publications like *Harper's Monthly*, the *Progressive,* the *New South Students, Liberation, Ramparts,* and *Z Magazine.* While Zinn biographer and fellow activist and academic Martin Duberman calls *Harper's* and the *Nation* "prestigious national journals" and touts Zinn's "*national* prominence,"[57] the fact is that while exposure in such popular media outlets may be welcomed by colleges' public relations departments, most tenure committees do not see it as evidence of academic achievement. By traditional academic standards, a dossier like Zinn's perhaps should have been cause for denial of tenure and possibly of employment.

And there was another reason. In 1964, Robert Van Waes, the AAUP staff member handling Zinn's case, asked him to come to Washington to talk. Manley, in his correspondence with the AAUP, had alluded to a "morals charge" against Zinn dating back to 1960, which had become "fairly common gossip on campus." The college president had previously informed Zinn that if the AAUP decided to investigate his case, "there are certain documented facts concerning your personal and private relationships with a student, which are extremely relevant to your fitness to serve as a faculty member in this or any other institution, along with the fact that you have not been truthful with the College on this matter."[58]

Friendly Zinn biographer Duberman reports, "As one anonymous student had put it, 'Howie tried to "lay a dame."'" Mrs. Benjamin Mays (wife of the president of Morehouse College, in the same complex with Spelman and Atlanta University), however, told a "more elevated" version of the story, "referring simply to the so-called incident with a student—who, it turned out, had been the winner of a much-coveted Merrill scholarship to study abroad."[59]

In his autobiography, Zinn does describe getting caught in a car with a student, Roslyn Pope, but presents the arrest as a case of harassment by racist police. Zinn writes that "she and I had been arrested together as I drove her off-campus one evening to her parents' home in Atlanta. Flooding my car with their searchlight, two policemen ordered us into their patrol car." The way he tells the story, when the two of them were arrested for disorderly conduct, Zinn asked, "What's disorderly about our conduct?" At that point, "Smacking his flashlight into his palm, [the policeman] said, 'You sitting in a car with a nigger gal and asking me what's disorderly conduct?" Zinn makes it appear as if he had been pulled over for simply giving a ride to "a friend of the family."[60]

But according to Duberman, Zinn changed his story in the course of briefing the AAUP's Van Waes about the incident. Zinn told Van Waes that the girl was a minor who was confiding in him about boyfriend problems. Duberman recounts details that Zinn left out as his story shifted, but the bottom line is that Zinn was parked with a female student on a dead-end street far from her destination late at night. And Zinn did not want his "ailing" wife to find out. Zinn said he would sue for libel if Manley tried "to ruin him," but then considered the damage from airing such a suit and said he was open to a settlement. Van Waes mentioned an additional year's salary and the opportunity to resign. But Zinn reconsidered yet again and wrote Manley a nasty letter, charging the college president with allowing his sexual imagination to "[work] overtime in order to manufacture some tidbit of gossip about me." Zinn detected "'the sincere moralizing of a true Puritan'" in Manley and charged him with hypocrisy for turning a blind eye to the homosexuality and alcoholism on his campus.[61]

In response, Manley threatened to publish an "official" police report, corroborating statements, and statements from neighbors. By 1965, however, Zinn had been offered an associate professorship at Boston University and the matter was dropped.[62]

But even in later years, Zinn did not want his wife, who was depressed, to know the story.[63] There was a reason for Roz's "darker moods," as Duberman explains: "her discovery in the early 1970s that Howard had been having an affair with another woman that had become serious. The few details we know come not from the vacuumed Zinn archives but from material in the archives of others and from a few close friends who've spoken frankly...." Zinn chose to confide in his daughter, Myla, when she was in her mid-twenties, "telling her that he'd fallen in love with another woman—though he still loved Roz as well." Duberman describes the daughter's response to this sick situation: "if he expected understanding, he was quickly undeceived. Myla (in her own words) 'was shocked and upset not only because I had had no idea that anything like this had ever happened, but also because he hadn't told my mother. His seeking my support and approval showed me how little he knew me and how little he understood what a huge betrayal this was of my mother.'"

Zinn ultimately chose to stay with his wife, but "did continue to have 'flings,' making sure that Roz didn't find out."[64]

In 2016, when she was seventy-seven, Roslyn Pope, the girl Zinn was caught in the car with in 1959, told Robert Cohen, who was doing research for his *Howard Zinn's Southern Diary: Sit-Ins, Civil Rights, and Black Women's Student Activism,* that she had been humiliated by the arrest and then offended by Zinn's writing about it without discussing it with her. She adamantly denied having an affair with Zinn. At the time, rumors continued to swirl around campus about another student, and Alice Walker, a student of Zinn's at Spelman, did not dismiss them when she talked to Cohen. "We were all in love with Howie," she told him. Cohen, however, maintains that Manley sexualized the incident in order to "shock and intimidate Zinn into dropping the appeal of his firing."[65]

In his autobiography, Zinn explains that persecution followed him to his new job at Boston University. He was promised that he would be granted tenure a year after he was hired for the new job, but was put off with excuses, such as secretarial errors. "Finally, in early 1967 [actually only a few months more than a year after he was hired] the Department of Political Science held a meeting to vote on my tenure. There were a few professors opposed, saying flatly that my actions against the [Vietnam] war were embarrassing the university. On the other hand, student evaluations of my teaching were enthusiastic, and my fifth book was being published that spring. The department voted for tenure."

So did the dean and the Board of Trustees, in quick order. In the following years, Zinn regaled students with the story of how, when students asked him to be the speaker at their anti-war protest in front of the hotel where Secretary of State Dean Rusk was speaking on the very same day the board would vote on his tenure, Zinn risked it all and spoke out against the war as Rusk and the trustees stepped out of limousines. He did receive tenure—but only because the board voted on it before the speech.[66]

But when John Silber became Boston University president, a battle royale ensued. In the spring of 1972, as one of his first acts as president and as an affront to Zinn's political sensibilities, Silber invited the U.S. Marines onto the campus to recruit students! Students protested and obstructed other students from meeting with recruiters. Silber called the police and was on the scene, according to Zinn, "with a bullhorn, acting like a general in a military operation as the police moved in, using police dogs and clubs, to arrest the demonstrators." Zinn was ill at home at the time, but the next day from his sick bed he wrote an article about the "history of the U.S. Marines, the philosophy of civil disobedience, and the concept of an 'open university'...." Silber continued to battle Zinn by enacting a "censorship policy" because the Zinn-advised student newspaper, *Exposure*, had printed "bold criticism of the administration." The ACLU stepped in to defend a student punished for hanging a "divest" sign from his dormitory window. Zinn was denied teaching assistants and pay raises.[67] (He sued and won back pay.)

Zinn was not much of a scholar or historian. He was continually in danger of losing his job. But he was a brilliant, mesmerizing political activist. He had persuaded his students at Spelman to defy their college president and the wishes of their parents, to risk expulsion and physical harm, and spend time in jail. Alice Walker wrote that Spelman girls "swooned over" the "tall, rangy, good-looking professor."[68] At Boston University, his rhetoric inspired tears in draft resisters and in young women reading *Black Boy* for class. Zinn's classes routinely filled up and had students waiting on overflow. Former student Alice Walker was still gushing about him decades later. One of his students was so inspired that he would go on to commit a portion of the fortune he earned later to establishing the Zinn Education Project.

As of 1970, by his own account, Zinn had "spoken against the war at hundreds of situations around the country—teach-ins, rallies, debates."[69] In the 1970s, Zinn continued to radicalize students in the classroom—including William Holtzman, who later in life co-founded the Zinn Education Project with his wealth, and who recalls how Zinn regaled students with stories told in his "spell-binding manner." When Holtzman raised his hand to ask a question about American history, compromise, and tenure, Zinn replied in "a Buddha-like manner," relating his story about risking tenure by speaking in protest during Rusk's visit.[70] In high school, Emily Rentz was subjected to intensive Zinn study and then a visit from the man himself. He was "extremely charismatic," with most of the students either in "awe" of him when he came to visit her class in 2005 or acting like it to get a good grade. Zinn was "a powerful" speaker, "manipulative." He spoke with "conviction." As Rentz told me, "He spoke eloquently and articulately with deliberate pauses that dramatized his points as he spoke. He was very animated and sarcastic," and directed criticisms at the "government, corporate America, capitalism in general and Republicans as a whole. But he did it carefully and cleverly.... He made us feel like we had to be intellectually idiots to think differently.... [and to] feel ashamed to be American...." She found that Zinn was also "idolized" at Boston University, which she attended after graduating from high school in 2006.[71]

Zinn used his teaching podium to agitate, assigning readings and activities that kept students at a high emotional pitch. In the 1960s and 1970s, he took them on civil rights and anti-war protests and continued his work with SNCC, encouraging the group to take an anti-war position. After the war, he found causes in the Black Panther cases and in activism against "prisoner abuse." His students did field research interviewing prisoners and, in the early 1980s, to his admiration, made shantytowns to protest apartheid. (During a trip to South Africa in the summer of 1982, Zinn visited Crossroads, "a real shantytown outside of Capetown.") This was in a period, as Zinn noted, when "there was wide-spread head-shaking over the 'apathy' of the student generation."[72]

Zinn believed that much could be learned *in* jail: "An encounter with police, even one night in jail, is an intense and unique educational experience." This insight opens a chapter of his autobiography in which Zinn regales the reader with the story of his own overnight stay in a Massachusetts jail for failing to show up in court after having blocked the transport of soldiers, and then in a D.C. jail for failing to move off the White House lawn.[73] He writes that "the ordeal of imprisonment demands a concentration on one's own needs, to sacrifice for others,"[74] but Zinn himself rarely went to jail. When he was at Spelman in Atlanta during the civil rights protests in Albany and Selma, Zinn observed and recorded from a safe distance. It was his students and the members of SNCC who went to jail. In the same way, at Boston University he was known to instigate protests—including takeovers of the president's office—then disappear before the protesters suffered the consequences for the protests he had instigated. National Association of Scholars president Peter Wood, who worked at Boston University as a librarian in 1984 while finishing his dissertation (and then became assistant to the provost, associate provost, and eventually president's chief of staff), remembered Zinn as always having "a half smirk on his face and the more trouble he could cause the happier he looked."[75]

Zinn was failing to do what he was paid to do—teach and engage in scholarship. In a 1979 interview, Boston University president Silber said, "[Zinn] has to decide if he thinks he has a higher market value in the academic community some place else.... I think he is paid all he can get in the academic marketplace." When asked, "Do you feel he's not worth any more than he's making?" Silber replied that "he did not think Zinn's 'standards of scholarship' were very high."[76] Peter Wood recalls that Zinn was part of a group known as BSASH, "Before Silber and Still Here"—a "collection of mediocrities that hung on after Silber had dramatically raised academic standards for faculty appointments."[77]

Zinn, however, claimed that his activism frightened "the guardians of traditional education." In the classroom, he wrote, "I didn't pretend to an objectivity that was neither possible nor desirable. 'You can't be neutral on a moving train,' I would tell them." (That phrase, which he used as the title for his autobiography, recalled Karl Marx's 1850 statement that "revolutions are the locomotives of history.") As Zinn explained, "Events are already moving in certain deadly directions, and to be neutral is to accept that." Zinn claimed that he was not imposing his views "on blank slates, on innocent minds" because his students had had a "long period of political indoctrination before they arrived in my class—in the family, in high school, in the mass media." He just wanted to offer his "wares along with others" in a "marketplace.... long dominated by orthodoxy"[78]

Students in Professor Zinn's classes did not need to recall historical facts on exams, because no exams were given.[79] They did not need to go to the library and present their research in footnoted papers because the only "research" Zinn required was from their involvement in community organizations and interviews with such individuals as prisoners. Writing assignments consisted of journal entries and "day-to-day reactions" to such activities and the freewheeling class discussions. But Zinn's students were not even required to adhere to these standards, for Zinn made it a policy to never fail any student.[80] Instead of textbooks[81] or standard history books, students read poetry, fiction, drama, and polemics.[82]

Zinn had been hired to teach history and some political science at Spelman. At Boston University, he was asked to join the political science department. "They apparently didn't care that I was really a historian, but I didn't care really what department I was in," Zinn told Davis Joyce in 1997, "'cause I knew I was going to teach the way I was going to teach anyway." He did what he wanted to do "no matter what the description in the catalog was." This was his "guerrilla warfare with administration." Over the course of his academic career, Zinn taught classes in American history, American government, Russian history, and Chinese history, as well as an Introduction to Political Theory, a senior seminar on Marxism and anarchism, and a graduate seminar called Politics of History. He also offered a course at first called "Civil Liberties" and then changed to "Law and Justice in America." Zinn gave the vague title to his "Law and Justice in America" course so that he could, as he said, do "whatever I wanted in there." He put together "a selection of diverse readings," including "Arthur Miller's play *The Crucible* when talking about McCarthyism; *Johnny Got His Gun* by Dalton Trumbo or *Born on the Fourth of July* by Ron Kovic when dealing with war; and Langston Hughes's poetry or Richard Wright's *Black Boy* when covering race, as well as excerpts from Emma Goldman's anarchist autobiography, Studs Terkel's oral histories, and Howell Rains's [sic] *My Soul Is Rested*." In his "Introduction to Political Theory," Zinn sometimes paired "Plato with Daniel Berrigan...or Machiavelli with Henry Kissinger."[83] What his students learned can be gleaned from nine excerpts of students' journals that Zinn provides in his autobiography. A young woman cried after reading *Black Boy* and a young man in ROTC had come to hate the Vietnam War.[84]

The literary works Zinn taught—such as the novel *Johnny Got His Gun* by screenwriter Dalton Trumbo, a member of the CPUSA—tended to push the Communist Party line.[85] *The Crucible*, an allegory about the HUAC "witch hunts," was a favorite among those who subscribed to the Communist publications that Miller wrote for, such as *New Masses*.[86] Langston Hughes, a Zinn favorite, used his writing talents to serve the party. In the 1930s, he had recruited black "actors" to travel to the Soviet Union to make an anti-American film. The film was canceled, but Hughes accepted an offer to stay and write for *Izvestia*. After his return to America, his plays, articles, poetry, and memoirs continued to praise the Soviet Union. Richard Wright had made something of a devil's bargain with the party as a young aspiring writer during the Depression, being lured into its John Reed Club for a chance to write—though he later broke with the party.

Zinn avoided debates with his peers. He did not publish in peer-reviewed journals or present papers at conferences. His audience was young people in the classroom, or on the quad, in a rally, protest, or teach-in. He spoke at "counter-commencements"—one at his alma-mater, Columbia University—while, as he explained, "the historian who had chaired my dissertation defense, Richard Hofstadter was giving the official commencement address nearby." Zinn shared the "counter-commencement platform" at Wesleyan University with radical clergyman William Sloane Coffin and leftist historian Henry Steele Commager.[87] He also did one at his neighborhood high school, setting students against parents.

In addition to hundreds of anti-war rallies, Zinn participated in an anti-war symposium in Hiroshima in 1966 where he met David Dellinger, who, in 1968, called and asked him to go to Hanoi with the radical priest Daniel Berrigan to bring back three American POWs.[88] In Laos, the soldiers were hustled into a military plane—thus sabotaging a prime opportunity for the publicity that North Vietnam had sought from an airport arrival by Zinn. The *New York Times* reported that Zinn had a "heated 40-minute argument" with Ambassador William H. Sullivan on the mode of transport. Zinn told the reporter, "I feel that this was a violation of the spirit of the release. The attitude and feelings of the North Vietnamese should have been considered." Berrigan reported on the conversation they had had with North Vietnamese premier Pham Van Dong that afternoon, relaying the North Vietnamese official's message to President Johnson: "We repeat our demand for unconditional cessation of the bombing of North Vietnam."[89]

In 1971, Zinn helped RAND Corporation military analyst Daniel Ellsberg hide the "Pentagon Papers"—U.S. government documents on the Vietnam War that Ellsberg had stolen. They were first published in the *New York Times* and then in other newspapers. The four-volume *Pentagon Papers*, Gravel edition, was edited by Zinn and Noam Chomsky, but it did not include "80% of the documents in Part V.B.," which are titled "Justification for the War," and parts of the peace negotiations.[90] The *New York Times* published an even more highly selective book with its own editorial commentary in 1971. When Ellsberg and his co-conspirator were indicted on eleven counts, including violation of the Espionage Act,[91] Zinn served as an "expert" witness tracing the history of U.S. involvement in Indochina from World War II to 1963. Zinn wrote that "it was like teaching class."[92] The case ended in a mistrial after the office of Ellsberg's psychiatrist was broken into during the Watergate scandal.

After Zinn retired in 1988, he had time for speaking tours. In Boulder, he met David Barsamian, "an ingenuous impresario of radical broadcasting" who would become one of the major promoters of his work. Zinn was "impressed again and again by how favorably people reacted to what, undoubtedly, is a radical view of society—antiwar, anti-military, critical of the legal system, advocating a drastic redistribution of the wealth, supportive of protest even to the point of civil disobedience." This was even when he was "speaking to cadets at the Coast Guard Academy in Newport, Rhode Island, or to an assembly of nine hundred students at the reputedly conservative California Polytechnic in San Luis Obispo."[93] In 2009, Zinn—referring to a colleague who had complained that students were missing classes for protest—told the assembled group at the University of Wisconsin, Madison, listening to him being interviewed by *Nation* sportswriter David Zirin that "this guy could not know what education was. The best kind of education you can get is when you're involved in social struggles for a cause." The interview was published in *International Socialist Review.*[94]

By the 1990s, *A People's History* had made its way into classrooms and Zinn was still a favorite radical on the college lecture circuit—and even in some high school classes. Both during and after his teaching career, Zinn enjoyed a number of European junkets. He spent a semester in 1974 teaching with Herbert Marcuse at the University of Paris, "'at the Vincennes Campus—Paris VIII, set up after the 1968 uprisings as a kind of haven for left-wing faculty and open-admissions students.'" Zinn taught there again in 1978 and in 1980.[95] In 1995, he went to Bologna, Italy, on a Fulbright.

Zinn also had plenty of time for political activism. He co-founded the New Party, the socialist party that helped Barack Obama win his Illinois Senate seat, and then worked on the Obama presidential campaign with the now defunct ACORN. He worked for or was associated with the Democratic Socialists of America, the Committees of Correspondence for Socialism and Democracy, Standing Together to Organize a Revolutionary Movement (STORM, a Marxist-Maoist collective), and International ANSWER, the anti-war organization controlled by the communist Workers World Party. In June 2004, Zinn spoke at an event put on by the International Socialist Organization, reuniting there with former students Alice Walker and Marian Wright Edelman. In October 2004, he signed a statement calling for an investigation into the possibility that the 9/11 attacks had been orchestrated by the Bush administration. Zinn served as an original board member for the Movement for a

Democratic Society (MDS), a revived SDS. In 2009, young MDS members shut down Congressman Tom Tancredo's speech at the University of North Carolina by chanting loudly and breaking windows. In 2005, Zinn was the commencement speaker at Spelman College, obviously a much-changed institution from when Albert Manley had served as president.

Howard Zinn died in 2010, but *A People's History of the United States* lives on and carries the rhetoric of past decades of leftist politics forward with it. For students who missed the 1960s, it offers the drama of the anti-war struggle. The sharp demarcations between oppressors and oppressed and repeated references to the "struggle" in *A People's History* are reminiscent of the rhetoric of old issues of the *Daily Worker, New Masses, Negro Worker,* and *Southern Worker.* The explanations for all historical events follow the contours of CPUSA leader William Z. Foster's *Outline Political History of the Americas*, published in 1951. Zinn's is a crusading voice full of moral certainty that appeals to millennials and Generation Z, none of whom seem to be bothered by terms redolent of their grandparents' youth: "the System" and "the Establishment." Even Zinn's use of the word "Negro," which has been considered offensive since the 1960s, is accepted.

One indication of the success of *A People's History* is the far-reaching effect of the attack on Columbus with which Zinn opens the book. While former president George H. W. Bush, in his last Columbus Day proclamation, offered high praise to "one man who dared to defy the pessimists and naysayers of his day [and] made an epic journey that changed the course of history,"[96] Bill Clinton in his 1993 Proclamation commemorated "the mutual discovery of Europeans and Native Americans and the transformations, through toil and pain, that gave birth to brave new hopes for a better future."[97] And by 2017, Columbus Day was a "controversial holiday," according to *USA Today,* which noted President Donald Trump's *failure* to mention Native Americans, in contrast to Clinton's final proclamation in 2000 that acknowledged the "clash" between "Columbus and other European explorers and the native peoples of the Western hemisphere," and Obama's 2009 procla-mation that "noted how the European immigrants joined the 'thriving indigenous communities who suffered great hardships as a result of the changes to the land they inhabited.'"[98]

Howard Zinn was a far-left political activist—very possibly a mem-ber of the Communist Party USA. The stories he put into *A People's History of the United States* weren't balanced factual history, but crude morality tales designed to destroy Americans' patriotism and turn them into radical leftists. Recall Zinn's claim that "What Columbus did to the Arawaks of the Bahamas, Cortés did to the Aztecs of Mexico, Pizarro to the Incas of Peru, and the English settlers of Virginia and Massachu-setts to the Powhatans and the Pequots." Let us look at Zinn's version of this part of American history.

THREE

Howard Zinn's "Usable Indian"

**W**hat Columbus did to the Arawaks of the Bahamas, Cortés did to the Aztecs of Mexico, Pizarro to the Incas of Peru, and the English settlers of Virginia and Massachusetts to the Powhatans and the Pequots." Zinn has given fair warning. His account of the entire Age of Discovery is the same morality tale he has already told about Columbus: Europeans bad, Indians good. "The Aztec civilization of Mexico" is glorious, with "the heritage of the Mayan, Zapotec, and Toltec cultures." It "built enormous constructions from stone tools, and human labor, developed a writing system and a priesthood." (The Aztecs did not have the wheel or an alphabet, and much of the "human labor" was slave labor.) Zinn acknowledges that the Aztecs perpetrated "the ritual killing of thousands of people as sacrifices to the gods." (This "ritual killing" included children, slaves, and prisoners of war whose hearts were cut out of them while they were still alive as five priests held them down.) But for Zinn, the "cruelty of the Aztecs.... did not erase a certain innocence." (One might ask where was the "innocence" in the spectacle displayed at the inauguration of the Great Temple in 1487 when over eighty thousand captured prisoners were slaughtered at the rate of

fourteen per minute, which "far exceeded the daily murder record at either Auschwitz or Dachau," as Victor Davis Hanson points out. These killings were intended to be warnings to those who might defy the absolute rule of Aztec priests, who were seen as incarnations of gods whose faces could not even be looked at directly.)[1]

Zinn claims the Aztecs welcomed Cortés "with munificent hospitality" and gifts of gold and silver. They would not have been so munificently hospitable if their king Montezuma had not believed that the pale-skinned Cortés was "the legendary man-god" of their mythology, "the mysterious Quetzalcoatl." In their innocence, as Zinn explains, the Aztecs could not have known that he had really "come from Spain with an expedition financed by merchants and landowners and blessed by the deputies of God, with one obsessive goal: to find gold."

Montezuma began having doubts about Cortés's divinity and begged him "to go back." But what did Cortés do? He began "his march of death from town to town, using deception, turning Aztec against Aztec, killing with the kind of deliberateness that accompanies a strategy—to paralyze the will of the population...."[2]

Well, no. In fact, there was a battle of epic proportions before Cortés and his men, along with their Tlaxacan allies, escaped—losing half of their force to the Aztecs.

Nor did Cortés turn "Aztec against Aztec." His allies were people of other tribes who had been persecuted by the Aztecs for a century—especially the Tlaxcalans, who had had their women and children "butchered," their fields stripped, and their populations raided for "material and human tribute."[3] In fact, "Tlaxcala became the magnet for every Indian who had something to lose if the Aztecs won." Warriors came from all around, and soon Cortés had "over fifty thousand Indians" that he was training "in the Spanish fighting methods."[4] This enabled Cortés to complete his conquest in two years instead of a decade or more.[5]

Zinn, however, is not concerned with such details; he is happy to lump all Indians into one group. In Zinn's scheme, individuals don't matter so much as the group to which they belong: Indian or European, good guy or bad guy.

So we quickly get to the next heartless Spanish conquistador: Pizarro in Peru, who, in Zinn's narrative "used the same tactics, and for the same reasons—the frenzy in the early capitalist states of Europe for gold, for slaves, for products of the soil, to pay bondholders and stockholders of the expeditions, to finance the monarchical bureaucracies rising in Western Europe, to spur the growth of the new money economy rising out of feudalism, to participate in what Karl Marx would later call 'the primitive accumulation of capital.'"[6]

Notice how Karl Marx—the inventor of the Communist political philosophy whose implementation has resulted in the murders of tens of millions—is subtly introduced as a trustworthy authority.

Next, Zinn marches on to the colonies the English established in North America—where he sees the same "pattern" as in the Spanish conquests: "In the North American English colonies, the pattern was set early, as Columbus had set it in the islands of the Bahamas. In 1585, before there was any permanent English settlement in Virginia, Richard Grenville landed there with seven ships. The Indians he met were hospitable, but when one of them stole a small silver cup, Grenville sacked and burned the whole Indian village."[7]

But as Gary Nash, on whose 1974 book, *Red, White, and Black,* Zinn relies heavily, makes clear—while Zinn does not—Grenville was not representative of the permanent settlers of the English colonies. Nash describes him as a member of the "generation of adventurous seadogs and gentlemen" whose exploits "ended mostly in failure."[8] These men were not settlers, but adventurers; the gentlemen in the group, thinking themselves above doing manual labor, refused to farm. Zinn, though, makes no such distinctions in his eagerness to see the same Europeans bad, Indians good "pattern" everywhere.

Then comes the conflict with the Indian chief Powhatan at Jamestown over his refusal to return some runaways during the "starving time" in 1610. Zinn quotes from a text he doesn't identify, describing the colonists' bloodthirsty "Revendge" in response to Powhatan's "prowde and disdaynefull Answers": killing fifteen or sixteen Indians plus the queen and her children, burning their house, and destroying the crops.[9]

Zinn calls his source simply "the English account," and devotes over half a page to a speech by Powhatan to John Smith that even Zinn admits may never have really been made. Only Zinn waits to make that admission until he has first got it firmly fixed in his readers' minds that it really did happen, claiming that "Powhatan had addressed a plea to John Smith that turned out prophetic." Only then does the slippery Zinn admit that the authenticity of the speech "may be in doubt." And he follows that admission up with the dubious claim that "it is so much like so many Indian statements that it may be taken as, if not the rough letter of that first plea, the exact spirit of it."[10] Note the whole bag of rhetorical tricks Zinn is using here. He calls the "letter" of the speech—the literal words that Powhatan actually spoke (or that he didn't speak)—"rough" and the "spirit" of the speech "exact." Those clever word choices lend rhetorical force to Zinn's claim that we should take it seriously even if it never actually happened. If there are, in fact, as Zinn claims, many similar Indian statements from which he could have picked to make his point, one wonders why he didn't choose one of *them*, instead of this dubious one.

When, twelve years after the colonists' killing of fewer than two dozen Indians, the Indians kill 347 colonists, including women and children, Zinn presents the massacre as a reasoned decision on the part of the Indians in light of their alarm at the growth of the English population.[11]

That 1622 massacre was instigated by Opechancanough, who had succeeded his brother Powhatan upon his death in 1618 and was resentful of white settlement and "English efforts to assimilate his people into their culture." Opechancanough saw an opportunity after "the English murdered a highly regarded warrior and prophet named Nemattanow...on suspicion of killing a white trader." The 347 lives lost represented "almost a third of the English population in Virginia."

As Larry Gragg comments in *American Indian History*, "[m]ore would have died had not a Pamunkey [a tribe in the Powhatan confederacy] servant informed his master, who, in turn, warned the main settlements in and around Jamestown.... in response, the English launched a vigorous counterattack, including military expeditions, the destruction of crops, and the burning of villages...."[12]

Zinn doesn't bother with such details. His characterization of the situation is crude: the colonists, unable to "enslave the Indians" and unable to "live with them," simply "decided to exterminate them." *A People's History* reserves such language for the Europeans' intentions, not the *Indians'*—even in the case of King Philip's War in the 1670s, which, as historian Bert M. Mutersbaugh explains, was intended to be a "war of extermination against the English."[13]

From Virginia, we're off to New England to the next atrocity—this time by the Puritans, who, Zinn tells us, "appealed to the Bible.... to justify their use of force to take the land."[14] Zinn makes little distinction between the settlers at Jamestown (originally single young men seeking their fortunes) and those in Massachusetts Bay (families seeking religious freedom). Like Las Casas, the Puritans sought to save and convert the Indians. The converts lived in "praying towns" where they enjoyed "considerable autonomy," according to Thomas Woods. Missionary John Eliot developed a written language for the Algonquins and translated the Bible for them. Nor did the Puritans use "force"—as Zinn puts it—to steal the Indians' land. As Woods explains, while "the king had issued colonial land grants," the "Puritan consensus" was that this "conferred *political* and not *property* rights.... Roger Williams obtained title from the Indians before settling in Providence," and "Connecticut and New Haven followed [his] pattern...." In the Connecticut Valley, settlement "was positively *encouraged* by some tribes in the 1630s, who hoped the English might prove a useful obstacle to the ambitions of the Pequots, a hated tribe that had begun to force its way into the area. Once settled, these New England colonies went on to purchase whatever additional land they desired," allowing Indians hunting rights on these lands.

Although Zinn claims that Governor Winthrop justified the forceful taking of land that had not been "subdued," Woods explains, "The colonists did believe that deserted or desolate land could be occupied by whoever discovered it, but this idea was never used to dispossess Indians of their lands."[15]

Woods takes much of his information from Alden T. Vaughan's 1965 study *New England Frontier: Puritans and Indians, 1620–1675*, a work ignored by Zinn. In 1995, reflecting on his work and the criticism of his detractors, Vaughan said he had originally been impressed by the Puritans' "attempt, marked by failure in the long run but partly successful in the early years, to deal justly and peacefully with their Indian neighbors. For example, in 1638 Plymouth Colony hanged three Englishmen for murdering an Indian.... in their educational and judicial system and in their missionary efforts, the Puritans revealed a paternalistic but genuine concern for the Indians.... by mid-century, Harvard College welcomed Indian students, as the colony's common and grammar schools had for many years."

The failure at conversion, Vaughan said in retrospect, had to do with the colonists' "cultural absolutism," but not "color prejudice," for they believed that the Indians had descended from the ten lost tribes of Israel.[16]

Zinn's discussion of the war with the Pequot Indians is also topsy-turvy. His explanation is simplistic: the colonists "wanted their land." Thus, the "murder of a white trader, Indian-kidnapper, and troublemaker" was only "an excuse to make war on the Pequots in 1636." In fact, more than one rather shifty European had been killed by the Pequot, as is clear from the account of the war by Governor Winthrop, who reported that the men who were sent out against the Indians were authorized "to go to the Pequods to demand the murderers of Captain Stone and other English." As even Zinn has to admit, "Massacres took place on both sides." But the massacres by the English are somehow worse because "The English developed a tactic of warfare used earlier by Cortés and later, in the twentieth century, even more systematically: deliberate attacks on noncombatants for the purpose of terrorizing the enemy." This claim is intended to establish in the reader's mind the idea that Europeans, beginning with Cortés, uniquely attacked noncombatants.[17] Zinn never gets around to describing the Pequots' massacre of the English, or the attacks upon noncombatants in the Tuscarora War, which began on September 22, 1711, when "approximately five hundred Tuscaroras and their allies attacked at widely scattered points along the Neuse, Trent, and Pamlico Rivers. Men, women, and children were butchered and their homes destroyed by fire. The Indians' frenzy was slowed only by fatigue and drunkenness. At the end of the two-day rampage more than 130 whites were dead and nearly 30 women and children had been captured...." The reason for the attack was that the Tuscarora felt that they were being cheated by the settlers; they were additionally inspired by "unscrupulous traders" who described "the settlers as easy targets with no government backing or protection."[18] Then there was the Yamasee War over trade grievances when the Yamasee joined with Creeks and Catawba and "began a war against South Carolina in April 1715. The Yamasee and their allies attacked Carolina traders and settlements, killing four hundred English...."[19] These are just two examples of surprise attacks upon civilians, which were the early settlers' greatest fears. Such attacks, "terrorizing the enemy," were a continuation of Indian practices from before European settlement.

The Pequot were nothing like the stereotype of the peaceful, innocent, gentle Indians that Zinn had been carefully building up from his first introduction of the "Arawak" on page one of *A People's History*. C. George Fry explains in *American Indian History*, "As suggested by their name (from *pekawatawog*, 'the destroyers'), the Pequots were once the most formidable tribe in New England." They had "a virtual hegemony over their adjacent nations...." That was why the Mohegans and the Narragansetts helped the English in their attack on the main Pequot fort on the Mystic River in 1637 after two English traders were killed and outlying English settlements, including Wethersfield, were attacked.[20]

Zinn says nothing about the fearsomeness of the Pequots. After the colonists found their "excuse," according to Zinn's narrative, "a punitive expedition left Boston to attack the Narragansett Indians on Block Island, who were lumped with the Pequots." Zinn then quotes from Governor Winthrop about the expedition's "commission" to "put to death the men of Block Island, but to spare the women and children.... take possession of the island," and then demand that the "murderers of Captain Stone and other English" be turned over. The English were able to kill only "some Indians," with the rest hiding in the forest. So, they burned deserted villages and crops. Zinn quotes from an account by "one of the officers of that expedition" to provide "insight into the Pequots they encountered: 'The Indians spying of us came running in multitudes along the water side, crying What cheer, Englishmen, what cheer, what do you come for? They not thinking we intended war, went on cheerfully....'"

This quotation evokes the scene of Columbus meeting the Arawak and serves to establish the idea that although "[m]assacres took place on both sides" the English were the aggressors, while the Indians were innocent and wronged. "So the English set fire to the wigwams of the village," continuing that "tactic of warfare" so favored by the Europeans to "terroriz[e] the enemy," and launched the Pequot War. Zinn quotes "ethnohistorian" Francis Jennings' "interpretation" of the attack led by Captain John Mason on the Pequot village on Mystic River as an example of cowardly warfare on noncombatants.[21]

But Zinn is being very selective about the historical record. The quotation from the unnamed "officer" of the expedition who coldly ignores friendly Pequot overtures—Captain John Underill, as Underhill himself describes in his *History of the Pequot War*—further enhances this impression. The passage Zinn quotes about the Indians who "went on cheerfully," not understanding that the colonists "intended war," comes after Underhill's account of an attack by Indians that killed the colonists' Indian interpreter. And while Zinn wants the reader to believe that the Pequots were crying out "cheerfully" in innocent trust that the colonists came in peace, what follows in Underhill's account tells a very different story. After the English made no answer, the Indians continued to call out, asking, "are you hoggery, will you cram us? That is, are you angry, will you kill us, and do you come to fight?" This is so contrary to the impression Zinn has been careful to create. In fact, the Indians were trying to ascertain whether they needed to prepare for battle—and quickly figured out that they did. According to a part of Underhill's account that Zinn does *not* quote: "That night the Nahanticot Indians, and the Pequeats, made fire on both sides of the river, fearing we would land in the night. They made most doleful and woful cries all the night, (so that we could scarce rest) hallooing to one another, and giving the word from place to place, to gather their forces together, fearing the English were to come war against them."[22]

In Underhill's account, the attempted negotiations with the Indians to get the murderers handed over are met by stalling and taunting. Fort Saybrook, defended by Underhill and Mason and their twenty men "armed with corselets, muskets, bandoleers, rests, and swords...did much daunt" the Indians, who after six weeks, "fell upon...[nearby] Wethersfield, with two hundred Indians" and slew "nine men, women, and children" and held "two maids" captive in their canoe decked out with "sails" made from the slain Englishmen's clothes, taunting the English until they fired, narrowly missing the captive girls.[23]

Underhill also recounts some events—not mentioned by Zinn—that led up to the conflict. The Pequots had made threats against the settlers at Fort Saybrook and were running "up and down as roaring lions" and "threatening persons and cattle to take them, as indeed they did." He also describes what happened to a "Master Tilly, master of a vessel" anchored in the Connecticut River. Tilly came ashore, "not suspecting the bloody-mindedness of those persons, who fell upon him and a man with him, whom they wickedly and barbarously slew; and, by relation, brought him home, tied him to a stake, flayed his skin off, put hot embers between the flesh and the skin, cut off his fingers and toes, and made hatbands of them; thus barbarous was their cruelty!"[24]

The company sent to Fort Saybrook after the attack on Wethersfield included "one hundred armed soldiers" and "threescore Mohiggeners, whom the Pequeats had drove out of their lawful possessions." Underhill gives details about the fighting, which resulted in the deaths of two Puritans before the colonists resorted to fire-setting. And afterward, the Narragansets asked for help against the Pequots who were after them, and the English fought them off.[25]

Underhill is telling the Puritans' side of the story. But historian Shannon Duffy weighs the evidence and explains that the Pequots had raided the new Connecticut settlements and that their siege of Fort Saybrook "continued for months." In addition, "Other attacks killed nine other Englishmen, including one trader, John Tilly, who was ritually tortured before his execution. Connecticut declared war on April 18, 1637.... Massachusetts followed suit on May 1, and Plymouth on June 7." The colonists' May 26 attack on Fort Mystic, which killed between six hundred and seven hundred Pequots, "apparently caused the Pequots to lose heart." Duffy, unlike Zinn, does her best to see both sides of the story, noting that the contemporary accounts "insisted that the war was a defensive one," but that "[s]ince the 1970s...historians have become more critical of Puritan motives and actions." Some see the Puritans using the murders of John Oldham in 1636 and Captain John Stone in 1634 as an "excuse to destroy the Pequots for materialistic reasons." Even at the time, William Bradford, because of Stone's less than reputable character, believed the Indians' story that Stone had kidnapped two Pequots and been killed along with seven of his men in a rescue attempt. The "Pequot refusal to negotiate on either death," however, "seems to have been at least a partial cause of mounting Puritan frustration," according to Duffy. And contributing to the idea that the Indians posed a threat was "Mohegan sachem Uncas, leader of a breakaway faction of the Pequots" who circulated "rumors that the Pequots were plotting against the English communities." And Captain John Endecott's "expedition to Block Island" was "not intended" to start a war. Endecott had orders only to "assert Massachusetts' claims by force." John Winthrop, writing to "aggrieved" Plymouth governor William Bradford, explained apologetically that the "first intentions" of the organizers of that raid were "only against Block Island." Duffy judges that the colonists "did not realize.... that the Pequots would be required to respond...or risk losing face with other indigenous groups," and the Indians "seem to have failed to recognize how the English would interpret their raids on the Connecticut settlements." She cites Underhill's account as one of the contemporary ones claiming that "the decision to fire the fort was not premeditated," but was done only when the English "encountered stiff resistance and realized that they had lost the element of surprise." It may even "have been partly an accident."[26]

But there is not the slightest question of who is to blame in Zinn's account. According to Zinn's favorite "ethnohistorian" Francis Jennings, the Indians took three lessons to heart from the Pequot War: that Englishmen would break their pledges when it advantaged them, that their warfare "'had no limit of scruple or mercy,'" and that Indian weapons were "'almost useless'" against the Europeans. Zinn adds that the New England "Indians were used against each other"—just like the Aztecs![27] But Jennings allows his ideology to blur any kind of balance. Like Zinn's other favorite historian, Hans Koning, Jennings slips into polemics, providing political commentary—in his case, on Watergate, which was going on at the time he was writing *The Invasion of America* in 1975. The "Watergate deceits," he opines in the preface to the book, "do not seem to be a new thing in history."[28] And all the deceits in early American history are deceits of the colonists against the Indians. As Oscar Handlin noticed, Jennings's call "for a turn away from legend to history, 'from heroes and demons to conflicting persons'" was "honorable" in "intention," but not in "execution." Handlin points out, "Jennings' evidence would have sustained a portrayal of the Puritans as confused, well-intentioned, and incapable of adapting to differences a universalistic faith could not recognize. Instead they became pious hypocrites, their ideas 'cant,' who all along wanted to do the original inhabitants out of their land." In this version of American history "settlement" was transformed into "conquest," then "invasion."[29]

Thus, we should not be surprised by Zinn's discussion of King Philip's War, forty years later, which presents another murder "attributed" to an Indian as only another "excuse" for a "war of conquest." Actually, as Duffy explains, Wampanoag leader Metacom, "known to the English as Philip," began the war in June 1675 by attacking Plymouth Colony. On top of his usual canards against Western civilization, Zinn manages to drag in a little more Marxist class theory: "Jennings says the elite of the Puritans wanted the war; the ordinary white Englishman did not want it and often refused to fight."[30] "For a while, the English tried softer tactics," Zinn says. "But ultimately, it was back to annihilation."[31]

While Zinn goes further than most in depicting the Indians as the peaceful, blameless victims, the cliché was already a well-known trope that Richard R. Johnson—in 1977, three years before the publication of *A People's History of the United States*—identified as "the usable Indian": the Native American as a prop in furtherance of a predetermined agenda. Just as the caricature of the savage Indian was convenient to some in earlier times, the caricature of the innocent, generous, pacifist Indian was convenient to collectivists of the 1960s and beyond. In correction of both myths, Johnson offered a more nuanced and accurate account of the complex relationship between the white settlers and the American natives.[32]

As Johnson explains, in 1675, "the pressures of advancing English settlement finally drew several of the major tribes into unprecedented coalition against the whites. In ... King Philip's War, over half of New England's towns were attacked and nearly a quarter destroyed or heavily damaged." Eventually, the settlers and their Indian allies gained the victory, but with high casualties. In Connecticut, the "powerful Mohegans" offered their services to the colonists, and several hundred of them served as scouts and auxiliaries, along with Pequots and Niantic: "In March 1676, the authorities devised a tactic so effective that it became the pattern of New England's offensive operations for many years to come—the dispatch of combined parties of white and Indian volunteers in search of the enemy with the promise of pay, provisions, and the profits of their plunder." Massachusetts and Plymouth soon followed Connecticut's example. When war "blazed" on New England borders "a dozen years later," Indians made up to 25 percent of the forces fighting for the English. They took part in expeditions against Canada in 1690. "Indians formed a substantial proportion—one-seventh in 1707 and one-eighth in 1710—of colonial forces mustered for the assaults on Canada," according to Johnson.[33]

As Johnson explains, "Though mercenaries in all but name, [Indians], like the whites, were fighting to defend their homes; and they proved to be loyal and dependable allies." They knew the woods, could act as spies among the enemy, and were mobile and effective fighters. These alliances in New England went back to when the Pilgrims and Wampanoag formed "a common front against the Narragansetts"; the latter, in turn, joined forces with the Connecticut settlers in 1637 against the Pequot. (The Mohegans, who with the "Praying Indians" made up the bulk of the colonists' Indian allies in Prince Philip's War from 1675–1678, had seceded from the Pequots in 1636.) Some genuine friendships also developed between whites and their Indian allies. As Johnson notes, "wartime comradeship often spun lasting bonds of loyalty and friendship."[34]

Such detail and nuance are absent from *A People's History*. Instead, Zinn fills space with anti-capitalist polemic: "Behind the English invasion of North America, behind their massacre of Indians, their deception, their brutality, was that special powerful drive born in civilizations based on private property...." Then comes a quotation from Roger Williams about the colonists' "depraved appetite" for "great portions of land." Of course, Zinn fails to acknowledge the fact that Williams, just like Bartolomé de Las Casas before him, makes his criticism from the Christian perspective. Williams's complaint is about "the great vanities, dreams and shadows of this vanishing life.... which the living and most high Eternal will destroy"[35]

Zinn also does some alliterative editorializing: "Was all this bloodshed and deceit—from Columbus to Cortés, Pizarro, the Puritans—a necessity for the human race to progress....?" This bit of rhetoric is used to set up Zinn's suggestion that anyone who tries to put the suffering of the Indians in context is guilty of crimes on the order of Stalin's. According to Zinn, historians who provide that kind of balance are making the very same case that "was made by Stalin when he killed peasants for industrial progress in the Soviet Union." Zinn asks histrionically whether "miners and railroaders of America, the factory hands...who died by the hundreds of thousands from accidents or sickness" were also "casualties of progress?" It's a bloody tradeoff that may not be worth it—even for the oppressor, Zinn suggests—as he will always have to be looking over his shoulder: "And even the privileged minority—must it not reconsider, with that practicality which even privilege cannot abolish, the value of its privileges, when they become threatened by the anger of the sacrificed, whether in organized rebellion, unorganized riot, or simply those brutal individual acts of desperation labeled crimes by law and the state?"[36]

This part of the chapter on "Columbus, the Indians and Human Progress" is a rhetorical tour de force. Whipping boy Samuel Eliot Morison is dragged into the argument again as an example of the wicked, old, and balanced history supposedly guilty of "burying the story of genocide inside a more important story of human progress." Who can argue with Zinn when he asks, "We can all decide to give up something of ours, but do we have the right to throw into the pyre the children of others, or even our own children, for a progress which is not nearly as clear or present as sickness or health, life or death?" And then it's back to that monster Columbus: "Beyond all that, how certain are we that what was destroyed was inferior? Who were these people who came out on the beach and swam to bring presents to Columbus and his crew, who watched Cortés and Pizarro ride through their countryside, who peered out of the forest at the first white settlers of Virginia and Massachusetts?"[37]

He answers, we "call them Indians, with some reluctance," because they are "saddled with names given them by their conquerors," and then launches into an encomium. Their farming methods were so advanced. "They perfected the art of agriculture, and figured out how to grow

maize (corn), which cannot grow by itself and must be planted, cultivated, fertilized, harvested, husked, shelled." His enthusiasm at the
Indians' agricultural prowess knows no bounds: they "ingeniously developed a variety of other vegetables and fruits, as well as peanuts and
chocolate and tobacco and rubber."[38]

Furthermore, their lifestyles were light years ahead of European
civilization: "While many of the tribes remained nomadic hunters and
food gatherers in wandering, egalitarian communes, others began to live
in more settled communities where there was more food, larger populations, more divisions of labor among men and women, more surplus to
feed chiefs and priests, more leisure time for artistic and social work...."[39]
The Iroquois lived in proto-hippie communes, with land "worked in
common" and hunting "done together," with their catch "divided among
the members of the village. Houses were considered common property
and were shared by several families. The concept of private ownership
of land and homes was foreign to the Iroquois."[40] In this portrait of the
Indians as Communists ahead of their time, Zinn draws heavily on Gary
Nash's *Red, White, and Black: The Peoples of Early North America*,
which Oscar Handlin put alongside Jennings's as an "atonement book"
that "pivoted on the hostility to whites," with the portrayal of Indian
culture varying "with the preference of the author." As Handlin points
out, for Nash the Indians were "California countercultural rebels, defenders of women's rights, and communist egalitarians—to say nothing
of their anticipation of Freudianism."[41]

On the topic of the Iroquois, Zinn leans heavily on Nash just as he
leaned on Koning on the subject of Columbus—following the earlier
historian's text too closely and lifting his quotations of original sources
without giving him credit for doing the research. Zinn's pages 19–21 follow Nash's 13–23. Zinn quotes most of Nash's quotation from the 1899
*Jesuit Relations and Allied Documents: Travels and Explorations of the
Jesuit Missionaries in New France, 1610–1791* about the Indians' willingness to share with each other. But neither Nash nor Zinn quote the passage about the Iroquois's torture of the priest Father Jean de Brébeuf by

the usual methods of beating, burning, scalping, cutting off of flesh, but also adding a mock baptism with boiling water. Nash at least mentions that the Jesuits were willing to be "martyred."[42] Not Zinn.

Iroquois culture was superior in the way women are treated, according to Zinn: "Families were matrilineal. That is, the family line went down through the female members, whose husbands joined the family, while sons who married then joined their wives' family.... when a woman wanted a divorce, she set her husband's things outside the door."[43] That's one of many Zinn passages suspiciously close to his source. Compare Nash on page twenty: "the Iroquois family was matrilineal, with family membership determined through the female line... Sons and grandsons remained with their kinship group until they married; then they joined the family of their wife. Divorce was also the woman's prerogative; if she desired it, she merely set her husband's possessions outside the longhouse door."[44]

In another sign of feminist advancement, the senior woman in the village chose the men who represented the clans at the village and tribal councils, as well as the forty-nine chiefs for the ruling council for the Five Nation confederacy. You can't help noticing that even in Zinn's (or Nash's) telling, these supposedly liberated Indian women were choosing *men* to rule them—and that women did not speak at clan meetings, where the women all stood *behind* the men. Zinn: "The women attended clan meetings, stood behind the circle of men who spoke and voted, and removed the men from office if they strayed too far from the wishes of the women."[45] Nash: "the senior women were fully in attendance, caucusing behind the circle of men who did the public speaking and lobbying with them, and giving them instructions."[46] Nash anticipates the reader's skepticism: "To an outsider it might appear that the men ruled, because it was they who did the public speaking and formally reached decisions. But their power was shared with the women. If the men of the village or tribal council moved too far from the will of the women who had appointed them, they could be removed, or 'dehorned.'"[47] After cribbing several pages from Nash's book in this manner, Zinn quotes approvingly from it: "As Gary B. Nash notes in his fascinating study...*Red, White, and Black,* 'Thus power was shared between the sexes and the European idea of male dominancy and female subordination in all things was conspicuously absent in Iroquois society."[48]

Edmund Morgan, however, another of Zinn's sources—though he naturally does not follow him on this point—reports that things weren't so good in Virginia, where "nearly any activity that could be designated as work at all was left to the women.... man counted on [his wife] to support him. He could make canoes, weapons, and weirs without losing his dignity, but the only other labor he ordinarily engaged in was clearing fields for planting, and the method employed [girdling trees and burning brush around them] made this less than arduous.... the next year the women worked the ground between the trees, using a crooked stick as a hoe...."[49]

Zinn, however, presents such drudgery as women's empowerment: "The women tended the crops and took general charge of village affairs while the men were always hunting or fishing." In other words, the women were in charge—when there were no men around! Zinn's idea of women's power in military matters includes stitching, hoeing, and grinding meal: "And since they supplied the moccasins and food for warring expeditions, they had some control over military matters."[50] This, too, comes from Nash, who had written, "While men were responsible for hunting and fishing, the women were the primary agriculturalists of the village. In tending the crops they became equally important in sustaining the community...."[51] Of course, one can always say that a housewife is "equally important" to her breadwinner husband in sustaining her family, and, by extension, the larger community, and claim that women's work in the traditional division of labor—cooking, cleaning, sewing—means she has control over matters in the larger world. But that's not exactly a feminist take.

In Zinn's telling, there is really nothing in which the Indians are not superior to Europeans, right down to potty-training. Zinn borrows Nash's Freudian analysis to claim the Iroquois "did not insist on early weaning or early toilet training, but gradually allowed the child to learn self-care." They learned "solidarity with the tribe" and "to be independent, not to submit to overbearing authority."[52] They were taught to think of themselves as equals and to share. Of course this enlightened Indian approach was completely unlike the Europeans' authoritarian attitude exemplified by the Pilgrim pastor John Robinson, whom Zinn (once again cribbing from Nash) quotes on breaking children's "natural pride."[53] "Other Indian tribes," Zinn assures us—on no particular evidence—"behaved in the same way."[54] Of course they did.

Zinn's purportedly diligent "note-taking" seems to have stopped before the last page of Nash's chapter, where Nash tries for a modicum of scholarly judgment and historical context, warning, "It would be mistaken to romanticize Iroquois culture or to judge it superior to the culture of the European invader." Nash, although clearly an admirer of the Indians to a fault, warns that "grading cultures" is an "exercise in ethnocentrism." Unlike Zinn, Nash looks honestly at the Iroquois' own aggression and violence: In addition to advancing in agricultural techniques, "[t]hey were also emerging as one of the strongest, most politically unified, and militaristic native societies in the Northeast woodlands. Even after the formation of the League of Iroquois, which had as one of its objectives the abatement of intertribal warfare, an impressive amount of fighting seems to have occurred between the Five Nations and surrounding Algonkian peoples. Many of these conflicts involved a quest for glory and some of them may have been initiated to test the newly forged alliance of the five tribes against lesser tribes which could be brought under Iroquoian subjugation."

What? Subjugation? Alliances? Militarism? These are supposed to be *European* traits! Maybe that's why Zinn skips this page, on which Nash also notes that "the Iroquois on the eve of European arrival were feared and sometimes hated by their neighbors for their skill and cruelty in warfare." Furthermore, "[t]heir belief in the superiority of their culture was as pronounced as that of the arriving Europeans."[55]

Nash's book—which, alas, has been updated and imposed upon innocent students in American classrooms—skims over Indian acts of cruelty while providing vivid descriptions of those by Puritans. But Nash, unlike Zinn, at least acknowledges that there was "enmity" between Indians (the Hurons and Iroquois, for example) before the Europeans arrived.[56]

Zinn leaps beyond his counterculture colleagues in simplistically blaming all the violence and oppression on "European values as brought over by the first colonists, a society of rich and poor, controlled by priests, by governors, by male heads of families."[57] (Ah, those Puritan priests!) And little did the Europeans realize how superior a culture—for Zinn lumps all Indian tribes into one mythical pre-Columbian utopia—they were despoiling: "So, Columbus and his successors were not coming into an empty wilderness, but into a world which in some places was as densely populated as Europe itself, where the culture was complex, where human relations were more egalitarian than in Europe, and where the relations among men, women, children, and nature were more beautifully worked out than perhaps any place in the world." Poetry and history were passed on in an "oral vocabulary more complex than Europe's, accompanied by song, dance, and ceremonial drama."[58] Shakespeare and Dante, apparently, don't come up to the standard of Amerindian poetry—or to the little bit we know about it, given the fact that they didn't have a written language.

Indian culture was also communal and self-actualizing: "They paid careful attention to the development of personality, intensity of will, independence and flexibility, passion and potency, to their partnership with one another and with nature."[59] In short, Columbus and the European civilization he represents are the serpent that destroyed the real-live Garden of Eden.

And just as in the Garden of Eden, there was perfect peace before the serpent destroyed paradise. "Human relations" were "egalitarian" and "beautifully worked out"—except that in reality the Indians did more than just grow corn and follow the orders of their women. As we have seen, native cultures were plagued by warfare and fighting—not unlike European cultures. When the Iroquois raided other Indian communities, they took women and children as prized slaves and tortured the men to death. As Karim M. Tiro, chair of the department of history at Xavier University, explains, "Communal torture and even cannibalism was regarded as another way to extract the spiritual power that inhered in human beings."[60] Abraham D. Lavender points out that "prior to European contact, slavery had been practiced by some American Indians, who frequently sold captives as slaves...."[61]

Indians engaged in warfare, kidnapping, torture, slavery, and profit-seeking—not exactly the idyllic, hippie lifestyle Zinn depicts. Men were the hunters. Women took care of the home front and grew and cooked the food. And life was harsh. As Francis Parkman described long ago in *The Jesuits in North America*, "Female life among the Hurons had no bright side. It was a youth of license, an age of drudgery."[62] The Hurons, targeted by the Iroquois, also engaged in torture and cannibalism:

> Warlike expeditions...were always preceded by feasting, at which the warriors vaunted the fame of their ancestors' and their own past and prospective exploits. A hideous scene of feasting followed the torture of a prisoner. Like the torture itself, it was, among the Hurons, partly an act of vengeance, and partly a religious rite. If the victim had shown courage, the heart was first roasted, cut into small pieces, and given to the young men and boys, who devoured it to increase their own courage. The body was then divided, thrown into the kettles, and eaten by the assembly, the head being the portion of the chief. Many of the Hurons joined in the feast with reluctance and horror, while others took pleasure in it.[63]

This is not to single out Native Americans and imply that they alone in history committed acts of cruelty and barbarity, or to deny that gross injustices were perpetrated against them (as we recall such things as the Trail of Tears). The objective is to point out how false Zinn's caricature is. Zinn never gets beyond a second-grade level of description, dwelling on happy topics like sharing, farming, hunting, and fishing.

In fact, Indians were proud of their warrior skills and served honorably in both World Wars. During World War I, Indians enlisted—mostly in the Army—and "in greater proportion than any other population." During World War II, "tribes with strong warrior traditions volunteered," again, "in disproportionate numbers"—some even bringing their own rifles to the induction stations. Writes Carole A. Barrett, "On all the reservations there was a great deal of enthusiasm and pride in the young men and women who volunteered for military service. It was common for the family members or the tribal community to honor the new recruits by sponsoring a feast and having old men talk about tribal traditions of warfare...." The media "almost universally" praised the men "for natural fighting instincts, endurance, and ferocity." Pima Indian and paratrooper Ira Hayes appears in the iconic photograph of the Marines raising the U.S. flag on Iwo Jima.[64] And there are the 420 famous Navajo "code talkers" who sent vital encrypted messages in their language. Participating in battles at Saipan, Tinian, Bougainville, Okinawa, Tarawa, Guadalcanal, Iwo Jima, and the Solomon Islands were thirty-six hundred Navajos. They have been recognized for their service by American presidents, most recently by President Donald Trump.[65]

Zinn acknowledged none of this. He was bent on exploiting "the usable Indian" to indict America, Western civilization, capitalism, and the traditional family. This kind of rhetoric has a long history in the annals of the polemics of the radical Left.

In his 1974 *Last Americans: The Indian in American Culture,* William Brandon described the use to which the Indian had been put. He quotes Columbus, the nineteenth-century Frenchman Alexis de Tocqueville, and the twentieth-century anthropologist Franz Boas, who remarked on the lack of acquisitiveness among primitive peoples. In this tradition, claims Brandon, was the "pioneer American evolutionary anthropologist" Lewis Henry Morgan, who compared property-less Indian society to modern materialistic culture in his 1877 *Ancient Society*, which became a classic of socialist literature and thought.[66]

According to National Association of Scholars president Peter Wood, who holds a Ph.D. in anthropology, *Ancient Society* is Morgan's "least good book" and is not representative of his excellent scholarship as America's first scientific ethnographer. Morgan, a lifelong Christian, "admired the Iroquois" but did not "romanticize them." He did not live long enough to voice objections to the misrepresentation of his ideas by Marxists.[67] Marx saw Morgan's work as a "corroboration of 'the materialistic conception of history.'" He was only able to take notes on Morgan's work before he died. His partner, Friedrich Engels, then added Marx's misinterpretation of Morgan's ideas to the 1888 English edition of *The Communist Manifesto* and then to *The Origin of the Family, Private Property and the State*.[68] In his introduction to the Penguin Classics edition of *The Origin of the Family*, Tristram Hunt describes the excitement that Engels felt even as he sorrowfully sorted through Marx's papers after his death in 1883. At that time, Engels wrote to his own "acolyte" Karl Kautsky, "There is a *definitive* book— as definitive as Darwin's was in the case of biology—on the primitive state of society." Morgan had found "downright communist postulates" in that primitive state—postulates that could be applied to modern society.[69] In presenting "the tribe and its communal forms of land ownership and family structure" as "the first, natural state of man," Morgan's book seemed to have demolished "the bourgeois myth that the modern, monogamian, 'nuclear' household had existed since the dawn of human society."[70]

According to Marxist theory, the patriarchal family came in with capitalism. It was at that point that men became obsessed with monogamy so that fathers could be sure that the children who would inherit their accumulated capital were their own. And monogamy led to the oppression of women:

Marx and Engels had first hinted at [a] sex/class comparison in *The German Ideology* where they connected the modern system of the division of labour back to household injustices. The nucleus of private property and inequality, they suggested, "lies in the family, where wife and children are the slaves of the husband. This latent slavery in the family...is the first form of property...." In *The Origin of the Family,* Engels went further to suggest that antagonism between the social classes was first predicated upon male oppression of the female within the monogamian family.... "The modern individual family is founded on the open or concealed domestic slavery of the wife...."[71]

That's the line Zinn takes in *A People's History of the United States.* He calls women "invisible" and titles chapter six "The Intimately Oppressed."[72] As Zinn complains, in 1960, there were slots in nursery schools for only 2 percent of the children of working mothers so that the rest of them "had to work things out for themselves."[73] In early America, says Zinn, women were actually "something like black slaves."[74] This was all because of capitalism: "Societies based on private property and competition, in which monogamous families became practical units for work and socialization, found it especially useful to establish this special status of women, something akin to a house slave in the matter of intimacy and oppression...." Echoing Marx and Engels, Zinn maintains, "Earlier societies—in America and elsewhere—in which property was held in common and families were extensive and complicated, with aunts and uncles and grandmothers and grandfathers all living together, seemed to treat women more as equals than did white societies that later overran them bringing 'civilization' and private property."[75]

Here Zinn is touting anthropology now so thoroughly debunked that even honest leftists no longer rely on it. Tristram Hunt is a former member of the Labour Party in Britain and is still sympathetic to the views of Marx and Engels, but he admits the problems with their argument that the nuclear family is a byproduct of capitalism. *The Origin of the Family* by Engels, Hunt concedes, is "widely dismissed on account of its flawed anthropological foundations." As he explains, research has demonstrated that the view of the state of women in pre-modern societies was "far too rosy." Nuclear families *did* dominate society before industrialization.[76]

But Howard Zinn's presentation of American history follows the old-style Marxist line. His line of rhetoric in *A People's History* about the proto-Communism of the Indians is not all that different from the propaganda one can find in official Communist Party USA "histories." Take, for example, William Z. Foster, leader of the Russia-run CPUSA during the Stalin era. His *Outline Political History of the Americas* was published in 1951 by the official publishing house of the CPUSA (Soviet-funded), International Publishers, when Zinn was probably an active Communist Party member and teaching a class in Marxism at the Communist Party headquarters in Brooklyn, as his FBI file indicates.

Consider Foster's account of "The Conquest of the Western Hemisphere," a chapter that presents the Age of Exploration as a "tragic sea of violence, bloodshed, slavery, exploitation, poverty, and general misery" on account of the "brutal greed...of the ruling classes of all the feudal-capitalist colonizing states." The Indians, on the other hand, "as a natural result of their primitive democratic system of society, were infused with high conceptions of honor and fair dealings with one another and with outsiders," with "none of the frightful poverty, neglect of the aged, exploitation of children, and general misery that has been the Indians' lot since they were conquered by the technically far superior and supposedly civilized capitalist nations."[77]

The "tribal communalism prevailing throughout the Americas" was "profoundly democratic." Citing Morgan and Engels, Foster claimed that before Columbus the Indian woman "held an honored position in the primitive society within which she lived, indeed far more so than she has had since in America." The Indian woman had great authority: "She was the mistress of the home and of all its associated industries, including agriculture in its early stages; she took full part in tribal elections, and in certain stages the tribal lineage was traced solely through her." Foster quotes the anthropologist Clark Wessler: "She was a strong laborer, a good mechanic, a good craftsman, no mean artist, something of an architect, a farmer, a traveler, a fisherman, a trapper, a doctor, a preacher, and, if need be, a leader."[78] One is reminded of the post-war photographs of kerchiefed middle-aged Soviet women doing heavy outdoor labor.

Few women desire the kind of "equality" that Engels, Foster, and Zinn offer. Marxists may present monogamy as a capitalist trick for enslaving women, but the fact is that most women desire lifelong, monogamous marriages—which redound to their benefit, compared to any other arrangement in which men can use women and then discard them. Few women in the United States wanted to trade places with women in the Soviet Union or would want to live the life of an Indian woman. American women today have more freedom than women have ever enjoyed anywhere on the globe at any time in world history. And even in early America, women's rights here were greater than in England, and certainly than in most places in the world.[79] Women in colonial America enjoyed the benefits of chivalry and security and respect in the family. Some women were tavern-keepers, merchants, dress-makers, midwives, teachers, writers, and landed proprietors, as the 1924 study *Colonial Women of Affairs: A Study of Women in Business and the Professions in America before 1776* tells us.[80]

There were women who were slaves, but not all women were slaves, as Zinn implies. This brings us to our next chapter, which addresses a real historical injustice that provides more fodder for Zinn's anti-Western polemic: slavery.

FOUR

America the Racist

Writing in the December 1991 issue of *Academic Questions*, Fred Siegel, associate professor of history at Cooper Union and then a self-described liberal and Democrat, bemoaned a fashionable trend in history writing. The "New Historians," he quipped, saw American life as "a story of defeat, despair, and domination. American history became a tragedy in three acts: what we did to the Indians, what we did to the African-Americans, and what we did to everyone else."[1]

That's a pretty fair description of *A People's History of the United States*. Zinn winds up Act 1 of his book on the oppression of Indians and women only to launch into Act 2 on slavery—beginning with an eight-line description from J. Saunders Redding's 1950 *They Came in Chains* of the ship carrying the first slaves to the colonies in 1619: "a strange ship, indeed, by all accounts, a frightening ship, a ship of mystery.... through her bulwarks black-mouthed cannon yawned. The flag she flew was Dutch; her crew a motley. Her port of call, an English settlement, Jamestown, in the colony of Virginia.... her cargo? Twenty slaves."

They Came in Chains was the work not of an historian, but of a Hampton Institute English professor. Arna Bontemps, in *Saturday*

Review, described it as "a deeply felt, sometimes impassioned account," "a fever chart of rising and falling hopes."[2] Zinn quotes from this dramatic description to set up his own contention that "there is not a country in world history in which racism has been more important, for so long a time, as the United States. And the problem of 'the color line,' as W.E.B. Du Bois, put it, is still with us." In light of America's uniquely horrible racism, Zinn wonders, "Is it possible for whites and blacks to live together without hatred?"[3]

As usual, capitalism is the culprit. Zinn plays fast and loose with numbers and sources in his effort to prove that capitalism is at the root of racism. He misreports and distorts the slaves' truly horrific suffering for his own purposes. For example, he claims that "perhaps one of every three blacks transported overseas died"[4]—allowing the "perhaps" to do a lot of work. In fact, according to the best quantitative evidence, 12 to 13 percent of slaves died in transit from Africa to the Americas during the history of the Middle Passage.[5] Sometimes a larger percentage of the slave ship's crew died on the voyage. In the Dutch slave trade, one in five crewmen died at sea.[6] But it suits Zinn's purpose to exaggerate the true numbers and to ignore the historical context of a time and place when life was more perilous for all.

Zinn acknowledges that slavery existed in Africa—where, in fact, it predated the discovery of America—but presents it as a kinder, gentler kind of slavery: "Slavery existed in the African states, and it was sometimes used by Europeans to justify their own slave trade. But...the 'slaves' of Africa were more like the serfs of Europe—in other words, like most of the population of Europe." The difference was the still-powerful "tribal life" of Africa: "Africa had a kind of feudalism, like Europe based on agriculture, and with hierarchies of lords and vassals. But African feudalism did not come, as did Europe's, out of the slave societies of Greece and Rome, which had destroyed ancient tribal life. In Africa, tribal life was still powerful, and some of its better features—a communal spirit, more kindness in law and punishment—still existed. And because the lords did not have the weapons that European lords had, they could not command obedience as easily."[7]

Here Zinn is simply romanticizing life in pre-colonial Africa—just as he romanticized life in pre-colonial America. "Tribal life," as Zinn presents it, was "communal" and gentle in "law and punishment." In contrast, "American slavery" is categorically "the most cruel form of slavery in history."[8] For his account of slavery and the Middle Passage, Zinn relies on Basil Davidson's 1961 *The African Slave Trade*. Davidson did do groundbreaking work in the field of pre-colonial African history. But by 1971, well before Zinn published his *People's History* in 1980, many of his generalizations were coming under fire from specialists in African history.[9] Zinn didn't care enough to keep up with the literature. It might have interfered with his desire to indict capitalism: "African slavery is hardly to be praised," Zinn concedes. But it lacked "the frenzy for limitless profit that comes from capitalistic agriculture; the reduction of the slave to less than human status by the use of racial hatred, with that relentless clarity based on color, where white was master, black was slave."[10] The real problem between blacks and whites in America wasn't so much slavery itself—owning other human beings as chattels—but "class exploitation."[11]

Thus, the Civil War was a tragic missed opportunity. If only it had been fought to overthrow the capitalist system that undergirded the particularly cruel American form of slavery, it might have ended racism (not to mention, presumably, ushering in a worker's paradise). But sadly, the Civil War, as Zinn presents it, was fought "to retain the enormous national territory and market and resources."[12]

So why *did* such an evil, capitalist system fight a bloody war to end slavery? After all, within the capitalist system, slavery was profitable: it "remained a profitable investment at the time it was abolished regardless of country," write Robert Paquette and Mark M. Smith.[13] So there was something beyond the profit motive that ended slavery in the West. Yes, within the capitalist country that Zinn condemns, slavery was killed for moral reasons. As early as the American Revolution, the fight for liberty inspired debates about slavery. Then, by the early nineteenth century, the slave trade had been abolished in England and the United States and the

American abolitionist movement was in full swing. Abolitionists were arguing against slavery from Christian and Enlightenment principles (and some, wrongly, on economic grounds). Yet, in 1842, when the Sultan of Morocco was asked by the British consul general what his country was doing to abolish slavery or to reduce its trade, he replied that he was "not aware of its being prohibited by the laws of any sect." Indeed, the question was absurd to him. Why would anyone even ask such a thing? The sultan thought that the rightness of slavery "needed no more demonstration than the light of day."[14]

In fact, the campaign to abolish slavery was a Western thing, and a relatively new thing at the time. As the late great Orientalist historian Bernard Lewis put it, "The institution of slavery had…been practiced from time immemorial. It existed in all the ancient civilizations of Asia, Africa, Europe, and pre-Columbian America. It had been accepted and even endorsed by Judaism, Christianity, and Islam, as well as other religions of the world."[15] And it was not only African peoples who were enslaved. Slavery was "a ubiquitous institution" in the early modern period, writes Allan Gallay. "Contemporary to the rise of African slavery in the Americas, millions of non-African peoples were enslaved." These included "over a million Europeans…in North Africa, and perhaps more in the Ottoman Empire," as well as the European settlers taken in captivity in the New World by Indians—not to mention the enslavement of Indians by Indians of other tribes.[16]

The Civil War not only led to the emancipation of American slaves but inspired leaders in the slave-holding nations of Cuba and Brazil to take steps to end slavery and avoid a similar outcome.[17] The Civil War also had an impact in Europe, where it brought "the issue of slavery sharply before European opinion." It "coincided with a renewed and determined British effort, by both diplomatic and naval action, to induce Muslim rulers in Turkey, Arabia, and elsewhere to ban, and indeed suppress, the slave trade," writes Lewis.[18]

A People's History does not provide such historical and global context. Instead, Zinn's reader gets the impression that American capitalism produced the cruelest slavery in the world—and that Americans invented racism. Zinn blames "the new World" for the development of racial hatred, which he pretends did not exist before the discovery of America. "Slavery," he claims, "developed quickly into a regular institution, into the normal labor relation of blacks to whites in the New World. With it developed that special racial feeling—whether hatred, or contempt, or pity, or patronization—that accompanied the inferior position of blacks in America for the next 350 years—that combination of inferior status and derogatory thought we call racism."[19]

In fact, racism is not an invention of Western culture. Let's consider Zinn's pseudo-philosophical claim: "This unequal treatment, this developing combination of contempt and oppression, feeling and action, which we call 'racism'—was this the result of a 'natural' antipathy of white against black?" This is a rhetorical question. Zinn suggests that if "racism can't be shown to be natural, then it is the result of certain conditions, and we are impelled to eliminate those conditions." So, Zinn claims, "All the conditions for black and white in seventeenth-century America were...powerfully directed toward antagonism and mistreatment."

These "conditions" have everything to do with capitalism and class. Zinn tells us, "There is evidence that where whites and blacks found themselves with common problems, common work, common enemy in their master, they behaved toward one another as equals." He cites Kenneth Stampp's claim that "Negro and white servants of the seventeenth century were 'remarkably unconcerned about the visible physical differences.' Black and white worked together, fraternized together. The very fact that laws had to be passed after a while to forbid such relations indicates the strength of that tendency."[20] So once the proletariat—black and white—unite again, racism will be eliminated.

Histories in the Soviet Union airbrushed certain facts, as they did certain personages from photographs. Zinn does the same thing, airbrushing out evidence that contradicts his claims. But the facts show that racism has existed all over the world, not only in the West, and that it was not only in the West that blacks were singled out for slavery of the most demeaning kind. Nor was racism only directed against those with darker skins.

The Muslim role in slavery and the slave trade is ignored by Zinn, but, in fact, it was "through the Moslem countries of North Africa" that" black slaves were imported into Europe during the Middle Ages."[21] By "the end of the eighteenth century," the Islamic Middle East held "the majority of the world's white chattel slaves."[22] Whites to the north and blacks to the south were both seen as inferior and therefore legitimate slave material. As Bernard Lewis points out, "The literature and folklore of the Middle East reveal a sadly normal range of traditional and stereotypical accusations against people seen as alien and, more especially, inferior. The most frequent are those commonly directed against slaves and hence against the races from which slaves are drawn—that they are stupid; that they are vicious, untruthful, and dishonest; that they are dirty in their personal habits and emit an evil smell."

The Arabs, like many in the West, held stereotypes about black men and women as highly sexed.[23] When blacks appear in Islamic illustrations of "court life, domestic life, and various outdoor scenes," they are depicted doing the lowly tasks assigned to them—"carrying a tray, pushing a broom, leading a horse, wielding a spade, pulling an oar or a rope, or discharging some other subordinate or menial task."[24] Slaves had limited rights under Islamic law,[25] but it did not mean that they had equal opportunities—even within the institution of slavery itself.

When white slaves were available—before the Russians put up barriers—black slaves usually held positions below them. The Ottoman Empire had at first acquired slaves from Central and Eastern Europe and by raiding "the Caucasians—the Georgians, Circassians, and related people." These sources dried up when Russia annexed Crimea in 1783 (a shipping off point for the slaves) and conquered the Caucasus in the early nineteenth century. The Ottomans then went to Africa, and by the nineteenth century that continent provided "the overwhelming majority of slaves used in Muslim countries from Morocco to Asia."[26] Once white slaves were no longer available, black slaves sometimes "were given tasks and positions which were previously the preserve of whites."[27]

Some of the worst suffering came when Arab slave traders transported slaves, as Thomas Sowell notes in *Ethnic America: A History*. The "massive commercial sales of Negro slaves began after the conquest of northern Africa by the Arabs in the eighth century," when "Arab slave traders penetrated down into the center of Africa and on the east coast." With the "cooperation" of local tribes, "they captured or purchased slaves to take back with them across the Sahara Desert, which eventually became strewn with the skeletons of Negroes who died on the long march...." Sowell comments, "The Arabs were notable as the most cruel of all slave masters."[28] The suffering continued into the nineteenth century as slave traders went into more remote areas as "scrutiny" by the Ottoman Empire and European powers increased. In 1849, sixteen hundred black slaves died of thirst as they were driven from Bornu to southern Libya.[29]

In the nineteenth century, it was Africa that provided highly prized slave eunuchs. Between one hundred to two hundred boys between the ages of eight and ten were castrated "every year at Abu Tig in Upper Egypt, on the slave caravan route from the Sudan to Cairo." The castrated boys could be sold at twice the normal price. As Louis Frank wrote in 1802, "it is this increase in price which determines the owners, or rather usurpers, to have some of these wretches mutilated."[30] These atrocities took place thousands of miles from American shores.

Muslim nations' adherence to Islamic law, which sanctions slavery (except of free Muslims), made it more difficult to eliminate. As Bernard Lewis explains, "From a Muslim point of view, to forbid what God permits is almost as great an offense as to permit what God forbids—and slavery was authorized and regulated by the holy law." Most Muslim states did not enact slavery abolition until the years between the World Wars. Yemen did so only when it became a "newly established republican regime" in 1962; that same year, Saudi Araba did, as well, "by royal decree." The last Muslim country to abolish slavery was Mauritania in the year Zinn's book came out, 1980.[31]

Zinn chose not to include such information, but instead limited his discussion to earlier centuries of the Atlantic slave trade. He does admit that slaves were captured "in the interior" of Africa—frequently by blacks. Yet the African slave traders are absolved of responsibility. They were "caught up in the [Atlantic] slave trade themselves."[32] And yet, Bernard Lewis quotes a *ninth century* writer who observed that "the black kings sell blacks without pretext and without war."[33]

Far from being hapless victims lured into a new kind of commerce, the Africans' legal system actually "fueled the Atlantic slave trade," according to Boston University professor John Kelly Thornton in *Africa and Africans in the Making of the Atlantic World, 1400–1680*, published by Cambridge University Press.[34] And while slaves in America and Europe "typically had difficult, demanding, and degrading work, and they were often mistreated by exploitative masters who were anxious to maximize profits," in Africa a slave could be arbitrarily sacrificed on an altar.[35]

Although the English colonies, and then the United States, accounted for a relatively small percentage of the purchases of African slaves in the New World, they "held the largest number of slaves of any country in the Western hemisphere—more than a third of all the slaves in the hemisphere—in 1825." The reason was that it was "the only country in which the slave population reproduced itself and grew by natural increase. In the rest of the hemisphere, the death rate was so high and the birthrate so low that continuous replacements were imported from Africa."[36]

The life of a slave was full of uncertainty, subject to the owner's whims and circumstances, to be sure. Cruel punishment was meted out arbitrarily and family members could be sold without warning, as Thomas Sowell acknowledges. Yet he also states that conditions were "generally more brutal in other countries" than in the United States (in contrast to Zinn's claim of the opposite). Thornton provides some sample cases—including the Ridgley estate in mid-seventeenth-century Maryland—where slaves could raise crops on a portion of the estate and sell them in exchange for some of the profits. Virginia slave John Graweere raised pigs and sold them for "one half the increase."[37]

American slaves were sometimes given their legal freedom or partial freedom, such as the "half freedom" of Dutch areas. "In these situations, clearly, slaves had some mobility and could form families and socialize their children. That they might not choose to forget their African background is revealed in the fact that one of the most successful of these small-holding former slaves, Anthony Johnson, named his farm 'Angola,'" according to Thornton. Their culture was changed, to be sure, partly because slaves from various African cultures were thrown together. There is evidence that even on slave ships and during the Middle Passage new cultural relationships were formed between Africans of different societies. The result was a new culture, with "the many and varied African cultures" serving as "building blocks" and European culture providing "linking materials."[38]

Many slaves adopted the ideals of Western culture, including Frederick Douglass, the great abolitionist. Zinn quotes Douglass several times—but as is to be expected, selectively. The discussion of Douglass's autobiography comes on the heels of that of another black abolitionist, David Walker, the "son of a slave" from whose pamphlet, *Walker's Appeal,* Zinn quotes extensively, adding his own comment, "There was no slavery in history, even that of the Israelites in Egypt, worse than the slavery of the black man in America, Walker said."[39] While we might sympathize with Walker's cause, we should also remember that he was writing not history, but polemic.

Douglass's autobiographies, *Narrative of the Life of Frederick Douglass, an American Slave* first published in 1845, and *My Bondage and My Freedom* from ten years later, offer not only an account of a firsthand experience of being a slave, but also a more nuanced investigation of the institution. Zinn's discussion of this classic begins, "Some born in slavery acted out the unfulfilled desire of millions. Frederick Douglass, a slave, sent to Baltimore to work as a servant and as a laborer in the shipyard, somehow learned to read and write, and at twenty-one, in the year 1838, escaped to the North, where he became the most famous black man of his time, as lecturer, newspaper editor, writer."[40] Douglass also described the differences between the treatment of slaves in urban areas and on isolated plantations, where the slave owner was far enough from his neighbors that they did not hear "the cries of his lacerated slave" or see how ill fed or clothed he was.[41]

In the first edition of the *Narrative*, Douglass, clearly hoping to inspire antislavery sentiment, described the beatings and hunger he and others endured, the abandonment of his aged grandmother as the property was divided up upon the death of the original owner, and men selling off the children they had fathered with slave women. Douglass was also careful to explain how the institution of slavery transformed inherently good people, like his mistress, who changed for the worse after her husband pressured her to treat the eight-year-old Douglass like a slave, in a dehumanizing manner. The "poison of irresponsible power," Douglass wrote, "commenced its infernal work. That cheerful eye, under the influence of slavery, soon became red with rage...."[42] In his writings and his speeches, Douglass appealed, against the institution of slavery, to the ideals of the Bible and the Declaration of Independence. He repeatedly pointed to the inconsistency between the treatment of slaves and the precepts of Christian charity and the American ideals of liberty and equality. These principles were irrelevant, of course, to the Sultan of Morocco around that same time.

The climactic moment of the *Narrative* comes when the sixteen-year-old Douglass fights back against Edward Covey. After enduring weekly beatings for six months and facing more punishment for having fainted from overwork, Douglass fought off Covey and an assistant as the infamously cruel "breaker" of slaves was attempting to tie him up. Douglass described the "battle" as the "turning-point in my career as a slave," because it "rekindled the few expiring embers of freedom, and revived within me a sense of my own manhood."[43]

This kind of spirit was not unusual among slaves. Douglass showed incredible will, but many slaves practiced other forms of resistance, with "work slowdowns, sabotage, and running away," depending upon the circumstances, which varied.[44] As the 1960s and 1970s brought greater interest in black history, scholars such as Edgar McManus, in his *A History of Negro Slavery in New York*, countered the stereotype of "Negroes as a passive mass, harnessed and driven by a white elite." McManus pointed out that in New Netherland, prejudice was more religious than racial in nature. While Jews could not "own realty" or join the militia, "Negroes could." Some even "owned white indentured servants" and "intermarried with whites." Although slaves engaged in domestic and farm work, they were also employed as skilled workers—goldsmiths, naval carpenters, coopers, tanners, and masons.[45]

As Lorena Walsh points out, the discussions about liberty in the years leading up to and during the War of Independence affected slave owners and slaves. It also affected slave status. Loyalists and Patriots vied for slaves' allegiance by promising them freedom and had their own authority compromised when they employed slaves.[46] Over four thousand blacks "served in the Continental Army, and thousands more in the local militia." Those serving from New York State enjoyed the prospect of freedom, thanks to a law passed by the New York State Assembly in 1781.[47] Nearly all the Revolutionary War leaders were inspired to condemn slavery. In fact, "Jefferson's first draft of the Declaration of Independence contained a sweeping condemnation of the slave trade and England's refusal to allow legislation 'to prohibit or restrain this execrable commerce.'" Washington, Jefferson, and Madison—all slaveholders—expressed support of "gradual emancipation."[48]

Zinn acknowledges this passage in the original Declaration, but then casts suspicion upon Jefferson's motives: "This seemed to express moral indignation against slavery and the slave trade (Jefferson's personal distaste for slavery must be put alongside the fact that he owned hundreds of slaves to the day he died.)" And Zinn suggests a possible self-serving motive: the fear of slave insurrections. "Because slaveholders themselves disagreed about the desirability of ending the slave trade," Zinn writes, "Jefferson's paragraph was removed." Zinn concludes with dripping sarcasm, "So even that gesture toward the black slave was omitted in the great manifesto of freedom of the American Revolution."[49] As usual,

Zinn presents anything short of immediate utopian results as evidence of hypocrisy and greed. Any suggestion that injustices should be cured by changes that are gradual, and lawful—and safe—is taken as evidence of insincerity. No credit is given to such American Founders as John Jay, Alexander Hamilton, and Philip Schuyler for their roles in the newly formed New York Manumission Society, organized in 1785, which became the "working organization of the antislavery movement," keeping the pressure up "on state officials" and "the issue before the public"—and that ultimately succeeded[50] in phasing out slavery in New York State. Full abolition was achieved in 1827.

There is still slavery in Africa to this day. "[A]n estimated 9.2 million" Africans "live in servitude without the choice to do so" at "the highest rate.... in the world," according to the 2018 Global Slavery Index. Slavery is "especially prevalent" in Eritrea and Mauritania, countries noted for the collusion of the government in the practice. In Eritrea, the "one-party state of president Isaias Afwerki has overseen a notorious national conscription service" for forced labor. In Mauritania, "the world's last country to abolish slavery," "the situation is more acute," with the "black Haratin group" inheriting its slave status.[51]

In 2018, photojournalist Seif Kousmate traveled to Mauritania, where he was imprisoned for a time. His photos of the Haratine in Mauritania, published at the *Guardian,* are images of abject poverty and misery. Mauritania is a place where "up to 20% of the population is enslaved, with one in two Haratines forced to work on farms or in homes with no possibility of freedom, education or pay." And contrary to Zinn's assertion that racism is a uniquely American trait, Kousmate writes, "For centuries, Arabic-speaking Moors raided African villages, resulting in a rigid caste system that still exists...with darker-skinned inhabitants beholden to their lighter-skinned 'masters.'" Many of the subjugated can conceive of no other system and accept their status. The government, however, "denies that slavery exists," and "prais[es] itself for eradicating the practice."[52]

As Zinn was writing *A People's History,* Mauritania had not yet made slavery officially illegal. Yet, Zinn obscures the practice of slavery in other parts of the world besides America—in the past and in his present—and focuses on American slavery, falsely presenting American slavery as the most cruel, and America as the most racist. He preemptively discounts statistical evidence to the contrary. For example, he writes, "Economists or cliometricians (statistical historians) have tried to assess slavery by estimating how much money was spent on slaves for food and medical care." But then, to keep the reader from paying any attention to this evidence, Zinn immediately asks, "But can this describe the reality of slavery as it was to a human being who lived inside it? Are the *conditions* of slavery as important as the *existence* of slavery [emphasis in the original]?"[53] The suggestion that they're not, however, contradicts Zinn's earlier excuse-making for African slavery, when he argued that the conditions of slavery there under their pre-capitalist society—"tribal life," "a communal spirit"—made the *existence* of slavery not so bad.

Zinn's aim is to present all American slave owners as wicked Simon Legrees. So, he brings up the whipping of slaves "in 1840–1842 on the Barrow plantation in Louisiana with two hundred slaves." Zinn quotes from *Time on the Cross* by Robert William Fogel and Stanley Engerman: "The records show that over the course of two years a total of 160 whippings were administered, an average of 0.7 whippings per hand per year. About half the hands were not whipped at all during the period." Zinn adds an editorial note: "One could also say: 'Half of all slaves were whipped.' That has a different ring." Zinn also points out that though "whipping was infrequent for any individual," nonetheless "once every four or five days, *some* slave was whipped [emphasis in the original]." Zinn claims that the amount of cruel physical punishment on Barrow's plantation was typical because "Barrow as a plantation owner, according to his biographer, was no worse than the average."[54] But do we know what "average" is? Zinn has presented only one isolated case.

In another case of selective reporting, Zinn tells his readers, "A record of deaths kept in a plantation journal (now in the University of North Carolina Archives) lists the ages and cause of death of all those who died on the plantation between 1850 and 1855." Zinn doesn't tell his reader what plantation these numbers are from, but he does report the ages: "Of the thirty-two who died in that period, only four reached the age of sixty, four reached the age of fifty, seven died in their forties, seven died in their twenties or thirties, and nine died before they were five years old."[55] Those certainly seem like young ages, but they are records from only one plantation—which for all we know was chosen by Zinn precisely for the short life-spans of slaves there.

Comparative statistics tell a very different story. Nobel Prize-winning economic historian Robert William Fogel has shown that American slaves were better nourished than many other groups, including "most European workers, during the nineteenth century." At that time, "all of the working classes…probably suffered some degree of malnutrition," in comparison to modern standards. The malnutrition of American slaves was not "as severe as that experienced by…Italian conscripts, or the illiterate French conscript," he writes. Height is an indicator of nutrition, and slaves born in the United States were "about an inch shorter than U.S.-born whites in the Union Army," but "taller than French and Italian conscripts, British town artisans, and British Royal Marines."[56] No wonder Zinn wants his reader to disregard the findings of "[e]conomists and cliometricians." It better serves his purpose to discount and rely on isolated, misleading examples, instead.

Consider the sources provided by Zinn: a diary kept by a plantation owner identified only by last name and state, and an unidentified plantation journal in the "archives" at the University of North Carolina. Can we find a grosser violation of the American Historical Association's standards for evidence? As if this weren't bad enough, Zinn then refers to "two northern liberal historians" who he says authored the "1932 edition of a best-selling textbook." That unnamed book by unnamed authors allegedly excuses slavery "as perhaps the Negro's 'necessary transition to civilization.'"[57] Who are the straw men who are supposed to have made this appalling observation? We have no way of knowing, so we can't check Zinn's accusations.

Zinn switches back and forth from presenting untraceable isolated incidents, to discounting rigorous statistics, to posing leading questions:

"But can statistics record what it meant for families to be torn apart, when a master, for profit, sold a husband or a wife, a son or a daughter? In 1858, a slave named Abream Scriven was sold by his master, and wrote to his wife: 'Give my love to my father and mother and tell them good Bye for me, and if we Shall not meet in this world I hope to meet in heaven.'"[58] In the face of such human suffering, which was very real, only a heartless cliometrician could be interested in actual data—so let's not worry about the documented facts.

Such forced family break-ups did happen to an estimated third of slave families—as conservative historians have acknowledged[59]—and they were horrific. Abolitionist writers, including Frederick Douglass, pointed to such inhumane practices to appeal for abolition, and Americans came to see slavery as wrong.

The arguments that persuaded Americans to end slavery are grossly distorted by Zinn. Take Frederick Douglass's July 5, 1852, speech in Rochester, New York: "What to the Slave Is the Fourth of July?" Zinn quotes from the early part of the speech which was intended to arouse the emotions of the audience, to make them empathize and understand the hypocrisy of celebrating the Declaration of Independence in a nation that denies freedom to slaves. But, not surprisingly, he ignores the patriotic climax of the speech. Thus, the only idea that Zinn takes away from it is that the "whole nation" was "complicit" in the "shame of slavery."[60] Zinn spares readers the passage in which Douglass expresses faith in the Constitution, calling it a "GLORIOUS LIBERTY DOCU-MENT." Those caps are in the original speech by Frederick Douglass, who had actually broken with fellow abolitionist William Lloyd Garrison over Garrison's abandonment of faith in the Constitution and the American system.[61] At the climactic moment of the speech, Douglass declared, "I hold there is neither warrant, license, nor sanctions of the hateful thing [for slavery, that is, in the Constitution]; but, interpreted as it ought to be interpreted, the Constitution is a GLORIOUS LIB-ERTY DOCUMENT." Contrary to Zinn's representation, Douglass's speech expressed his optimistic faith in America. "I do not despair of this country," Douglass proclaimed, expressing confidence that "the doom of slavery is certain." His "spirit" was "cheered" by "drawing encouragement from the principles of the Declaration of Independence...and the genius of American Institutions....''[62]

Zinn quotes Douglass at length, though always selectively, but he says nothing about Douglass's role in the Civil War—the war that Zinn casts as simply a means to perpetuate a racist capitalistic state. In fact, Douglass served as a recruiter of black troops—Douglass's own sons served in the war—and as adviser to President Lincoln. Zinn also fails to mention the appointment of this stalwart Republican to political office as federal marshal (1877–1881), recorder of deeds for the District of Columbia (1881–1886), and chargé d'affaires for Santa Domingo and minister to Haiti (1889–1891).

Zinn ignores Douglass's relationship with Lincoln so that he can portray the president as a cowardly racist politician beholden to powerful money interests. To Zinn, Abraham Lincoln "combined perfectly the needs of business, the political ambition of the new Republican party, and the rhetoric of humanitarianism." Lincoln used abolition for political advancement. It was only "close enough to the top" of his "list of priorities" that "it could be pushed there temporarily by abolitionist pressures and by practical political advantage." Zinn contrasts Lincoln's statement "that the institution of slavery is founded on injustice and bad policy, but that the promulgation of abolition doctrines tends to increase rather than abate its evils" with "Frederick Douglass's statement on struggle, or Garrison's 'Sir, slavery will not be overthrown without excitement....'" But Zinn does not tell the reader where the Lincoln quotation is from: a resolution that the future Great Emancipator made when he was a twenty-eight-year-old state house representative. It can be found in one of Zinn's favorite sources, Richard Hofstadter's *The American Political Tradition*, from which Zinn purloins not only quotations, but also Hofstadter's jaundiced view of Lincoln, whom Zinn excoriates for being concerned about public opinion (imagine that, in an elected official!) and for following the Constitution (!)[63] The only kind of abolitionist Zinn approves of is a violent abolitionist like John Brown, whose "last written statement, in prison, before he was hanged" for the raid on Harper's Ferry, as Zinn approvingly notes, declared, that "the crimes of this guilty land will never be purged away but with blood."[64]

Zinn ignores the fact that Brown's raid led to the deaths of ten in his party, including two of Brown's sons, as well as several civilians, including two slaves and a free black man. This was after Brown and his band of men had killed five settlers in Kansas, where the issue of slavery was being contested. The method was to drag "the man of the house from his house and butche[r] him as his family screamed in horror." These victims were not even slave owners, just settlers who believed in allowing slavery into the territory. Brown succeeded only in sowing fear and mistrust in the South, in the opinion of Thomas Woods.[65] Zinn naturally approves of purging injustices "with blood," so John Brown is a hallowed martyr to him. A People's History expresses Zinn's disappointment that "it was Abraham Lincoln who freed the slaves, not John Brown."[66]

Lincoln's original hope to eliminate slavery gradually by beginning to outlaw it in the territories while keeping the nation together is not good enough for Zinn. He prefers Brown's vigilante terrorism. As Zinn tells the story, Southern states seceded from the Union after Lincoln's election not because of slavery, but out of "a long series of policy clashes between South and North."

> The clash was not over slavery as a moral institution—most northerners did not care enough about slavery to make sacrifices for it, certainly not the sacrifice of war. It was not a clash of peoples (most northern whites were not economically favored, not politically powerful; most southern whites were poor farmers, not decisionmakers) but of elites. The northern elite wanted economic expansion—free land, free labor, a free market, a high protective tariff for manufacturers, a bank of the United States. The slave interests opposed all that; they saw Lincoln and the Republicans as making

continuation of their pleasant and prosperous way of life impossible in the future. [67]

Zinn ignores a little fact: that Lincoln had been *elected* on an anti-slavery ticket. The "decisionmakers" were the voters. The "clash" which had been building up for years before his election was over slavery. As one textbook notes, "The causes of secession, as they appeared to its protagonists, were plainly expressed by the state conventions [of the Deep South]. 'The people of the Northern states,' declared Mississippi, 'have assumed a revolutionary position towards Southern states.' 'They have enticed our slaves from us,' and obstructed their rendition under the fugitive slave law. They claim the right 'to exclude slavery from their territories,' and from any state henceforth admitted to the Union."

The North was charged with "'a hostile invasion of a Southern state to excite insurrection, murder and rapine'.... South Carolina added, 'They have denounced as sinful the institution of slavery; they have permitted the open establishment among them' of abolition societies, and 'have united in the election of a man to the high office of President of the United States whose opinions and purposes are hostile to slavery.'" The textbook authors conclude:

> On their own showing, then, the states of the Lower South seceded as the result of a long series of dissatisfactions respecting the Northern attitude toward slavery. There was no mention in their manifestoes or in their leaders' writings and speeches of any other cause. Protection figured as a 'cause' in the Confederate propaganda abroad and in Southern apologetics since; but there was no contemporary mention of it because most of the Southern congressmen, including the entire South Carolina delegation, had voted for the tariff of 1857, and because the Congress of the Confederacy re-enacted it.... or was any allusion made to states [sic] rights apart from slavery; on the contrary, the Northern

states were reproached for sheltering themselves under states [sic] rights against the fugitive slave laws and the Dred Scott decision.[68]

As Vice President of the Confederate States of America, Alexander H. Stephens stated, "'Our new Government is founded...upon the great truth that the negro is not the equal of the white man. That slavery—subordination to the superior race, is his natural and normal condition.'"[69]

But in Zinn's history, "Lincoln initiated hostilities."[70] Oh, really? In fact, Confederate forces fired the first shot of the war. When Confederate forces took over Fort Sumter, Lincoln notified them that he would be sending supplies only, leaving the ball in the court of the Confederates. On April 6, Lincoln notified the governor of South Carolina "to expect an attempt will be made to supply Fort Sumpter [sic] with provisions only; and that, if such attempt be not resisted, no effort to throw in men, arms, or ammunition will be made, without further notice, or in case of an attack upon the Fort.'" On April 12, Confederate forces fired on Fort Sumter.[71]

Zinn is engaging in a kind mental gymnastics. The fact is, Zinn will do anything to make America look bad; he simply cannot allow his reader to give the first Republican elected president credit for freeing the slaves—and for going about it in a principled and prudent manner. That would mean giving the American people credit for abolishing slavery, and it would undermine Zinn's picture of America as a uniquely racist country.

So, Zinn has to make out that Lincoln's actions always fall short. Even the Emancipation Proclamation did not arise out of a sincere desire to free the slaves, but only from political and military expediency: "When in September 1862, Lincoln issued his preliminary Emancipation Proclamation, it was a military move, giving the South four months to stop rebelling, threatening to emancipate their slaves if they continued to fight, promising to leave slavery untouched in states that came over to the North." The Proclamation made the Union Army open to blacks—but that was just for propaganda purposes: "And the more blacks entered the war, the more it appeared a war for their liberation."[72]

Was Lincoln's Emancipation Proclamation a cynical move? Was it issued only for military advantage and public relations? To the contrary, in issuing the Proclamation, Lincoln put his military powers as commander-in-chief at the service of his moral convictions. That was the *only* way Lincoln could issue the proclamation. As James Oakes explains:

> Lincoln was freeing slaves by virtue of the power vested in the president as commander in chief of the army and navy "in time of actual armed rebellion against the authority and government of the United States, and as a fit and necessary war measure for suppressing rebellion".... Except in time of war or insurrection the Constitution forbade the federal government from directly interfering with slavery in the states where it existed. Military necessity was the only constitutional ground on which Lincoln could justify federal "interference" with a state institution.[73]

James McPherson believes that Lincoln may have been influenced by a pamphlet by William Whiting, a leading lawyer and abolitionist in Boston. In *The War Powers of the President, and the Legislative Powers of Congress in Relation to Rebellion, Treason, and Slavery*, Whiting had argued "that the laws of war 'give the President full belligerent' right as commander in chief to seize enemy property (in this case slaves) being used to wage war against the United States...."[74]

But, as McPherson also points out, Lincoln "recognized with regret that white racism was a stumbling block to emancipation." Thus, in the months leading up to the Proclamation, he advanced "the colonization of freed slaves abroad." It was "a way of defusing white fears of an influx into the North of freedpeople." So, Lincoln met with "five black men from Washington" on August 14, 1862, to "urg[e] them to consider the idea of emigration."[75]

Zinn ignores Lincoln's reasons for seeking to send freed blacks to Africa, charging that Lincoln "opposed slavery, but could not see blacks as equals, so a constant theme in his approach was to free the slaves and to send them back to Africa." He also ignores many efforts to end slavery short of war, claiming, "It was only as the war grew more bitter, the casualties mounted, desperation to win heightened, and the criticism of the abolitionists threatened to unravel the tattered coalition behind Lincoln that he began to act against slavery."[76] This is false. Lincoln had supported outlawing slavery in the new territories, hoping that that would lead to gradual abolition. And he gave the border states multiple opportunities to accept compensated abolition.[77]

Zinn, who quotes Hofstadter's claim that the Emancipation Proclamation "had all the grandeur of a bill of lading,"[78] either misses or purposely obscures Lincoln's intentions and his political genius in promulgating it—for example, in his reply to Horace Greeley's open letter accusing Lincoln of deferring to "Rebel Slavery." James McPherson calls Lincoln's presidential letter a "stroke of genius" in "preparing public opinion" for the Proclamation. McPherson explains that "to conservatives who insisted that preservation of the Union must be the sole purpose of the war, Lincoln said that such *was* his purpose. To radicals who wanted him to proclaim emancipation in order to save the Union, he hinted that he might do so. To everyone he made it clear that partial or even total emancipation might become necessary...to accomplish the purpose to which they all agreed."[79]

Howard Zinn claims that Lincoln, in his efforts to eliminate slavery, was simply reacting to "abolitionist pressures" and angling for "practical political advantage." In fact, Lincoln was putting pressure on radical abolitionists—and on opponents of abolition, too—to win the war, preserve the Union, and free the slaves. To achieve those worthy goals, he had to take political risks and exercise his formidable political skills. As Debra Sheffer writes, "Lincoln believed predictions that the proclamation would seriously hurt the Republican Party in the [1862] elections, but he forged ahead with the plan in order to win the war and save the Union.

The Republican Party did indeed suffer losses as a result of the proclamation, but the damage was minimal, with Republicans still holding a majority in both the Senate and the House." Lincoln's annual address to Congress in December included "one final plea for the Border States to consider emancipation."[80]

But Howard Zinn is unimpressed. Zinn is determined to knock Lincoln off his pedestal. He wants to replace "Lincoln freed the slaves"— a true fact of history, learned by generations of Americans for a century—with the notion that Lincoln was a small-minded political operator who "skillfully" blended "the interests of the very rich and the interests of the black" and "link[ed] these two with a growing section of Americans, the white, up-and-coming, economically ambitious, politically active middle class."[81] In other words, the Civil War didn't so much free the slaves as enable bourgeois oppression. Only Zinn could present Lincoln—the American president with the humblest background, a man who worked his way up from poverty and was often ridiculed by the elites—as a member of the elite ruling class. Zinn simply cannot give Abraham Lincoln—and thus the American people who elected him and fought to win the Civil War—credit for ending slavery.

Frederick Douglass saw it differently. In 1876, more than a decade after the president had been assassinated for his anti-slavery position, Douglass said, "Abraham Lincoln was at the head of a great movement and was in living and earnest sympathy with that movement, which, in the nature of things, must go on until slavery should be utterly and forever abolished in the United States."[82]

Of course, that estimate of Lincoln is not included in A People's History. And of course, Zinn neither quotes nor even refers to Douglass's 1865 speech, "What the Black Man Wants":

> What I ask for the Negro is not benevolence, not pity, not sympathy, but simply justice.... everybody has asked the question, and they learned to ask it early of the abolitionists, "What shall we do with the Negro?" I have had but one

answer from the beginning. Do nothing with us! Your doing
with us has already played the mischief with us. Do nothing
with us! If the apples will not remain on the tree of their own
strength, if they are wormeaten at the core, if they are early
ripe and disposed to fall, let them fall! I am not for tying or
fastening them on the tree in any way, except by nature's plan,
and if they will not stay there, let them fall. And if the Negro
cannot stand on his own legs, let him fall also. All I ask is,
give him a chance to stand on his own legs! Let him alone![83]

For Howard Zinn, it was not a good thing to simply treat former
slaves as men, to leave them free to run their own lives. He was unwilling to acknowledge Douglass's accomplishments in national affairs,
preferring to present Douglass as a pitiful and angry militant waiting
for a revolutionary leader, and the Civil War as a tragic missed opportunity for a leftist social revolution against the "deeply entrenched
system" of capitalism.[84]

For Zinn, the very real horrors of slavery are simply more fodder for
his war against America and Western civilization. The nearly three-
quarters of a million dead in the Civil War are just casualties of a military
machine, and blacks are no better off than they were under slavery. The
irony is that, as historian Robert Paquette, a specialist in the history of
slavery, has remarked in his criticism of the use of Zinn's history as a text
in high school classrooms:

An assessment in a classroom of, say, the history of slavery—
the peculiar institution—by a professional historian should
take into consideration the fact that the institution was not
peculiar at all in the sense of being uncommon, and that it had
existed from time immemorial on all habitable continents. In
fact, at one time or another, all the world's great religions had
stamped slavery with their authoritative approval. Only at a
particular historical moment—and only in the West—did an

evolving understanding of personal freedom, influenced by evangelical Christianity, emerge to assert as a universal that the enslavement of human beings was a moral wrong for anyone, anywhere.[85]

Or as President Lincoln reminded the nation at the dedication of the new cemetery at Gettysburg: the dead had "not died in vain" because "a new nation, conceived in Liberty, and dedicated to the proposition that all men are created equal" would "endure."[86]

FIVE

Casting a Pall on the Finest Hour

oward Zinn has made dishonest use of the discovery of America, slavery, and the Civil War to indict America and promote communist revolution. But in his treatment of World War II, he hits a new low. Through a series of four long, leading questions about "imperialism, racism, totalitarianism, and militarism," Zinn insinuates that the "enemy of unspeakable evil," "Hitler's Germany," was no worse than the United States and her allies.[1] Imperial Japan, too, was a victim of American aggression.

We weren't really fighting against racist totalitarianism, but rather to maintain the evil capitalist system. World War II was "a war waged by a government whose chief beneficiary—despite volumes of reforms—was a wealthy elite." Just like all of America's wars: "The alliance between big business and the government went back to the very first proposals of Alexander Hamilton to Congress after the Revolutionary War. By World War II that partnership had developed and intensified. During the Depression, Roosevelt had once denounced the 'economic royalists,' but he always had the support of certain important business leaders."[2]

Zinn's theory that all American wars have been fought to benefit plutocrats is not an original one. It was in wide dissemination in the 1930s during Zinn's teenage years as Americans suffering from the Great Depression looked back on World War I. During that decade, "An avalanche of lurid articles and books poured from American presses condemning the munitions manufacturers as war-fomenting 'merchants of death,'" according to an American history text by Thomas Bailey: Many "naïve souls" leapt to "the illogical conclusion that [the arms manufacturers] had caused [World War I] in order to make money. This kind of reasoning suggested that if the profits could only be removed from the arms business, America could keep out of any World conflict that might erupt in the future."[3]

President Franklin Roosevelt, as is well known, had a contentious relationship with business and military leaders. It began early. In his second "Fireside Chat" on May 7, 1933, he announced his massive and numerous New Deal programs, as well as a policy of "a general reduction of armaments," which he said would reduce costs and remove "the fear of invasion and armed attack."[4] Roosevelt's plan to reduce an "already small Army of 140,000 men as a way to free up money for relief" caused General Douglas MacArthur, the army chief of staff, to "explode" in anger.[5] When it came time to help Britain, many feared that the United States would be vulnerable because of the weakened military.[6] During the 1930s, both Germany and Japan expanded through military force, with Germany taking over Czechoslovakia, Austria, and then Poland in 1939 and Japan brutally invading China with the rape of Nanking in 1937.

Fortunately, once the order was given to increase production for armaments and other military supplies, American factories were able to get close enough to meeting President Roosevelt's "seemingly impossible yearly production goals" to vaunt the Allies to victory, according to Victor Davis Hanson. The United States had "over twelve million in uniform," but "suffered only about 416,000 combat casualties," which was just slightly above "3 percent of those enrolled in the military" and was "proportionally the fewest combat casualties of the major powers." American industries might have helped save American lives and win the war.[7]

But Howard Zinn's account of World War II is a pacifist fantasy riddled with conspiracy theories. The tone is set on the first page of his chapter on the war, where he opens with a long quotation from "a skit put on in the United States in the year 1939 by the Communist party" suggesting that America fought World War II for "imperialist" reasons. Later—after Germany violated its pact with the Soviet Union and invaded Russia in 1941—the CPUSA called World War II "a 'people's war' against Fascism." But, "Was it?" Zinn asks. He doesn't seem to think so. Momentarily presenting himself as a critic of the Soviet Union, he asks whether "England, the United States, the Soviet Union," really represented "something significantly different" from the "unspeakable evil" of Nazi Germany. The Allies' victory, Zinn suggests, would not really "be a blow to imperialism, racism, totalitarianism, militarism, in the world."[8]

Citing the massive involvement of Americans on the war front and the home front, Zinn asks, "could this be considered a manufactured support, since all the power of the nation—not only of the government, but the press, the church, and even the chief radical organizations—was behind the calls for all-out war? Was there an undercurrent of reluctance; were there unpublicized signs of resistance?"[9]

Of course, there was internal opposition to the war. There was a very strong and public anti-interventionist movement. One of the fears that the anti-interventionists had was about allying with the Soviet Union, whose executions and mass starvations were already known. They were rightly concerned about the Soviets' imperialist ambitions. As Melvyn Leffler noted, "Almost a third of all Americans" continued to distrust our military ally the Soviet Union even at the height of the fighting against the Nazis, and "most polls showed that fewer than half of all Americans expected cooperation to persist in the postwar period."[10] But after the attack on Pearl Harbor, many anti-interventionists, including future president Gerald Ford and aviator Charles Lindbergh, gave the war effort their full support.

But this is not the opposition to the war that Zinn has in mind. This important part of history is not even given a mention in Zinn's book. Instead he is interested in how "blacks, looking at anti-Semitism in

Germany, might not see their own situation in the United States as much different."[11] As we shall see in more detail below, Zinn grossly exaggerates the degree to which African Americans opposed World War II. To be sure, bitterness was expressed in the black newspapers about the attention given to Nazi persecution of the Jews even as African Americans faced discrimination at home.[12] But Zinn ignores the fact that African Americans were fighting for the right to fight.

Years before the United States entered the war, black leaders were supporting bills by Congressman Hamilton Fish to expand the opportunities for African Americans in the military beyond the support services to which they were relegated. The exploits of black soldiers in the Civil War, the Indian Wars, the Mexican-American War, and in the Philippines were the subjects of lectures by black leaders that boosted the pride and morale of African Americans and also provided arguments for equal rights. In World War II, Africans Americans would once again exhibit their fighting ability, beginning with Dorie Miller on the ship *West Virginia* in Pearl Harbor rushing to wield an anti-aircraft gun (in spite of having been denied combat training), to the Tuskegee Airmen and the 761st Tank Battalion, the original "Black Panthers." During 183 days of combat in the last two years of the war, the 761st "captured or liberated more than 30 major towns and four airfields," "pierced the Siegfried line into Germany and fought in the Battle of the Bulge," and liberated "at least one concentration camp, the Gunskirchen camp in Austria."[13] They received their Distinguished Unit Citation only in 1978.

Their overdue recognition was in the news as Zinn was writing his history,[14] but Zinn ignores such events. (Instead, he harps on President Jimmy Carter for the generic sins of all the American presidents and glorifies the *other* Black Panthers). Nor does Zinn bother to read about their performance in the black newspapers from the accounts by Trezzvant Anderson, the black "combat journalist assigned by the War Department to cover the battalion."

Joe Wilson Jr., son of First Sergeant Joseph Wilson Sr. of the 761st Battalion, wrote in his history of his father's unit, "In another one of the war's ironies, Jewish-American soldiers helped to liberate black inmates from Nazi concentration camps." These were the "Rhineland Mulattoes," children from the German African colonies.[15]

Zinn, however, sets out to debunk the myth that "seemed clear at the time…that the United States was a democracy with certain liberties, while Germany was a dictatorship persecuting its Jewish minority, imprisoning dissidents, whatever their religion, while proclaiming the supremacy of the Nordic 'race.'" Zinn will set the record straight![16]

Zinn sets out to correct his readers' belief in "the United States…as a defender of helpless countries." In contrast to that "image" being promulgated "in American high school history textbooks," the true "record in world affairs" is a long train of abuses: The United States:

> had opposed the Hatian [sic] revolution for independence from France.… It had instigated a war with Mexico and taken half of that country. It had pretended to help Cuba win freedom from Spain, and then planted itself in Cuba with a military base, investments, and rights of intervention. It had seized Hawaii, Puerto Rico, Guam, and fought a brutal war to subjugate the Filipinos. It had "opened" Japan to its trade with gunboats and threats. It had declared an Open Door Policy in China as a means of assuring that the United States would have opportunities equal to other imperial powers in exploiting China.[17]

The list goes on. America created the "'independent" state of Panama "in order to build and control the Canal," sent "marines to Nicaragua in 1926 to counter a revolution," and "intervened" in the Dominican Republic, Haiti, Cuba, Nicaragua, Panama, Guatemala, and Honduras. As a result—the horror!—"By 1935, over half of U.S. steel and cotton exports were being sold in Latin America." And to top it off, American troops interfered in the Bolshevik Revolution![18]

What is the purpose of this litany of supposed American sins? To demonstrate that the U.S. didn't have the moral standing to oppose Nazi

Germany. "In short, if the entrance of the United States into World War II was (as so many Americans believed at the time, observing the Nazi invasions) to defend the principle of nonintervention in the affairs of other countries, the nation's record cast doubt on its ability to uphold that principle."[19] Zinn suggests that the American government's "main interest was not stopping Fascism but advancing the imperial interests of the United States." That's why "when Japan and Germany threatened U.S. world interests, a pro-Soviet, anti-Nazi policy became preferable."[20]

The fact that the United States declared war after the attack on Pearl Harbor instead of when Hitler invaded Austria, took over Czechoslovakia, or attacked Poland (the simultaneous Soviet attack on Poland is not mentioned) is supposed to prove our imperial ambitions. If we had really cared about fighting injustice, we might have gone to war with the Japanese back in 1937 when they attacked China and raped Nanking. But America waited to go to war until America was attacked. Why? Because we're wicked imperialists: "It was the Japanese attack on a link in the American Pacific Empire that did it."

Besides, President Roosevelt told lies! While Zinn pretends to eschew "the wild accusations against Roosevelt (that he knew about Pearl Harbor and didn't tell, or that he deliberately provoked the Pearl Harbor raid....),"he suggests in the same sentence that "it does seem clear that [Roosevelt] did as James Polk had done before him in the Mexican war and Lyndon Johnson after him in the Vietnam war—he lied to the public for what he thought was a right cause. In September and October 1941, he misstated the facts in two incidents involving German submarines and American destroyers."[21] But Zinn does not even identify these "incidents"—the clashes between the U.S. destroyers *Greer, Kearney,* and *Reuben James,* and German U-boats in September and October 1941— much less acknowledge the danger they represented.

In any case, in the estimation of Thomas Bailey, the *Greer* incident, the only one of the three in which there was no damage or loss of life, "was the only one of the three clashes that raised grave doubts as to Roosevelt's basic honesty. This destroyer...was carrying passengers, mail, and freight to the American outpost on Iceland" and "had been trailing a German submarine and broadcasting its position to British aircraft and warships, who dropped bombs nearby." The Germans retaliated. Even though the *Greer* was the "aggressor.... Roosevelt delivered a shoot-on-sight radio message" a week later, on September 11, 1941.[22]

Does this prove that American involvement in World War II was based on a lie and thereby illegitimate through and through? Some conservative critics, such as Larry Schweikart and Michael Allen, suggest military action should have been taken *sooner.* They maintain that with the sinking of the *Reuben James* on October 31, 1941, "the United States would have been fully justified by international law in declaring war on Germany and her allies." In their judgment, the neutrality acts harmed such states as Ethiopia and China, which were "attempt[ing] to resist the Italian and Japanese aggressors," and Roosevelt's advisors fell short in advising him of the threats: "Had the United States deliberately and forcefully entered the war in Europe earlier, on its own timetable, perhaps some of Hitler's strategic victories (and, possibly, much of the Holocaust) might have been avoided." Schweikart and Allen speculate that if America had entered World War II earlier, the Battle of Britain "would not have been close" and that Hitler might have "scrapp[ed] the German invasion of Russia."[23] They fault Roosevelt for following public opinion and failing to lead.

President Roosevelt, like all American presidents, has his fans and his critics. But Zinn's purpose is not to offer a critique of one specific U.S. president or one particular set of policies, but to indict *all* American presidents—Polk, Roosevelt, Lyndon Johnson—and pretend they're all the same because all of them, regardless of party or individual character, are irredeemable, greedy, capitalist war-mongers. Zinn's project is to destroy the credibility of the American presidency—and of America, itself.

Thus, Zinn refers to "one of the judges in the Tokyo War Crimes Trial...Radhabinod Pal," who "dissented from the general verdicts against Japanese officials and argued that the United States had clearly provoked the war with Japan."[24] According to Wikipedia, Pal was the only one to maintain that all the defendants were "not guilty."[25] Zinn quotes from Richard H. Minear's *Victors' Justice*, which, he says, "sums up Pal's view" that American "embargoes on scrap iron and oil" were to blame for "provok[ing] the war with Japan." According to the Indian judge, "these measures were a clear and potent threat to Japan's very existence."[26] But Victor Davis Hanson, drawing on numerous sources, points out that Japan could have obtained oil "in the Dutch East Indies without attacking Pearl Harbor and Singapore."[27] As Harvard professor Fredrik Logevall has written, Japan attacked Pearl Harbor to "destroy the American fleet" and buy "time to complete its southward expansion."[28] Schweikart and Allen, citing the fact that "Japan was already on a timetable for war," judge the claims that "Roosevelt provoked Japan" as "absurd." Japan's policies were taking it toward bankruptcy, which would make war necessary. Intercepts beginning in December 1940 revealed that Japan was planning to "expand" to the southwest, the south, or the east—or in more than one of those directions.[29]

Immediately after quoting Pal, Zinn asserts, "The records show that a White House conference two weeks before Pearl Harbor anticipated a war and discussed how it should be justified."[30] No further details about the mysterious "conference" are given. Zinn simply juxtaposes the fact of this murky meeting with Pal's claim that the U.S. provoked the Japanese attack on Pearl Harbor and allows the power of suggestion to implant the idea of a conspiracy. It would take a bit more work to describe the events actually taking place with names and dates. But no one should be surprised that the White House was anticipating possible entry into World War II in November 1941. So, of course the Roosevelt administration had to prepare for that contingency. Tensions were rising steadily. As Bailey points out, "Congress, responding to public pressures and confronted with a shooting war, voted in mid-November, 1941, to pull the teeth from the now-useless Neutrality Act of 1939."[31] None of that was a secret.

Thus during "negotiations with Japan" in Washington in "November and early December of 1941," the State Department "insisted that the Japanese clear out of China but, to sweeten the pill, offered to renew trade relations on a limited basis." But the Japanese were "unwilling to lose face by withdrawing at the behest of the United States."[32] *New York Times* readers could have read about a November 25, 1941, "parley" at the White House involving discussions between representatives of the United States, Britain, China, and the Netherlands about "the Far Eastern situation."[33] On December 4, the giant, front-page headline in the *Chicago Daily Tribune* announced, "FDR's War Plans!" The president was dismayed at the leak. But as Secretary of War Henry Stimson asked reporters a couple of days later, "What would you think of an American general staff which in the present condition of the world did not investigate and study every conceivable type of emergency which may confront this country and every possible method of meeting that emergency?"[34]

The next stick Zinn uses to beat Roosevelt—and the United States—with is the truly tragic "plight of Jews in German-occupied Europe." Zinn cites "Henry Feingold's research" showing "that, while the Jews were being put in camps and the process of annihilation was beginning that would end in the horrifying extermination of 6 million Jews and millions of non-Jews, Roosevelt failed to take steps that might have saved thousands of lives. He did not see it as a high priority; he left it to the State Department, and in the State Department anti-Semitism and a cold bureaucracy became obstacles to action."[35]

Zinn here is distorting Feingold's words. It is not completely true that "Roosevelt failed to take steps." Feingold indicates that Roosevelt could have done more, while acknowledging the economic, legal, and diplomatic challenges during an economic depression and then wartime. The United States had no power to force Germany "to cease and desist." Additionally, infighting among American Jewish leaders sometimes stymied efforts. Peter Bergson defied them with advertising campaigns and rallies, spurring a humanitarian response. Enlisted was Swedish diplomat Raoul Wallenberg, who rescued at least 20,000 Hungarian Jews before he was killed by the Soviets. As for Zinn's sweeping charge about anti-Semitism within the State Department, most of the "obstacles to action" came from Breckinridge Long, the assistant director, who vented in his diary about "communists, extreme radicals, Jewish professional agitators, refugee enthusiasts." Long had received "strong support" from his Jewish ally and friend in the State Department's Foreign Service, Laurence Steinhardt, for his "close relatives" ruling in June 1941, "which made it virtually impossible for any refugee with relatives remaining under Nazi control to come to the United States." According to Feingold, Steinhardt "buttressed Long's already strong anti-Semitic predilections by articulating his own prejudices against 'eastern' Jews." Long wrote that Steinhardt was "right not as regards the Russian and Polish Jew alone," but also "the lower level of all that slav population of Eastern Europe and Western Asia—the Caucasus, Georgia, Ukraine, Croat, Slovene, Carpatho-Ukraine, Montenegro, etc. . . ."[36] Historians, even admirers of FDR, wish that he had displayed more "political courage" to stop the tragedy.[37]

But such distinctions are not for Zinn. His point is that America was no better than Nazi Germany. Not only was the Roosevelt administration responsible for the deaths of Jews who were not allowed to emigrate to the United States, but the U.S. was enforcing "Nordic supremacy" just like the Third Reich—as evidenced in the treatment of black troops. Naturally, this suggestion is presented in the form of a question: "Was the war being fought to establish that Hitler was wrong in his ideas of white Nordic supremacy over 'inferior' races? The United States' armed forces were segregated by race. When troops were jammed onto the *Queen Mary* in early 1945 to go to combat duty in the European theater, the blacks were stowed down in the depths of the ship near the engine room, as far as possible from the fresh air of the deck, in a bizarre reminder of the slave voyages of old."[38]

Zinn knows that black soldiers in World War II suffered nothing remotely like the conditions he himself had described in an earlier chapter of slaves "chained together . . . in different stages of suffocation,"[39] but he elides the differences to make America seem no better than Nazi Germany.

And Zinn has another victim class whose sufferings advance his America the Fascist thesis: women were oppressed, too! "The Fascist nations were notorious in their insistence that the woman's place was in the home. Yet, the war against Fascism, although it utilized women in defense industries where they were desperately needed, took no special steps to change the subordinate role of women." The evidence? "The War Manpower Commission, despite the large numbers of women in war work, kept women off its policymaking bodies."

And it only gets worse. While the treatment of blacks and women was bad, the U.S. came "close to direct duplication of Fascism," according to Zinn, "in its treatment of the Japanese-Americans living on the West Coast." FDR "calmly signed Executive Order 9066, in February 1942, giving the army the power, without warrants or indictments or hearings, to arrest every Japanese-American on the West Coast—110,000 men, women, and children—to take them from their homes, transport them to camps far into the interior, and keep them there under prison conditions."[40]

Not all Americans were in favor of the internment of the Japanese. FBI director J. Edgar Hoover, Republican congressman Robert Taft, and the prominent black journalist George S. Schuyler all opposed it. But it would probably be safe to say that most Americans were angered and frightened by the Pearl Harbor attack. One can get a sense of just how much the nation was on edge by perusing the newspapers from the time or by reading Schweikart and Allen's description of the mood in 1942, when "a Japanese sub surfacing off the coast of Oregon" was taken as a sign of "an imminent invasion of San Francisco, San Diego, or the Los Angeles area." "Bunkers were thrown up at Santa Barbara; skyscrapers in Los Angeles sported antiaircraft guns on their roofs; and lights on all high-rise buildings were extinguished or covered at night to make it more difficult for imperial bombers to hit their targets. Local rodeo associations and the Shrine Mounted Patrol conducted routine reconnaissance of mountains, foothills, and deserts, checking for infiltrators." German Americans and Italian Americans also came under "the close scrutiny" of the FBI. But by 1942, threats to American soil on the East coast were not very serious.[41] Following the attack on Pearl Harbor, the Canadian government interned twenty-two thousand people of Japanese origin, as well.[42]

One now oft-forgotten part of this history is related by political science professor Ken Masugi, whose parents were interned first at Tule Lake (until it became "a segregation center to house ethnic Japanese who proved troublemakers in other camps") and then at the Minidoka Center in Idaho. According to Masugi, "Any honest study of the relocation or WWII will discuss the Niihau episode." This event occurred on the afternoon of December 7, 1941, hours after the attack on Pearl Harbor, when a Japanese fighter-bomber landed on the remote Hawaiian island of Niihau. A native Hawaiian, Hawila Kaleohano, approached the pilot and grabbed his gun and papers. He then brought back two American-born inhabitants of Japanese heritage to act as interpreters. These two, a farmer and his wife—after they learned about the earlier attack on Pearl Harbor—decided to *help* the *pilot* and claim "the island for the Emperor." Once the Hawaiians learned about their plot, a battle ensued, ending with the deaths of both the Japanese farmer and the pilot at the hands of the Hawaiians. The incident was included in the Roberts Commission Report released on January 24, 1942; understandably, it inspired alarm. Masugi comments, "Here was a simple farmer, neither agent nor nationalist, joining the cause of Japan in its moment of glory...."[43]

"The war posed loyalty tests," Masugi explains, describing the divided loyalties of his own family, with his Japanese-born father favoring Japan and his American-born mother favoring the U.S. One of Masugi's uncles "joined the army and was decorated; another, obeying his immigrant mother's demand, went to prison rather than be drafted."[44] Masugi believes that the "initial phase of relocation could be justified without reducing it to racism or war hysteria."[45]

But Zinn obscenely compares internment camps for the Japanese to Nazi concentration camps, claiming that the "prison conditions" represented an almost "direct duplication of Fascism." Consider what American soldiers saw when they came upon Ohrdruf, a subcamp of Buchenwald, which Charles Sasser describes in his book about the 761st Black Panthers: "'No more war, no more war!' one bony creature chanted with hysterical glee, staggering and clapping her hands. All her teeth were gone. It was hard to tell if she were young or old." Seared into the memory of Johnnie Stevens was "the stench of discarded, decaying flesh, burning bodies, piles of human excrement, sewer pits buzzing with flies." Captain Johnny Long watched inmates "totter" over to the "bloating carcass" of a horse and throw themselves "upon it like starving jackals, ripping and tearing at the bloody thing with their bare hands as they ate the flesh raw." Not knowing any better, the soldiers left food for the prisoners, which killed some of them, so far gone were their starved bodies.[46] Zinn somehow never brings up such details. While arguably a violation of civil rights, the American relocation bears absolutely no resemblance to the Holocaust. At their camps, Japanese Americans "published their own newspapers," tended gardens, and established schools, glee clubs, and "baseball teams for their children." Eventually, internees were paid reparations.[47]

Zinn not only ignores such facts; he also implies that the internments were kept secret from the public, claiming, "Not until after the war did the story of the Japanese-Americans begin to be known to the general public. The month the war ended in Asia, September 1945, an article appeared in *Harper's Magazine* by Yale Law professor Eugene V. Rostow, calling the Japanese evacuation 'our worst wartime mistake.'"[48]

Was Japanese American internment, in fact, a secret from the "general public" until after the war ended in Asia? Absolutely not. One only needed to open a newspaper. Articles by Lawrence Davies in the *New York Times*, for example, described the developments in the internment of the Japanese blow by blow. Davies's January 29, 1942, dispatch from San Francisco began, "An anti-fifth column campaign aimed at ridding State and city payrolls of all persons of Japanese ancestry, even though they themselves are American citizens, and moving all Japanese nationals to internment camps or at least out of the coastal war zone, made progress today." The city of Los Angeles, like county and state governments, would dismiss public employees of Japanese ancestry.[49] A few days later, on February 3, Davies reported that the state had "intensified its drive against potential fifth columnists" with "a surprise 'raid' by Federal agents against the big Japanese fishing colony on Terminal Island at Los Angeles, with more arrests at San Diego and San Francisco...." The 255 "enemy aliens regarded as dangerous" in custody "so far" included Germans and Italians, along with the Japanese. Apparently internment camps were being discussed, as Davies reported that "demands still were heard in some quarters for whole-sale removal of Japanese from the 'combat zone' to internment camps or inland places."[50] Subsequent dispatches reported on a "curfew zone" for enemy aliens, more raids on Japanese colonies (Puget Sound), discussions about internment camps—though they were said not to be "indicated" at "the present time"[51]—FBI raids uncovering stashes of ammunition, weap-ons, and contraband, and arrests and apprehensions, including those of German American Bund members, someone of Czech ancestry,[52] a "so-called Buddhist priest,"[53] former members of the Japanese military, and a number of Italians and Germans.[54]

Executive Order 9066, which authorized military commanders to designate military exclusion zones, was signed by President Roosevelt on February 19, 1942. The February 24 New York Times reported that "almost 800 Japanese aliens who were seized in raids in California were started off for internment camps" and that the "residential fate of about 100,000 other enemy aliens on the West Coast was being marked out."[55] Detailed accounts about the process of relocation kept coming. A February 28 article reported that Japanese leaders were waiting "with an air of resignation" for the orders for between 75,000 and 125,000 to be interned.[56]

Interestingly, "quite a few" Japanese Americans were waiting with anticipation for having a safe place, writes Brian Hayashi. For them, the camps might provide "refuge from the anti-Japanese violence they saw around them" like the "drive-by shootings, knife stabbings, and murder of a handful of California Japanese by Filipinos and others...." And some others felt a "sense of honor" in being "'prisoners of war'"—as a display of sacrifice for "the old country."[57]

And Harper's, the very same magazine whose 1945 article Zinn cited, ran a ten-page article in its September 1942 issue about life in the intern-ment camps. Carey McWilliams described his visit in June—a mere four months after the executive order—to the camp established at the Santa Ana race track. With a population 18,562, it had "almost everything that any California city of comparable size would have: newspaper, hospital, police and fire departments, recreational centers, stores, ball parks, workshops, and libraries." There was a city council. After sampling some of the food, he wrote, "The food is good, there is enough of it, and the kitchens are clean." Not quite Auschwitz. Inconveniences included waiting in line for meals and enduring two roll calls a day. Shelter was described as adequate. In stark contradiction of Zinn's obscene suggestion, McWilliams reported, "It would certainly not be accurate to characterize Santa Anita as a 'concentration camp.' To be sure, the camp is surrounded by a small detail of soldiers; searchlights play around the camp and up and down the streets at night; and the residents cannot leave the grounds." At the same time, though, it was "quite common to see American flags and service flags.... here are twenty-nine World War veterans...and a flourishing post of the American Legion."[58]

Masugi recalls learning from family members that camp conditions were "Spartan" but with amenities developing "over the years." Residents were encouraged to leave the camps and go to work, in the fields and elsewhere. Three of Masugi's mother's siblings chose to move to Chicago, because "A job or place in college could get one out of the centers."[59]

In 1942, the Office of War Information released a ten-minute film distributed by the War Activities Committee of the Motion Picture Industry. Narrator Milton Eisenhower, director of the War Relocation Authority, reassured viewers that most Japanese were loyal and were being treated well and explained the reason for the internments: after Pearl Harbor, "the West Coast became a potential combat zone." The footage in the film matches McWilliams's description in *Harper's*.[60]

How did the actual "people" Zinn presumes to speak for feel about the internments? Surprise. Not all agreed with him. For example, a June 19, 1942, article in the *New York Times* reported that Japanese organizations were divided on internment. While Mike M. Masaoka, national secretary of the Japanese American Citizens League, asserted that the internments represented a larger threat to civil liberties and members of the American Friends Service Committee and the ACLU charged that the camps went against American democratic values, Miss Teru Masumoto of the Japanese American Committee for Democracy put forth a resolution (narrowly defeated) proclaiming that "as all loyal Americans we support every measure that will help to insure victory...despite any personal hardships or sacrifices."[61]

A year later, the Senate Military Affairs Committee was recommending a draft for Japanese men and reporting that "more than 7,500 Japanese" were already in the Army.[62] A December 14, 1943, article about an exchange of prisoners noted that "about 110,000 Japanese and Japanese-Americans" were being interned and that any of them could "apply for return to Japan."[63] The Swedish General Secretary of the Y.M.C.A. on a tour of war prisoner and civilian internment camps praised the U.S. camps as "the cleanest he has seen anywhere in the world."[64]

Disregarding all the evidence, including the news accounts he would have seen as a young man, Zinn goes so far as to suggest that the internment of the Japanese is proof that America fought World War II *for* racism rather than against it. "Was it a 'mistake'—or was it an action to be expected from a nation with a long history of racism and which was fighting a war, not to end racism, but to retain the fundamental elements of the American system?" These racist "elements" of America were so "fundamental" that they went back to...Alexander Hamilton. According to Howard Zinn, World War II "was a war waged by a government whose chief beneficiary—despite volumes of reforms—was a wealthy elite," with "the alliance between big business and the government" going back "to the very first proposals of Alexander Hamilton to Congress after the Revolutionary War."[65]

Americans did not relish the idea of going to war, but it was not because of their allegiance to memories of the capitalist villain Alexander Hamilton. Still reeling from World War I, they were in an isolationist mood in the years leading up to Pearl Harbor. In 1937, 70 percent of Americans said that U.S. involvement in World War I had been a mistake, and a majority were angry about the European nations defaulting on their war debts.[66] But by 1941, even before the attack on Pearl Harbor, "89 percent of American men" said they "would spend one day a week training for homeland defense" and "78 percent of all Americans" said they "would 'willingly' pay a sales tax on everything and cut gasoline consumption by a third in the event of war." Once war was declared, boys, men, and women volunteered in an unprecedented manner. Older men and teenage boys lied about their age to enlist, and many celebrities volunteered.[67] Immediately after Pearl Harbor, the anti-interventionist group America First called for support of the war efforts and closed up shop. Former skeptics even got on board. Famous aviator Charles Lindbergh volunteered his services. Representative Hamilton Fish said, "The time for debate is past. The time for action has come...." And Senator Burton Wheeler said, "Let's kick hell out of them."[68] At that time, 97 percent of Americans "approved of Congress's declaration of war against Japan," according to a Gallup poll,[69] and they demonstrated their support in efforts that ranged from buying war bonds to planting Victory Gardens to working extra hours in factories.

In fact, the Allied victory was due in large part to an American workforce that worked with resolve and to a free market system that supported industrial output and innovation by the so-called arms merchants, including Nebraskan Andrew Jackson Higgins, a builder of "fishing and pleasure boats," who designed the "Higgins boats"—the landing craft that made D-Day possible. After the war, President Eisenhower, who was certainly in a position to know, said that Higgins was "'the man who won the war.'"[70] Military historian Victor Davis Hanson credits the American free enterprise system: "In critical areas such as transport planes, merchant ships, locomotives, food supplies, medicines, oil production, and metals production," the Allies far "outproduced" the Axis powers, who often relied on "coerced" workers.[71]

But in Zinn's world, businessmen are always exploiters: "Despite the overwhelming atmosphere of patriotism and total dedication to winning the war, despite the no-strike pledges of the AFL and CIO, many of the nation's workers, frustrated by the freezing of wages while business profits rocketed skyward, went on strike. During the war, there were fourteen thousand strikes, involving 6,770,000 workers, more than in any comparable period in American history."[72]

These numbers are technically correct; they match those from the United States Bureau of Labor. What Zinn fails to say, though, is that only 29.2 percent ever came to the attention of the National War Labor Board, according to a report published in 1950, which also noted that "many of the stoppages were not considered important to the war program" and "many others were of short duration." According to the *Encyclopedia of Strikes* (2009), "Most strikes during the war involved a small number of workers, a single plant or department, and lasted a short time...."[73]

Many of these were "wildcat" strikes conducted by workers without the blessings of the unions. They were usually not over wages, but over working conditions, such as speed-ups, or having to work with black co-workers. Joshua Freeman, who is pro-labor, is one of the few scholars in the field who acknowledges that "workers," especially those who were "militant," could also be racist. Some of the wildcat strikes were led by local union officials and some were "taking place outside of union structures." Contrary to Zinn's claims, "The most frequent causes of these true wildcats included disciplinary action—particularly the firing of union officials or militant workers, working and safety conditions, long hours, and speed ups.... only infrequently were wages a cause of wildcats." Some of the wildcat strikes were "hate strikes," "walkouts by white workers protesting the hiring or upgrading of blacks," which sometimes led to riots, including at shipyards in Chester, Pennsylvania; Mobile, Alabama; and Sparrows Point, Maryland. Freeman admits that "wartime racist strikes present a tricky problem for those historians who uncritically extol all militant labor action in and of itself." They are so much of a tricky problem for Zinn that he does not mention them.

Freeman attributes many of the strikes to "militants." At one of the early strikes at the North American Aviation plant in Inglewood,

California, in early June 1941 (before Hitler's invasion of Russia), "communist-led workers" walked out and then "kept other workers from entering the plant through threats and beatings," according to Burton and Anita Folsom. To the applause of the public, President Roosevelt finally gave the orders and twenty-five hundred soldiers "marched on the plant with their bayonets fixed," "restor[ing] order" and allowing workers to return to work and "reorganize" the union. Non-communist workers were probably very happy to have their jobs because, as Freeman explains, "For the majority of workers the war was an experience of opportunity rather than limitation. Their wartime income was larger than ever before.... the men of draft age were also aware that every day in the shipyard was a day not spent in a barracks or a foxhole."[74]

Zinn, however, simply lets the reader believe that the strikes were all part of a general revolt against the capitalist-controlled war-mongering Establishment, a revolt which included "350,000 cases of draft evasion, including technical violations as well as actual desertion, so it is hard to tell the true number." Zinn also speculates that "the number of men who either did not show up or claimed C.O. [conscientious objector] status was in the hundreds of thousands—not a small number." It was, he claims, "hard to know how much resentment there was against authority, against having to fight in a war whose aims were unclear, inside a military machine whose lack of democracy was very clear. No one recorded the bitterness of enlisted men against the special privileges of officers in the army of a country known as a democracy."[75] Instead of giving hard statistics, Zinn would rather throw around possible numbers with the caveat that it was "hard to know" exactly how many soldiers in the 1940s expected a "democracy" within the *military*. But it's easy to guess that that number was vanishingly small—though perhaps not as small as the number who thought that the war's "aims were unclear."

Zinn then uses anecdotal and problematic evidence to make a claim about the black community in order to buttress his own argument about "manufactured" support for the war and the country. He claims that "there seemed to be widespread indifference, even hostility, on the part of the Negro community to the war despite the attempts of Negro newspapers and Negro leaders to mobilize black sentiment." Laurence Wittner (*Rebels Against War*) quotes a black journalist who states, "the Negro.... is angry, resentful, and utterly apathetic about the war." In addition, "A student at a Negro college told his teacher: 'The Army jim-crows us. The Navy lets us serve only as messmen. The Red Cross refuses our blood.... lynchings continue.... what more could Hitler do than that?'" Zinn also quotes a "Draftee's Prayer" that appeared in "a Negro newspaper" in January 1943.[76]

Sam Wineburg points to these references cited by Zinn as misleading evidence by which "Zinn hangs his claim" that African Americans had only one aim in World War II—for "victory over racism." In actuality, there was a popular "Double V" campaign: for victory here and abroad, over racism *and* over the enemy. Many of Zinn's readers "will likely conclude" that the sentiments selectively quoted in *A People's History* "represented broad trends in the black community." But that is far from the truth. Wineburg went to Wittner's source and found that when Horace Mann Bond, "president of Georgia's Fort Valley State College and the father of civil rights leader Julian Bond," was asked by the editors of *Annals of the American Academy of Political and Social Science*, "Should the Negro care who wins the war?" Bond "bristled at ...the insinuation that blacks were apathetic to America's fate." The very question, Bond said, implied that the Negro was "divested of statehood.'" Similarly, in the pages of the African American newspaper the *Pittsburgh Courier*, editor P. L. Prattis and labor leader A. Philip Randolph argued in early 1941 in favor of ramping up efforts to aid the Allies. NAACP leader William Pickens and other black leaders were also in support.[77]

As usual, Zinn omitted statistics that cut against his polemic. In just the same *two pages* from the passage in *Rebels Against War* from which Zinn pulled his anecdotes, there are statistics demonstrating that African Americans were far *less* likely than the general population to register as conscientious objectors. Of the total 10,022,367 American males (ages 18–37) eligible to serve, 2,427,495, or 24 percent, were black. The total number of conscientious objectors was 42,973. "If the number of black conscientious objectors were proportional" to their numbers in the population, Wineburg explains, "there would have been 10,000 African-American conscientious objectors...." But the "total number of black conscientious objectors" was only four hundred. Blacks were also far less likely than whites to be draft evaders; they were "only 4.4 percent of the Justice Department cases."[78] While Zinn's source, Lawrence Wittner, presents anecdotes as evidence of the "smoldering discontent of America's Negro population," he also describes "the peace movement" as being in a "debilitated state," so bad that "it was unable to turn this rebellion into antiwar activity." There was a "virtual disappearance of peace sentiment" among the working class.[79] In Zinn-world, however, African Americans and the working class *were* united against the war because it was only being perpetuated to promote racism, which, in turn, supports capitalism.

Not only was America's cause in World War II tainted by our racism at home, but the war effort was actually *fueled* by racism: only racial hatred of the Japanese can explain why "the vast bulk of the American population was mobilized" for war. This racism explains the bombings of Hiroshima and Nagasaki. And those bombings were only the culmination of the Allied bombing campaign, which was worse than the Nazi one: "These German bombings were very small compared with the British and American bombings of German cities." Zinn cites a 1943 agreement of the Allies "on large-scale air attacks to achieve 'the destruction and dislocation of the German military, industrial and economic system'" as if that were evidence that military leaders gleefully wanted to commit mass murder of civilians. Zinn claims, "The English flew at night with no pretense of aiming at 'military' targets; the Americans flew in the daytime and pretended precision, but bombing from high altitudes made that impossible."[80]

According to Wineburg, Zinn is "on solid ground" only in "a technical sense" when he compares Allied bombing to Nazi bombing: "In the bombing of Rotterdam on May 14, 1940, there was an estimated loss of a thousand lives, and in the bombing of Coventry on November 14, 1940, there were approximately 550 deaths. In Dresden, by comparison, somewhere between 20,000 and 30,000 people lost their lives." But as Wineburg points out, "fourteen months before bombing Coventry," the Nazis had "unleashed Operation Wasserkante, the decimation of Warsaw," where "smoke billowed 10,000 feet into the sky" and 40,000 Poles died. As Wineburg notes, "Zinn is silent about Poland."[81]

Zinn gives a much larger number—"[m]ore than 100,000"—than Wineburg for Dresden. But as Wineburg points out, this is the number "long favored by Nazi sympathizers who held up the Allies' bombing of Dresden as tantamount to Nazi atrocities at Auschwitz." As a matter of fact, it is the number given by the discredited historian David Irving in his 1963 book, *The Destruction of Dresden*, in which, as Wineburg explains, Irving "credulously (or calculatingly) drew on mortality figures provided by the Nazis for propagandistic purposes."[82]

But surely there must be some excuse for leftist icon Howard Zinn retailing Nazi propaganda and citing a Hitler apologist for his supposed facts? David Irving must not have come out as a Hitler fanboy at the time Zinn was writing *A People's History*. In fact, he had. Three years earlier, in 1977, Irving had published *Hitler's War*. Reviewers blasted the book. Walter Laqueur in the *New York Times* stated that there was "no shred of evidence" for Irving's claim that Hitler's subordinates had "killed several million Jews without his knowledge and against his wish." John Lukacs in *National Review* called it "appalling" because of its errors, misuse of sources, and attempt to present Hitler as "morally superior to his opponents."[83]

A bit of statistical context is needed here, in light of Zinn's insinuation that the Allies gleefully outdid the Axis in mass murder. As Victor Davis Hanson points out, "The Axis losers killed or starved to death about 80 percent of all those who died during the war. The Allied victors largely killed Axis soldiers; the defeated Axis, mostly civilians."[84] Hanson lists five causes of noncombatant deaths:

(1) the Nazi-orchestrated Holocaust and related organized killing of civilians and prisoners in Eastern occupied territories and the Soviet Union, as well as Japanese barbarity in China; (2) the widespread use of air power;...(3) the famines that ensued from brutal occupations, mostly by the Axis powers; (4) the vast migrations and transfers of populations, mostly in Prussia, Eastern Europe, the Soviet Union, and Manchuria; and (5) the idea prevalent in both totalitarian and democratic governments that the people of enemy nations were synonymous with their military and thus were fair game through collective punishments.[85]

As Hanson explains, "Despite German brutality in 1914, there had been nothing quite similar to the *Waffen SS*...and nothing at all akin to Dachau or the various camps at Auschwitz. The Kaiser's Germany would not have exterminated seventy to ninety thousand of its own disabled, chronically ill, and developmentally delayed citizens, as the Third Reich had by August 1941. The idea of Japanese kamikazes might have been as foreign in 1918 as it was largely unquestioned in late 1944."[86]

But in Zinn's account of World War II, the Japanese aggressors are the victims—just like the Nazis. Zinn drags out the old canard that Japan was already on the verge of surrender before the atomic bombs. The Japanese "had begun talking of surrender a year before this, and the Emperor himself had begun to suggest, in June 1945, that alternatives to fighting to the end be considered." Zinn takes the word of the Japanese Foreign Minister that "[u]nconditional surrender is the only obstacle to peace...."

"If only," Zinn wails, "the Americans had not insisted on unconditional surrender—that is, if they were willing to accept one condition to the surrender, that the Emperor, a holy figure to the Japanese, remain in place—the Japanese would have agreed to stop the war." Then Zinn launches into full conspiracy mode: "Why did the United States not take that small step to save both American and Japanese lives? Was it because too much money and effort had been invested in the atomic bomb not to drop it?"[87]

In fact, the insistence on "unconditional surrender" was intended to prevent remilitarization of a nation that had sought "world conquest," as the Potsdam Proclamation of July 26, 1945, stated. Zinn ignores this fact and presents U.S. unwillingness to allow a "holy figure" to remain on his throne as the only stumbling block. Germany had surrendered, but the Japanese would fight to the death, as evidenced by the increasing use of kamikaze fighters and villagers committing suicide instead of surrendering. Zinn ignores the fact that the Potsdam Proclamation, which demanded unconditional surrender, also promised "eventual establishment of a 'peacefully inclined and responsible' Japanese government 'in accordance with the freely expressed will of the Japanese people.'" The Japanese rejected this offer on July 28. And in fact, when the Japanese did surrender, Hirohito was allowed to "remain on his ancestral throne as nominal Emperor."[88]

Next, Zinn asks another—somewhat more reasonable—question:

> Or was it, as British scientist P. M. S. Blackett suggested (*Fear, War, and the Bomb*), that the United States was anxious to drop the bomb before the Russians entered the war against Japan? The Russians had secretly agreed (they were officially not at war with Japan) they would come into the war ninety days after the end of the European war. That turned out to be May 8, and so, on August 8, the Russians were due to declare war on Japan. But by then the big bomb had been dropped, and the next day a second one would be dropped on Nagasaki; the Japanese would surrender to the United States, not the Russians, and the United States would be the occupier of postwar Japan.[89]

And thank goodness for that. Zinn tries to make the fact that the Japanese didn't surrender to the Soviets—and, like the Eastern

Europeans, suffer half a century of Communist oppression—into some kind of tragedy.

And what about Zinn's suggestion that Hiroshima and Nagasaki were completely unnecessary because Japan was already ready to surrender? As Sadao Asada pointed out in the *Pacific Historical Review* in critique of the "revisionist" line followed by Zinn, "Most assuredly Japanese sources do not support the *ex post facto* contention of the U.S. Strategic Bombing Survey (1946) that 'in all probability' Japan would have surrendered before November 1 'even if the atomic bombs had not been dropped, even if Russia had not entered the war and even if no invasion had been planned or contemplated." He placed Zinn's sources—Blackett, Gar Alperovitz, and Martin Sherwin—in the camp of revisionists who have argued that "the bomb was meant as a political-diplomatic threat aimed against the Soviet Union in the emerging cold war." This was also the view of Japanese apologists after the war. The monograph "Why Were the Atomic Bombs Dropped?" that "recapitulate[es] the Blackett thesis" that the victims were "killed as human guinea pigs for the sake of [America's] anti-Communist, hegemonic policy" was originally published in Japan in 1968.

The argument that Japan was "virtually a defeated nation" when the bombs were dropped in 1945, Asada explains, "confuses 'defeat' with 'surrender': Defeat is a *military fait accompli,* whereas surrender is the formal acceptance of defeat by the nation's leaders, an act of decision-making." Because Japan's "governmental machinery was, to a large extent, controlled by the military and hampered by a cumbersome system that required unanimity of views for any decision, Japanese leaders had failed to translate defeat into surrender. In the end it was the atomic bomb, closely followed by the Soviet Union's entry into the war, that compelled Japan to surrender." The bomb enabled "the prime minister to bring Hirohito directly into a position where his 'sacred decision' for surrender could override the diehards." The bomb helped the military "save 'face,'" by giving them the excuse that they had been beaten by science.

As Asada points out, "Alperovitz makes much of Togo's cable to [Ambassador] Sato [Naokake] dated July 12 [which] conveyed Hirohito's message 'the war be concluded speedily.'" But "what the deciphered Japanese dispatches reveal, however, were indecision and contradiction in Tokyo; the Japanese government could never agree on surrender terms," with the military presenting obstacles and delays. Asada describes the militaristic fanaticism that contradicts Zinn's claim that the Japanese no longer posed any threat: "Women practiced how to face American tanks with bamboo spears," and the Japanese were committed to "glorious deaths" in "kamikaze planes as human rockets, in midget submarines as human torpedoes, and in suicide charges in ground units." Japan's surrender probably "forestalled sacrifices on both sides far surpassing those at Hiroshima and Nagasaki." Even after Hiroshima, some Japanese military leaders did not believe that the U.S. had more than one bomb, or that they could be dropped quickly—one after the other—until we dropped the bomb on Nagasaki.[90]

But Zinn conjectures, "The dropping of the second bomb on Nagasaki seems to have been scheduled in advance, and no one has ever been able to explain why it was dropped. Was it because this was a plutonium bomb whereas the Hiroshima bomb was a uranium bomb? Were the dead and irradiated of Nagasaki victims of a scientific experiment?"[91]

In case the suggestion about experimentation on human beings that exceeded even that of the Nazis is lost, Zinn turns back to Europe, claiming that Germany was "crushed primarily by the armies of the Soviet Union on the Eastern Front, aided by the Allied armies on the West.... the Fascist powers were destroyed."

And then: "But what about fascism—as idea, as reality? Were its essential elements—militarism, racism, imperialism—now gone? Or were they absorbed into the already poisoned bones of the victors?"[92]

Zinn answers the question: "The war not only put the United States in a position to dominate much of the world; it created conditions for effective control at home."[93] The "control" of Americans by means of a purportedly ginned-up and needless "Red Scare" is the subject of our next chapter.

CHAPTER
SIX

Writing the Red Menace
Out of History

he U.S. government had learned "that war solves problems of control." Or so claims Zinn. Thus, after World War II, the Truman
administration "worked to create an atmosphere of crisis and cold
war." It "presented the Soviet Union as not just a rival but an immediate
threat. In a series of moves abroad and at home, it established a climate
of fear—a hysteria about Communism—which would steeply escalate
the military budget and stimulate the economy with war-related orders.
This combination of policies would permit more aggressive actions
abroad, more repressive actions at home."[1]

In reality, Americans did not need propaganda to feel fear about the
Soviet Union. Not only did they retain the distrust they had felt even in
the war years—as the polls cited above show—but they could also see
how the Soviets had "broken their promises in regard to Poland, violated
self-determination in Eastern Europe, and provoked trouble in both Iran
and Turkey," as historian Howard Jones has pointed out in *"A New Kind
of War": America's Global Strategy and the Truman Doctrine in Greece*.[2]

Zinn acknowledges that "the rivalry with the Soviet Union was
real," but presents the Communist regime in a way that would surprise

most: "that country had come out of the war with its economy wrecked and 20 million people dead, but was making an astounding comeback, rebuilding its industry, regaining military strength. The Truman administration, however, presented the Soviet Union as not just a rival but an immediate threat."[3] And so it was. At the end of the war, the Red Army had a "disproportionate conventional force advantage in Europe" over the United States, according to Yale Cold War historian John Lewis Gaddis. And Stalin "launch[ed] a massive program to build a Soviet bomb that imposed a considerably greater burden on his country's shattered economy than the Manhattan Project had on the United States—the use of forced labor and the wholesale neglect of health and environmental hazards were routine."[4]

Anne Applebaum would disagree with Zinn's claim of the USSR's "astounding comeback." In fact, the "nationalization of the economy prolonged the shortages and economic distortions created by the war. Central planning and fixed prices distorted markets, making trade between individuals as well as between enterprises difficult. These problems were compounded by weak, nonexistent, or competing national currencies" in Poland, Soviet-occupied Germany, and Hungary. After factory workers went on strike in Budapest in 1947, for example, the regime used informers to "identify and dismiss 'troublemaking' workers."[5] Soon, of course, there were no more labor strikes.

According to Zinn, "revolutionary movements in Europe and Asia" were presented to "the American public as examples of Soviet expansionism—thus recalling the indignation against Hitler's aggressions"— in order to make it appear that the Soviet Union was a "threat." In Zinn's telling, these were nothing more than democratic movements for self-rule.

For example, in China, according to Zinn, "a revolution was already under way when World War II ended, led by a Communist movement with enormous mass support. A Red Army, which had fought against the Japanese, now fought to oust the corrupt dictatorship of Chiang Kai-Shek, which was supported by the United States." Actually the Red

Army had been fighting *Chinese nationalists,* and for nearly a "quarter of a century," in what Gaddis describes as a "civil war."[6] Zinn continues: "In 1949, when the Chinese Communist forces moved into Peking," the civil war was ended and China had the "closest thing...to a people's government, independent of outside control."[7] That is another lie. At Yalta, Stalin was given "hegemony" over Manchuria, from which he "protected and supported the Chinese Communists, under Mao Tse-Tung."[8] The U.S. State Department held out hope that Mao would break with Stalin in the way Yugoslav communist dictator Marshal Josip Broz Tito had. But Mao was "a dedicated Marxist-Leninist who was more ready to defer to Stalin as the head of the international communist movement," as he indicated in a June 1949 announcement about allying with the Soviet Union. Mao intended to follow Stalin's example as a dictator. His two-month visit to Russia in December 1949 resulted in the Sino-Soviet Treaty, "in which the two communist states pledged to come to the assistance of the other in case of attack."[9] In 1950, Stalin gave the "'green light'" to North Korean dictator Kim Il-sung to invade South Korea—"part of the larger strategy for seizing opportunities in East Asia that he had discussed with the Chinese." Shortly afterward, Stalin "encouraged Ho Chi Minh to intensify the Viet Minh movement against the French in Indochina."[10]

If Mao was a popular leader of the people, as Zinn claims, he had a strange way of showing it. After becoming appalled by Nikita Khrushchev's denunciation of "the Stalinist 'cult of personality' early in 1956," Mao decided to defiantly double down and outpace the Soviet Union to make China the real "revolutionary country." In addition to his "industrialization and collectivization campaigns," he also followed Stalin's example in conducting "his own purge of potential dissidents," luring followers to criticize him in his "Let a hundred flowers bloom, let a hundred schools of thought contend" campaign. Mao ordered peasants to abandon their crops and melt down farm implements to make steel in an effort to make them proletarians. Private property and self-sufficiency even on the peasant level could not be tolerated. Mao's "Great Leap

Forward" was "the greatest single human calamity of the 20th century," in Gaddis's estimation. Over 30 million died in the famine that resulted between 1958 and 1961, "the worst on record anywhere."[11]

The fact is, the American people had very good reasons to be afraid of Communism, which has left a trail of murderous carnage everywhere it has been tried. And in the 1940s, it was going from triumph to triumph on the international scene. A Brookings Institution report stated that "the indefinite westward movement of the Soviet Union...must not be permitted 'whether it occurs by formal annexation, political coup, or progressive subversion.'"[12] This was good advice—confirmed by what a CIA agent reported in September 1946—about secret remarks made in May of that year by Soviet Vice-Consul Araniev in Shanghai about seeking "worldwide communist revolution by means other than war," such as establishing "communist cells in China" and elsewhere. Araniev "remarked that World War II had been only a truce between Russia and its ideological enemies—the capitalist countries, now led by the United States.... the 'new fires' in Greece and China were 'rehearsals' and 'trials of strength' that were political and psychological in nature." Communist ideas would be propagated "on a worldwide scale" through establishment of communist cells of three to five members inside trade unions, the army, transport factories, and any other organization of workers'" so that "[s]trikes, sabotage and other means" would "discredit capitalist governments."[13]

Howard Jones explains, "The Kremlin sought a temporary relaxation of hostilities to allow 'economic and ideological rehabilitation at home and the consolidation of position abroad.'" While the Soviets tried "by legal or revolutionary means" to "establish communist regimes" in France, Italy, Spain, and Greece, they simultaneously "sought economic and political penetration of the Middle East, Far East, and Latin America." And, "[t]o obscure these activities, they would engage in propaganda designed to convince the world of their peaceful intentions."[14] The Soviets were financing communist candidates in Europe. And according to Gaddis, during the 1948 elections in Italy, the "large communist party generously financed from Moscow looked likely to win."[15]

But to this day, Zinn serves as a propagandist for the Soviet Union's "peaceful intentions," insisting in *A People's History* that the regime not only had nothing to do with the rise of Mao, but it also had nothing to do with similar events in Greece and the Philippines. According to Zinn, after World War II in Greece, the National Liberation Front (the EAM), just "a popular left-wing" movement, was "put down by a British army of intervention." When another "left-wing guerilla" movement sprang up against the reestablished "right-wing dictatorship" and "Great Britain said it could not handle the rebellion," the United States came in under the "Truman Doctrine" that would infuse Greece and Turkey with four hundred million dollars in military and economic aid to resist Communist takeovers. The effort was described by President Truman as "resisting attempted subjugation by armed minorities or by outside pressures." Zinn comments sarcastically:

> In fact, the biggest outside pressure was the United States. The Greek rebels were getting some aid from Yugoslavia, but no aid from the Soviet Union.... the United States moved into the Greek civil war...with weapons and military advisers.... two hundred and fifty army officers, headed by General James Van Fleet, advised the Greek army in the field. Van Fleet started a policy—standard in dealing with popular insurrections—of forcibly removing thousands of Greeks from their homes in the countryside, to try to isolate guerillas, to remove the source of their support.

After the "rebellion was defeated in 1949," Greece was safe for the flow of "[i]nvestment capital from Esso, Dow Chemical, Chrysler, and other U.S. corporations" and access to oil in the Middle East.[16]

These short paragraphs are peppered with many lies. The Soviets had their sights set on Greece, which was "under German occupation until late 1944," during the war, as the actions of Soviet agent Donald Maclean, a high-ranking official of the Foreign Ministry, showed. The decrypted Venona messages—radio messages from KGB agents in Washington and New York to Moscow recorded by the U.S. Army Signal Corps—show that in 1944 and 1945, Maclean sent the KGB almost a dozen messages about discussions between Churchill and Roosevelt—including about Greece, which was facing "chaos" as "pro- and anti-Communist Greek resistance forces and the Greek government-in-exile battled for control." Maclean messaged the Russians that he hoped "we will take advantage of these circumstances to disrupt the plans of the British." He was also advising the Soviets in 1944 about Allied plans regarding the liberation of other parts of Europe, such as France and Italy.[17]

After the war the leaders of the EAM (Zinn's "a popular left-wing" movement) joined the KKE, the Greek communist party. A KKE delegation in early 1946 had gone "to Moscow to seek aid," but had been told to "focus on political means"—in line with the new strategy of using "means other than war."[18] And "the Soviet delegation" at the United Nations "lashed out at Greece for allegedly causing unrest in the Balkans by seeking unwarranted territorial claims in the north," "criticized the British for maintaining troops in Greece" ("in part to counter Western complaints about the continued Soviet presence in Iran"), and "expressed interest in Turkey, Iran, and a base in the Dodecanese islands." Significantly, as Jones explains, "Greece was the chief obstacle to Soviet penetration of the eastern Mediterranean, making it evident that the antagonistic policies of Yugoslavia, Albania, and Bulgaria toward Greece paralleled Soviet interests in the region...."[19]

Was this a "popular insurrection," with guerilla freedom fighters supported by the people? No. As Jones points out, "In Greece anti-communist groups were in the majority and the country's leaders were receptive to aid and advice. Most importantly, the Greek populace was favorably disposed toward the United States."[20]

And what about Zinn's claims that as part of "standard" procedure, "thousands of Greeks were removed from their homes in the countryside, to try to isolate the guerillas, to remove the source of their support"? In fact, the guerillas did not have the support of the people in the country-side. Communists "infiltrated cells of workers in the cities, towns, and large villages. Referred to as 'self-defense personnel,' the cells built an intelligence and supply network that worked behind the lines of the Greek army in recruiting, raising money, gathering information about troop movements, and terrorizing the population."[21] The "Democratic Army" "raid[ed] and pillag[ed]" villages, used forced recruitment, and carried out "terrorist executions by guns, knives, and axes."[22] This certainly does not sound like the popular movement that Zinn represents it to be.

The Communist guerillas also sabotaged American relief efforts to such an extent that a *Time* magazine correspondent in Athens in 1948 described the Truman Doctrine as "failing." Jones explains, "Houses, shops, schools, public utilities, railroads, bridges, trains, animals, food—nothing was safe from the growing number of raids on towns and villages." Over four hundred thousand refugees were "living in tents, shanties, mud huts, or abandoned public buildings and warehouses.... and many of these evacuated by the government from guerilla territory because the Greek army could not protect them."[23] Contrary to Zinn's claim, Greeks had to be removed from their own homes for their own protection from the Communists!

Zinn cites Douglas Miller and Marion Nowak, the authors of *The Fifties: The Way We Really Were*, to the effect that Communist victories in Czechoslovakia and China, the blockade of Berlin, and the explosion of the atomic bomb by the Soviets produced a "wave of hysteria" and a massive "Red hunt" by the Truman administration that failed to uncover "a single case of espionage." While hysterical "Americans became convinced of the need for absolute security and the preservation of the established order," really all that was happening was an "upsurge all over the world of colonial peoples demanding independence,"—"in Indochina against the French, in Indonesia against the Dutch; in the Philippines armed rebellion against the United States.... China, Korea, Indochina, the Philippines, represented local Communist movements, not Russian fomentation." American leaders knew that keeping down this "general wave of anti-imperialist insurrection" would require "national unity for militarization of the budget, for the suppression of domestic opposition to such a foreign policy." Thus, the U.S. government conspired to depict such "local" movements as being fomented by the Russians to create an "atmosphere" of fear in which "Senator Joseph McCarthy of Wisconsin could go even further than Truman."[24]

In fact, the Communist movements in "China, Korea, Indochina, the Philippines" did indeed result from "Russian fomentation." We have already looked at Soviet involvement in China. John Lewis Gaddis explains that Korea, which had been "part of the Japanese empire since 1910," was "jointly occupied by Soviet and American forces at the end of World War II," with the Soviets in the north and the Americans in the south. There had been no agreement about "who would run the country," but the "American-supported Republic of Korea" controlled the south "by virtue of an election sanctioned by the United Nations." Syngman Rhee in the south wanted to invade the north and unify the country, but the U.S. withdrew troops, not wanting to get involved in a potential war. In the meantime, in the north, Kim Il-sung finally received a long-desired "encouraging response" from his "superpower sponsor," the Soviet Union, in 1950. Stalin believed that a "'second front' was now feasible in East Asia, that it could be created by proxies, thus minimizing the risk to the U.S.S.R., and that the Americans," who "had done nothing...to save the Chinese nationalists," would again do nothing. Stalin read with care the announcement on January 12, 1950, by Secretary of State Dean Acheson "that the American 'defensive perimeter' did not extend to South Korea" and the "top-secret National Security Council study upon which it was based"—thanks to British spies.

Not only did Stalin give Kim Il-sung the "green light" to invade South Korea, but he also "encouraged Ho Chi Minh to intensify the Viet Minh offensive against the French in Indochina." This strategy had the advantage of not requiring "direct Soviet involvement." Both the North Koreans and the Viet Minh would operate "under the pretext of unifying their respective countries. And the Chinese, still eager to legitimize their revolution by winning Stalin's approval, were more than willing to provide backup support, if and when needed."[25] Stalin was emboldened by the fact that, thanks to spies, the Russians had successfully detonated their own atomic bomb the previous year.[26]

Zinn admits that North Korea, "a socialist dictatorship" in "the Soviet sphere of influence" invaded South Korea, but calls South Korea "a right-wing dictatorship, in the American sphere" and portrays the American response as overkill. According to Zinn, the Americans reduced Korea to "shambles" and "provoked the Chinese into entering the war."[27] So both the Soviet Union and the United States supported dictatorships, and the United States was more at fault. And any concern about the series of betrayals by Communist spies that led to the war is evidence of paranoia ginned up by an American government intent on keeping its citizens in line.

The situation in the Philippines was another result of the actual "Russian fomentation" that Zinn is so sarcastic about. The Huk Rebellion was not a simple movement for democracy. It began as an uprising by starving peasants who wanted better treatment from their landlords in the 1930s.[28] It then became a resistance movement against the invading Japanese. But in 1948, the PKP, the Philippine Communist Party, with leaders from the cities—some of them trained in Moscow—set out to take over the Huk movement, despite the fact that "many supporters of the 'armed struggle' had a 'deep prejudice against communism and communists.'"[29] A Labor Day PKP statement in 1950 encouraged workers to join with them by pointing to "economic recoveries in the Soviet Union and the New Europe, the victory of New Democracy in China," and the Soviet Union's "atomic and hydrogen bombs." The objective was to fight "'American imperialism and its puppets....'"[30]

As *Philippine Freedom* author Robert Aura Smith has noted, "The various manifestoes that were issued were couched in the familiar Marxist jargon, although there was heavy emphasis upon 'landlordism,' just as there was in China. And the government was always pictured as the 'tool of American imperialism.'" So, "direct" "day-to-day or even month-to-month" "orders from Moscow" were not needed. But "Communist agents in the United States Army in the Philippines" were in contact with the Huks.[31]

Zinn claims that this was one of the "upsurges" of "colonial peoples demanding independence,"[32] forgetting or overlooking the fact that the United States had granted the Philippines independence in 1946 in the Treaty of Manila after fighting off the Japanese invaders during World War II. Or maybe Zinn is in agreement with the PKP that the Filipino government was a "puppet" government, a "tool of American imperialism." As in Greece, the population in the countryside was terrorized by Communist guerillas until the second president of the independent Philippines put them down.

What Zinn presents as "a general wave of anti-imperialist insurrection in the world," is really a wave of terrorized peasants. But he is writing a book about American history, and one of the most terrifying periods for those of Zinn's political persuasion is the Cold War era. In his view, ginning up needless fear of the Communist threat was a way to defeat indigenous freedom movements abroad and repress free thinkers and dissidents on the domestic front with "executive order on loyalty oaths, Justice Department prosecutions, and anti-Communist legislation." Senator Joseph McCarthy—always an easy mark for the Left—is presented as representative of all anti-Communists. But it's a fact that Soviet expansion was enabled by Americans' *lack* of due diligence when it came to weeding out Communist spies.

There was genuine cause for concern. Americans were justifiably upset by the Communist takeover of China in 1949. In 1945, it had been discovered that the journal *Amerasia* had published "several lengthy paragraphs lifted from a secret OSS [Office of Strategic Services, the U.S.'s first central intelligence agency] report." The FBI found out that "three government employees were supplying the journal with information," and "arrested Emmanuel Larsen, a mid-level State Department official.... Lieutenant Andrew Roth, a navy intelligence officer; John Service, an up-and-coming foreign service officer; Philip Jaffe, editor and publisher of *Amerasia*...Mark Gayn, a well-known journalist...and Kate Mitchell, another *Amerasia* editor."

Then, in 1947, the "Hollywood Ten"—film directors, screen writers, and producers, including nine hardcore Communist Party members and a tenth "close ally"—refused to answer questions before the House Committee on Un-American Activities (HUAC), and as a result were briefly imprisoned and then blacklisted in the industry.[33] In 1948, Whittaker Chambers testified against spy Alger Hiss, and on January 25, 1950, Hiss was sentenced to five years in prison "for perjury in denying espionage charges before a Grand Jury." The day before, Klaus Fuchs had started confessing his "wartime espionage at Los Alamos" to "British interrogators."

A week later, Senator Joe McCarthy made his famous speech in Wheeling, West Virginia, about the list of Communists in the State Department. Christopher Andrew and Vasili Mitrokhin, among other anti-Communists, claim that "McCarthy ultimately did more for the Soviet cause than any agent of influence the KGB ever had."[34] Admittedly, McCarthy had political reasons for going after Communists and attacking Democrats who had been soft on them, or at least not vigilant enough. He also was not careful in making his charges, and he became more reckless as his drinking, some say, got worse. But the nearly universal condemnation of McCarthy betrays a double standard. As John Earl Haynes has pointed out, the standard to which McCarthy is regularly held is not applied to the Dies Committee hearings of the 1930s, when Representative Samuel Dickstein "led the congressional attack on domestic fascism" and "often published in the *Congressional Record* lists of people he regarded as fascists and Nazis." Dickstein went beyond anything McCarthy would do when he responded to a congressman's complaint "that six people Dickstein had named as Nazis swore they were not" with the reply, "If out of these hundreds of names that I have buttonholed as fascists and Nazis...only six filed a protest, I think I have done a pretty good job."[35]

Contemporary opinion was kinder to McCarthy than history has been. In January 1954, he still had a 50 percent "favorable" rating in "opinion polls," with only 29 percent opposed.[36]

Zinn discounts McCarthy's list, claiming it was based on a list of one hundred dossiers "from State Department loyalty files," which "were three years old," with "most of the people...no longer with the State Department." Zinn huffs indignantly, "but McCarthy read from them anyway, inventing, adding, and changing as he read,"—for example, changing one description from "liberal" to "communistically inclined." He "kept on like this for the next few years," going so far as to criticize books in the Voice of America libraries.[37] In fact, the VOA library did include an estimated thirty thousand books promoting Communism, some by Communist leaders Earl Browder and William Z. Foster, and others favorable to the Chinese Communists by Owen Lattimore and others, and by Philip Foner, official labor historian of the Communist Party, the author of "more than a dozen books extolling the CPUSA."[38] The CPUSA, in which Browder, Foster, and Foner were all officials, was controlled by Stalin's Soviet Union. Many of the individuals who left the State Department went on to spread their poison elsewhere. Even those just "communistically inclined" were able to do great damage to our nation's security.

William Henry Chamberlin, a journalist who had been based in Moscow, knew this first-hand. He described how the Office of War Information was influenced by Communist sympathizers, like when the New York office had suggested that he "broadcast to the Netherlands East Indies about the successes of Soviet industrialization and collective farming." When he informed them that he would have to "emphasize the heavy cost of these experiments in suffering and human lives, the offer was dropped." Chamberlin described pro-Communist media messages that swayed public opinion in favor of the Soviet Union.[39]

As William Buckley and L. Brent Bozell wrote in 1954, in the case of Harold Glasser and in nine similar cases, McCarthy "merely quoted from derogatory reports developed by other investigators, with a view to persuading the Senate that at least a *prima facie* case existed for questioning the operating standards of a loyalty program that had cleared them." Scholars John Earl Haynes and Harvey Klehr, and Alexander

Vassiliev, former KGB officer, in their book *Spies: The Rise and Fall of the KGB in America* (based upon Soviet intelligence records copied by Vassiliev in 1993), call Glasser "one of the KGB's most productive spies in Washington." Twice in 1953, Glasser appeared "before the Senate Internal Security Subcommittee and the Permanent Subcommittee on Investigations of the Committee on Government Operations (Joseph McCarthy's committee). In both cases, he invoked the Fifth Amendment. By 1954, he was working for Liberty Brush Company" and then "faded from public sight." Glasser had joined the Treasury Department as an economist in 1936, and his role in Soviet intelligence had been known since 1948 when former Communists Whittaker Chambers and Elizabeth Bentley had identified him. Klehr, Haynes, and Vassiliev describe over a dozen documents that Glasser passed on to the KGB, including one from the Treasury Department about "Allied policies with regard to neutral countries," "a conversation" between officials about "Poland's attitude to postwar Germany and about Sov.-Polish relations," and about "civilian deliveries for liberated regions."[40]

Another one of McCarthy's cases was Stanley Graze, whose name was on the list he gave to the Tydings Committee. Graze was an agent who began his work for the Communist Party as a college student and continued it after being drafted into the army in 1943. In 1945, he "obtained a post in the Russian Division of the OSS" and became "an active espionage source via Victor Perlo." He moved on to the State Department, then resigned in 1948 after learning that "he had come under investigation for suspected Communist ties," according to Stan Evans. He wound up at the United Nations, a not unusual landing place for those leaving the State Department under similar circumstances.[41]

When he appeared before Congress in 1952, Graze invoked the Fifth Amendment. Haynes, Klehr, and Vassiliev learned that the KGB tried to re-recruit him up until 1962, but "Stanley Graze took a different direction in life.... he turned into a criminal capitalist," becoming fund manager for Investors Overseas Services. In 1969, Graze and his associates helped Robert Vesco "loo[t]...more than $200 million," and in

1972, he found himself an object of a civil fraud complaint by the Securities and Exchange Commission. After again invoking the Fifth and refusing to testify at an SEC hearing in 1973, Graze left the country and settled in Costa Rica, where he died in 1987. But according to a KGB officer who had a conversation with Graze at a wedding reception in Costa Rica in 1976, Graze was still a dedicated Marxist.[42]

Another name "included among State Department security risks by Senator McCarthy in 1950" was that of Franz Neumann, "a Soviet source in the OSS," an agency especially open to Communists. The Soviets suspected him of passing on disinformation, but reconsidered reestablishing contact in 1944, though there is "nothing indicating that contact was reestablished." Before he died in an automobile accident in 1954, Neumann had served "on Justice Robert Jackson's prosecutorial staff at the Nuremberg War Crimes trials" and "plunged into German politics and supported a merger of the German Social Democratic Party with the Communists." But he was disillusioned by Soviet repression in East Germany and "helped found the Free University of Berlin and in 1948 accepted a professorship at Columbia University." According to Haynes, Klehr, and Vassiliev, Neumann "never publicly disclosed his clandestine wartime cooperation with the KGB, and no congressional investigating committee called him to testify."[43]

In the preface to Spies, John Earl Haynes and Harvey Klehr ask, "Was the hunt for Communist spies in fact a witch hunt, a search for fictional demons, that tells us more about the paranoia and madness of the inquisitors, or was it a rational, if sometimes excessively heated, response to a genuine threat….?" While McCarthy's charges came "late in the game" and "were wildly off the mark,"[44] Haynes and Klehr present evidence that the damage was worse than suspected. In Venona, they condemn McCarthy for making accusations against such individuals as Dean Acheson and George C. Marshall.[45] As early as 1954, anti-Communist authors Buckley and Bozell, too, had convicted McCarthy of overreach in imputing "treasonable motives" against Marshall in his sixty thousand-word speech on the Senate floor in June 1951, which listed seventeen charges against the general, including Marshall's pro-Stalin positions at Tehran and Yalta, giving the Soviets access to Eastern Europe and to Berlin and Prague "ahead of the allies," helping to formulate an "anti-Chiang" policy, and refusing "to prosecute vigorously the war against the North Koreans." As much as these accusations seem to indicate softness on Communism, there was no evidence that Marshall was a Communist agent, just probably "America's most disastrous general," said Buckley and Bozell.[46]

Nevertheless, the CPUSA was in fact quite successful in placing individuals "in selected government agencies in order to gain information or influence policy."[47] Screening was lax. William Henry Chamberlin, writing in 1950, wondered how the major spy ring leader Nathan Gregory Silvermaster was able to retain his employment after "Naval Intelligence protested against his employment early in the war," and the Civil Service Commission had reported "in 1942" about "considerable testimony in the file indicating that about 1920 Mr. Silvermaster was an underground agent of the Communist Party." Witnesses said that Silvermaster had "been everything from a 'fellow traveler' to an agent of the OGPU [Soviet political police]."[48]

It was not only spies, but also Communist sympathizers who manipulated American foreign policy—including at the Treasury Department, where a "policy of financial strangulation" could determine outcomes, according to Stan Evans in 2007. He described the "cast of characters" involved, including Harry Dexter White, Lauchlin Currie, V. Frank Coe, Harold Glasser, and Alger Hiss. Evans understood that Marshall was not a Communist agent, but he pointed out how his bad policies could have been influenced by his mentor, John Vincent, "a close ally of [John Stewart] Service and Soviet agent Laughlin [sic] Currie," who came to oppose the anti-Communist leader Chiang Kai-shek. Curiously, when Marshall "arrived in China," in December 1945, "the Nationalists were winning.... the Communists hadn't had sufficient time to be equipped and trained adequately by their Soviet sponsors...." But Marshall got Chiang "to call off his armies." That move on the American general's part was determined by China experts Anthony Kubek and Freda Utley to be "foremost among a number of crucial measures that turned the tide in favor of Mao." Under the Truman Doctrine, military aid was provided to Greece and Turkey, but was denied to Chiang. On January 5, 1950, President Truman announced that "no military aid would be provided" even "to help Chiang protect Formosa." The later—and even more per-fidious—developments occurred after Marshall had left the department under Dean Acheson, who became secretary of state in 1949.[49]

Playing a significant role in all this was Owen Lattimore, a "scholar of the little-known cultures of the Chinese borderlands of Mongolia, Manchuria, and the Turkish-speaking regions of inner Asia." Recom-mended by the spy Lauchlin Currie, he "served in Chiang's headquar-ters...during 1941 and 1942" and then as "deputy director of Pacific operations for the Office of War Information. In 1950 he was director of the School of International Relations at Johns Hopkins University." After the FBI found him to be "pro-Communist in his sympathies," but with "no reliable evidence that he was a Soviet agent or even a secret member of the CPUSA," the Tydings Committee "exonerated him." He was then brought before the McCarran committee, where under a more probing examination, Lattimore was revealed to have defended the Moscow Show Trials and to have "been a close associate of several of those who stole government documents in the *Amerasia* case," along with serving "on *Amerasia*'s editorial board for several years." At the Institute for Pacific Relations (IPR), he had advised a colleague about surreptitiously advancing policy to the benefit of the Chinese and Russian Communists, and, in 1949, "just before the Communist invasion of South Korea," letting "South Korea fall—but not to let it look like we pushed it." Lattimore was charged with seventeen counts of perjury, but "federal courts twice rejected the indictment as involving states of mind and judgments that did not lend themselves to judicial determination in a criminal case." Still, "the revelations of his past sympathy for Soviet policies disqualified him for faculty status in programs training Ameri-cans for U.S. government foreign service."[50]

As Haynes acknowledges, Senator McCarran, who as a Democrat had sway in the Truman administration, was finally able to drum Lattimore out of government service. But while Lattimore may have been a scholar and not a spy, he was still able to influence policy—perhaps even more so because of the assumptions about scholarly objectivity and expertise. While detractors of the anti-Communist "Red Scare" may point to Lattimore as a victim of a "witch hunt," most Americans during this period would probably not have wanted someone like him teaching foreign service officers, or even their own children at a university.[51]

Lattimore, however, was a featured guest speaker at—Spelman College! Invited by—Howard Zinn! We wonder what the students heard about Communist China. The invitation attracted the attention of the FBI. In *A People's History*, Zinn presents Lattimore as a victim, someone who could not even get the full support of the ACLU. As Zinn points out, Lattimore was a target of a speech by then-congressman John F. Kennedy in January of 1949. Zinn quotes Kennedy's speech at length, inserting explanatory information in brackets: "So concerned were our diplomats and their advisers, the Lattimores and the Fairbanks [both scholars in the field of Chinese history, Owen Lattimore a favorite target of McCarthy, John Fairbank, a Harvard professor] with the imperfection of the democratic system in China after 20 years of war and tales of corruption in high places that they lost sight of our tremendous stake in non-Communist China...."[52]

As a matter of fact, Kennedy was absolutely right—except that he gave too much of the benefit of the doubt to Lattimore, whose concern about the "imperfection" of Chinese democracy served as a cover for his larger goal: Professor Lattimore avoided formal ties to the Communist Party, but did everything to advance the Soviet agenda from his position as a "scholar."

And yet, Zinn presents the House Committee as paranoid: "interrogating Americans about their Communist connections, holding them in contempt if they refused to answer, distributing millions of pamphlets" that claimed that Communists could be found "'everywhere—in

factories, offices, butcher shops, on street corners, in private business...."[53] Well, they were there. And, we would add, in classrooms.
While some professors at American universities were actual Communists, many more were opposed to the committee. In 1947, fifty profes-
sors from Dartmouth College signed a letter in opposition. In 1962,
William F. Buckley addressed charges from "the Kenyon (College)
Council to Abolish the House Committee on Un-American Activities."
In response to one of the twenty-eight professors who wanted to abolish or radically reform the committee (only five favored keeping it),
Buckley wrote that "Professor F." had complained, *"I have not heard
that the Committee has ever questioned the objectives of the Ku Klux
Klan ...* [emphasis in the original]." But as Buckley pointed out, "But
the Committee has; see, e.g., Special Com. on HUAC Vol. 1-6, 9-12,
14; Exec. Hearings, made public, Vols. 1, 2, 6-7. Appendix I, IV, and
divers references, 1946-1960."[54]

Alas, where was a Communist to go when, as Zinn complains, even
"the liberals in the government were themselves acting to exclude, per-
secute, fire, and even imprison Communists"?[55] David Horowitz, in his
autobiography, relates how his father, a member of the Communist Party,
lost his teaching position for refusing to answer questions about Communist Party membership. But he placed it in perspective: "In the entire
Cold War period less than two hundred leaders and functionaries of the
Party ever went to prison, in most cases serving less than two years."
Horowitz comments, "Considering the Party's organizational ties" to
the Soviet Union, it was not too large a price to pay.[56] Despite the fact
that the CPUSA was controlled by a hostile foreign power, the Party "was
never outlawed, membership in the party was never a crime, and even
during the height of the anti-Communist era it operated legally, maintained offices, published literature, recruited members, and sustained a
network of auxiliary organizations."[57]

But according to Zinn, professors just exploring ideas—persons
such as himself—faced the prospect of concentration camps because
of the anti-Communist hysteria. He charges, "in 1950, the Republicans

sponsored an Internal Security Act for the registration of organizations found to be 'Communist-action' or 'Communist-front,'" and "liberal senators did not fight...head-on." This bill, also called the McCarran Act after Senator McCarran, was passed on September 23, 1950. To Zinn's horror, Democrat opponents of the act, "including Hubert Humphrey and Herbert Lehman, proposed a substitute measure, the setting up of detention centers (really concentration camps) for suspected subversives, who, when the President declared an 'internal security emergency,' would be held without trial. The detention-camp bill became not a substitute for, but in addition to, the Internal Security Act, and the proposed camps were set up, ready for use." Fortunately, the 1960s came to save the day: "In 1968, a time of general disillusionment with anti-Communism, this law was repealed."[58]

And who were these Communists that lawmakers wanted to imprison—in "concentration camps," no less? According to Zinn, by 1954 the "list of organizations [the government had] decided were 'totalitarian, fascist, communist or subversive...or as seeking to alter the form of government of the United States by unconstitutional means,'" as well as those in "sympathetic association" with them, included "the Chopin Cultural Center, the Cervantes Fraternal Society, the Committee for the Negro in the Arts, the Committee for the Protection of the Bill of Rights, the League of American Writers, the Nature Friends of America, People's Drama, the Washington Bookshop Association, and the Yugoslav Seaman's Club."[59] Howard Zinn pretends that there were no such things as Communist front groups.

Contrary to Zinn's claim that the McCarran Act was meant to imprison dissident writers, professors, and classical music buffs, it was meant to be used in the case of "a national security emergency," such as a war with the Soviet Union. As Haynes explains, those to be detained were "potential saboteurs and spies." Thus, "after the Korean War ended and Stalin died, the Eisenhower administration regarded the plans as unneeded. The government sold or leased the sites for other uses." Contrary to Zinn's claim that "the camps were set up, ready to use," Haynes explains, "No detention camps were ever built, and no one was ever detained under the McCarran Act."[60]

Were the congressmen overreacting? Consider the harm that had been done during the World War II years. In their book on the decrypted Venona Papers, Haynes and Klehr call the CPUSA "a fifth column working inside and against the United States." A "disturbing number of high-ranking U.S. government officials...had passed extraordinarily sensitive information to the Soviet Union that had seriously damaged American interests."

"Harry White," for example, "the second most powerful official in the U.S. Treasury Department...part of the American delegation at the founding of the United Nations—had advised the KGB about how American diplomatic strategy could be frustrated."

Maurice Halperin, "head of a research section" of the OSS, "then America's chief intelligence arm, turned over hundreds of pages of secret American diplomatic cables."

William Perl, a "government aeronautical scientist, provided the Soviets with the results of the highly secret tests and design experiments for American jet engines and jet aircraft" and thus helped them to "overcom[e] the American technological lead."

Physicists Klaus Fuchs and Theodore Hall, and technician David Greenglass (brother-in-law of Julius Rosenberg) "transmitted the complex formula for extracting bomb-grade uranium from ordinary uranium," allowing the Soviet Union to make their own bomb in 1949 and emboldening Stalin to authorize North Korea to invade South Korea in 1950.

And Lauchlin Currie, "trusted personal assistant" to President Roosevelt, "warned" the KGB about the FBI's investigation of "key" Soviet agent and spy ringleader Gregory Silvermaster.[61]

Soviet archive records opened in the 1990s revealed that Currie had also passed on information about President Roosevelt's attitudes toward Charles de Gaulle (June 1944) and his willingness "to accept Stalin's demand that the USSR keep the half of Poland that it had received under the Nazi-Soviet Pact of 1939 and that FDR would put pressure on the Polish government-in-exile to make concessions to the Soviets." Currie lied to the FBI in 1947 and lied again during his testimony to Congress in 1948. The FBI continued to investigate him, but in 1950, Currie moved to Colombia, "lost his naturalized American citizenship" (he had been born in Nova Scotia), and "later became a Colombian national."[62]

Had the government acted sooner—that is, immediately after ex-Communist Whittaker Chambers came forward—"significant damage to U.S. national interests would have been avoided and a great deal of the basis for the bitter postwar domestic controversy about communism and subversion would have been removed," say Haynes and Klehr. In 1939, Chambers gave information to Adolf Berle, assistant secretary of State, including the names of eight people who have now been confirmed by the Venona decryptions to have "cooperated with Soviet espionage": Alger Hiss, State Department; Laurence Duggan, State Department; Frank Coe, Treasury Department; Charles Kramer, National Labor Relations Board; John Abt, "prominent labor lawyer with wide contacts in the Congress of Industrial Organizations"; Isaac Folkoff, California Communist party leader; Lauchlin Currie; and Harry Dexter White. Five others were confirmed to be spies by means outside of Venona: Julian Wadleigh, State Department; Vincent Reno, a "civilian official at the Army Aberdeen Proving Grounds"; Noel Field, State Department; Solomon Adler, Treaury Department; and Philip Rosenblit, who, "unknown to Chambers" by that time was a victim of Stalin's terror.[63]

The delay came about because a number of individuals failed to act. According to Allen Weinstein, author of *Perjury: The Hiss-Chambers Case*, Berle "never filed the memo, before or afterward, with either State Department security officers or military intelligence agencies." Chambers had sought an audience with the president for a guarantee of immunity, a meeting that the journalist Isaac Don Levine unsuccessfully tried to arrange. He and Chambers did meet with Berle who "assured [Chambers and Levine] that the information would go directly to Roosevelt." But when Berle "talked to both Felix Frankfurter and Dean Acheson about the loyalties of Alger and Donald Hiss," he was told "that the charges were groundless." According to Levine, Berle brought Chambers's revelations to the attention of the president, but FDR "scoffed at the charges of Soviet espionage rings within the government." Levine "tried doggedly" for over a year "to stir interest in Chambers's allegations among influential political figures," including Representative Martin Dies. Levine also went to "Loy Henderson…chief of the State Department's Russian Section; Republican Senator Warren R. Austin; Ambassador William Bullitt…; labor leader David Dubinsky; and gossip columnist Walter Winchell…. Bullitt, Dubinsky, and Winchell all brought the charges to Roosevelt's attention, according to Levine, but the President continued to brush the story aside." Berle contacted the FBI several times in February and March 1941 about Chambers's information, but the FBI did not request the documents until 1943.[64]

Chambers did not get his day in court until 1948. Although leftists continued to maintain that Alger Hiss was caught in a frame-up by Red hunters, Hiss's guilt has been definitively established by Weinstein, who began as a skeptic, as well as by Haynes, Klehr, and Vassiliev, who proclaimed, "cased closed."[65] Allen Weinstein, a man of the Left, had set out to write his book about Alger Hiss to prove his innocence—but then came across the evidence that showed his guilt.

The same thing happened when then-leftist historian Ron Radosh undertook the investigation of the case of Julius and Ethel Rosenberg, who were executed in 1953 for espionage. In the book he co-wrote with Joyce Milton, *The Rosenberg File*, Radosh explained how, though when he began the research for the book he "no longer subscribed to the pro-Soviet views" of his adolescence, he had "continued to hold" to his "earnest belief in the Rosenbergs' total innocence, always thinking that in the future new evidence might emerge to prove the complicity of the government in a frame-up. When the Rosenbergs' two sons, Michael and Robert Meeropol, finally sued the U.S. government for all FBI files pertaining to the case, [he] assumed that the release of this material would lead to [their] final vindication…." The opposite was true, as Radosh and Milton found after interviewing "scores of individuals" and going through over two hundred thousand "pages of documents" released by the FBI and other agencies.[66]

Some witnesses, speaking to Radosh and Milton on the condition they not be identified, acknowledged that the Rosenbergs were guilty but argued that there was "the historical truth and the Party's truth." One attorney gave Radosh a lecture "on the necessity of presenting the Rosenbergs solely as victims of Cold War hysteria." Another "venerable and well-established Communist party lawyer, whose career goes back to the late 1920s," asked, "What was so bad about helping Stalin get the A-bomb? It was the responsibility of a good Communist to do whatever he could to help the Red Army gain victory."[67]

Before the book's publication in 1983, a June 23, 1979, *New Republic* article in which Radosh and Sol Stern raised questions about the Left's defense of the Rosenbergs had garnered considerable attention. That was the year that Zinn was writing *A People's History*. But nothing stopped Zinn from sticking to the old line that the Rosenbergs were the victims of a frame-up—through all editions of *A People's History*. Zinn simply repeated the old conspiracy theories, often presenting them as leading questions: "Did [witness Harry] Gold cooperate in return for an early release from prison? and "How reliable was Gold's testimony?" Zinn repeated long-demolished claims about meetings between judges and prosecutors that supposedly proved that the Rosenbergs were framed. For Zinn, the execution of the Rosenbergs was "a demonstration to the people of the country...of what lay at the end of the line for those the government decided were traitors."[68]

In 2008, Rosenberg codefendant Morton Sobell, who had spent nineteen years in Alcatraz and other prisons and at that point was ninety-one years old, admitted that he and Julius Rosenberg had been spies. Zinn mentions Sobell on page 434, claiming that the case against him was so "weak" that Sobell's attorney had "decided there was no need to present a defense."[69] Sobell's admission led the Rosenbergs' two sons to acknowledge for the first time that their father had been a spy. Writing about this development in the *Los Angeles Times,* Radosh bemoaned the fact that most college textbooks still presented the "innocent" Rosenbergs as being deprived of a fair trial, or guilty only of passing inconsequential information. In truth, the Rosenbergs not only tried "their best to give the Soviets top atomic secrets from the Manhattan Project, they succeeded in handing over top military data on sonar and on radar that was used by the Russians to shoot down American planes in the Korean and Vietnam wars."[70] When Howard Zinn was contacted by a *New York Times* reporter on the occasion of these revelations in 2008, he claimed, "I never was going along saying I know that they were innocent, and I'm not shocked by the fact that they turned out to be spies," but, "to me it didn't matter whether they were guilty or not. The most important thing was they did not get a fair trial in the atmosphere of cold war hysteria."[71]

No amount of proven treason, agitation for violent revolution, or, for that matter, mass murder and the immiseration of millions by socialist governments across the globe would ever persuade Zinn to dial down his indignation at what he characterized as "hysteria" about Communism.[72] He was concerned not about the victims of the malevolent Communist ideology, but about Communist Party leaders who were prosecuted on evidence he claimed consisted "mostly of the fact that the Communists were distributing Marxist-Leninist literature, which the prosecution contended called for violent revolution. There was certainly not evidence of any immediate danger of violent revolution by the Communist party."[73] Well, how about Karl Marx's statement in "The Victory of the Counter-Revolution in Vienna" that "the very cannibalism of the counterrevolution will convince the nations that there is only one way in which the murderous death agonies of the old society and the bloody birth throes of the new society can be shortened, simplified and concentrated, and that way is revolutionary terror"?[74] Or Lenin's *Lessons of the Commune*: "there are times when the interests of the proletariat call for ruthless extermination of its enemies in open armed clashes."[75] In fact, one need not go farther than

The Communist Manifesto to see that Communists do not advocate social change through peaceful political means. In fact, Marx and Engels mock Socialists' "fantastic pictures" of "peaceful means" and "small experiments." In contrast, "The Communists openly declare that their ends can be attained only by the forcible overthrow of all existing social conditions."[76] It's the only way to get things done.

In Zinn's history, though, sheer fear-mongering through a "series of invented scares about Soviet military build-ups, a false 'bomber gap' and a false 'missile gap,'" led to an unnecessary U.S. arms build-up, which by 1962 had produced "the equivalent, in nuclear weapons, of 1,500 Hiroshima-size atomic bombs." Zinn claims "The Soviet Union was obviously behind…. but the U.S. budget kept mounting, the hysteria kept growing, the profits of corporations getting defense contracts multiplied…." There are those "profits" again! "By 1970, the U.S. military budget was $80 billion, with two-thirds of the $40 billion spent on weapons systems going to 'twelve or fifteen giant industrial corporations.'"[77] Contrary to Zinn's claims, the U.S.S.R. was not "obviously behind" in the arms race. In fact, the U.S. was not spending *enough*. By around 1968, "the U.S.S.R. had at last achieved strategic parity with the United States: if there was to be a 'missile gap' now, the Americans were likely to find themselves at the short end of it," according to *Cold War* author Gaddis.[78]

Of course, Zinn is following the Communist Party line in presenting the Soviet Union as no threat at all. We recall his condemnation of the 1948 Marshall Plan, which rebuilt Western Europe and kept it out of Communist hands, for its "political motive": the real purpose was to "creat[e] a network of American corporate control over the globe," "to build up markets for American exports," and to "use pressure and money to keep Communists out of the cabinets," such as in France and Italy where the Communist parties "were strong."[79] Well, yes they were, thanks to funding from Moscow. Just as we have seen before, Zinn's take on history is suspiciously similar to the Soviet propaganda pushed by CPUSA boss William Z. Foster in his *Outline Political History*. Naturally, he didn't like the Marshall Plan either, charging, "The Marshall Plan, presented to the world as a project of rehabilitation of war-torn Europe, is fundamentally designed to arm and mobilize the European capitalist countries for an all-out war against the U.S.S.R. and the People's Democracies of Eastern Europe."[80]

Zinn updated Foster's litany of injustices against Communism by adding President Kennedy's Alliance for Progress in Latin America. Nor did he approve of the 1953 overthrow of the Iranian government that had "nationalized the oil industry," or the 1954 overthrow of the Guatemalan government of Jacobo Árbenz. All were about the U.S. military and industry conspiring to install right-wing dictatorships for their own benefit. Arbenz was "a left-of-center Socialist" whose government was "the most democratic Guatemala had ever had." His overthrow was at the behest of "American business interests" because he had "expropriated 234,000 acres of land owned by United Fruit." When U.S. Marines were sent to Lebanon in 1958, it was all about blood for oil—"to make sure the pro-American government was not toppled by a revolution, and to keep an armed presence in that oil-rich area."[81]

But Cuba is Zinn's favorite case: "The Democrat-Republican, liberal-conservative agreement to prevent or overthrow revolutionary governments whenever possible—whether Communist, Socialist, or anti-United Fruit—became most evident in 1961 in Cuba." Castro is Robin Hood, because, after assuming power on January 1, 1959, he "moved to set up a nationwide system of education, of housing, of land distribution to landless peasants." And America is the enemy. The United States did not want to lend Cuba money and refused to let the International Monetary Fund do so. After the U.S. "cut down" on the amount of sugar we bought, Cuba was forced to turn to the Soviet Union. Then the U.S. government armed and trained Cuban exiles for the Bay of Pigs invasion, a mission outrageously kept secret by the *New Republic*, part of the "liberal-conservative coalition," at the request of Arthur Schlesinger. Zinn can't get over the fact that even liberals, like Schlesinger, applauded the effort.[82] But so did most Americans, as the rise in Kennedy's poll numbers after the invasion indicated.[83]

The American people may have been happy with the state of the world in the early sixties, characterized as it was by an economic boom, American military strength, and Communism held at bay. But it made Zinn sad. Not only had the U.S. interfered in budding Communist (really communitarian) movements around the globe on behalf of greedy fruit growers and oil companies, but "the fifteen-year effort since the end of World War II to break up the Communist-radical upsurge of the New Deal and wartime years seemed successful. The Communist party was in disarray—its leaders in jail, its membership shrunken, its influence in the trade union movement very small.... The military budget was half of the national budget, but the public was accepting this."[84]

But he did his part to change all that! A new field remained to be plowed, new potential sources of "revolt" to be exploited. There was dissatisfaction among "Negroes." Black Americans had proven their patriotism and competence in World War II, and no doubt, most Americans would agree that equal rights and opportunities for them were long overdue. But for Howard Zinn, equal economic and legal rights fell far short of his goals. He would not be happy with such things as Supreme Court decisions to desegregate the schools, civil rights laws guaranteeing equal rights, or access to jobs and voting. The title of his next chapter "Or Does It Explode?" gives a good indication of what he had in mind.

SEVEN

Black Mascots for a Red Revolution

"The black revolt of the 1950s and 1960s—North and South—came as a surprise. But perhaps it should not have. The memory of oppressed people is one thing that cannot be taken away, and for such people, with such memories, revolt is always an inch below the surface. For blacks in the United States, there was the memory of slavery, and after that of segregation, lynching, humiliation. And it was not just a memory but a living presence—part of the daily lives of blacks in generation after generation."[1]

While the African Americans among whom Zinn lived in Atlanta certainly suffered from the indignities of segregation and prejudice, it would be an exaggeration to say that daily life for Spelman professors and students consisted of fear of an imminent lynching, that "revolt" was always "an inch below the surface," or that mid-twentieth century African Americans remembered slavery. Zinn relies on an inordinate amount of creative literature to sell this take on the black experience in the twentieth century.

For example, Zinn quotes a famous poem by Harlem Renaissance author Claude McKay to illustrate the supposed "dangerous currents among young blacks," which he claims Senator Henry Cabot Lodge warned about, but which Zinn himself celebrates:

> If we must die, let it not be like hogs
> Hunted and penned in an inglorious spot....
> Like men we'll face the murderous cowardly pack,
> Pressed to the wall, dying but fighting back![2]

As it happens, McKay himself, who had been inspired to write "If We Must Die" by the race riots as soldiers returned from World War I and published the poem in 1919 in the *Liberator*, "insisted that the sonnet had universal intent." Though the poem, he said, "makes me a poet among colored Americans.... frankly, I have never regarded myself as a Negro poet. I have always felt that my gift of song was something bigger than the narrow confined limits of any one people and its problems." These words of McKay are reported in *Harlem Renaissance* by Nathan Huggins, the 1971 book that Zinn references on page 445 of *A People's History* and includes in his bibliography. But Zinn ignores McKay's own understanding of the appeal of his poetry beyond the confines of race. After "learn[ing] that a white American soldier, who had died on the Russian front in World War II, had this poem among his belongings," McKay said, "I felt profoundly gratified and justified. I felt assurance that 'If We Must Die' was just what I intended it to be, a universal poem."[3]

Zinn seems to want to confine black poets to a black ghetto. Rather than having universal appeal, their work is always about racial anger. He continues the literary redlining with his treatment of Countee Cullen's poetry. By choosing to discuss only two of Cullen's poems—"Scottsboro, Too, Is Worth Its Song" and "Incident"—Zinn gives the impression that he wrote mostly about race.[4] In fact, Countee Cullen's work transcends any single issue. He studied under Hyder E. Rollins, a John Keats scholar, at New York University from 1922 to 1925, graduating Phi Beta Kappa, and earned a graduate degree at Harvard. He expressed little interest in politics and less in an Afro-centric identity. In fact, Cullen wrote for the February 10, 1924, *Brooklyn Daily Eagle* that "If I am going to be a poet at all, I am going to be POET and not NEGRO POET [emphasis in the original]." Excessive focus on race, he felt, was hindering the "artists among us." He asserted, "I shall not write of Negro subjects for the purpose of propaganda." It was precisely for such bourgeois and what he called "white" values that the far-left author Langston Hughes attacked Cullen implicitly in his famous 1926 essay, "The Negro Artist and the Racial Mountain."[5]

But for Zinn, literature by African Americans is all about racial resentments that—here's hoping!—might fuel a leftist revolution in the United States: "It was all there in the poetry, the prose, the music, sometimes masked, sometimes unmistakably clear—the signs of a people unbeaten, waiting, hot, coiled."[6] Here Zinn is on the same page with both the American Communist Party and the Soviet propaganda machine. "The first discussion on record of the Negro problem by an American Communist took place in Russia...." wrote Theodore Draper in his 1960 classic *American Communism and Soviet Russia*. It was part of the subject of the "national and colonial question" and "on the agenda of the Comintern's Second Congress in 1920," the fourteenth point of the sixteen theses Lenin submitted to the delegates: "The Negroes in America." In 1921, Lenin sent the American Communists a letter urging them to recognize Negroes "as a strategically important element in Communist activity." The party's position was articulated in the November 1921 issue of the *Communist*: "The most important point in our agitation must be to *fix responsibility for the Negro's sufferings where it rightly belongs: on the bourgeoisie and the Capitalist-Imperialist System!*" [emphasis in the original].[7]

According to Zinn, "black Communists in the South had earned the admiration of blacks by their organizing work against enormous obstacles. There was Hosea Hudson, the black organizer of the unemployed in Birmingham, for instance. And in Georgia, in 1932, a nineteen-year-old black youth named Angelo Herndon, whose father died of miner's pneumonia, who had worked in mines as a boy in Kentucky, joined an Unemployment Council in Birmingham organized by the Communist party, and then joined the party."

Zinn insinuates that the Communists were the only ones concerned about blacks. They were on the right side of the notorious Scottsboro Case, in which several young black men were sentenced to death for raping white women, though the evidence was in their favor. Zinn has to admit, "The [Communist] party was accused by liberals and the NAACP of exploiting the [Scottsboro] issue for its own purposes...." But he admits only to "a half-truth" in the accusations, arguing that "black people were realistic about the difficulty of having white allies who were pure in motive."[8]

Actually, there were plenty of white allies who *were* pure in motive. They were working with and for the NAACP, which had an integrated leadership with blacks in the most prominent roles. Clarence Darrow, probably the most famous lawyer in America, heeded the call of NAACP executive secretary Walter White to take on the Scottsboro case.

The NAACP could also brag about their own brilliant African American attorneys, such as Scipio Africanus Jones and Charles Hamilton Houston, some of whom argued cases before the Supreme Court, thank you very much. This is not to mention thousands upon thousands of African Americans who contributed hard-earned wages to the defense of the Scottsboro boys when the alarm was first raised by black ministers and field organizers of the NAACP. By the early 1920s, a little over a decade after its founding, the NAACP had switched from being white-run to black-run.[9] Zinn ignores the black supporters that the Scottsboro Boys had in the NAACP, in the black churches, and among black journalists and working class citizens. These black crusaders for civil rights are wiped out of African American history by Zinn—and, increasingly, by the historians who have followed him.

Instead, he presents Hudson and Herndon—two unusual black men lured into the Communist Party—as examples of black empowerment. Hudson, Zinn writes, was "a black man from rural Georgia, at the age of ten a plowhand, later an iron worker in Birmingham," who had been "aroused by the case of the Scottsboro Boys in 1931."[10] According to *Let Nobody Turn Us Around*, an anthology edited by Manning Marable and Leith Mullings, Hudson "subsequently worked in the Works Progress Administration (WPA), served as vice president of the Birmingham and Jefferson County locals of the Workers Alliance, was president of Steel Local 2815, and vice president of the Alabama Political Education Association. Hudson used several aliases and often worked underground, especially during the 1950s when he was a Communist organizer in the South. In 1971 he visited the Soviet Union for the first time."[11]

Herndon was from Ohio and had been recruited in Cincinnati by the Communists to come to Atlanta to lead marches. Zinn quotes—though he does not cite—a ten-line passage from *You Cannot Kill the Working Class*, published by the International Labor Defense and League for Struggle for Negro Rights around 1937, in which Herndon—who was put on trial for violating a Georgia statute against insurrection—complains about how passages from the Communist literature that he possessed were read to the jury and about how he was asked, "Did I believe in the demand for the self-determination of the Black Belt?..."[12] The "Black Belt" was the scheme the Soviets had put forth in 1928 to carve out of the eleven black majority states of the American South a separate black republic.

George Schuyler, the popular Harlem-based columnist for the *Pittsburgh Courier*, thought that Herndon was being used by white Communists. As Schuyler recounts in his 1966 autobiography *Black and Conservative*, "A Greenwich Village Communist woman whom I knew had previously asked me to go down there [Atlanta] for that purpose, and I laughed aloud." He adds with his characteristic sarcasm, "So they got Herndon; he carried out his Red assignment, and he was promptly nabbed, jugged, tried and sentenced to the Georgia chain gang; then released on bail. Soon the Communists were parading him around the country at mass meetings that proved very lucrative."[13]

In *Blacks and Reds: Race and Class in Conflict, 1919–1990*, Earl Ofari Hutchinson also describes Hudson and Herndon as prizes for the white Communist organizers: "Communists were rewarded in Alabama and Georgia when they found two young black men who emerged as daring leaders. Hosea Hudson in Alabama and Angelo Herndon in Georgia would give the Party greater visibility and stature among blacks." Herndon was "another martyr" for the Communists.[14] Herndon enjoyed his Communist Party role for only about another decade. "By the end of the 1940s" he had returned to the Midwest to lead a bourgeois life as a salesman. He died in 1997.[15]

Zinn claims, "The Negro was not as anti-Communist as the white population. He could not afford to be, his friends were so few—so that Herndon, Davis, Robeson, Du Bois, however their political views might be maligned by the country as a whole, found admiration for their fighting spirit in the black community."[16] Zinn—surprise, surprise—provides no statistics for his claim, and the reality is the opposite. Blacks were *less* supportive of Communists than whites because African American leaders believed, correctly, that the Communist Party was exploiting them. Black newspapers warned their readers. In the *Afro-American* in 1939, for example, Claude McKay advised readers to "avoid blindly following any 'isms,' especially communism...." The *Amsterdam News,* which "supported FDR...in the 1936 and 1940 elections" but then endorsed Governor Thomas Dewey in 1944 and 1948, ran "a hostile account of a September 1939 Communist meeting...in which Benjamin J. Davis Jr. and other communists denounced the 'imperialist war' after having been vocal anti-fascists since the Popular Front." One of the paper's reporters "expressed bewilderment" when the black singer and actor Paul Robeson, who had suddenly—when the Hitler-Stalin pact was signed—shifted to an anti-war position after having been "a vocal anti-fascist for several years." According to Davidson College professor Daniel Aldridge, the NAACP kept a "vigilant watch for communist activity in NAACP branches and youth groups" after receiving reports, in November 1946, of attempted Communist takeovers of several branches. W. E. B. Du Bois, though a founder of the NAACP, was dismissed from the group for his Communist views. Black Communist Ben Davis was elected to the New York City Council in 1945. But that was under a citywide "proportional representation system," so that he benefited from the white leftist vote. After the rules were changed in 1947, Davis lost his Harlem district by a three-to-one "margin."[17]

In 1948, presidential candidate Henry Wallace and running mate Glen Taylor, the candidates of the Communist-controlled Progressive Party, fared poorly among blacks. Wallace's decision to call lawmakers who opposed civil rights "murderers" didn't seem to help him with black voters. Neither did his party's platform, which followed the "Marxist line" in rejecting the Marshall Plan and the Truman Doctrine, and in calling "for disarmament talks" to outlaw nuclear weapons, and for the "nationalization of banks and railroads."[18] According to Wilson Record in *The Negro and the Communist Party* it was estimated that "considerably less than ten percent" of the two million votes for Wallace came from blacks. "In Harlem, Wallace ran a poor third to Truman and Dewey," and "the Progressive Party's Negro candidate for the State Senate" was beat out by the white Democratic Party candidate, 55,784 votes to 12,719 votes.[19] Aldridge describes African Americans as "cool" towards Wallace's campaign, even though the Progressive Party had made a "concerted effort" to "address black issues" and run black candidates. He explains, "While prominent African Americans such as Robeson and Du Bois strongly supported Wallace, others, including Roy Wilkins and widely read black journalists such as Pittsburgh Courier's P. L. Prattis and Amsterdam News political columnist Earl Brown advised black voters to reject Wallace, precisely because of alleged communist domination of the Progressive Party." And black New York City voters went for Truman 4-to-1.[20] Record looked at other heavily black areas, such as "[i]n Chicago," where "three congressional candidates in 'Black Metropolis' divided the vote as follows: Democrats 98,204; Republican, 43,620; Progressive, 5,188. A similar distribution was found elsewhere." Record explained in 1951, "The [1948] election results were a blow to the Communist Party, which had placed its entire apparatus behind the Progressives. They were likewise a blow to its Negro program.... the Progressive

Party, contrary to its claims, was not the party of the farmer, the worker, or the Negro."[21] More than a half-century later, David Aldridge countered the thesis that had arisen in the interim among academic historians: that "black anti-communism" was due to a "postwar Red Scare," or fear of government persecution. Aldridge demonstrates that it was actually "grounded in a deep distrust of the Communist Party and the Soviet Union" that had "roots in the prewar period." Black voters voted for anti-Communist Democrats whom they perceived as pro-civil rights.[22]

In a 1951 *Ebony* magazine article, the NAACP's Walter White accused one-time friend Paul Robeson of abandoning blacks for "adulation…from the Soviet Union and from white leftists."[23] Robeson is still cast as a victim of anti-Communist witch hunts. But White's charge is borne out by observations made by David Horowitz, who recalls that there was a "palpable reverence" in the air for Robeson at the Progressive rallies Horowitz attended in his youth: "As he entered the room, a hush stilled the audience, virtually all white, which rose as one and began to clap rhythmically, Soviet style…."[24] Interestingly, Howard Zinn's FBI file indicates that an informant advised agents on July 14, 1948, that Zinn had filed a property damage claim on New York State arising from the Peekskill Riots,[25] which began as protests of a planned Robeson concert. As the October 1, 1950, issue of *Commentary* put it, Peekskill residents could see that the Robeson concerts—which had been taking place yearly since 1946—"could no more be considered mere musical events than a Communist rally in Madison Square Garden." In 1946, one of the Robeson "ushers" had stabbed a local resident and veteran. Sponsored by the Civil Rights Congress, a Communist front group, the concerts "were primarily fund-raising events and Communist demonstrations," and the residents of Peekskill knew it. Military veterans, especially, were angered by Robeson's allegiance to the Soviet Union, which he had publicly announced in 1946 and then reiterated in 1949, stating, "I love this Soviet people more than any other nation…it [is] unthinkable that the Negro people of America or elsewhere in the world could be drawn into war with the Soviet Union."

James Rorty, who wrote the *Commentary* article, described what the Communists were up to: "As for the Communist-controlled Civil

Rights Congress which again sponsored Robeson, its avowed interest in the defense of free speech and assembly was...wholly hypocritical. Those familiar with the Communist program have long recognized that it requires the exploitation of the civil rights issue only with the objective of polarizing extremist passions and sowing the seeds of discord—the more violent the better—that will disrupt the democratic process. What the Communists wanted was another propaganda harvest...."[26]

Howard Zinn would like the reader to believe that the Communist Party helped blacks and treated them with respect, so he does not tell us the story of the first black Communist, Lovett Fort-Whiteman. In 1924, Fort-Whiteman became the first African American to attend a Comintern training school in Moscow and the first national organizer of the American Negro Labor Congress, a Communist Party organization. In 1930, he moved to the Soviet Union. And in 1939, he died there—in the Gulag. In 1998, Harvey Klehr, John Earl Haynes, and Kyrill M. Anderson published *The Soviet World of American Communism*, which drew on Soviet secret police records. They learned from archives in the newly independent Kazakhstan that on July 1, 1937, Fort-Whiteman had been sentenced to five years of internal exile for "anti-Soviet agitation"— largely because *he had criticized Langston Hughes's short stories*. William L. Patterson and James Ford, "high-ranking black CPUSA leaders," were called to lead a meeting with "all the Negro comrades" to decide the fate of Fort-Whiteman after he criticized Hughes.[27] His punishment was changed to five years' hard labor on May 8, 1938, and he died on January 13, 1939, at the age of forty-four[28] after being starved and overworked and then beaten when he could not make quota.[29]

Homer Smith, who moved to the Soviet Union in 1932 to work in the post office and then served as a correspondent for black publications, met Fort-Whiteman, who with Langston Hughes and a cast of about twenty, were to make the anti-American propaganda film *Black and White* (the project was abandoned when the Soviets sought diplomatic relations with the U.S.). Smith described Fort-Whiteman in his 1964 memoir, *Black Man in Red Russia*, as someone who had acted as the "mentor" of other black

Americans living in Russia, thus continuing the work he had done in the U.S. On speaking tours, Fort-Whiteman "pleaded fervently for...support for the Scottsboro boys and Angelo Herndon" and "expounded loud and long on lynchings, Jim Crow and the oppression of his people in America, and condemned with fiery emotions the enslavement of black people in the African colonies of European imperialist nations." But none of that saved him from death in the Gulag. And Smith himself only narrowly escaped Fort-Whiteman's fate.[30]

Robert Robinson, a black machinist and engineer who also moved to the Soviet Union, found himself trapped there for forty-four years. In his 1988 book *Black on Red: A Black Man's Forty-Four Years inside the Soviet Union*, Robinson recalled meeting Fort-Whiteman and noted his disappearance. During his time in the Soviet Union, he met Paul Robeson and asked for help in getting out. Robeson refused. Robeson also betrayed Jews. In the 1950s, after returning from trips to the Soviet Union, Robeson lied to those who asked about the Yiddish poet Itzik Feffer, claiming that he was being treated well. Soon Feffer and other Jews "vanished" into the Gulag.[31]

Meanwhile, real African American heroes—blacks who fought and won the battles for civil rights—don't figure largely in Zinn's account. The significant achievements of black labor and civil rights activist A. Philip Randolph, for example, are obscured by Zinn—perhaps because Randolph was an anti-communist who quit the National Negro Congress in 1940 because it "had fallen under the control" of Communist Party allies.[32] There are only three mentions of Randolph in *A People's History*—two of them quotations that have no bearing on what Randolph accomplished and are adduced simply to support Zinn's picture of the black population "in the streets" and spoiling for a socialist revolution.[33] The single substantive mention of Randolph is in relation to the protest that brought about the Fair Employment Practices Committee (FEPC), which Zinn claims "had no enforcement powers and changed little."[34]

But, in fact, Randolph and NAACP leaders succeeded in opening up opportunities for blacks, including via the FEPC. They politically maneuvered FDR by appealing to his sympathetic wife. Their actions on behalf of black soldiers and black federal workers raised the standard of living for many blacks. The FEPC, reports William J. Collins in the *American Economic Review*, "was the direct outcome of A. Philip Randolph's threat to lead 100,000 people in a march on Washington to protest the meager opportunities for black workers in defense-related employment, including the armed forces." Collins's research contradicts Zinn's claims that "the nation...kept blacks in low-paying jobs."[35] The FEPC, which was "established to receive, investigate, and resolve complaints of discrimination by Executive Order 8802," which outlawed discrimination in defense industries, did have some success and started the upward trajectory in terms of wage growth for blacks. Collins explains that "between 1940 and 1950 the proportion of black male workers classified as operatives (semi-skilled workers) in the Census rose from 12.6 to 21.4 percent (whites went from 19.0 to 20.2 percent), and the proportion of manufacturing industries rose from 16.2 to 23.9 percent (whites went from 25.5 to 27.7)." In a previous study, he had found that "black men who worked in war-related industries during the 1940's and who were still working in such industries in 1950 earned a substantial premium (around 14 percent) over observationally similar black men who did not enter these industries." True, improvement did not come instantaneously and uniformly. But Collins describes what the FEPC *was* able to do: "FEPC intervention altered the racial balance some firms struck in their hiring decisions by (1) providing advice on how to integrate the workplace, (2) giving managers a ready excuse for hiring blacks if white workers objected, (3) threatening to bring more powerful government agencies into the fray...(4) publicly embarrassing firms and unions that refused to hire blacks." In summary, "The FEPC appears to have accelerated the pace of black economic advancement," according to Collins, who also notes that this economic advancement continued through the twentieth century.[36]

The FEPC came as a consequence of the campaign for an integrated military and for African Americans' "right to fight"—rather than just serve in support positions in the military. In 1938, the ten-member bipartisan *Pittsburgh Courier* National Steering Committee had campaigned for Republican congressman Hamilton Fish's House Bills 10164, 10165, and 10166, which would "abolish discrimination in the Army," "provide for the creation of a Negro division," and "appoint Negroes to West Point."[37] These efforts had only limited success at the time on account of opposition by FDR and the Southern Democrats. But Randolph was satisfied for the time being with Executive Order 8802 on June 25, 1941, at a time when it looked like the U.S. would become involved in war. He did not want to interfere with the war efforts, so an end to segregation in the military would have to wait.[38]

But in 1947, Randolph and Grant Reynolds, commissioner of correction for New York State, founded the Committee Against Jim Crow in the Military Service and Training—which expanded early in 1948 into the League for Nonviolent Civil Disobedience Against Military Segregation, as Jervis Anderson recounts in his 1972 biography of Randolph: "On March 22, 1948, after Randolph had made it clear that the civil disobedience movement would be satisfied with nothing less than an executive order against military segregation, President Truman invited a group of black spokesmen to the White House to discuss the subject. Among them were Randolph, Walter White, Mary McLeod Bethune, Lester Granger, and Charles Houston, a special counsel for the NAACP."

Randolph told the president that the "mood among Negroes of this country is that they will never bear arms again until all forms of bias and discrimination are abolished."

Nine days later, Randolph testified on the universal military training bill in Congress, telling the committee, "This time Negroes will not take jim crow lying down. The conscience of the world will be shaken as by nothing else when thousands and thousands of us second-class Americans choose imprisonment in preference to permanent military slavery...." Randolph threatened to advise blacks to refuse to serve. And during the Democratic National Convention in Philadelphia in July 1948, when Hubert Humphrey "was waging his historic fight against the Dixiecrats to obtain a strong civil rights plank in the party's platform, scores of blacks led by Randolph were picketing the convention hall." According to Anderson, it was "the combined pressure of the Randolph campaign, the Humphrey civil rights floor fight, and the need to retain the black vote in the November election" that led President Truman to issue Executive Order 9981 ending racial discrimination in the military. When he received confirmation from Truman's spokesman that segregation would be ended, "Randolph called off the civil disobedience campaign and wired congratulations" to Truman for his "high order of statesmanship and courage."[39] The reader of *A People's History* will learn none of this.

Besides failing to celebrate individual heroes of the fight for civil rights, Howard Zinn was also not a big fan—either as an author or as an activist—of the black group that was most responsible for African Americans' legal progress in the Civil Rights Movement: the NAACP. We have seen how in 1960 he was instrumental in organizing the Student Nonviolent Coordinating Committee (SNCC). That radical group soon pushed its way into the civil rights spotlight and elbowed aside the NAACP.[40]

Along with Ella Baker, the executive director of the Southern Christian Leadership Conference who spearheaded the initiative, Zinn attended the initial SNCC conference in 1960 as one of the "middle-aged radicals"—adults who served as mentors to the college and high school students. Zinn describes the founding in his autobiography: "SNNC...had been formed...when veterans of the recent sit-ins got together in Raleigh, North Carolina. Inspiring and overseeing its beginning was the extraordinary Ella Baker, veteran of struggles in Harlem and elsewhere...." Later, Zinn was asked to join SNCC's executive committee as one of their two "'adult advisers,' along with [Baker]."[41] He was "principal speaker" at the 1963 annual meeting in Atlanta and returned to speak again in 1964, when he reminded attendees that in spite of integration of schools in the South and of communities in the East and the "liberalizing" of hiring policies in the West, they should not "become oblivious of Negroes in Mississippi where Jim Crow and terror still rule supreme."[42] Zinn just loved to tell young people how *bad* things were. And as we have already seen, he had more sway in the organization than he let on.

SNCC, unlike the NAACP—which in the 1950s heeded Justice Department memos warning that Communists were targeting its youth divisions—was friendly to Communists and Communist sympathizers.[43] In its first year, the John F. Kennedy administration had ended government programs to educate the public about Communism, and military leaders were dissuaded from speaking out against it.[44]

And Zinn did what he could to move young black activists in a more radical direction—closer to Communism. Zinn had made clear in a 1960 article in the *Nation* that it was his goal to transform Spelman College into a "school for protest."[45] In his 1964 book *SNCC: The New Abolitionists*, he described the traditional classroom experience as "pallid and unrewarding" because it is "divorced from the reality of social struggle." He criticized "Negro colleges" for their "century-long traditions of conservatism and obsequiousness." Only "militant students," he stated, could become civil rights leaders.[46] On the question of whether SNCC was Communist—suspicions arose because the group received support from Carl Braden's Southern Conference Education Fund and the National Lawyers Guild—Zinn wrote that "SNCC workers are young, and they have grown up in a world where there is no longer any single meaning of 'Communism' or 'Communist,' where varieties of communism develop in different parts of the world...."[47]

Apparently, Zinn was responsible for the solo trip of one of his favorite students, Marian Wright Edelman, in 1959 as a nineteen-year-old to study and travel in Europe and summer at a youth camp in the Soviet Union. He had nominated her for the Merrill Scholarship and dissuaded her from traveling with a group from a women's college.[48]

According to his FBI file, Zinn was "host for [a] soviet youth delegation in 1961," had sponsored the Student Peace Union Group in 1962, and was reportedly trying to recruit students to attend the Soviet-sponsored Eighth World Youth Festival in Finland in 1962—exactly the kind of thing the NAACP had been steering youth leaders away from. And in his role as founder and head of the Non-Western Studies Program, funded by the Ford Foundation, Zinn had hosted Owen Lattimore of Johns Hopkins University, and formerly of the Institute of Pacific Relations, as a speaker in 1961. Zinn's FBI report referred to the Senate Judiciary Report #2050 of July 2, 1952, which called IPR "a vehicle used by the Communists to orientate American...policies toward Communist objectives." The youth festival was a project, in part, of the International Union of Students, which was described as a "communist organization" in HUAC's "Guide to Subversive Organizations and Publications."[49] (Lattimore's role in the disastrous Communist takeover of China has been noted in the previous chapter.)

SNCC members were happy to cooperate with the CPUSA, for example on behalf of the National Committee to Abolish the House Un-American Activities Committee (HUAC). Letters from executive director Frank Wilkinson, a member of the CPUSA,[50] and other members inviting SNCC to join their efforts began arriving soon after SNCC was launched.[51] On May 22, 1964, Wilkinson lobbied John Lewis and James Forman of SNCC and Robert Moses of the Council of Federated Organizations (COFO), which included SNCC, on behalf of two individuals who wanted to participate in the Mississippi Summer Project.[52]

SNCC used the NAACP for travel expenses, attorney fees, bail, and fines—while pushing it aside. On September 1, 1961, NAACP executive secretary Roy Wilkins wrote to Edward King, executive secretary of SNCC, complaining, "We cannot commit ourselves to free-wheeling activity planned and launched by another organization." He added in a postscript, "We have received persistent reports, which we hope very much are in error, that your Committee has had a more or less formal intention of 'involving the NAACP whether they like it or not in situations where they cannot escape embarrassment unless they come along.' We don't intend to be embarrassed, if at all possible, and especially in a voter-registration campaign that, so far, seems to have put more workers in jail than it has voters on the books."[53]

In another letter in November of the same year, Wilkins complained that SNCC's Mississippi voter drive had "added only 18 names to the registered voter list," but saddled the NAACP with "a minimum $15,000 in bills for fines, bail, appeal bonds, lawyer's fees, travel and other expenses."[54]

Eventually, the NAACP did "come along," changing course to keep up with the "direct action" campaigns of SNCC—much to the dismay of NAACP stalwarts like George Schuyler, and to the delight of Howard Zinn, who wrote in his 1964 book *SNCC: The New Abolitionists*, that "the student movement galvanized the older organizations into a new dynamism" and "won the support of some of the established Negro leaders who quickly sensed that a new wind was blowing."[55]

Zinn may have had more to do with the pressure put on the NAACP than he has let on. In his diary entry of January 13, 1963, he confided that someone from the NAACP had told another activist, Dotty Dawson, that Zinn was a "controversial figure," and that someone from the Anti-Defamation League told another activist that Zinn was "a Communist." Five days later, Zinn described a conversation with Spelman colleague Les Dunbar about Communism. Dunbar had told the ADL person that Zinn's "ideological and policy stances, from what Dunbar knew, precluded my being a Communist." In response to Zinn's query about having Communists in a civil rights organization, Dunbar had replied, "I don't want them." Zinn expressed his opinion that "the only basis for acting against a person was specific empirical data showing this person was acting in a harmful way." It was difficult to "*know* if a person is a Communist," Zinn had told Dunbar; charges from HUAC and the FBI were unreliable, he claimed.[56]

Zinn did not like the NAACP, which was founded in 1909, and which grew out of the Niagara Movement, a group of twenty-nine prominent African Americans led by W. E. B. Du Bois and William Trotter, who were representative of the assertive, educated, and independent "New Negro." They met near Niagara Falls in 1905 and drew up a manifesto for full civil rights. The NAACP was so highly esteemed that its principals met with presidents. It had won several significant legal cases, among them the *Sweet* case of 1925 in which a black Detroit homeowner was exonerated after protecting his home from a mob of whites by shooting and killing one of them in self-defense and the Elaine, Arkansas, riots trials—which culminated in a 1925 Supreme Court ruling that a trial conducted in a mob atmosphere violated legal due process. Neither case is mentioned in Zinn's history. He does discuss the 1905 Niagara meeting, but attributes the "formation" of the NAACP (erroneously, in 1910) to "a race riot in Springfield, Illinois" (only the partial reason). Zinn presents the founders of the NAACP not as the interracial group they were, but as dominated by whites, with W. E. B. Du Bois as its "only black officer." Zinn leaves it at that, not mentioning the fact that by the 1920s the organization's leadership was black-dominated. When the Ku Klux Klan resurged in the 1920s, Zinn comments, "the NAACP seemed helpless in the face of mob violence and race hatred everywhere."[57] Far from being helpless, the NAACP was at the forefront of the effort to stop lynchings and improve the lot of blacks in the Jim Crow South. But Zinn ignores the work of black NAACP attorney Charles Houston and downplays that of Thurgood Marshall; he omits the daring forays to the South by Walter White to investigate lynchings, and by Roy Wilkins and George Schuyler in the 1930s to investigate abuses of black Southern levee workers.

In downplaying the role of the NAACP in the battle for civil rights and exaggerating that of the Communist Party, Howard Zinn was, once again, following the Communist Party propaganda line. In his 1951 *History of the Communist Party of the United States*, Communist Party USA general secretary William Z. Foster had claimed that it was the party's legal arm, the International Legal Defense (ILD), that had made the Scottsboro case known. It had sent "its lawyer, the veteran Communist Joseph Brodsky" to prevent the legal lynching. According to Foster, "the A.F. of L., the S.P., A.C.L.U., and even the N.A.A.C.P. displayed no interest in the case."[58]

That's the Communist Party line—from the time of the original events to Zinn's *A People's History*. The April 10, 1931, *Daily Worker* printed a statement from the Central Committee of the Communist Party USA claiming that "'reformist' organizations…such as the National Association for the Advancement of Colored People, the Universal Negro Improvement Association, the Urban League, etc" would "betray the Negro masses." It also announced that a telegram had informed the governor that the Communist ILD was sending an attorney to offer the defendants legal services.[59]

Black weekly newspapers soon reported the dire situation in Alabama, with the *Chicago Defender* reporting briefly on April 4,[60] and then providing more extensive coverage two weeks later along with the other major black newspapers, the *Pittsburgh Courier* and the *Afro-American*.[61] At that point, readers learned that the NAACP was putting together a legal strategy. As the *Afro-American* was reporting on the NAACP's progress in its May 2 issue, in the same issue it was reporting how the CPUSA was undermining the organization by sponsoring riots. On May 2, the *Afro-American* reported on a riot started in Harlem by an interracial group of Communist protestors who carried signs calling to "Smash Scottsboro Frame-Up."[62] This was the first of many riots fomented and paid for by the Soviet Union and supported by a propaganda campaign in its multiple publications.

· After NAACP Executive Secretary Walter White secured an agreement for representation of four of the Scottsboro defendants, the Communist ILD sent out a statement that the defendants had "repudiated it."[63] A few days later, the *Courier* quoted a statement from White saying, in part, that the NAACP "cannot cooperate with the Communists who have vilified the N.A.A.C.P., accused it in documents submitted for the signature of the boys' parents of being traitorous, and have stopped at nothing to exclude the N.A.A.C.P. from the case, then proceed[ed] to charge the N.A.A.C.P. with failure to cooperate."[64] The Communists were denounced by the *Pittsburgh Courier*[65] and the Chattanooga City Interdenominational Ministers' Alliance of Negro Divines.[66]

Throughout that summer, Communists tried to shut down NAACP meetings. On Chicago's south side, they "heckled" NAACP assistant field secretary William Pickens and were charged with "inciting a riot."[67] Pickens was again heckled and "jostled" at meetings in New York and Boston.[68] Communists even showed up at the NAACP's annual meeting in Pittsburgh and distributed flyers stating, "The workers of Pittsburgh must brand the leaders of the N.A.A.C.P. as traitors of the Negro masses."[69]

The *New York Times* reported that the NAACP's Pickens had accused the Communists of a willingness to "sacrifice these Negro boys to their party ambitions"[70] and that German Communist newspapers were "making capital of the Scottsboro convictions" and "fervently appealing to Reds everywhere to 'save the victims of judicial murder.'" Everywhere included the American Consulate in Berlin, where windows were smashed, and Dresden and Leipzig, where riots took place.[71]

While the eight defendants (the case against twelve-year-old Roy Wright, the youngest, had ended in a mistrial) languished in prison that summer, black sharecroppers in nearby Camp Hill, Alabama, organized by Communists into the "Share Croppers' Union" met to protest the Scottsboro case and to "press...demands" on landowners. At least one African American was killed, thirty-four were imprisoned, and four others disappeared.[72] The Communist organizers had fled the scene.

The NAACP's White expressed his frustrations in a lengthy article in the December 1931 *Harper's Magazine* on the "'united front'" ruse, and the suspicion "in the Negro mind...more than confirmed—that at least some of the Communists did not want the nine boys saved but sought instead to make 'martyrs' of them for the purposes of spreading Communist propaganda among Negroes."[73] But by January 1932, the ILD had wrested the case away from the NAACP.[74]

More bloodshed came in December 1932, when, as James Goodman relates in *Stories of Scottsboro*, "Tallapoosa County sharecroppers, encouraged by Communists to form a union, picked up guns in resistance to whites," who had simply "served a writ of attachment to cover a bad debt." As a result, "several sharecroppers were killed."[75]

The Communists made "trouble" not only among Alabama share-croppers, but also among mill workers, miners, and the unemployed, and they imposed themselves "whenever and wherever a Negro was accused of rape." In Tuscaloosa, in July 1933, when "three Negroes" were arrested for the rape and murder of a young woman, an ILD lawyer on the first day of the hearing "insisted that he and his two associates had been retained by the defendants," even though relatives of the accused had already hired other lawyers and told the judge so. "A few thousand Tuscaloosans" who had "gathered outside the courthouse" had also made it clear that the Communist involvement in the case was not welcome, but the ILD from New York "immediately announced it would continue to fight for the defense and sent a telegram to the judge," which "warned that 'two hundred thousand members' were prepared to expose his 'illegal maneuvers' as another Scottsboro." Before the trial, rumors that the ILD would be back insisting on a "change of venue" and that the prosecution had made "a secret deal" against prosecution "fueled reports that a lynch mob was planning to storm the Tuscaloosa jail." As a result, the prisoners were ordered to be transferred to Birmingham. During transit, twelve masked men hijacked the vehicle, and shot the prisoners, killing two of the three.[76]

Apparently, Zinn, who presents the Communist Party as the only hope for African Americans, wasn't disturbed by the bloodshed. Journalists and members of the NAACP spoke out against the Communists' recklessness with black lives, but of course Zinn doesn't quote their statements of protest. George Schuyler, for example—beginning when he heard about the Scottsboro case in 1931 up through his 1966 autobiography and on— expressed his anger at the Communists' callous use of blacks. Schuyler, who grew up in a working-class family in Syracuse and had served two enlistments in the segregated army, began his journalistic career in 1923 at the black socialist magazine the *Messenger*. The next year, he also started writing for the *Pittsburgh Courier*, which by the 1930s was the leading black newspaper.

On August 15, 1931, he charged "the Communist racketeers" with giving "the murderous Southern Neanderthals the very opportunity and excuse they are looking for to commit additional homicide."[77] Two weeks later, he accused the Communists of wanting "electrocutions, massacres and savage sentences in order that they may have concrete cases on which to base their propaganda." He charged, accurately, that the CPUSA's purported help to American blacks was undertaken at the behest and for the benefit of the Kremlin. Schuyler also took note of self-contradictions in the Communist propaganda: the Communists had found a "score of 'mothers'" for the "eight condemned lads" and they were busy collecting donations for a defense fund while at the same time "maintain[ing] that no justice" could be "obtained in the capitalist courts."[78]

In his May 6, 1933, column, Schuyler claimed that "Communist liars" had got to the boys and their parents by "swearing the N.A.A.C.P. wanted the defendants electrocuted. They were also doubtless influenced by the fact that the I.L.D. was a white organization. Even then the N.A.A.C.P. offered to cooperate, but the Communists, thinking this case an excellent wedge to get the colored brother with Red propaganda, refused." Then the Communists had "bungled matters almost beyond repair"[79]—by, for example, intentionally prolonging the fundraising period by not filing a bill of exceptions in time for a new trial.[80] It was the Communists' total disregard for the safety and well-being of actual African Americans that opened the eyes of the originally socialist Schuyler and inspired his steady stream of denunciations—which, in turn, inspired threats from the Communists, prompting the journalist to keep a loaded pistol next to his typewriter. The headline of Schuyler's June 23, 1934, *Pittsburgh Courier* editorial complained about "Another Communist 'Victory'"—in the Ku Klux Klan's resurgence.[81]

The assistance of the NAACP was eventually instrumental in freeing the Scottsboro defendants, but only after many wasted years behind bars thanks to the Communists' bungling of the case. The last two "Scottsboro Boys" were not paroled until 1944. The record shows that the

Communist Party exploited those who needed help most. It was willing to sacrifice black lives.

Zinn similarly prioritizes revolutionary violence over the real lives of the actual "people" he claims to be speaking for. So, naturally, he was dismayed to report that the "black militant mood" that had been "flashing here and there in the thirties" was "reduced to a subsurface simmering during World War II, when the nation on the one hand denounced racism, and on the other hand maintained segregation in the armed forces and kept blacks in low-paying jobs." Zinn casts aspersions on the motives of the reformers of the post–World War II era and on the very real improvements they helped bring about for African Americans. For Zinn, President Harry Truman's postwar civil rights efforts were nothing more than "cold war rivalry" efforts to "calm a black population," and "to present to the world a United States that could counter the continuous Communist thrust at the most flagrant failure of American society."[82]

Zinn couldn't muster any enthusiasm for Truman's Committee on Civil Rights, which, in 1947, recommended expanding the civil rights section of the Justice Department, establishing a permanent Commission on Civil Rights, and passing laws against lynching and job and voting discrimination. He charges that these reforms weren't being pushed for purely "moral" reasons: "there was also an 'economic reason'—discrimination was costly to the country, wasteful of its talent. And, perhaps most important, there was an international reason"—namely "world supremacy."[83]

Not only were Truman's reforms for the wrong reasons, but they also weren't fast enough. The United States took "small actions." He grudgingly admits that "Truman—four months before the presidential election of 1948, and challenged from the left in that election by Progressive party candidate Henry Wallace—issued an executive order asking that the armed forces, segregated in World War II, institute policies of racial equality 'as rapidly as possible.'" But again, for the wrong motives: "The order may have been prompted not only by the election but by the need to maintain high morale in the military, as the possibility of war grew." Plus, Truman could have done more: "Truman could have issued executive orders in other areas, but did not. The Fourteenth and Fifteenth Amendments, plus the set of laws passed in the 1860s and early 1870s, gave the President enough authority to wipe out discrimination." Even given Zinn's exaggeration of the president's power—he seems to have forgotten not only the other branches of government, but also the political constraints on what office-holders can get away with—no federal action could ever completely "wipe out discrimination." Even Zinn knows this, as he himself points out in regard to the sweeping 1954 *Brown v. Board of Education* decision by the Supreme Court: "By 1965, ten years after the 'all deliberate speed' guideline, more than 75 percent of the school districts in the South remained segregated."[84]

Nevertheless, as even Zinn acknowledged—in his August 1959 article for *Harper's Monthly*, "A Fate Worse Than Integration"—racial barriers were coming down in the post-War years. Thanks, in part, to capitalism. As Zinn observed in the late fifties, Southerners' concerns with profit-making, peaceful coexistence, manners, and law-and-order were naturally leading to improved race relations and increased voting and economic power for blacks. When a "bold Negro student" would take a seat in a white section of a bus, no one would say anything, and black bus drivers were accepted. "Growing Negro purchasing power" meant that at Rich's Department Store in Atlanta, black women tried on and purchased the same clothing as white women and that white salesmen sometimes addressed Negro customers with "Yes, Sir." White men made deliveries to the back doors of the homes of affluent Negro lawyers and "white employees of a contractor [dug] ditches on the campus of a Negro university."[85] In an October 1959 article in the NAACP's *Crisis*, Zinn described the uneventful way that the Atlanta public library was desegregated—through a steady stream of Spelman professors and students asking to check out materials but also preparing for a lawsuit. The pressure worked. The library's board of trustees voted to desegregate.[86] Zinn reported these peaceful, incremental civil rights victories as they happened, but in *A People's History* he was never going to acknowledge the reality of such quiet social change.

Instead, he reports with excitement that blacks "rose in rebellion all over the South" and that "in the late 1960s they were engaging in wild insurrection in a hundred northern cities. It was all a surprise to those without that deep memory of slavery, that everyday presence of humiliation, registered in the poetry, the music, the occasional outbursts of anger, the more frequent sullen silences. Part of that memory was of words uttered, laws passed, decisions made, which turned out to be meaningless."

Zinn casts the peacefully conducted and effective Montgomery Bus Boycott as part of the "wild insurrection"; in fact, he introduced it as an example of "revolt" in the immediately following paragraph: "For such a people, with such a memory, and such daily recapitulation of history, revolt was always minutes away, in a timing mechanism which no one had set, but which might go off with some unpredictable set of events. Those events came, at the end of 1955, in the capital city of Alabama—Montgomery."[87]

Unsurprisingly, Zinn downplays the role of the NAACP and its moderate leaders in the Bus Boycott. The first two editions of A People's History omitted any mention of E. D. Nixon, the Alabama NAACP leader who organized the Boycott. Zinn had apparently ignored a letter from Walter G. Hooke, a reader in Cambridge, New York, about including the courageous leader. Hooke wrote Zinn again in July 1995 when the newly released second edition did not include any mention of Nixon.[88] Finally in the 2003 edition, Zinn included a line about Nixon: "Montgomery blacks called a mass meeting. A powerful force in the community was E. D. Nixon, a veteran trade unionist and experienced organizer. There was a vote to boycott all city buses. Car pools were organized to take Negroes to work."[89]

With that bland description of Nixon and the passive construction of the last sentence—"were organized"—Zinn sweeps away decades of work by Nixon. In contrast, contemporary dispatches from the South by Pittsburgh Courier "roving reporter" Trezzvant Anderson give one a sense of how many hours of careful strategizing, often in secret, went into the boycott. And in a retrospective article in 1957, Anderson described how Nixon had built the local NAACP organization up from "400 to nearly 2,000 members," "organized" a local for the Pullman Porters, taken "an active role" in Randolph's planned March on Washington, and gotten a USO for black soldiers during World War II. Nixon's work had eliminated a segregated "peephole window" at which black customers had had to buy tickets at the Montgomery train station, and he had "put up the bond" and gotten the attorney for his secretary, Rosa Parks, after she was arrested. Nixon was the organizer of the boycott, calling the first meeting and bringing together the principals. As Anderson wrote, "the beginning of the boycott was triggered by the same E.D. Nixon, who had for 25 years stood in the forefront of the battle for equal opportunity for Negroes in Montgomery." Anderson called Nixon "the real dynamo behind the Montgomery bus boycott." It was not "the Rev. Dr. King—despite all the publicity and awards since given him—but an unlettered, six-foot three-inch Pullman porter, E.D. Nixon...." But as Anderson explained, Nixon magnanimously stepped aside and let the more polished young Martin Luther King Jr. take the spotlight.[90]

If there ever was a good candidate to be one of the overlooked "people" whose history Zinn claimed to be writing, it would be E. D. Nixon. But Zinn has little time for the stories of African Americans who worked on peaceful campaigns for civil rights, especially when they did it without the help of Communists. Zinn clearly hoped that "the frightening explosiveness of the black upsurge"[91] could be useful in bringing about some kind of socialist revolution or other radical transformation of America.

Zinn himself spent time organizing in Albany, Georgia, which he describes as "a small deep-South town where the atmosphere of slavery still lingered." Mass demonstrations "took place in the winter of 1961 and again in 1962. Of 22,000 black people in Albany, over a thousand went to jail for marching, assembling, to protest segregation and discrimination. Here as in all the demonstrations that would sweep over the South, little black children participated—a new generation was learning to act." Triumphantly, Zinn writes, "There is no way of measuring the effect of that southern movement on the sensibilities of a whole generation of young black people...."[92]

SNCC and Southern Christian Leadership Conference (SCLC) workers were putting children in harm's way, going to schools and recruiting teenagers and even children over the wishes of their parents. This had to be done for lack of adult volunteers: the majority of Southern blacks, although in favor of ending segregation, were opposed to the mass demonstration strategies that Zinn celebrates, especially when they led to jail, as Zinn describes: "In Birmingham in 1963, thousands of blacks went into the streets, facing police clubs, tear gas, dogs, high-powered water hoses. And meanwhile, all over the deep South, the young people of SNCC, mostly black, a few white, were moving into communities in Georgia, Alabama, Mississippi, Arkansas. Joined by local black people, they were organizing, to register people to vote, to protest against racism, to build up courage against violence.... imprisonment became commonplace, beatings became frequent."[93]

Zinn has to acknowledge that "Civil rights laws were passed in 1957, 1960, and 1964," and the Voting Rights Act in 1965, and even that "The effect on Negro voting in the South was dramatic." But he pooh-poohs these victories, and the very civil rights for which blacks had been struggling for so long: "The federal government was trying—without making fundamental changes—to control an explosive situation, to channel anger into the traditional cooling mechanism of the ballot box, the polite petition, the officially endorsed quiet gathering."[94] Wait, we ask, weren't the protests *for* the right to vote? Yet Zinn casts the ballot box—and virtually every other element of political and civic life in a democracy—as a mere "cooling mechanism."

Even the March on Washington in 1963 was nothing for Zinn because it "was quickly embraced by President Kennedy and other national leaders, and turned into a friendly assemblage." If it isn't marked by violence and explosive anger, Zinn can't get excited about it. Though King's "I Have a Dream" speech was "magnificent oratory," it failed to capture "that anger that many blacks felt." SNCC chairman John Lewis, "a young Alabama-born SNCC leader, much arrested, much beaten," was censored, the sentences in his speech urging "militant action" taken out.[95] Zinn does not report the cut sentences, statements about the "the revolution" being "at hand" to free "ourselves of the chains of political and economic slavery," and a threat to march "through the heart of Dixie, the way Sherman did."[96]

In contrast, and despite its name, the Student Nonviolent Coordinating Committee that Zinn had helped to found had no problem with that kind of rhetoric. A September 25, 1966, article by *New York Times* reporter Gene Roberts opened with an anecdote about SNCC member Willie Ricks firing up a crowd of about a thousand at the fairgrounds in Yazoo City, Mississippi, with talk of "white blood flowing" and yells of "'black power.'" Roberts observed that "Rarely is a Snick [SNCC] office without an handful of copies of such publications as *The Worker* or *People's World*, both organs of the Communist party; *Freedomways*, a Marxist magazine; *The Militant*, a Trotskyite newspaper; *The National Guardian*, which is oriented toward both the Soviet Union and Communist China." SNCC Chairman Stokely Carmichael had turned a demonstration in Atlanta into a riot over Labor Day weekend. Understandably, SNCC members were not welcomed by black locals. In the Vine City section of Atlanta, residents drove out Bill Ware, a SNCC project director, when he tried to run out a white social worker with his sound truck. "At times, the anger of the poor has turned against Snick intellectuals," Roberts noted.[97]

In the summer of 1967, Hubert G. "Rap" Brown, Carmichael's successor as SNCC chairman, called for mob violence—on the very same day that President Lyndon Johnson, in an attempt to calm rampant rioting, was addressing and acknowledging "the conditions that breed despair and violence," such as "ignorance, discrimination, slums, poverty, disease, not enough jobs." In his August 1 column, David Lawrence noted the irony that the same day that the president was blaming "ignorance" for the riots, the college-educated Brown was "publicly urging Negroes to 'to shoot and loot,' calling the President 'a wild, mad dog, an outlaw from Texas,' and declaring that Johnson had sent 'white killers' and federal troops 'into Negro communities to kill black people.'" At a speech in Washington, Brown had called the killing of a white policeman a "'beautiful' example of black people controlling their community," and he had inspired a riot in Cambridge, Maryland.[98]

Black residents quite forcefully put out the unwelcome mat for black militants. The claim that Malcolm X "was probably closer to the mood of the black community" than the "quiet dignity'" of the March on Washington that President Kennedy had praised is another of Zinn's lies. As the young scholar Michael Javen Fortner shows in *Black Silent Majority,* his book about the drug and violence epidemics in Harlem, "Throughout the 1960s, polls consistently showed that only a tiny minority of blacks embraced black nationalists and militants." A 1964 survey in New York City showed that only 6 percent of blacks believed that Malcolm X was "doing the best for Negroes." In contrast, 55 percent said it was the NAACP and 22 percent said it was Wilkins, the NAACP's leader. "In a 1966 national Harris Poll, 62 percent of African Americans said Wilkins was 'helping' the 'Negro cause of Civil Rights,' while only 18 percent said black power advocate Stokely Carmichael was helping. In fact, 34 percent said Carmichael was hurting the cause." A *Newsweek* poll showed similar results. Fortner describes the divide between white liberals and African Americans who were surrounded by criminals and drug addicts in their neighborhoods. He points out, "While conservative white elites condemned the violent tactics of black militants and liberal white elites justified them, the black silent majority felt invisible—unheard and unanswered."[99] Black New Yorkers formed vigilante groups to keep trouble-makers out of their neighborhoods and lobbied for severe drug laws. Harlem pastor Oberia Dempsey, who packed a pistol as he led armed citizen patrols, clashed continuously with white liberals.[100]

But Zinn took no real interest in the problems of the working-class residents of Harlem or Vine City. Those aren't the "people" *A People's History* focuses on. Instead, Zinn valorizes black militants—who might be useful for the socialist revolution. He devotes nearly a full page to four paragraphs from Malcolm X's radical speech in Detroit, which happened two months after the 1963 Martin Luther King march he dismissed.

We have seen how Zinn was unimpressed by the passage of history-changing civil rights legislation and the upsurge in black voting. "It did not work," *A People's History* explains. "The blacks could not be easily brought into 'the democratic coalition' when bombs kept exploding in churches, when new 'civil rights' laws did not change the root condition of black people." Notice how he puts "civil rights" in quotation marks. Again, "The civil rights bills emphasized the voting, but voting was not a fundamental solution to racism or poverty."[101] This is four pages after Zinn has heralded SNCC's voter registration drives[102]—which, as we have seen, were more notable for inspiring outbreaks of violence than for actually registering voters. At the SNCC annual meeting in 1963, Zinn told students that voting does not matter.[103] An odd thing to tell young people, unless you want to disillusion them and make them want a revolution. It's almost as if Zinn wanted to sabotage the Civil Rights Movement. In fact, the Marxist class struggle, not civil rights for blacks, was his real agenda. He was obviously indulging in wishful thinking when he asked, with respect to developments during the Nixon administration, "Was there fear that blacks would turn their attention from the controllable field of voting to the more dangerous arena of wealth and poverty—of class conflict?" Why "more dangerous"? "The new emphasis was more dangerous than civil rights, because it created the possibility of blacks and whites uniting on the issue of class exploitation."[104] Zinn might as well go ahead and chant the old Soviet slogan: "Black and white, unite and fight!" Like any real leftist, Zinn was never satisfied with reforms; he wanted more radical, revolutionary change. He claimed in his 1974 book *Justice in Everyday Life: The Way It Really Works* that reforms "from Woodrow Wilson to Franklin Roosevelt to Lyndon Johnson have not changed the facts of a class structure in America," and "all the civil rights laws have not changed the fact that most blacks, on the job, in school, where they live, grow up knowing that they once were slaves, that whites know it too...."[105] In *A People's History*, Zinn did everything he could to foment bitterness and anger about that historical injustice—not for the sake of civil rights for blacks, but to further his socialist cause. In effect, it was a way to help promote his new "Marxian vision," adapted for the current situation, which he described in a 1969 article titled "Marxism and the New Left." There, Zinn proposed that the "Negroes in the ghetto" should replace Marx's "industrial proletariat as the revolutionary agent."[106]

Zinn seems to luxuriate in the racial violence of the 1960s, describing "black outbreaks in every part of the country." One of these, in Florida, was "set off by the killing of a Negro woman and a bomb threat against a Negro high school." Another, in Cleveland, was sparked by "the killing of a white minister who sat in the path of a bulldozer to protest discrimination against blacks in construction work," and another in New York was a result of "the fatal shooting of a fifteen-year-old Negro boy during a fight with an off-duty policeman." Zinn reports, on a note of triumph, "There were riots also in Rochester, Jersey City, Chicago, Philadelphia."[107] In the New York case, the grand jury, upon which George Schuyler served, determined that the policeman had acted in self-defense.[108]

Zinn claims the Watts riots of 1965 were "provoked by the forcible arrest of a young Negro driver, the clubbing of a bystander by police, the seizure of a young black woman falsely accused of spitting on the police. There was rioting in the streets, looting and firebombing of stores. Police and National Guardsmen were called in; they used their guns." He offers a short quotation from the preface of a book on the riots by Robert Conot: "the Negro was going on record that he would no longer turn the other cheek." There was a "new mood in SNCC and among many militant blacks."[109] Zinn absolutely revels in the replacement of Christian ethics and law and order with violence and mayhem. His project of transforming college students from devout Christians to revolutionaries has been completed, and he couldn't be any happier.

"In 1967, in the black ghettos of the country," Zinn says, "came the greatest urban riots of American history."[110] Is that "greatest" in the sense of largest, or in the sense of the *best* riots? We suspect the latter. Zinn expresses no dismay at innocent lives lost in these riots. He expresses no concern for African Americans who had to live in the midst of rioting and see their neighborhoods destroyed. As George Schuyler pointed out, the lawbreakers were terrorizing "the respectable bulk of Negroes."[111]

While the 1968 *Report of the National Advisory Commission on Civil Disorders*, usually referred to as the Kerner Report, blamed discrimination, segregation, and poverty for the riots, it also noted the growth of the black middle and upper class, along with gains in wages:

> The Negro "upper-income" group is expanding rapidly and achieving sizeable income gains. In 1966, 28 percent of all Negro families received incomes of $7000 or more, compared with 55 percent of white families. This was double the proportion of Negroes receiving comparable incomes in 1960, and 4 times greater than the proportion receiving such incomes in 1947. Moreover, the proportion of Negroes employed in high-skill, high-status, and well-paying jobs rose faster than comparable proportions among whites from 1960 to 1966. As Negro incomes have risen, the size of the lowest-income group has grown smaller, and the middle and upper groups have grown larger—both relatively and absolutely.[112]

Of course, Zinn didn't welcome this good news for African Americans. He called the Kerner Report "a standard device of the system when facing rebellion." It is intended to have "a soothing effect." Zinn's concern is not with the majority of blacks—the struggling "people" he claims to care about—but with the rabble-rousing advocates of "Black Power." Zinn suggests that there's some kind of unexplained conspiracy behind the assassination of its "most eloquent spokesman," Malcolm X: "After he was assassinated as he spoke on a public platform in February 1965, in a plan whose origins are still obscure, he became the martyr of this movement." [113] The "plan" was far from obscure. The assassination team was made up of followers of the rival Black Muslim leader, Elijah Muhammad; they carried out a carefully orchestrated hit in the Audubon Ballroom in Harlem after the police who routinely provided security for Malcolm X had followed the requests of Malcolm X's "senior people" and positioned themselves at a distance from the event. [114]

Assuming to speak for the black community, Zinn writes, "Martin Luther King, though still respected, was being replaced now by new heroes: Huey Newton of the Black Panthers, for instance. The Panthers had guns; they said blacks should defend themselves." [115] The Black Panthers killed at least sixteen law enforcement officers, including a National Park Service Ranger "on patrol near San Francisco in 1973." [116] Zinn does not mention that fact, nor the torture death of Alex Rackley, a young black man the Panthers accused of being an informer. [117]

Zinn wrote about the Black Panthers from a safe distance while enjoying tenure and jaunts to Europe. But David Horowitz, who was involved with the Panthers as an activist on the Left, saw them as they really were, "a criminal gang that preyed on the black ghetto itself," and who "pursued various avenues of criminal violence which included extortion, drug-trafficking and murder." He believes they murdered his bookkeeper, a supportive leftist woman who made the mistake of inquiring about their finances. The Black Panthers also attacked other blacks, such as "a leader of the Black Students Union at Grove Street College in Oakland," whom they murdered "because he had inadvertently insulted one of their enforcers." In 1973, Horowitz was introduced to Huey Newton by movie producer Bert Schneider. "At the time," reports Horowitz, "Newton was engaged in a life and death feud with Black Panther Eldridge Cleaver," who had "fled to Algiers after a shoot-out with Bay Area police." Horowitz points out that Eldridge has admitted to ambushing them. Former Panther Chairman Bobby Seale had "gone into hiding after Newton had expelled him from the Party." And no wonder. Horowitz later learned that "Seale had been whipped—literally—and then personally sodomized by [Newton] with such violence that he had to have his anus surgically repaired by a Pacific Heights doctor who was a political supporter of the Panthers."[118] And yet Newton is the man Zinn names as the prime example of the "new heroes" replacing King among black Americans.[119]

Zinn can't seem to muster any sympathy for the Black Panthers' victims. But he has plenty to spare for those thugs themselves. He characterizes the investigation and prosecution of this violent gang as "a planned pattern of violence against militant black organizers, carried on by the police and the Federal Bureau of Investigation" and asks, "Was the government turning to murder and terror because the concessions— the legislation, the speeches, the intonation of the civil rights hymn 'We Shall Overcome' by President Lyndon Johnson—were not working?" He claims, "It was discovered later that the government in all the years of the civil rights, while making concessions through Congress, was acting through the FBI to harass and break up black militant groups."[120] Nothing, of course, about what the "militant" groups were up to, such as the crime and murder described by Horowitz. And no mention of the fact that the FBI had been equally instrumental in investigating and prosecuting white "militant" groups, such as the Ku Klux Klan.

Martin Luther King Jr. enjoys a sudden rise in Zinn's esteem only on account of his quixotic, chaotic, and ineffective "Poor People's Encampment" in Washington, undertaken without the "paternal approval of the President." Zinn notes that the Encampment "went on," after King's assassination in Memphis, Tennessee. But in the context of his previous glorification of rioting, what follows is particularly perverse: "The killing of King brought new urban outbreaks all over the country, in which thirty-nine people were killed, thirty-five of them black."[121]

As usual, blacks suffered the brunt of the violence that Zinn's heroes—the "black militants" so useful to him as mascots for the socialist revolution—fomented. As we have already seen, most African Americans did not side with these violent troublemakers; they wanted them punished to protect their communities. George Schuyler railed against the white radicals who inspired black troublemakers to riot and then blamed police. Citing polls of blacks, he went so far as to quip, "They want *more* police brutality."[122] Professor Michael Fortner has pointed out that while "White reformers and law enforcement officials agitated for more rehabilitative resources for the 'innocent victims' of the drug trade and practical sentences for dealers who would seek to corrupt youngsters.... working and middle-class Harlemites pleaded with the police to expand their campaigns against pushers and other progenitors of vice."[123]

Zinn clearly hoped to exacerbate class conflict by portraying blacks as poor victims ripe for revolt against the evil capitalist system. These are some of the "people" of his history. A Mrs. Unita Blackwell from Greenville, Mississippi, was one of seventy "poor black people" who in 1966 had "occupied an unused air force barracks" and then been evicted. Her thoughts were that "the federal government have proven that it don't care about poor people." Another "black woman, Patricia Robinson, in a pamphlet distributed in Boston in 1970 (*Poor Black Woman*) tied male supremacy to capitalism and said the black woman 'allies herself with the have-nots in the wider world and their revolutionary struggles.' She said the poor black woman did not in the past 'question the social and economic system' but now she must, and in fact, 'she has begun to question aggressive male domination and the class society which enforces it, capitalism.'"[124]

But there are glimmers of hope, in Zinn's opinion. For example, "whites and blacks were crossing racial lines in the South to unite as a class against employers. In 1971, two thousand woodworkers in Mississippi, black and white, joined together to protest a new method of measuring wood that led to lower wages. In the textile mills of J. P. Stevens where 44,000 workers were employed in eighty-five plants, mostly in the South, blacks and whites were working together in union activity. In Tifton, Georgia, and Milledgeville, Georgia, in 1977, blacks and whites served together on the union committee of their plants."[125]

No more specific information is given in this "history," so it is unclear about what message is conveyed other than a vague awareness of workers, "black and white," uniting and fighting the bosses.

In Zinn's estimation, the progress that came from the civil rights struggle included the fact that by the late sixties and early seventies, prisoners were referring to themselves as "revolutionaries" and opposing the Vietnam War. So the "explosions" of the Civil Rights Era were just preludes of more revolutionary action to come: "The events of those years underlined what prisoners already sensed—that whatever crimes they had committed, the greatest crimes were being committed by the authorities who maintained the prisons, by the government of the United States. The law was being broken daily by the President, sending bombers to kill, sending men to be killed, outside the Constitution...."[126]

EIGHT

Ho, Ho, Ho Chi Minh! Howard Zinn and the Commies Win!

C hapter 18 of *A People's History of the United States* is titled "The Impossible Victory: Vietnam." Did Zinn call victory in Vietnam "impossible" because, like a lot of leftist anti-war protesters, he wanted everyone to believe that the American cause in that war was hopeless? Yes, but he also wanted students to be glad about America's defeat and the "victory" of the plucky North Vietnamese Communists. Zinn claims, "From 1964 to 1972, the wealthiest and most powerful nation in the history of the world made a maximum military effort, with everything short of atomic bombs, to defeat a nationalist revolutionary movement in a tiny, peasant country—and failed. When the United States fought in Vietnam, it was organized modern technology versus organized human beings, and the human beings won."[1]

What it boils down to is that Howard Zinn took the side of America's Communist enemies—and, as we shall see, did his bit as an anti-war activist disseminating anti-American propaganda to help them beat us.

According to Howard Zinn, such events as the Soviet takeover of Eastern Europe—during which the Communists blockaded Berlin and "ousted non-Communists from the government" (that's Zinn's description of a Communist coup in Czechoslovakia, and in a way it's accurate: the Czech Foreign Minister was literally "ousted" from an upper-story window to die when his body hit the courtyard below)[2]—Mao's conquest of China, Communist spies stealing the secret of the atom bomb for the Russians, and Communist North Korea's unprovoked attack on the South were irrationally "portrayed to the public as signs of a world Communist conspiracy." One wonders, what would the signs have been if there *had* been an international Communist plot?

Zinn has an explanation. It was simply an "upsurge all over the world of colonial people's demanding independence," which the U.S. government found "disturbing." In Zinn's telling of the story, "In fact, China, Korea, Indochina, the Philippines, represented local Communist movements, not Russian fomentation. It was a general wave of anti-imperialist insurrection...."[3] As was established earlier in the book, Zinn is wrong on China, Korea, and the Philippines. He is also—not surprisingly—wrong on Indochina. But Zinn maintains that the Vietnam War was due to the brutal suppression of the local nationalist movement in Indochina by the imperialistic United States. It was a modern-day David and Goliath story with the giant imperialistic power justly humiliated: America represented "technology," while the Communist North Vietnamese were "human beings."

Yes, America had lost her humanity, but Ho Chi Minh was Thomas Jefferson—only more human.

> Led by a Communist named Ho Chi Minh, the revolutionists fought against the Japanese, and when they were gone held a spectacular celebration in Hanoi in late 1945, with a million people in the streets, and issued a Declaration of Independence. It borrowed from the Declaration of the Rights of Man and the Citizen, in the French Revolution, and from the American Declaration of Independence, and began: "All men are created equal. They are endowed by their Creator with certain inalienable rights; among these are Life, Liberty, and the

pursuit of Happiness." Just as the Americans in 1776 had listed the grievances against the English King, the Vietnamese listed their complaints against French rule.[4]

The valiant freedom fighters won Vietnam's independence from France, but "Western powers were already at work to change" it back.[5]

Vietnam, though, was not much like the American colonies, and Ho Chi Minh was no Thomas Jefferson. One notable difference: the Vietnamese leader was a Marxist-Leninist revolutionary. According to Harvard professor Fredrik Logevall, Ho had joined the French Communist Party when he was living in Paris after World War I and was impressed by the connections Lenin drew "between capitalism and imperialism" and by the Communist dictator's vision for "nationalist movements in Africa and Asia," as well as his pledge of Soviet support "through the Comintern, for nationalist uprisings throughout the colonial world as a key first step in fomenting worldwide socialist revolution against the capitalist order."[6] In other words, Ho was hoping to join on to the very "world Communist conspiracy" that Zinn paints as a fiction dreamed up by American imperialists.

In June 1923, Ho had set out to Moscow in disguise hoping to meet Lenin, who, however, died in January 1924. So that month he paid his respects to the deceased Lenin, "participated in meetings of the Comintern," and received training. That autumn he was sent by the Soviets to southern China, "ostensibly to act as an interpreter for the Comintern's advisory mission to Sun Yat-sen's Nationalist government in Canton, but in reality to organize the first Marxist revolutionary organization in Indochina. To that end, he published a journal, created the Vietnamese Revolutionary Youth League.... and set up a training institute...." Early in 1930, he "presided over the creation of the Vietnamese Communist Party in Hong Kong," which was later that year, "on Moscow's instructions...renamed the Indochinese Communist Party (ICP)." Its responsibility was to spur "revolutionary activity throughout French Indochina."[7]

In contrast to the claims of his fans, Ho's dedication to nationalism was limited to the "revolutionary nationalism" of Lenin—described by Stephen J. Morris in the *Weekly Standard* as "nationalism as a temporary expedient in the struggle against 'imperialism.'" In fact, Vietnamese Communists adhered to "a Marxist-Leninist view of international affairs" and rejected nationalism "as an ideology of the feudal and capitalist social classes."[8] Ruth Fischer, a former Communist German revolutionary who knew Ho from their time in Moscow during the 1920s, described him as "the model of the disciplined Communist."[9]

Ho spent the 1930s in China and the USSR. Ho's work "benefitted" from a new political mood, as "the Soviet Union and Western democracies cooperated against the common threat of global fascism." From 1936-1939, "a Popular Front government in Paris allowed Communist parties in the colonies an increased measure of freedom."[10] Although "he witnessed the arrests and killings of his Bolshevik and Comintern comrades, including many fellow Vietnamese Communists," by the Soviets, Ho remained a dedicated Stalinist.[11]

"By mid-June 1940," Logevall explains, "France stood on the brink of defeat at the hands of invading Nazi German forces, Japan, on friendly terms with Germany and sensing an opportunity to expand southward, prepared to seize French Indochina, and Ho Chi Minh, meeting with associates in southern China, said he saw 'a very favorable opportunity for the Vietnamese revolution....'"[12]

In the spring of 1941, Ho Chi Minh returned to Vietnam, set up camp, and held a plenary meeting of the Indochinese Communist Party's Central Committee. In July, Japanese bases were established in southern Indochina. On July 24, the White House learned that "Japanese warships had appeared off Cam Ranh Bay." Soon thereafter came the U.S. embargo of Japan, and then Japan's attack on Pearl Harbor on December 7. On December 8, Charles de Gaulle, under the presumption that the French colonies lent his Free French government legitimacy, "proclaimed common cause with Washington and declared war on Japan."[13]

Although both de Gaulle and Winston Churchill wanted to keep their colonies, FDR, motivated by "smug[ness]," pressure by "Japanese anti-colonial propaganda," and Wilsonian idealism, had put forward the Atlantic Charter in August 1941. It included a clause respecting "the right of all peoples to choose the form of government under which they will live." The lofty statement provided inspiration and justification to nationalist leaders in colonies around the globe.[14] It also provided a pretext for those like Ho Chi Minh, who were using nationalism to further the spread of international Communism.

By 1944, the Communists' designs were becoming apparent. In China, Chiang Kai-shek had to dedicate resources to fighting the Communists instead of the Japanese. Stalin's ambitions in Europe and Asia involved a strategy of "weaken[ing] the European colonial powers," including France.[15] In that same year, Ho Chi Minh "helped put together a coalition known as the Vietnam Revolutionary League," which included "several non-Communist groups operating from exile in southern China." But as Logevall points out, "The ICP was from the start the central force in this coalition, and Ho the leading personality." Ho downplayed "his background as an agent of the Comintern and talked up the need for nationalist unity, even telling a Chinese general, 'I am a communist but what is important to me now is the independence and the freedom of my country, not communism.'" This was part of his pattern of lying. "By late 1944," Ho was "back in Tonkin" and "could see the endgame. He predicted that Japan would lose the Pacific War, France would seek to regain Indochina, and before that Tokyo would overthrow the [Jean] Decoux regime.... the result would be a power vacuum the [Communist] Viet Minh could fill."[16] After the Japanese successfully ousted the French administration in a March 9 coup, the Viet Minh formed an army under the command of General Giap, Ho's military man.[17]

Ho Chi Minh gained the support of the peasants and the Allies through more deception. Massive floods in 1944 helped cause a devastating famine. By February 1945, "Viet Minh operatives" were leading "'rice struggles,' breaking open warehouses and distributing food to the hungry. These efforts, though growing out of grassroots popular protest more than Viet Minh initiative per se," left a positive impression about the Viet Minh.[18] At that time the Viet Minh actually worked with the OSS (the Office of Strategic Services, the precursor to the CIA), helping to collect intelligence and rescue Allied soldiers whose planes had been shot down.[19]

After Japan surrendered on August 14, Ho Chi Minh assassinated non-Communist nationalist rivals and Trotskyites. He made his triumphant entry into Hanoi on August 26. Mark Moyar recounts in *Triumph Forsaken: The Vietnam War 1954–1965*, "As he had hoped, he preempted the Allied powers as well as the Vietnamese nationalist leaders...many of whom were still in China. Vietnamese Communist guerrillas marched unopposed into Hanoi and other cities with the rifles and submachine guns that they had received from their Chinese and American benefactors." Avoiding mention of their Communist ideology or plans, Ho's followers appealed to anti-colonialist sentiment and "nullified the most hated French policies, including high taxes and the government monopolies on salt, alcohol, and opium." Land was confiscated and given to peasants, landlords and village leaders were killed, nationalists were neutralized, and printing presses were seized. Exuding both modesty and power, Ho Chi Minh gained the confidence of the masses and future leaders of his movement.[20]

Ho Chi Minh's charisma also captivated many Americans. Ho used a combination of lies, evasion, and flattery on OSS men, including officer Archimedes Patti, who was "charmed by Ho's political sophistication," his seeming modesty, and his apparent desire for American-style democracy, as evidenced by a draft of a speech that quoted from the Declaration of Independence.[21] But Patti was not entirely taken in. On August 30, the OSS officer "forwarded" to President Truman a message from Ho asking that "the Viet Minh be involved in any Allied discussion regarding Vietnam's postwar status."[22] In a cable the day before, though, Patti had warned Washington that "'Red elements' were leading the new Viet Minh regime astray...."[23]

On September 2, "unaware that the Americans had already consented to France's return" to Vietnam, Ho, wearing a borrowed khaki suit and pith helmet, was driven to the Place Puginier square in Hanoi in a black American car. Coincidentally, at the time, two American P-38 Lightening fighters flew "overhead." Several American officers from the OSS, whom Ho had invited, stood near the platform. All this gave the impression that the United States government was endorsing him. Ho read from the Declaration of Independence, as well as from the French Revolution's Declaration of the Rights of Man. He accused "the French colonialists of violating these American and French principles" and claimed that his objective was an independent Vietnam.[24] The performance impressed Colonel Patti so much that that evening he sent a radio report to U.S. authorities advising them that "these people mean business."[25] The French, who were on their way, would soon find that out.

A People's History of the United States is still pushing Ho's propaganda. Zinn's 1980 history follows the same line he had argued in his *Vietnam: The Logic of Withdrawal,* a book he had written in 1967, when the War in Vietnam was still ongoing—before the Communist takeover of the South, before a million "Boat People" risked drowning to flee their tyranny, before another million human beings died in the Cambodian killing fields—when there was perhaps some excuse for naivety about the Communists' intentions. In that book Zinn presented Ho's Communism as an "indigenous" movement that was "a unique resultant of Marxist theory and local conditions."[26] Zinn was repeating the same lie that Ho Chi Minh told to American reporters when, shortly after the Communist takeover of China in 1949, he denied that the Viet Minh would be getting outside aid. But by the following year, a news report indicated that twenty thousand to thirty thousand of his troops were receiving food, arms, and training in China. A December 1954 article indicated a "continued influx from Red China."[27] By 1953, the Soviet Union was also supplying "trucks, anti-aircraft artillery, and heavy mortars."[28] Far from being a local movement, Ho Chi Minh benefited from "$670 million in military assistance before 1965" from China and then "approximately $2 billion over the following decade." The Soviet Union provided "$705 million in aid in 1967 alone" and more support came from the Warsaw Pact nations.[29] And yet, in 1967, Zinn wrote that Vietnam could expect to be as independent as Yugoslavia under Tito. Zinn presented Ho's government as preferable to the "elitist dictatorship" of South Vietnam and lectured, "We need to get accustomed to the idea that there will be more Communist countries in the world, and that this is not necessarily bad."[30]

Zinn himself was so ready to welcome that result that he pitched in to make it happen. Between 1967—when he published *Vietnam: The Logic of Withdrawal,* and 1980, when his *People's History* first came out—Zinn did his bit to help the Vietnamese Communists. In the celebrated "Pentagon Papers" episode of 1971, it was Zinn who hid top-secret documents stolen and leaked by Daniel Ellsberg, a military analyst working for the RAND corporation. He also served as a witness for Ellsberg at his trial on charges under the Espionage Act.

What harm did the publication of these top-secret documents do to the American war effort in Vietnam? The worst damage came from the fact that the events covered ended in May 1968—just when the successful CORDS (Civil Operations and Revolutionary Development Support) campaign "had begun its work," according to William Colby, the CIA officer who headed up the effort. The *Pentagon Papers* obscured what had been accomplished between May 1968 and June 1971,[31] giving the American public the false impression that the war was unwinnable. Left-wing journalists exploited the "revelations" in the *Pentagon Papers* and distorted the material in them, thus contributing to defeat in Vietnam. In doing so, they were following a line of propaganda that would successfully undermine the American public's support for the war and thus prove instrumental to our defeat—and ultimately to the subjection of millions of East Asians to bloody Communist tyrannies. The American Left did everything they could to create the impression that our war against the North Vietnamese Communists was unwinnable—and also unjust. And in *A People's History*, Zinn continues those distortions, quoting from the *Pentagon Papers* selectively to give the impression that government officials refused to help a democratic leader and then lied to the American public. Suggesting that there were nefarious secret plans behind America's war in Vietnam, Zinn writes that according to the "secret memoranda of the National Security Council...there was talk in 1950 of...the 'domino theory,'"—that is, the idea that the fall of one country to Communism would lead to the fall of others.[32]

Zinn does his best to obscure the honorable reasons for U.S. involvement in Vietnam—and to distract attention from the fact that the actual results of the Communist victory were exactly what the "domino theory" predicted. "Why was the United States doing this?" he asks, of the large amounts of aid we gave the French after Communist victories in China in 1949 and in Korea the following year. His answer? "To the public, the word was the United States was helping to stop Communism in Asia, but there was not much public discussion. In the secret memoranda of the National Security Council (which advised the President on foreign policy) there was talk in 1950 of what came to be known as the 'domino theory'—that like a row of dominoes, if one country fell to Communism, the next one would do the same and so on...."[33]

Contrary to Zinn's suggestion, the domino theory was not discussed only in "secret memoranda." The literal "domino" analogy was first used by President Eisenhower at a 1954 news conference when he replied to a reporter's question about Indochina by referring to the "the 'falling domino' principle."[34] But, though not under that name, the principle had been part of the Truman Doctrine. In 1947, when President Truman asked Congress for aid to Greece and Turkey, he warned about the likelihood that Communism would spread south to Iran and east to India if those countries should fall.

And there is no better proof of the wisdom of the domino theory—or of the horrific consequences that were certain to be visited on millions once leftists like Zinn succeeded in persuading America to abandon it—than the results of the Communist victory in Vietnam, with neighboring Laos and Cambodia falling under Communist tyranny shortly thereafter. Zinn and his political allies bear a large measure of responsibility for the suffering of the hundreds of thousands of Vietnamese "boat people" who risked drowning to escape the horrors of Communism in the 1970s—many of whom died. To anyone not seeing the Vietnamese Communists through rose-colored glasses, the tragic results were predictable from the beginning.

Beginning two decades before, Vietnamese in the hundreds of thousands had fled from the parts of their country where the Communists were taking over. A headline in the September 18, 1954 *New York Times* read "250,000 Vietnamese Flee Reds, Far Exceeding Expected Exodus." On October 10, in a letter to the editor of the *New York Times*, Nguyen Duc Thanh, president of the American Vietnamese Foundation, pleaded for help for the Vietnamese who had left their homes in North Vietnam to relocate to the South. He stated, "The overwhelming majority of the Vietnamese, given proper support, would elect to stay on the side of freedom despite whatever hardships." A November 7, 1954, article reported that a total of 479,431 persons had left North Vietnam.[35] By May 1955, "over 900,000 refugees, most of them Roman Catholic," had moved to the south. An estimated 50,000 to 90,000 Viet Minh moved north; about 10,000 Viet Minh, instructed "to engage in 'political struggle,'" remained in South Vietnam.[36] Ultimately, over a million Vietnamese fled the north.

In 1961, the *New York Times*, *Washington Post*, *Time*, and *Newsweek* were writing in support of the government's fight against "Communist aggression" in Vietnam.[37] And yet Zinn claims that in 1954—the very year in which the *New York Times* was reporting the flight of nearly half a million people from the Communist North Vietnam— "Vietnamese popular support…was overwhelmingly behind Ho Chi Minh and the revolutionary movement."[38]

In Zinn's telling, the Communists are the popular good guys. All the problems are caused by the evil, capitalist imperialists—especially the Americans. According to *A People's History*, an "international assemblage at Geneva presided over the peace agreement between the

French and the Vietminh" in 1954, in which "[i]t was agreed that the French would temporarily withdraw" to the south until two years later when an election would be held to "enable the Vietnamese to choose their own government." But "the United States moved quickly to prevent the unification," set up a puppet government under Ngo Dinh Diem, and persuaded him to prevent elections that were predicted to favor the Communists.[39]

But as Oscar Handlin pointed out in his review of *A People's History* in the *American Scholar*, the 1954 Geneva assembly "did not agree on elections in a unified Vietnam; that was simply the hope expressed by the British chairman when the parties concerned could not agree."[40] And Zinn's answer to Handlin, in a letter to that journal full of hysterical accusations—claiming, among other things, that Handlin had misled readers and created "historical facts by fiat"—proudly quoted the "'Final Declaration of the Geneva Conference (July 21, 1954), in *Great Britain Parliamentary Sessional Papers*, XXXI, pp. 9-11:'...general elections shall be held in July, 1956." Patiently, Handlin acknowledged that Zinn was quoting from "the final declaration by the British chairman"—but pointed out that it was a statement "to which the Saigon government never agreed" and which "the United States, not a party in 1954, did not support."[41]

Handlin's point is supported by commentators and historians both Right and Left. As Norman Podhoretz explains in *Why We Were in Vietnam*, "since neither the United States nor South Vietnam had signed the Geneva agreements, they were under no legal obligation to carry them out." Furthermore, "the Pentagon Papers reveal that the United States did not, as was often alleged in the subsequent debates over the war, 'connive with Diem to ignore the elections. U.S. State Department records indicate that Diem's refusal to be bound by the Geneva accords...were at his own initiative.'"[42] Mark Moyar has described the tricky situation surrounding the Geneva agreement, which "lacked the endorsement of the new south Vietnamese government and the U.S. government": "At a meeting of the National Security

Council [Secretary of State John Foster] Dulles explained that the United States would not sanction the Geneva agreement because 'we can't get ourselves into the "Yalta business" of guaranteeing Soviet conquests.' But at the same time, the Americans avoided criticizing the settlement, so as not to offend the French, whom the Americans were attempting to entice into the European Defense Community."[43]

Logevall too points to the challenges faced by the Eisenhower administration, including "congressional pressure to prevent any territorial loss to the Communists" *and* "to avoid 'another Korea.'" He writes, "At a press conference in Washington [on July 21, 1954], President Eisenhower expressed satisfaction that an agreement had been reached to stop the bloodshed in Indochina. But he emphasized that the United States was not a party to the accords or bound by them...." Eisenhower's plan was to use the "two years before the elections...to build up the South Vietnamese government, free of the taint of French colonialism."[44]

Even critics of America's policy in Vietnam acknowledged that elections there would not be free and fair under the conditions. Theodore Draper, who, as Podhoretz explained, was "no friend either of Diem or of American foreign policy in Vietnam," nevertheless pointed out that Ho Chi Minh "'might have taken power democratically, but he would not have kept power democratically, which is far more important. In 1960 the "elections" in North Vietnam resulted in a 99.8 percent majority for the ruling Communist Party and its two small satellite groups, with one permitted to run on an opposition platform.'"[45] But Zinn dishonestly suggests that America's failure to support an election in these conditions was anti-democratic. The Diem regime in South Vietnam is cast as repeatedly blocking elections with the help of "American money and arms."[46]

While in Zinn's telling the Communists were frustrated democrats, the American-allied government of South Vietnam was "increasingly unpopular. Diem was a Catholic, and most Vietnamese were Buddhists; Diem was close to landlords, and this was a country of peasants. His pretenses at land reform left things basically as they were." Diem "replaced locally selected provincial chiefs with his own men, appointed in Saigon" and "imprisoned more and more Vietnamese who criticized the regime for corruption, for lack of reform."[47] As Moyar points out, Diem's "Denounce the Communists" campaign did result in some false accusations, but he was addressing real threats—such as assassination.[48] As we shall see, some of Diem's supposedly Buddhist opponents in the south were Communist imposters; others were real Buddhists dedicated also to Communism.[49] Zinn, the proponent of redistributing property, does not mention the tens of thousands of landlords that were murdered by the Communists when they took over in the north in 1954.[50] Nor does he mention the fact that the Communist "land reform," or the redistribution of these lands to peasants, was followed by the standard Communist "'second stage' in which the land is taken back...and turned over to collective farms."[51] Zinn fails to mention such information, as he praises Communists as reformers. Diem, to be sure, was more authoritarian than a Western leader, but as Moyar points out, his culture and the chaotic conditions required a firm hand. Even so, "Diem did not stifle religion or kill tens of thousands in the process of redistributing land as Ho Chi Minh did, and he was more tolerant of dissent than his northern counterpart."[52] Stephen Morris has pointed out in the *Weekly Standard* that "South Vietnam was never even a fully authoritarian state." It allowed "organized political opposition...including opposition newspapers."[53]

Consider, in contrast, the description of Communist North Vietnam provided by Fredrik Logevall, who believes that Ho, with U.S. support, "might well have opted for an independent Communist course of the type Yugoslav leader Josip Broz Tito would follow."[54] Even so, Logevall admits that between 1946 and 1949, in Maoist fashion, the Viet Minh conducted indoctrination meetings in the villages. They also imposed taxes, or, more accurately, "cash extortions in the towns and rice levies in the villages." And "when the situation demanded, the cadres reinforced education and propaganda with terror tactics, including assassination of village leaders." Terror was "utilized selectively, not only in the military sense but in the sociological sense, targeting only those people who by virtue of their positions or their extensive landholdings weren't very popular anyway." Military General Giap kept the number of killings below a number that would provoke an insurrection.[55] As Morris notes, Giap created a "secret police organization modeled on the Soviet and Chinese equivalents." Ho Chi Minh's ruthless adherence to Stalinism is illustrated by the fact that he and his comrades continued to celebrate Stalin's "ideology and political practice," "[l]ong after" the dictator's death in 1953.[56]

Moyar, in contrast to Logevall, believes that Ho's commitment to Communist internationalism meant that "he would not have sacrificed Communist solidarity for the sake of Vietnam's narrow interests." Diem, in contrast, "ultimately suffer[ed] death for refusing to yield to the demands of his American allies."[57] But Zinn's picture of the Communist revolution as a spontaneous response to Diem's authoritarian rule, to which Ho sent "aid" and "encouragement," is accepted by historians neither of the Right or Left. This is Zinn's fanciful take:

> Opposition grew quickly in the countryside, where Diem's apparatus could not reach well, and around 1958 guerrilla activities began against the regime. The Communist regime in Hanoi gave aid, encouragement, and sent people south— most of them southerners who had gone north after the Geneva accords—to support the guerrilla movement. In 1960, the National Liberation Front was formed in the South. It united the various strands of opposition to the regime; its strength came from South Vietnamese peasants, who saw it as a way of changing their daily lives.[58]

In support of this take, Zinn quotes the "U.S. government analyst Douglas Pike," selecting—and that, as we shall see, is the operative word—from his book *Viet Cong: The Organization and Techniques of the National Liberation Front of South Vietnam*: "In the 2,561 villages of South Vietnam, the National Liberation Front created a host of nation-wide socio-political organizations in a country where mass organiza-tions...were virtually nonexistent.... aside from the NLF there had never been a truly mass-based political party in South Vietnam."[59] Zinn's use of ellipses here is quite deceptive; it allows him to pretend that a network of Communist front organizations was some kind of indigenous political organization—and that U.S. government analysis recognized it as such. In fact, the parts of this passage that Zinn left out make it clear that the NLF was simply a particularly effective way for the North Vietnamese Communists to infiltrate the South. Pike's purpose in Vietnam as a for-eign service officer with the U.S. Information Agency was to become "knowledgeable in the field of communication of ideas in an insurgency," as he wrote. As part of his work, since his arrival in 1960 he had come to understand the culture, for which the tightly knit villages were the center of life. Pike writes, "To the 2,561 villages of South Vietnam, where live two thirds of the people, came the Communists, openly or behind a front, determined to turn each village into an instrument for revolution, a drive aimed not at the people as individuals so much as at the village as a unit. The Southern village was weak and vulnerable to this kind of assault...."[60] In Pike's analysis, there was a "Communist" "assault" being carried out in some cases by "a front" in order "to turn each village into an instrument for revolution." The NLF *wasn't* the indigenous and spontaneous political movement that Zinn suggests it is with his cleverly selective quotation of Pike. It was a Communist front organization, specially adapted to the conditions on the ground in Vietnam.

Pike, on the same page, also describes how the NLF fooled the Vietnam-ese and the Americans into believing that the NLF was "only a phantom edifice" by " revers[ing] the usual order for front formation: Instead of beginning with the organizations and creating the front, it began with the front and created the organizations and then assigned them the task of engag-ing in revolution through the mechanism of the struggle movement."[61]

Further selective quotation by Zinn promotes the idea that the Communists were benign political organizers, rather than bloody revolutionaries. Zinn quotes from Pike's preface, page ix, saying in *A People's History,* "Pike wrote: 'The Communists have brought to the villages of South Vietnam significant social change and have done so largely by means of the communication process.' That is, they were organizers much more than they were warriors."[62] A reader would get the idea that "Communists" were setting up town hall meetings something like the one depicted by Normal Rockwell in his painting of "The Freedom of Speech" in his "Four Freedoms" series. But on the same page, Pike also says that the NLF "threw a net of associations over the rural Vietnamese that could seduce him into voluntarily supporting the NLF or, failing that, bring the full weight of social pressure to bear on him, or, if both of these failed, could compel his support. It could subject him effectively to surveillance, indoctrination, and exploitation. It could order his life. It could artificially create grievances and develop voluntary support where logically such support ought not to have been forthcoming."[63] Even the reference to a "communication process" in the passage that Zinn did quote was not a reference to honest political persuasion. The "NLF communication process," as Pike revealed, included "mass psychological techniques such as rallies, demonstrations, parades, movements, neighborhood and work meetings, and group criticism and individual denunciation campaigns"; "agit-prop work" directed at the masses; and pragmatic appeals "rooted in fundamental Communist doctrine."[64] This is Maoist indoctrination, not grassroots politics or townhall meetings.

And it was backed, in the final instance, by terror. As Pike explains, to "restructur[e]...the social order," the Communists tried successive escalating levels of "communication" strategies. But these so-called "communication" strategies began with "seduc[ing] [the villager] into voluntarily supporting the NLF." They became successively forceful: "social pressure," then "surveillance, indoctrination, and exploitation."[65] While the "agit-prop cadres" hoped to convert the South Vietnamese "to such a degree that the villager would support the cause of his own volition," when this was not possible they tried to "confuse the opinions and emotions of the villager so that he became indecisive and thus ineffectual in providing support to the GVN [South Vietnam]." They were engaging in standard Communist strategies: "the agit-prop cadres sought to instigate strife along class lines. They dealt in misinformation, exaggeration, and distortion. They concealed or mistated Communist intentions. They drew attention to and inflated real or trumped-up village grievances."[66] And ultimately, the Communists backed up these psychological and social strategies with real violence, killing individuals within the village to form "a scar of fear." Pike describes three cases that he had personally investigated. These were the killing of a priest by driving bamboo spears into him and then shooting him in the head; two school teachers forced to witness the execution and decapitation of two farmers; and the shooting death after a "people's tribunal" of a sixty-seven-year-old farmer for "purchasing two hectares of rice land and ignoring NLF orders to turn [it] over to the tenant...."[67]

It is difficult to imagine a more deliberate misrepresentation of a book than Zinn's of Pike's. Pike charges the NLF, in fact, with *genocide*. Here is page 248 of Pike's *Viet Cong: The Organization and Techniques of the National Liberation Front of South Vietnam*:

> Steadily, quietly, and with a systematic ruthlessness the NLF in six years wiped out virtually an entire class of Vietnamese villagers. The assassination rate declined steadily.... from 1960 to 1965 for the simple reason that there was only a finite number of persons to be assassinated. Many villages by 1966 were virtually depopulated of their natural leaders, who are the single most important element in any society. They represent a human resource of incalculable value. This loss to South Vietnam is inestimable, and it will take a generation or more to repair the damage to the society. By any definition, this NLF action against village leaders amounts to genocide.[68]

But you don't need to read hundreds of pages to understand Pike's position. He makes it as clear as day in his preface (Pike's book was originally published in 1966, with a second edition in 1967, before the outcome of the Vietnam War was known):

> I have to a degree put down roots [in Vietnam] and have come to care very deeply about what happens. The plight of the Vietnamese people is not an abstraction to me, and I have no patience with those who treat it as such. Victory by the Communists would mean consigning thousands of Vietnamese, many of them of course my friends, to death, prison, or permanent exile.... My heart goes out to the Vietnamese people—who have been sold out again and again, whose long history could be written in terms of betrayal and who, based on this long and bitter experience, can only expect that eventually America too will sell them out. If America betrays the Vietnamese people by abandoning them, she betrays her own heritage.[69]

Zinn was one of those betraying the Vietnamese people—and then he turned around and made use of Pike's own book to justify that betrayal, distorting Pike's analysis to make it appear to support the opposite case. Talk about adding insult to injury. What should be Douglas Pike's lasting legacy has been hijacked to promote the very cause Pike was urging the American people to defeat. Google searches of several quotations from Pike's *Viet Cong* lead the reader not to Pike's book, but to *A People's History* and another book in which Zinn's chapter is republished: *Against the War: Writings by Activists*, published in 1999.[70] Pike's book is out of print, and few students today bother to search for the few remaining copies on the shelves of college libraries. Zinn's book is ubiquitous.

After lying about the NLF, Zinn continues the Communist lies about a protest campaign that led to America's betrayal of Diem, which enabled his assassination: "One day in June 1963," begins a paragraph, "a Buddhist monk sat down in the public square in Saigon and set himself afire."

As more monks did the same, "Diem's police raided Buddhist pagodas and temples, wounded thirty monks, arrested 1,400 people, and closed down the pagodas." They killed nine demonstrators. "Then, in Hué, the ancient capital, ten thousand demonstrated in protest."[71]

But according to Mark Moyar, this "Buddhist protest movement" did not arise "from popular dissatisfaction with a government guilty of religious intolerance." Rather, it was a "power play by a few Buddhist leaders" who had "close ties to the Communists or were themselves covert Communists." There were also other Communist agents participating. Diem followed the suggestions of his generals and arrested the leaders and closed pagodas that served as headquarters.[72]

As Moyar reports, "A few captured Communist documents, available at the time to both the Americans and the South Vietnamese, revealed Communist participation in the Buddhist protest movement. One Communist document, dated July 27, 1963 and captured a few weeks thereafter, stated that in some areas Communist personnel 'have pushed the political struggle movement by initiating the demonstrations against the terrorization of Buddhism at the province and districts.'"

Also inspiring suspicion were the NLF's statements of support of the Buddhists' claims early on. Unfortunately, journalists rejected "the claim of Diem and many other South Vietnamese officials that some militant Buddhist leaders were secret agents of Hanoi." Among these was *New York Times* reporter Neil Sheehan, who obtained the Pentagon Papers from Ellsberg for publication and who won the 1988 Pulitzer Prize for *A Bright Shining Lie*. Beginning in the 1990s, Communist Vietnamese histories have confirmed Diem's claims.[73]

Later, when Buddhists really were persecuted under the Communist regime, they were ignored by most of the media, as Norman Podhoretz recalls about "the self-immolation of twelve Buddhist nuns and priests on November 2, 1975," and a "raid by the Communist police" on a Buddhist temple in April 1977.[74]

Moyar sees the assassination of Diem with cooperation from the U.S. as a tragic mistake. Upon the advice of Secretary of Defense Robert

McNamara, who was worried about "public opinion," President John F. Kennedy cut U.S. aid. This led to "portentous consequences that Kennedy had neither intended nor desired." The cut made Diem even "less cooperative." He released some Buddhist prisoners, but rejected "far-reaching political reforms demanded by the Americans." Instead, he enacted "austerity measures" and stalled on appointing generals. Ambassador Henry Cabot Lodge then agreed to allow South Vietnamese generals to stage a coup, disregarding key parts of the president's instructions.[75] Diem and his brother were captured on November 1, 1963, and killed the following day.

But to Zinn, American involvement in Vietnam was all about secret plotting by greedy capitalists to nip a freedom movement in the bud. As he says in *A People's History*, "A secret memo of the National Security Council in June 1952 also pointed to the chain of U.S. military bases along the coast of China, the Philippines, Taiwan, Japan, South Korea:

> Communist control of all Southeast Asia would render the U.S. position in the Pacific offshore island chain precarious and would seriously jeopardize fundamental U.S. security interests in the Far East.
> And:
> Southeast Asia, especially Malaya and Indonesia, is the principal world source of natural rubber and tin, and a producer of petroleum and other strategically important commodities....[76]

Without identifying the source of this "secret memo," Zinn comments that it also included the fact that "Japan depended on the rice of the region" and so was also vulnerable to Communist exploitation.[77]

The source is actually a June 25, 1952, report to the National Security Council by the Executive Secretary James Lay. It does indeed include Zinn's quoted material, but it also notes the importance of these resources *not* to the United States, but to countries in the region. Zinn quotes from item 2(c) of the document's "General Considerations" but conveniently leaves out this sentence, indicated by his ellipses: "The rice exports of Burma and Thailand are critically important to Malaya, Ceylon, and Hong Kong and are of considerable significance to Japan and India, all important areas of free Asia." One of the "courses of action" recommended was to "encourage and expand their commerce with each other and with the rest of the free world...." But one does not even need to read that far down. The objective was listed as the first item: "To prevent the countries of Southeast Asia from passing into the Communist orbit, and to assist them to develop the will and ability to resist communism from within and without...."[78]

Zinn marches on with more selective evidence, quoting from a 1953 "congressional study mission" that "reported: 'The area of Indochina is immensely wealthy in rice, rubber, coal and iron ore. Its position makes it a strategic key to the rest of Southeast Asia.'"[79] This quotation appears in the first volume of the four-volume Gravel Edition of *The Pentagon Papers*—the one that *Zinn* and Noam Chomsky edited. It comes from a report by "Representative Walter Judd, a recognized Republican spokesman on Asia." This is what follows the sentence Zinn chose to quote: "If Indochina should fall, Thailand and Burma would be in extreme danger, Malaya, Singapore and even Indonesia would become more vulnerable to the Communist power drive.... communism would then be in an exceptional position to complete its perversion of the political and social revolution that is spreading through Asia.... the Communists must be prevented from achieving their objectives in Indochina."[80]

Zinn's selective quotation gives the impression that the U.S. was just interested in the resources "rice, rubber, coal, and iron ore." Not only do the deleted sentences convey something quite different, but so does the explanation in the report that Secretary of State John Foster Dulles "regarded Southeast Asia a key region in the conflict with communist 'imperialism' and that it was important to draw the line of containment north of the Rice Bowl of Asia—the Indochina peninsula."[81] The concern was in fighting *Communist* imperialism.

One wonders if Zinn had simply not read the volumes that he presumably edited. Either that or he deliberately left out key information. In any case, he continues to pursue the line that a secret cabal of imperialists in the U.S. government used the pretext of Communism to grab Indochina's resources. Zinn presents another example, quoting from a speech that Under Secretary of State U. Alexis Johnson gave before the Detroit Economic Club: "What is the attraction that Southeast Asia has exerted for centuries on the great powers flanking it on all sides? Why is it desirable, and why is it important? First, it provides a lush climate, fertile soil, rich natural resources, a relatively sparse population in most areas, and room to expand. The countries of Southeast Asia produce rich exportable surpluses such as rice, rubber, teak, corn, tin, spices, oil, and many others...."

Zinn huffs, "This is not the language that was used by President Kennedy in his explanations to the American public." Instead, Kennedy deviously "talked of Communism and freedom. In a news conference February 14, 1962, he said 'Yes, as you know, the U.S. for more than a decade has been assisting the government, the people of Vietnam, to maintain their independence.'"[82]

But Zinn's four-dot ellipsis at the end of the "rice, rubber, teak, corn, tin, spices, oil" quotation indicates that he has deleted the next sentence from his source. And no wonder he deleted that sentence! It reads: "It [Southeast Asia] is especially attractive to Communist China, with its burgeoning population and its food shortages."[83]

Contrary to Zinn, this Kennedy administration official was expressing concern about the *Communists'* desire to conquer Southeast Asia for these natural resources. Alexis Johnson's speech shows that the real fear was *Communist imperialism.* Of course, Zinn doesn't include Johnson's quotation of Under Secretary Averell Harriman's statement to that effect: "Chinese communism and all communism is imperialist."

The fact is, President Kennedy's references to "Communism and freedom" in his "explanations to the American public" were not a smoke screen; they were the real reasons. And this speech that Zinn falsifies is also printed in *The Pentagon Papers.*

These are three strikes against Zinn—three times that he has presented Communist imperialism as American imperialism. Such lies are necessary in order to advance his picture of each and every American president as filled with war-mongering greed. The next is President Lyndon Johnson. "In early August 1964," Zinn claims, "President Johnson used a murky set of events in the Gulf of Tonkin, off the coast of North Vietnam, to launch full-scale war on Vietnam."[84] If only that were the truth! In fact, Johnson hastened to reassure the American public—and, incidentally, our Communist enemies in Vietnam—that "our response, for the present, will be limited...."[85] Johnson's political calculations told him that a too hawkish stance might make him look like a trigger-happy extremist of the sort he had been pretending his Republican opponent Barry Goldwater was. As Podhoretz recounts, Johnson "excoriated the Republicans for their belief in the 'wisdom of going North in Vietnam,'" and promised to "launch an offensive 'only as a last resort.'" "'Dropping bombs,'" he said, would likely "'involve American boys in a war in Asia with 700 million Chinese.'"[86]

We have since learned that, contrary to Johnson's expressed fears, Mao was not ready to go fight in Vietnam at that time. As Mark Moyar explains, "After the Tonkin Gulf reprisals, in violation of previous promises, the Chinese made clear to Hanoi that if American forces invaded North Vietnam, China would not send its troops to fight the Americans." Instead, the North Vietnamese were advised that in the case of an attack they should leave the cities and fight from the mountains; they made plans to do this.[87] In fact, Moyar speculates, "an American expedition to North Vietnam" at that time could have led to an anti-Communist government there, established by volunteers from the one million Northern refugees in South Vietnam.[88]

Zinn dedicates two pages to the My Lai Massacre—the execution of two hundred to four hundred villagers in the hamlet of My Lai in March 1968 by American troops—a case in which military rules were grossly violated. Much in Zinn's recounting consists of quoted material from the trial of U.S. Army Lieutenant William Calley, the leader of the massacre. Zinn makes the astounding claim that "My Lai was unique only in its details."[89] Sure—but only if you count as "details" all the significant facts: that the deed was done by American soldiers, that an American officer ordered the killings, and that—as a result of these actually unprecedented "details"—there was a high-profile court martial in which William Calley was found guilty of murder. As Norman Podhoretz wrote in 1982, "no evidence existed at the time—and none has materialized since—to substantiate the charge that My Lai was typical." He adds that "given the number of antiwar journalists reporting on Vietnam," it would not have been likely that other atrocities could have been kept secret. Podhoretz cites Telford Taylor, "a prosecutor at Nuremberg and…now a strong opponent of the war," who said he was "'unaware of any evidence of other incidents of comparable magnitude'" and noted that "'the reported reaction of some of the soldiers at [My Lai] strongly indicates that they regarded it as out of the ordinary.'" Even Zinn's friend Daniel Ellsberg said, "'My Lai was beyond the bounds of permissible behavior, and that is recognizable by virtually every soldier in Vietnam.'"[90]

In fact, American concern for civilians put American soldiers in danger. Military installations disguised as textile mills and residential buildings increased dangers for pilots, who, as one explained, were "'shot down because rules of engagement required approach angles and other tactics designed to reduce civilian casualties rather than to afford maximum protection to the attacking planes."[91] In contrast, the Viet Cong abided by no laws of war. They used civilians, "'clutching the people to their breast' by converting rural hamlets into fortified strongholds that were camouflaged to look like peaceful villages; by disguising themselves as civilians; and by using villagers of all ages and both sexes…to plant mines and booby traps and engage in other military activities."[92] Zinn, of course, makes no mention of the Communists' use of civilians as human shields, nor of multiple other war crimes by the Viet Cong.

And this is the way Zinn explains the "Tet Offensive":

The unpopularity of the Saigon government explains the success of the National Liberation Front in infiltrating Saigon and other government-held towns in early 1968, without the people there warning the government. The NLF thus launched a surprise offensive (it was the time of "Tet," their New Year holiday) that carried them into the heart of Saigon, immobilized Tan San Nhut airfield, even occupied the American Embassy briefly. The offensive was beaten back, but it demonstrated that all the enormous firepower delivered on Vietnam by the United States had not destroyed the NLF, its morale, its popular support, its will to fight. It caused a reassessment in the American government, more doubts among the American people.[93]

But as Oscar Handlin pointed out in the *American Scholar*, "'Tet' was not evidence of the unpopularity of the Saigon government, but a resounding rejection of the northern invaders."[94] Not to mention that "the offensive was not a success and that the [National Liberation Front] evoked no signs of popular support."[95] According to Stephen Morris, in South Vietnam, Tet made previously "neutral or fence-sitting segments of the population commit themselves more to the South Vietnamese government cause." It helped in the ongoing pacification program to "win hearts and minds" because "the southern Communist cadres who had surfaced in the campaign were able to be identified and either captured or killed. The expansion of the number of South Vietnamese troops and reconstitution of local village, district, and provincial armed forces brought new stability."[96] Lewis Sorley, author of *A Better War: The Unexamined Victories and Final Tragedy of America's Last Years in Vietnam*, agrees that the Communists in the South never recovered and progressively lost influence. The encounter with the "Communist guerrilla forces" who were "routed" made "fence-sitt[ers] commit themselves to the South Vietnamese government cause."[97]

Yet the media reported Tet as a Communist victory. They dwelt on the "photograph of South Vietnamese police chief Nguyen Ngoc Loan shooting a man in the head, claiming the man was a 'Vietcong suspect.'"

He was not a suspect, but was a man Loan knew, "a Viet Cong colonel in civilian clothes...and by the rules of war, a spy," as Schweikart and Allen, the authors of *A Patriot's History of the United States*, explain. Morris tells us that the executed Viet Cong spy had "been found with a pistol adjacent to a hastily dug grave that held the bodies of seven South Vietnamese policemen and their families." While Morris concedes that the execution "may still have been unjustified," Schweikart and Allen note, "Andrew Jackson had done almost exactly the same thing to British agents...."[98]

Podhoretz relates how the media falsely reported that rural areas had "fallen under Communist control," and characterized North Vietnamese General Giap as "a genius," when he actually had "made serious errors of military judgment." Newscaster Walter Cronkite, "who had earlier seen Vietnam as another expression of the 'courageous decision that Communism's advance must be stopped....'" portrayed Tet as so much of a defeat that the United States should give up hopes of victory and negotiate a way out.[99] The Tet Offensive did turn American *elite* opinion further against the war. But it did not cause a dramatic shift in [U.S.] public opinion. In fact, polls showed that Johnson consistently drew higher support when he restarted the bombing of the North.[100]

Zinn's account of the U.S. "Operation Phoenix" is—surprise!— equally distorted. In his telling, it was a secret operation directed against innocent civilians: "The CIA in Vietnam, in a program called 'Operation Phoenix,' secretly, without trial, executed at least twenty thousand civilians in South Vietnam who were suspected of being members of the Communist underground."[101] In fact, the Phoenix program was a joint effort by the U.S. and South Vietnamese governments to destroy the Viet Cong Infrastructure in South Vietnam "without direct engagement by the U.S. military." As Colonel Andrew L. Finlayson points out at the CIA website, the secret program was often falsely portrayed by "the antiwar movement and critical scholars" (attention, Howard Zinn!) as an "assassination program targeting civilians." In reality, the program targeted Viet Cong *agents*. After Phoenix identified Viet Cong operatives at the village level, U.S. or South Vietnamese forces attempted to arrest or capture the individuals for interrogation, and "if they resisted, they were killed." According to Finlayson:

> In 1972 CORDS [Civil Operations and Revolutionary Development Support, which oversaw all pacification programs] reported that since the 1968 Tet Offensive, Phoenix had removed over 5,000 VCI [Viet Cong Infrastructure, or party leaders of the Viet Cong] from action, and that conventional military actions and desertions—some prompted by Phoenix—accounted for over 20,000 more. The US claimed that Phoenix and the US military's response to the Tet Offensive, along with other rural security, and militia programs, had eliminated upwards of 80,000 VCI through defection, detention, or death.

"By most accounts," writes Finlayson, "including those of Vietnamese communists—Phoenix (which ended in 1971) and other pacification programs drove the VCI so far underground that it was unable to operate effectively. In the 1972 Easter offensive, and again in 1975, there was no sign of the VCI or the Viet Cong military because Phoenix and its allied activities had dealt them a very serious blow."[102] So, the program seemed to have accomplished its objective—that is, to neutralize the Viet Cong without bombing. But in Zinn's opinion, the Viet Cong are folk heroes. Zinn perpetuates the false image of a program that rescued South Vietnamese peasants from the "genocidal" Viet Cong as a CIA-led assassination team directed at civilians.

In spite of the hopeless picture that anti-war protestors—prominent among them Howard Zinn—were painting toward the end of the Vietnam War, there was a definite turnaround after Tet. The United States and the South came tantalizingly close to beating the Communists. Stephen Morris described his two visits to South Vietnam "in early 1970 and again in early 1972." By the second trip, he was able to drive in a car with official license plates and "in a taxi with Vietnamese locals." He comments that had "the Viet Cong...not been suppressed I would probably have been captured or killed."[103] William Colby had a similar experience there in 1971, as Lewis Sorley recounts in *A Better War: The Unexamined Victories and Final Tragedy of America's Last Years in Vietnam.* In fact, Sorley says that by "late 1970," "the war was won. The fighting wasn't over, but the war was won.... the South Vietnamese countryside had been widely pacified.... our million members of the People's Self-Defense Force, armed with 600,000 weapons...constituted an overt commitment to the government in opposition to the enemy."[104]

In 1972, there were fewer than seventy thousand American troops in Vietnam, down from the "peak more than half a million."[105] During the Easter Offensive that year, "practically no American combat forces participated in the defense of South Vietnam." The defeat of the North was the result of the pacification and Vietnamization (preparation of the Vietnamese Army), along with "lavish American logistical support in the form of ammunition, fuel, and advanced weaponry," according to CIA officer William Colby. With the South Vietnamese bearing "the main burden of the fight on the ground...." "[a] free Vietnam had proven that it had the will and the capability to defend itself with the assistance, but not the participation, of its American ally." That was in a fight against an enemy "assisted by Soviet and Chinese allies." And then comes the wistful refrain heard so often about Vietnam: "On the ground in South Vietnam, the war had been won."

But Colby also was beginning to "appreciate a new factor in the war—the virulence of the antiwar movement," which had "erupted over our incursion into Cambodia in 1970," an incursion that was clearly justified as an "effort to clean out the Communist base areas along the frontier with South Vietnam"—something that would become tragically clear after the American withdrawal.[106] Even the liberal Stanley Karnow admitted the effectiveness of Tet and the Easter Offensive as he reported the Communists' comments about them.[107]

The military draft in the United States ended in 1973. In 1974, "there were only 500 Communist cadres left in Saigon, a city of 2.5 million," and at least 70 percent of Southerners were opposed to reunification.[108] But between 1973 and 1974, as victory was within sight, a Democratic-controlled Congress "emboldened" by the Watergate scandal and encouraged by the protestors slashed aid to Vietnam. "When Congress ordered an end to American air support, South Vietnam's fate was sealed," writes Jonathan Leaf. The abandonment of South Vietnam "was guided by a clique of antiwar activists."[109]

Zinn, of course, was the elder leading the charge. The poor execution at the beginning of the war allowed him and his cadres to gain momentum: bad military decisions were made at the beginning of the war (such as the assassination of Diem), the attempt to fight it on the cheap, and the failure to make a bold moral case. Larry Schweikart and Michael Allen recount President Lyndon Johnson's problems arising after President Kennedy's assassination due to his lack of popularity with Kennedy's staff, except for Secretary of Defense Robert McNamara, who was "obtuse" about mission and strategy. McNamara ceded "the propaganda campaign to the communists and their allies [the protestors]," and Johnson himself displayed a lack of commitment to the war—he was more interested in winning praise for his grandiose social programs.[110] Lewis Sorley criticizes Johnson's unwillingness to call up the reserves, which produced too much reliance on young, inexperienced conscripts. Morale among the troops suffered after "it became clear that the United States no longer sought to win the war, but to disengage." And the "turmoil and upheaval" of the social revolution took their toll on the soldiers. These included such harmful things as challenges to "established authority, received wisdom, to long-standing customs, to concepts of individual freedoms and responsibilities," as well as recreational drug use.[111] This is not to mention the vilification of the military and the outright assaults on returning U.S. soldiers.

Howard Zinn did his bit to promote the societal breakdown that impacted the troops. The chapter of A People's History on Vietnam celebrates the *defeat* of the U.S., so it is fitting that Zinn devotes more than half of its pages to the "people" who brought defeat to the home front: the protestors and his fellow leaders in the anti-war movement. Zinn is at his most cheery when he can report, "In the course of that war, there developed in the United States the greatest antiwar movement the nation had ever experienced, a movement that played a critical part in bringing the war to an end."[112]

In his teaching and political activism, Zinn himself had done his best to turn the Civil Rights Movement into an anti-war movement. He celebrates the fact that in 1966 "six members of SNCC were arrested for an invasion of an induction center in Atlanta." He relives his glory days, repeating the slogans, "Hell no, we won't go!" and "LBJ, LBJ, how many kids did you kill today?"[113] He fills pages of his "History of the United States" with anecdotes about protesters and draft dodgers, including one Philip Supina, "a Boston University graduate student in history" (where Zinn was teaching at the time) who "wrote on May 1, 1968, to his draft board" advising them of his refusal to report for his pre-induction physical exam[114]—and Alice Herz, an eighty-two-year-old peace activist who followed the example of the Buddhist monks and self-immolated. For Zinn, these are positive signs.

The burning of draft cards was a great celebration among students. Adults, too—including Zinn's travel buddy to North Vietnam, Father Daniel Berrigan, and his brother Philip, along with seven others—went to a draft board office in Catonsville, Maryland, and then came outside and, before an audience that included reporters, burned the records. They "became famous as the 'Catonsville Nine.'" Zinn gives an account of Daniel Berrigan's escape from FBI agents by hiding inside a giant theater figure and remaining underground for four months. Not so lucky, according to his account, was Mary Moylan, a former nun, and "the one woman among the Catonsville Nine." (Actually, there was another woman in the group, Marjorie Bradford Melville.) Moylan "refused to surrender to the FBI," and as Zinn ominously notes, "She was never found." Zinn then devotes nearly an entire page to an extensive quotation about jail and the "black scene" from the journal of the woman presumably murdered by the FBI or other government agents.[115]

Moylan, however, surrendered in 1979. Both the *New York Times* and *Washington Post* reported this on June 21, 1979—news that should not have escaped Zinn's notice as he was writing his book. She had spent nine years underground but served only one year in prison. She then resumed her career as a nurse and worked for several years at Queen Anne's Hospital in Chestertown, Maryland. She died in 1995 at the age of fifty-nine.[116] As much as Zinn would like to make Moylan a martyr, the reality is that Moylan, in almost any other country, would not have gotten so light a punishment and then been allowed to resume her job as a *nurse*.

Indeed, most anti-war activists got off with light or no punishment. That is probably why there were so many protests. According to Zinn's count, in the first six months of 1969, 215,000 students in 232 of the nation's 2,000 institutions of higher education had participated in protests, 500 underground newspapers existed in high schools, and two-thirds of the 1969 graduating class at Brown University turned their backs on Henry Kissinger's commencement address.[117] Zinn reports happily that students at 400 colleges and universities went on strike—"the first general student strike in the history of the United States." The normally statistics-averse Zinn wraps up, "During that 1969–1970 school year, the FBI listed 1,785 student demonstrations, including the occupation of 313 buildings." Polls showed an increasing opposition to the war, especially among the working class, and there was a "general change in the entire population of the country."[118]

The "climax," for Zinn, was Kent State, on May 4, 1970, "when students gathered to demonstrate against the war" and "National Guardsmen fired into the crowd," killing four students and paralyzing one.[119] Zinn, however, ignores the fact that one of the students had pointed a gun at the guardsmen after pistol-whipping another student with it. This came after "looters and arsonists" had taken over the campus, "torching the Air Force ROTC building," setting fire to the president's building, and then rioting downtown and at an airstrip, stealing a truck, attacking six planes, and starting a fire. When the guardsmen were facing the gun, they had already had rocks thrown at them by students and had become trapped, "caught behind a chain-link fence of a practice football facility." The disorder had started on that campus earlier in the semester, under the leadership of "self-professed Communist Robert Franklin." The protesters occupied buildings. On May 1, students buried a copy of the Constitution, burned a draft card and an American flag, and began more serious acts of arson. Before the four students were shot, "the ringleaders had organized" a large group of students around them "as human shields."[120]

The coup de grace was the shift in Americans' attitude toward the military. Zinn saw the drop in ROTC enrollment as a sign of "the capacity for independent judgement among ordinary Americans." The largest and most fervent opposition to the war in our armed forces began with "isolated protests," such as Richard Steinke's refusal to board an aircraft to a Vietnamese village in 1965. "The following year three army privates, one black, one Puerto Rican, one Lithuanian-Italian—all poor—refused to embark for Vietnam" and were "court-martialed and imprisoned." Later came the court martial of "a navy nurse, Lieutenant Susan Schnall" and displays of opposition by a sailor in Norfolk, Virginia, "an army lieutenant," and "two black marines, George Daniels and William Harvey."[121] As Zinn tells us, these "individual acts multiplied." Someone named Ray Kroll, who came from "a poor family," fled and deserted after being charged with drunkenness. He hid out in the chapel of Boston University (where Zinn was teaching at the time—not coincidentally, a great number of the anti-war protests seem to have taken place on the campus where Zinn was fomenting anti-war sentiment and activism). Michael S. Foley, author of *Confronting the War Machine: Draft Resistance during the Vietnam War*, describes Zinn and his friend and fellow Boston academic Noam Chomsky as "ubiquitous professors," who could be "heard at almost all antiwar demonstrations." Zinn inspired young men to the point of weeping. One named David Clennon told Foley that

Zinn "spoke so eloquently about the horrors of war that I was convinced all over again that turning in my draft card was the right thing to do" that he "was crying with relief...."[122]

More good news: "Underground newspapers sprang up at military bases," "We Shall Overcome" was sung at the Presidio in protest of a guard shooting "to death an emotionally disturbed prisoner for walking away from a work detail," GIs wore black armbands in Vietnam, black soldiers expressed their bitterness in recordings, cadets dropped out of West Point, and "[m]ore and more cases of 'fragging' were reported in Vietnam—incidents where servicemen rolled fragmentation bombs under the tents of officers who were ordering them into combat, or against whom they had other grievances. The Pentagon reported 209 fraggings in Vietnam in 1970 alone."[123]

In the "Winter Soldier" investigations, American solders testified "publicly about atrocities they had participated in or seen in Vietnam.... in April 1971 more than a thousand of them went to Washington, D.C., to demonstrate against the war. One by one, they went up to a wire fence around the Capitol, threw over the fence the medals they had won in Vietnam, and made brief statements about the war, sometimes emotionally, sometimes in icy, bitter calm."[124] One of those Winter Soldiers was John Kerry, who would become a U.S. senator representing Massachusetts; he was defeated in his 2004 run for the presidency in large part by the efforts of a group of Vietnam veterans called the Swift Boat Veterans for Truth, whose testimony refuted his claims about heroic service in Vietnam. Their open letter accused him of "seek[ing] to clad yourself in the very medals that you disdainfully threw away" and of endangering fellow servicemen (including prisoners of war) with falsehoods about their conduct in Vietnam.[125]

Howard Zinn was doing his part to make this history happen. Not only did he infuse his students with his ideas about war and Communism, but he did the same with American servicemen on a European teaching jaunt. As Zinn wrote to his former student, Alice Walker, he had been on a tour with "two days each in Rome, Naples, Paris, five days in Malta—yes, teaching sailors on a US ship in the harbor at Valetta, Malta, and teaching them (or rather talking with them about) international affairs including communism, democracy, Vietnam—not because the Navy has gone mad or I have suddenly been revealed as a CIA agent operating in the New Left—but because all large bureaucracies have their moments of amnesia."

He had also "been doing a huge amount of speaking in debates, teach-ins, etc. on Vietnam, several times each week, and sometimes almost every night, here and there to all sorts of odd groups—Catholics in Leominister, rich folk in Greenwich, Conn., students at Duke University (last night—a guest of Sam Cook, first Negro prof. at Duke)."[126]

According to Zinn, by 1972 there was "no victory in sight" and North Vietnamese troops "were entrenched in the South." (That's in contrast to what Morris and Colby reported from their time on the ground in Vietnam.) The U.S. made "one final attempt to bludgeon the North Vietnamese into submission" through bombings. "Many of the B-52s were shot down, there was angry protest all over the world," and Kissinger signed the peace agreement. "In late April 1975, North Vietnamese troops entered Saigon. The American embassy staff fled, along with many Vietnamese who feared Communist rule, and the long war in Vietnam was over. Saigon was renamed Ho Chi Minh City, and both parts of Vietnam were unified as the Democratic Republic of Vietnam."[127]

Of course, Zinn does not describe the real terror of the scene. As former Marine officer Philip Caputo reported for the April 28, 1975, *Chicago Tribune*, events of the "Communist drive on Saigon" were "almost Goyaesque in their horror," with enemy mortars exploding all around and body parts in the road, rotting in the rain. Communist tanks growled "like armored monsters" behind a procession of fleeing humanity, a "long, relentless column" of at least twenty miles, on foot, motor scooters, in cars, trucks, buses, and oxcarts.[128]

And this is how CIA veteran William Colby described the events as helicopters began lifting evacuees off rooftops and improvised landing pads:

Crowds of Vietnamese frantically tried to be included in the escape. Although literally every American was removed, the confusion made it impossible to take the thousands of Vietnamese clamoring to go—including many who had been assured that they would be taken care of by the power that had dominated their lives, and that they had served and relied upon, for so many years. A few Vietnamese officers put bullets to their heads, some as a gesture of honor in defeat, others to escape the draconian punishment that they knew awaited them in Communist "reeducation" camps.[129]

American servicemen, as is evident from surveys, were as disappointed as Colby by this outcome, with 82 percent angered by the fact that "political leaders in Washington would not let them win." Zinn did his part to paint a picture of abandonment of support of the war among the military. But surveys of Vietnam veterans tell a different story: 74 percent said they "'enjoyed' their service in Vietnam, 71 percent are 'glad' they went, and 66 percent report that they'd serve again." Veterans were also found to be "better educated" and earning "higher salaries than their peers who did not serve."[130]

As to the claim that what America was fighting against in Vietnam was a nationalist movement—or, as Zinn puts it, a movement for "local communism"—Morris points out that "after their victory in 1975, the Vietnamese Communists provided captured American weapons to the Soviet Union for use in Communist insurrections in other nations, most notably in El Salvador in the 1980s."[131] So, yes, Virginia, there *was* an international Communist conspiracy to bring about a worldwide Communist revolution, and Americans were properly "scared" of the Reds.

Like others around the globe, the Vietnamese suffered greatly at the hands of the Communists. The South Vietnamese armed forces had "lost 275,000 killed in action." Nearly twice as many Vietnamese civilians—465,000 men, women, and children—had lost their lives, "many of them assassinated by Viet Cong terrorists or felled by the enemy's indiscriminate shelling and rocketing of cities," wrote Sorley. A million became boat people; many died at sea in their desperate flight from Communist oppression. "Perhaps 65,000 others were executed by their liberators. As many as 250,000 more perished in brutal reeducation camps. Two million, driven from their homeland, formed a new Vietnamese diaspora."[132]

In a book that claims to celebrate the overlooked masses and the downtrodden, there is no mention of the Vietnamese refugees who were streaming to the United States when Zinn was writing his book in the late 1970s. But the only "people" Zinn was interested in were—as always—Communists, and people who can help the Communists win: "Traditional history portrays the end of wars as coming from the initiatives of leaders—negotiations in Paris or Brussels or Geneva or Versailles—just as it often finds the coming of war a response to the demand of 'the people.' The Vietnam war gave clear evidence that at least for that war (making one wonder about the others) the political leaders were the last to take steps to end the war—'the people' were far ahead."[133]

So, let us hear from one of the Vietnamese "people" whose story didn't make it into Zinn's book. In a *City Journal* article, *Triumph Forsaken* author Mark Moyar provides this testimony from Nguyen van Thai and Nguyen Phuc Lien: "We, Vietnamese.... fought because we understood the cruelty and dictatorship of the communists. We fought because we did not wish the communists to impose a barbarous and inhuman regime upon us. More than 1,000,000 people from North Vietnam fled their native land and emigrated to the South in 1954 in order to escape totalitarianism, which is ample evidence for this point. The second exodus of the 70's, 80's and early 90's also corroborated this fact."[134]

Zinn, in contrast, was jubilant about the triumph of the Vietnamese Communists—and the defeat of the United States. He quoted C. L. Sulzberger of the *New York Times* about the U.S. emerging "as the big loser.... we lost the war in the Mississippi valley, not the Mekong valley...." But he tops Sulzberger: "In fact, the United States had lost the war in both the Mekong Valley and the Mississippi Valley. It was the first clear defeat to the global American empire formed after World War II. It was administered by revolutionary peasants abroad, and by an astonishing movement of protest at home." More good news, from Howard Zinn's point of view: "From a long-range viewpoint, something perhaps even more important had happened. The rebellion at home was spreading beyond the issue of war in Vietnam."[135]

Zinn's distorted and anti-American version of the Vietnam War is widely promulgated in our educational system. Children watching videos produced and distributed by the Zinn Education Project (ZEP)—a plethora of educational materials is available from this organization—are presented with a film about the anti-war movement within the military or about hero Daniel Ellsberg who purloined the Pentagon Papers. My Lai is presented as "typical" of American involvement in Vietnam, as the *Young People's History* indicates with the claim, "An army officer admitted that many other tragedies like My Lai remained hidden."[136] Close to eighty-four thousand teachers have signed up at ZEP. Non-affiliated writers of history books for children also reference Zinn's history. One stamped "class book" in the Utica branch of my rural upstate New York library system features a five-paragraph excerpt from Ho Chi Minh's "Independence Day" speech of September 2, 1945, and quotes extensively from Zinn's book. The head note explains, "In his book, *A People's History of the United States*, historian Howard Zinn includes this selection of a Declaration of Independence and a list of grievances against the French proclaimed by Ho Chi Minh and his fellow revolutionists at the end of World War II in 1945." The text states, "The Vietnamese revolutionary carried with him a copy of the U.S. Declaration of Independence."[137]

Howard Zinn, the Founders, and Us

No assessment of Howard Zinn's *People's History of the United States* would be complete without some consideration of his perverse take on the founding of our nation. His chapter about the American Revolution is titled "A Kind of Revolution."[1] Why? Because American independence and the establishment of a republic on the basis that "all men are created equal, that they are endowed by their Creator with certain unalienable rights, that among these are Life, Liberty and the Pursuit of Happiness" is not revolutionary enough for Zinn. To satisfy him, the American Revolution should have smashed the capitalist system and toppled the "elite" to whom he refers sneeringly throughout the chapter.

In Zinn's telling, the revolution actually helped the "elite" keep their grip on power. How? "Ruling elites seem to have learned through the generations—consciously or not—that war makes them more secure against internal trouble."[2] Sure, laws were changed during the war to relieve poor debtors and require the rich to bear a larger part of the tax burden. But that was just "a sacrifice by the upper class to maintain power."[3] The revolution only enshrined a "new elite"[4]— including Alexander Hamilton, George Washington, and John Adams:

"The Continental Congress, which governed the colonies through the war, was dominated by rich men, linked together in factions and compacts by business and family connections."[5] In fact, America would "create the richest ruling class in history."[6] Zinn is much less interested in the conflict between the British and the colonists than he is in the "conflicts between rich and poor among the Americans."[7]

So, Zinn does his best to import the Communist class struggle into the American Founding—by "examining the Revolution's effect on class relations." According to *A People's History*, "land confiscated from fleeing Loyalists...was distributed in such a way as to give double opportunity to the Revolutionary leaders: to enrich themselves and their friends, and to parcel out some land to small farmers to create a broad base of support to the new government." This kind of massive redistribution—an ingenious tactic to shore up the ruling class and prevent a true revolution that would put the workers in control—"became characteristic of the new nation: finding itself possessed of enormous wealth, it could create the richest ruling class in history, and still have enough for the middle classes to act as a buffer between the rich and dispossessed."[8] (In Marxist theory, the middle class is always the real impediment to a true revolution. No wonder Karl Marx and Friedrich Engels said in *The Communist Manifesto* that the "bourgeois," "the middle-class owner of property" must be "swept out of the way...." and that the "first step in the revolution by the working class, is to raise the proletariat to the position of the ruling class, to establish democracy" and then "centralize all instruments of production in the hands of the state.")[9]

What a clever ruse by the wealthy! In actuality, from the very beginning, America offered opportunities and hope—even for the poorest. The late Wesleyan University economics professor Stanley Lebergott offered some historical perspective (sorely lacking in Zinn's history!). While life was challenging for most settling in the New World in the eighteenth and nineteenth centuries, it was much better than life in the Old. In Scotland, "men sold themselves into slavery because of poverty, and worked in the salt and coal mines." In France, "the ragged peasant...yoked his plow with a donkey in one trace and his wife in the other." In Switzerland, "women filled buckets with urine and manure, yoked them across their shoulders, and carried them uphill to fertilize the fields...." We've seen the statistics that show that even slaves in America were better nourished than many Europeans. In Switzerland, for example, "the simple people" had meat and bread only on holidays, while per capita meat consumption in Flanders in 1800 was estimated at "22 pounds per year"—in the United States, 360.[10]

As Alexis de Tocqueville commented in the 1830s, there were no peasants in America. At that time, Europe was still filled with them, many living in "absolute slavery" with no way to escape their lot, as Lebergott demonstrates. Peasants were not only "subject to taxes by central and local governments," but "also subject to even more rigorous charges imposed by landowners who took a substantial portion of their grain as payment for milling the rest into flour, forbidding them to do their own milling. Americans averaged less than a dollar a year in taxes. And anyone was free to set up a mill."[11]

That is why millions of these impoverished "left in an unplanned exodus," following "a handful of earnest religious leaders and believers, entrepreneurs and gold seekers, who had shown the way." The French-American writer Hector St. John de Crèvecoeur in his *Letters from an American Farmer*, published in 1782, described the situation in America: "The European does not find, as in Europe, a crowded society where every place is overstocked; he does not feel that...difficulty of beginning.... here is room for everybody, in America. Has he any particular talent, or industry? He exerts it in order to procure a livelihood, and it succeeds.... is he a laborer, sober and industrious? He need not go many miles...before he will be hired, well fed...and paid four or five times more than he can get in Europe."[12]

Zinn overlooks the fact that four centuries before the Communist scheme for land redistribution failed in Asia and Europe, "communal land cultivation" had already famously "failed in Massachusetts Bay."

After that abortive attempt, "virtually every white family owned its own farm," and "by 1774, of every four free families, three owned their own farm."[13]

The true, Communist-style revolution that Zinn wishes had happened in America actually did happen during the *French* Revolution just a few years later—with disastrous results: "Before his fellow French revolutionaries carted him off to be guillotined in 1794, Georges Danton had described his purpose: 'to put on top what was below.'"

But fortunately for Americans, dividing "the spoils among the conquerors," was not the zealous aim of the "American revolutionary leaders," despite the fact that "perhaps a quarter of the population were counterrevolutionaries." Amazingly—in comparison to the typical treatment of the defeated in any war—three-quarters of the "Loyalists remained in the United States," as Lebergott shows. While Zinn claims "Revolutionary leaders" divvied up the land of the Loyalists to "enrich themselves and their friends," in fact it was the "land holdings of the royal governors," "the massive holdings of King George III," and the "estates of wealthy Loyalists, chiefly those who fled" that were confiscated by the states. And "in the end...'less than 4 percent of the nation's real and personal estates changed hands.'"[14]

"The federal Constitution" *was* "the work of the commercial people in the seaport towns, of the slaveholding states, of the officers of the Revolutionary Army, and the property holders everywhere," as John Adams wrote. And what a good thing that was—in spite of the aspersions Zinn casts upon it for that reason. As Lebergott explains, Adams and his peers "recognized that by funding its debts and paying to defend its frontiers government would enhance the value of farms and land, as well as other property throughout the nation."[15]

None of these facts matter to Howard Zinn. He sets out to debunk the idea believed by "many Americans over the years"—that "the Constitution drawn up in 1787" was "a work of genius put together by wise, humane men who created a legal framework for democracy and equality."[16] Howard Zinn has a more up-to-date take he wants to sell his readers from a work published in 1913: *An Economic Interpretation of the Constitution of the United States* by Charles Beard. According to Zinn, Beard's updated 1935 version "arous[ed] anger and indignation," because it put forth the idea "that most of the makers of the Constitution had some direct interest in establishing a strong federal government: the manufacturers needed protective tariffs; the money-lenders wanted to stop the use of paper money to pay off debts; the land speculators wanted protection as they invaded Indian lands; slaveowners needed federal security against revolts and runaways; bondholders wanted a government able to raise money by national taxation, to pay off those bonds."[17]

But Beard's thesis that the Founders were solely motivated by such materialistic interests had been debunked several times over before Zinn wrote *A People's History*. It had been thoroughly demolished by Forrest McDonald, following Robert E. Brown's 1956 study, *Charles Beard and the Constitution: A Critical Analysis of 'An Economic Interpretation of the Constitution.'* Zinn makes a pretense of acknowledging what he calls Brown's "interesting point": "Granted that the Constitution omitted the phrase 'life, liberty and the pursuit of happiness,' which appeared in the Declaration of Independence, and substituted 'life, liberty, or property'—well, why shouldn't the Constitution protect property? As Brown says about Revolutionary America, 'practically everybody was interested in the protection of property' because so many Americans owned property."

But for Zinn, Brown's argument "is misleading. True, there were many property owners. But some people had more than others. A few people had great amounts of property; many people had small amounts; others had none." An estimated one-third "were small farmers." Such small property holders, including tradesmen, such as "bakers, blacksmiths, brewers,...coopers" acted—Marxist theory strikes again!—as "buffers against the blacks, the Indians, the very poor whites." The "slightly prosperous people.... enable the elite to keep control with a minimum of coercion, a maximum of law—all made palatable by the fanfare of patriotism and unity." Therefore, the Constitution and the Bill of Rights are suspect. Those *really* in power were the wealthy, and liberty was "shaky" "when entrusted to a government of the rich and powerful."[18] Zinn repeats the same old conspiracy theory—and the same old Marxist assumption that only equality of wealth can ensure democracy.

So, Zinn's argument is circular; he is simply reiterating Beard's idea that the Founding was a conspiracy of the rich against the poor. He does not answer Brown's objection to Beard's thesis. Nor does he consider the criticism of Beard by McDonald: "The idea of man as economic animal" is "simpleminded" because it fails to consider other "driving forces" like "love of power," and patriotism, which can "override selfish considerations of economic gain"—as displayed by two delegates, Nathaniel Gorham, "a wealthy Massachusetts merchant" who knew that the Constitution would raise the prices of securities, and lead to his losing his investments, but voted for it anyway, and Robert Morris, "who in 1787 was the richest merchant in America and who ended up in debtors' prison."[19]

But then we have to consider where Zinn is coming from, where he gets his theory of economic determinism. McDonald's critique of Beard applies equally well to Marx, who wrote in the *Critique of Political Economy*, "The mode of production of material life determines the social, political, and intellectual life process in general."[20] And also to Engels, who wrote in the introduction to the 1888 English edition of *The Communist Manifesto*, "the whole history of mankind (since the dissolution of primitive tribal society, holding land in common ownership) has been a history of class struggles, contests between exploiting and exploited, ruling and oppressed classes...."[21] That's all it is for Zinn, too.

Such a worldview cannot allow for the idea that men may be motivated by something other than material gain. Yes, many of the Founders, including Washington, Hancock, and Benjamin Franklin, were wealthy men. (George Washington was *not*, though, as Zinn claims, "the richest man in America.")[22] But the wealth of many of the Founders is the more reason to doubt Zinn's thesis that they "engineered the revolt" for financial gain. As David McCullough writes of Washington—who was not born to great wealth, who worked as a surveyor and speculated in property, and who then married the wealthy Martha Custis—"Washington's wealth and way of life, like his physique and horsemanship, were of great importance to large numbers of the men he led and among many in Congress. The feeling was that if he, George Washington, who had so much, was willing to risk 'his all,' however daunting the odds, then who were they to equivocate."[23]

As Lebergott points out, Beard is one of "a succession of historians" who mischaracterized the support for the Constitution—"as though that support had been restricted to holders of debt certificates, one of many species of property." Lebergott explains, "That somewhat myopic view has obscured the fact that over three-fourths of all American families owned property (land, farms, debts, certificates, etc.) and that nearly every species of property was likely to rise in value" with the adoption of the Constitution.[24]

In *Good Will Hunting*, Matt Damon—thoroughly indoctrinated by age ten, when he took Zinn's book to class—discounts Gordon Wood as a historian. Perhaps that's because Wood's history debunks Zinn's thesis. As Wood demonstrates, it was actually the Loyalists, not the Patriots, who came mostly from the upper level of society. The majority of the colonists were in the Whig tradition, the "'country' opposition to…the 'court,'"—in other words, it was the people who made the Revolution who were "the people."

The American revolutionaries were the heirs of the men who had agitated for increased representational voting power for the House of Commons.[25] Articulating their ideas was Thomas Paine, the author of *Common Sense*, who "rejected the traditional and stylized forms of persuasion designed for educated gentlemen." Paine carried on the project of the writers from the mother country, like Alexander Pope and Jonathan Swift, who had criticized the crown for supporting powerful commercial interests that corrupted "traditional values."[26] Colonists from all walks of life rebelled against trade restrictions and excessive taxation without representation through the Stamp Act rebellion and the Boston Tea Party. Farmers and speculators in search of new land resisted British control. They resented military intrusion into their homes through the Quartering Act.[27] In short, this was a revolution for the common man.

Zinn, who presumes to write a "people's history," does not consider that meetings called to resist the threat of British tyranny also made demands for inclusion of colonists who were not of the elite classes: in Philadelphia, radicals "demanded that seven artisans and six Germans" be added to that city's "revolutionary committee"; in Savannah, to the royal's governor's horror, revolutionaries "consisted of 'a Parcel of the Lowest People, chiefly carpenters, shoemakers, Blacksmiths etc. with a Jew at their head.'"[28] Colonists also took note of the prosecution of "English radical John Wilkes" for criticizing the Crown and his "four successive expulsions" from the House of Commons, "despite his repeated reelection by his constituents." As Wood explains, "Americans were involved not simply in a defense of their own rights, but in a worldwide struggle for the salvation of liberty itself. When they looked over the past several centuries of European history, all they could see were the efforts of monarchs everywhere to build up state power in order to extract money from their subjects for the waging of war"[29]— exactly the thing Zinn claimed to be fighting against.

Wood is Brown University's Alva O. Way University Professor and Professor of History Emeritus at Brown University and, according to the *Wall Street Journal*, has been called the "dean of 18th-century American historians." He has accumulated "virtually every award available to historians," including the Bancroft Prize, Pulitzer, and the National Humanities Medal in 2010.[30] But Howard Zinn simply dismisses Wood's work as the "Great Man" version of history, in contrast to his own "people's" history.[31] One wonders if he read the page on which Wood describes the "'carpenters, shoemakers, Blacksmiths'" who demanded a place on revolutionary committees.

In fact, if there is a "Great Man" in the history Wood writes, he is different from the "Great Men" before America—the Caesars and Napoleons of world history. In Wood's historical work, George Washington and the other Founders represent a new kind of character emerging in an America abandoning a "monarchical society" defined by "ties of blood, kinship, and dependency": "Americans offered a different conception of what people were like and new ways of organizing both the state and society. The Revolutionary leaders were not naïve and they were not utopians—indeed, some of them had grave doubts about the capacities of ordinary people. But by adopting republican governments in 1776 all of them necessarily held to a more magnanimous conception of human nature than did supporters of monarchy."[32]

Zinn contrasts the very real and very effective American Revolution with an imaginary egalitarian paradise in order to lure the young and ignorant to support the Marxist nightmare from which millions have fled—and by which millions who were unable to escape have been killed. He is uninterested in the ideas that undergird our American republic—which have made America so attractive to those fleeing totalitarian regimes. He's not satisfied with America's uniquely successful constitutional system of checks and balances. In fact, even pure democracy won't do: "For if some people had greater wealth and influence; if they had the land, the money, the newspapers, the church, the educational system—how could voting, however broad, cut into such power? There was still another problem: wasn't it the nature of representative government, even when most broadly based, to be conservative, to prevent tumultuous change?"[33] Notice Zinn's slippery rhetoric here: the posing of questions in rapid succession, with answers implied rather than asserted, and the presentation of a bloody Communist revolution as "tumultuous change" with those refusing it fearful enemies of the people. No revolution (certainly not the American Revolution) and no system of government (certainly not our Constitution) will satisfy Zinn until what he calls "the division of society into rich and poor" can somehow be made to vanish away. Those who know history know what this Marxist siren song leads to. The only way to disguise it is to ignore the more than one hundred million corpses that it produced in the twentieth century and to present the United States, the freest nation in world history, as a tyrannical, murderous, and imperialistic regime—which is exactly what Zinn has done in his *History*.

He has done this by lying, distorting and misusing evidence, hijacking other historians' work, and falsifying the facts, as we have seen again and again. The problem is not that, as Zinn liked to pretend in his own defense, he wrote a "people's" history, telling the bottom-up story of neglected and forgotten men and women. The problem is that he falsified American history to promote Communist revolution.

Howard Zinn laid out his communistic objectives openly and frequently, all the while denying that he was a Communist and charging Americans who called out Communists with delusions and paranoia implanted by the capitalists. He called them crazy. He smeared them as "red-baiters." Recall his high dudgeon about Columbus: "The treatment of heroes [Columbus] and their victims [the Arawaks]—the quiet acceptance of conquest and murder in the name of progress—is only one aspect of a certain approach to history, in which the past is told from the point of view of governments, conquerors, diplomats, leaders. It is as if they, like Columbus, deserve universal acceptance...." The "leaders" he wants to take down include "the Founding Fathers, Jackson, Lincoln, Wilson, Roosevelt, Kennedy...." Recall that he went on to assert that it was a "pretense" to believe that "there really is such a thing as 'the United States'" or a "'national interest' represented in the Constitution...." Such a statement sounds ludicrous, but not to a follower of Karl Marx, who states in *The Communist Manifesto*, "The Communists are...reproached with desiring to abolish countries and nationality. The workingmen have no country." Zinn does not believe in representative democracy. That is because, according to Marx, "[p]olitical power...is merely the organized power of one class for oppressing another."[34] Under that view, of course, voting has no meaning. As Samuel H. Beer explains, quoting Marx in his introduction to *The Communist Manifesto*, "Like the slave-owners' state and the feudal state, the modern representative state is a 'means of holding down and exploiting the oppressed class.'"[35] It sounds very much like Zinn's take on the entire history of the United States, doesn't it?

Or perhaps Zinn was borrowing from CPUSA leader William Z. Foster. Consider the way Foster casts the American founding. He quotes from *The Growth of the American Republic* by Samuel Eliot Morison and Henry Steele Commager: "The upper colonial class consisted of merchants, landed gentry, clergy of the established churches, lawyers, and officials.... they controlled the colonial assemblies, in certain colonies owned most of the land, sat on the county courts, controlled credits by individual loans [for as yet there were no banks] and set the social and cultural standards." So, in Foster's estimation, "The official leaders of the revolution came mainly from these exploiting classes." Like Zinn, Foster points out that among the signers of the Declaration of Independence, there "were no small farmers, workers, women, Negroes, or Indians, who constituted the overwhelming majority of the colonial population." Zinn repeats this point at least seven times. For example, on page 86, he claims that the "rebellion...allowed a certain group of the colonial elite to replace those loyal to England" and the Indians were "ignored by the fine words of the Declaration"; on page 89: "The inferior position of the blacks, the exclusion of Indians from the new society, the establishment of supremacy for the rich and powerful in the new nation...."; on page 91, in discussing Beard's theory about "four groups...not represented in the Constitutional Convention: slaves, indentured servants, women, men without property"; on page 101: "the Founding Fathers.... did not want a balance, except one which kept things as they were, a balance among the dominant forces at that time. They certainly did not want an equal balance between slaves and masters, propertyless and property holders, Indians and white"; and 102: "As many as half the people were not even considered by the Founding

Fathers.... were absent in the Constitution, they were invisible in the new political democracy.... the women of early America." (See also pages 97 and 99.) The idea is reinforced by sporadic examples, such as Shays's rebellion. Zinn simply repeats the idea the same way he repeated his nonsense about the equal distribution of wealth.

Communist leader Foster, like Zinn, describes the Revolutionists as "characteristic bourgeois self-seekers," many of them "brazenly speculat[ing] in army supplies, furnishing worthless munitions for the troops. They were the forerunners of those capitalists, of the same breed, who later sold antiquated muskets to the government during the Civil War, provided embalmed beef to the soldiers of the Spanish-American, and made billions in munitions orders during the two world wars."[36] Yes, all of the "same breed." Doesn't that sound familiar? Recall Zinn's attacks on the "arms merchants" he claimed were responsible for World War I. Remember his faulting Hamilton for World War II? All of "the same breed." A "pattern," to recall one of Zinn's favorite words—like "the System" and "the Establishment."

We can now see Zinn's purpose in calling on his fellow historians to abandon "disinterested scholarship" to effect "a revolution in the academy," and ultimately in the larger world.[37] That argument, in an essay often republished under the title "The Uses of Scholarship," but originally called "The Case for Radical Change," is of a piece with his attack on historical balance in the first chapter of *A People's History*. Zinn wanted to abandon disinterested scholarship and truthful history for ideology and propaganda, overturning all traditional academic standards. He wanted to do this because he thought the revolution in academic standards would lead to the Communist revolution in the larger world. He knew his history would not stand on the facts.

A People's History of the United States is intended to inspire anger of such magnitude that its readers want to overthrow the American Republic. As even fellow leftist Michael Kazin noted, in Zinn's opinion *nothing* works: Not the progressive reforms in labor laws and food safety. Not the legislation for civil rights and against discrimination in the workplace. All the improvements are dismissed or undercut by Zinn's cynical commentary. Here, again, Zinn is following the Communist script, specifically the closing words of *The Communist Manifesto:* "[The Communists] openly declare that their ends can be attained only by the forcible overthrow of all existing social conditions. Let the ruling classes tremble at a Communist revolution."[38] That's why John Brown and H. Rap Brown were Zinn's heroes. It's amazing to think that Zinn's book has become a respected and revered source for the teaching of American history in our schools, even a kind of sacred cow—as became evident with professors' reaction to the revelation in 2013 that three years earlier Indiana governor Mitch Daniels had questioned the use of Howard Zinn's book to teach children in Indiana public schools. In February 2010, in correspondence with state school officials, Daniels had questioned the use of Zinn's book in K-12 classrooms, in colleges of education, and in a National Endowment for the Humanities teachers' continuing education summer seminar titled "Social Movements in Modern America: Labor, Civil Rights, and Feminism." Daniels had argued that Zinn's history "should not be accepted for any credit by the state...." and had asked "how do we get rid of it before any more young people are force-fed a totally false version of our history?" He called *A People's History* "a truly execrable, anti-factual piece of disinformation that misstates American history on every page."[39] Daniels, of course, was absolutely right.

When the emails were revealed in 2013, Daniels stood firm, explaining that the K–12 curriculum was within the purview of state government. The leftist professoriate did not care and circled the wagons. Ninety outraged Purdue professors signed onto an open letter published by Academe, the site of the American Association of University Professors (AAUP), stating that Daniels's assessment of Zinn's scholarship went against their own "assessment," as well as that of "scholars around the world." Many in their group, they claimed, used Zinn's works in syllabi and published research. They lectured Daniels on the flaws of the "consensus school" of history—of which Arthur Schlesinger and

Oscar Handlin, who had criticized Zinn and whom Daniels had cited, were presumably members. They claimed that Zinn was *not* "anti-American," but rather committed to "bringing out our better collective selves." The professors avowed, "We trust our K–12 colleagues to know how and when to present challenges to received knowledge and how to encourage their students to judge such challenges for themselves." The letter contained a grandiloquent defense of "academic inquiry and the university's mission," claiming that "this issue transcends one author and one book" and "concerns the very legitimacy of academic discourse." They diverted attention from Daniels's criticism of Zinn's history, stating, "Scholarship emerges virtually every day that challenges the 'conventional wisdom' of prior generations. Do we assess such scholarship critically, or do we censor uncomfortable ideas out of hand?"

The letter was long on moral outrage and short on logic, on the one hand asserting that no one disputes Zinn's facts, just his conclusions, and then on the other implying that the shift in historical perspective from the old "consensus school" to Zinn's kind of history is how historiography has advanced.[40]

And the Purdue professors weren't the only ones contradicting themselves. In support of his entirely justified criticism of Zinn, Daniels had cited not only Schlesinger and Handlin, but two other historians: Sam Wineburg and Michael Kazin. You may remember Wineburg from his numerous telling criticisms of Zinn's World War II history. The Margaret Jacks Professor of Education at Stanford had attacked Zinn on the facts in the Winter 2012/2013 *American Educator*, calling *Zinn*'s history "educationally dangerous."[41] But just months later, he was blasting *Daniels* for his "shameless attempt to censor free speech" and asserting that he himself used Zinn's book in his classes. Wineburg claimed that the controversy was about "whether in an open democratic society we should be exposed—whether you're in ninth grade or seventh grade or a freshman at Purdue—whether you should be exposed to views that challenge your own cherished view."[42]

Michael Kazin had written in 2004 that *A People's History* was a "Manichean fable" suitable for "a conspiracy-monger's Web site."[43] In 2013, however, Kazin said that Daniels, who had quoted Kazin's critique of Zinn, should be "roundly condemned" for accusing Zinn of being "a biased writer." Daniels, Kazin claimed, had shown "how little he understands about how history is now written and has always been written." Although Kazin acknowledged that "Zinn's point of view is driven more by a desire to inspire his fellow leftists, instead of make them think about the complexities of the past, than I would like," he now had an excuse for the bias he had formerly condemned. So he wrote, "But I could list many other works of history—by conservatives, liberals, and radicals—which were also written to advance a political cause."[44]

Daniels had the public support of National Association of Scholars President Peter Wood, *National Review* editor Rich Lowry, and *New Criterion* editor Roger Kimball, but of very few historians. Alexander Hamilton Institute executive director Robert Paquette, a professor at Hamilton College, was an exception.[45] The American Historical Association—whose professional standards we have seen Zinn falls so woefully short of— and the Organization of American Historians sided with Zinn.[46]

Daniels capitulated in a lengthy response letter, which stated that he was "in strong general agreement" with the Purdue professors and "dedicated to the freest realm of inquiry possible at Purdue." He now conceded, "I understand that there are multiple competing theories of historiography," but in a final meek defense of his criticism of Zinn mentioned a supportive email that had referenced Zinn's disdain for objective truth as expressed in his essay, "The Uses of Scholarship."

The letter from Daniels inspired a *further* attack by the professors, who accused him of misunderstanding not only "academic freedom and the work of a university" but also "Zinn's brilliant critique of whether scholarship can be objective and disinterested." They demanded another statement asserting Daniels's "uncompromising support" for their free rein.[47] Then they set to work planning a "Read-In" of Zinn's writings, which took place a few months later on the Purdue campus, live-streamed, and "hosted in solidarity with 11 campuses" that held their own similar Read-In events. As *USA Today* reported, over a hundred students, professors, a state legislator, a French filmmaker, and at least one high school teacher who admitted to using the book in his class came to hear readings and speeches by, among others, Zinn's friends Staughton Lynd and Anthony Arnove, and by James Loewen, the author of *Lies My Teacher Told Me*. Over eight thousand dollars were pledged to fund a new graduate student scholarship in Zinn's name.[48]

Lawmakers' efforts to eliminate Zinn in the classroom usually go nowhere, as Arkansas State representative Kim Hendren learned in 2017 when he introduced House Bill 1834 to prohibit the use of Zinn's materials in Arkansas classrooms.[49] In fact, the Zinn Education Project used the controversy as a fundraising and outreach opportunity. After the bill was introduced, the website announced that "in solidarity with Arkansas educators and students" the organization would send a free copy of *A People's History* to any teacher requesting one. As of March 16, 2017, "700 middle and high school teachers and school librarians" had sent requests, and "more continue to come in." Tax-deductible donations were sought to pay for the books.[50]

One can understand teenagers being drawn to *A People's History of the United States*, but when professors who have personally pointed out egregious and deliberate historical misrepresentations defend it, we need to ask why. Is it all right to promote falsehoods in the service of your ideological cause, as long as it is your cause? Would Sam Wineburg apply such a standard to any other issue? Certainly, as Kazin asserts, history books have been written to "advance a political cause." Sometimes bias leads to unintentional misrepresentation. One example of a lapse of that sort would be the case of someone presenting a Founder like Thomas Jefferson as a Christian in order to bolster the claims about the Christian foundations of the nation, as is the case with David Barton's *The Jefferson Lies*. To their credit, a number of conservative scholars spoke out about the inaccuracies in the book. But no such effort has been made in regards to Zinn's book by historians on the left. Barton critics refused to use history as a weapon against the left, to rebalance a bias against Christianity. Of course, Zinn openly and proudly used history as a weapon. The real historian is grateful for legitimate corrections on points of fact from his peers, without regard for religious or ideological beliefs.

At one time, there *was* a court of peers. Oscar Handlin, in an essay on the deterioration of the historians' profession, recalled his first American Historical Association conference as a graduate student in 1936. That meeting was attended by 956 historians with different "background[s], interpretation[s], and points of view," but they were held together by "adherence to common standards and convictions." He recalled four of his teachers—Charles H. McIlwain, Frederick Merk, Samuel E. Morison, and Arthur M. Schlesinger—who "had treated the American Revolution, each in a distinctive fashion." But still, according to Handlin, "the student, confronting that array of divergent viewpoints, found no cause to doubt that a common standard of scholarship animated all four historians." He cited the philosopher Charles Peirce's description of the "'community of investigators' laboriously inching the world toward truth," as a "perfect term for our company."[51]

At one time, even some historians who were Communists had standards of scholarship—and they did not believe that Zinn met those standards. This was true of the internationally renowned historian of the South, Eugene Genovese, whom I knew in the five years before he died in 2012. Gene and his wife Betsey Fox-Genovese were well-known Marxist historians. But in the 1990s, Betsey converted to Catholicism and Gene followed her, returning to the faith of his childhood. In 2010, he told me that while he knew Zinn as a colleague and had admired his stand in the 1960s on integrating the Southern Historical Association, he refused to review *A People's History.*[52] When Zinn's sidekick Staughton Lynd, a proponent of the new "relevant" history that would combine scholarship with activism, ran for president of the American Historical

Association in 1969, Genovese objected. What Gene told me comports with David Greenberg's description in *The New Republic*:

> For all their leftist bona fides, [Genovese and colleagues Christopher Lasch and James Weinstein] agreed with their stodgy forebears that the intellectual had to hew to the highest standards of rigor; it was by the strength of their scholarship that they might revise entrenched beliefs that gave rise to the social conditions that, as a political matter, they decried. Genovese, most vociferously, flatly rejected the siren song of "relevant" history: he, too, hoped at the time for a socialist future, but he believed that it was best served by history that was true to the evidence, valid in its interpretations, and competent in its execution.[53]

Genovese's 1974 masterpiece *Roll, Jordan, Roll: The World the Slaves Made*, won the Bancroft Prize and is considered to be a classic in the field.

In spite of their claims about "academic discourse," we need to ask Zinn defenders if they would support distorted history in service of another goal. Would they accept the use of David Irving's books in the classroom? Or imagine what would happen to someone writing a history book that deliberately obscured the numbers of slaves and slave deaths and misrepresented the conditions under which they worked and lived. Imagine that historian focusing exclusively on the rare case of a slave who was treated as well as his owners' own children. Imagine such a historian citing a book by Frederick Douglass or another abolitionist, twisting the words around so that they became arguments *for* slavery. But that is *exactly* what Zinn did with the words of Douglas Pike: Pike accused the Viet Cong of genocide, but Zinn used selective quotations of Pike's work to make them the heroes of the Vietnamese people. Zinn, as we have seen, violated over and over the rules on which the American Historical Association prides itself and by which Richard

Evans and his team showed Irving to be a historian of disrepute. Zinn did everything—misrepresented sources, omitted critical information, falsified evidence, and plagiarized. His rhetorical strategies included leading questions, logical fallacies, and ad hominem attacks.

All Americans of good will, no matter their political views, should object to such perversion of the truth.

One of the classroom lessons on Christopher Columbus promoted by the Zinn Education Project involves trying the discoverer of America for the murder of the Indians. This role-play activity is designed for students as young as elementary school. One of the questions to the jury is whether "European life—the 'System of Empire,' [made] violence inevitable."[54] In effect such a trial is a show trial, with a jury of naive children who are manipulated by their teachers.

It is Zinn's book that should be put on trial. If the historian lies, there is no defense.

ACKNOWLEDGMENTS

I have had the good fortune to be surrounded by a number of exemplary scholars and historians at the Alexander Hamilton Institute for the Study of Western Civilization in Clinton, New York, where I have been a resident fellow since 2014. First, I want to thank the Institute's president and co-founder, Robert Paquette, who, during my initial visit to the AHI in the summer of 2010, made me feel warmly welcome and encouraged me to return to give a lecture, attend AHI's conferences, and apply for a research fellowship, which I did during the summer of 2011. When the program under which I was teaching at Emory University ended, I knew there was place for me at the AHI.

Bob Paquette, a prize-winning historian, is the dynamo of the AHI. He is known for his ability to motivate students with his exacting standards and his boundless enthusiasm for the study of history and the AHI. In spite of his myriad duties in administration, teaching, and writing, he gave a careful reading to a draft of a chapter and recommended sources from his vast store of knowledge about American history and slavery.

I have benefited greatly also from conversations with Hamilton College history professor and AHI co-founder Douglas Ambrose, as well as with Dr. David Frisk, AHI's other resident fellow, with whom I share an office. The AHI generously offered the research services of their undergraduate fellows, Alex Klosner and Edward Shvets, who, like the other AHI undergraduate fellows, stand head and shoulders above their peers in courage, intellectual curiosity, and conduct.

Helping to keep the AHI running smoothly by volunteering for countless tasks has been Bob's wife, Zoya Paquette. Her sincere interest in my work has been much appreciated, as has that of AHI co-founder James Bradfield and his wife, Alice.

While teaching at Emory University, I had the good luck to meet a top scholar in the field of American Communism, Harvey Klehr, who also directed the American Democracy and Citizenship program under which I was teaching during the latter part of my tenure there. Over the years, Harvey has readily answered questions about a topic that has consumed this daughter of parents who escaped Communist Yugoslavia (Slovenia). For this project, Harvey read two of my chapters and offered corrections. At Emory, Mark Bauerlein, who founded the American Democracy and Citizenship program, gave me valuable direction on early writing projects and served as an ally. On that campus, I also met philosophy professor Ann Hartle, then president of the Georgia state chapter of the National Association of Scholars. She has come through for me in my various pursuits and has become a good friend. I still hear her words of encouragement about this book during one of our lunch get-togethers. I miss the late Eugene Genovese, who understood the evils of Communism and could describe the practitioners in his unique, mockingly funny way.

Through the National Association of Scholars, I have met colleagues who still adhere to the old-fashioned high standards of scholarship. NAS president Peter Wood was helpful in reviewing chapters and sharing memories of Howard Zinn at Boston University. At NAS, both Peter Wood and David Randall have given me feedback and connected me with other scholars. Through that organization I met Will Fitzhugh, a selfless promoter of history writing for high school students. He also read a draft of a chapter and pointed me to additional sources.

Ken Masugi, political science professor in Washington, D.C., another member of the "Remnant" of scholars, expanded on his own article about the World War II relocation camps and suggested additional books. Robert Hager, retired Army Reserve Officer, former college professor, and now an editor in chief of *Communist and Post-Communist Studies*, whose acquaintance I made online, read my chapter on Vietnam and offered helpful suggestions.

From the website of Bill Humpf, patriot and Army National Guard veteran, in Mount Joy, Pennsylvania, I learned of an important document that helped expose yet another one of Zinn's lies about the Vietnam War.

My former neighbor, Lee Harris, author of fine and learned books on politics and history, gave me direction in my reading and shared his vast knowledge during our conversations. Marty Naparsteck, a stalwart friend of over three decades in spite of our differing political views, has happily served as my go-to guy for information on Vietnam writers and baseball.

This book has had a long genesis. Cliff Kincaid, president of America's Survival, Inc., commissioned a report on Howard Zinn that I presented at his conference in 2010. And it was at one of Cliff's conferences that I met Grove City College political science professor Paul Kengor, who through the years has been a great resource and has introduced me to some wonderful people. One was Ralph J. Galliano, director of the Selous Foundation for Public Policy Research, who, in turn, introduced me to historian Irwin F. Gellman, who dedicated many hours to coaching me and helping me get this book idea into the right hands. Through the intercession of Paul, I met Mike Shotwell, who has written about his Communist upbringing and read parts of my manuscript. He and his wife, Gwyneth, have become good friends.

I am thankful always for my son, Carson. Since childhood, he has cheerfully endured a mother often immersed in books and reminded her of the important things in life. My sister, Regina, and her husband, Eric, have provided encouragement and understanding of my need to postpone visits.

The librarians at the Kirkland Town Library in Clinton, at Hamilton College, and at Colgate University were generous with special dispensations in checking out the many books that I needed. The staffs at the Tamiment Library at New York University; Stuart A. Rose Manuscript, Archives, and Rare Book Library at Emory University; the Library of Congress; and the Library and Archives of the Martin Luther King Jr. Center in Atlanta were all very helpful and professional as I conducted research on Zinn and related topics.

Finally, I want to thank my agent, Alex Hoyt, and my editor at Regnery, Elizabeth Kantor. Both have ushered this project along with patience, enthusiasm, and good cheer.

I have sought out reliable and varied sources and the expertise of colleagues to refute Howard Zinn's lies, but I take responsibility for any errors within these pages.

NOTES

A Note from the Author

1. Gilbert T. Sewell, "The Howard Zinn Show," *Academic Questions*, May 2012, 209–17.

2. William Crum, "Cooper, Hamon Take OKC Council Seats," *Oklahoman*, April 10, 2019, https://newsok.com/article/5628297/cooper-hamon-take-seats.

3. Sarah Thompson, "New Year's Day Swearing-In Ceremony Kicks Off 2019 with Party," *Penobscot Bay Pilot*, January 1, 2019, https://www.penbaypilot.com/article/new-year-s-day-swearing-ceremony-kicks-2019-party/112193.

4. Naomi Schaefer Riley, "Reclaiming History From Howard Zinn," *Wall Street Journal*, May 17, 2019, https://www.wsj.com/articles/reclaiming-history-from-howard-zinn-11558126202; see also "Wilfred McClay on Teaching American History, the Trouble with Howard Zinn, and 'Land of Hope,' an Interview with Wilfred McClay," Encounter Books, May 15, 2019, https://www.encounterbooks.com/features/wilfred-mcclay-teaching-american-history-trouble-howard-zinn-land-hope/.

5. Evan Goldstein, "The Academy Is Largely Itself Responsible for Its Own Peril," *Chronicle of Higher Education*, November 13, 2018, https://www.chronicle.com/article/The-Academy-Is-Largely/245080.

6. Alex Beam, "Two-and-a-Half Cheers for Howard Zinn," *Boston Globe*, November 23, 2018, https://www.bostonglobe.com/opinion/2018/11/23/two-and-half-cheers-for-howard-zinn/HZPpBU8KrLhCHoMUb2aH0L/story.html.

7. Sam Wineburg, "Undue Certainty: Where Howard Zinn's *A People's History* Falls Short," *American Educator*, Winter 2012–2013, https://www.aft.org/sites/default/files/periodicals/Wineburg.pdf.

8. David Greenberg, "Agit-Prof, Howard Zinn's Influential Mutilations of American History," *The New Republic*, March 19, 2013, https://newrepublic.com/article/112574/howard-zinns-influential-mutilations-american-history.

9. Wineburg, "Undue Certainty."

10. Marion Smith, "VOC Releases Third Annual Report on Generational Attitudes Toward Socialism in America," October 30, 2018, https://www.victimsofcommunism.org/voc-news/third-annual-report-on-us-attitudes-toward-socialism.

11. Kathleen Elkins, "Most Young Americans Prefer Socialism to Capitalism, New Report Finds," CNBC, August 14, 2018, https://www.cnbc.com/2018/08/14/fewer-than-half-of-young-americans-are-positive-about-capitalism.html. The 52 percent of millenials broke down to 46 percent favoring socialism and 6 percent favoring communism.

Introduction: Howard Zinn: Icon, Rock Star

1. Matt Damon and Ben Affleck, *Good Will Hunting*, https://www.thescriptsource.net/Scripts/Good%20Will%20Hunting.pdf, 48.

2. "[Great Movie Scenes] Good Will Hunting— Bar Scene," Youtube, June 23, 2007, https://www.youtube.com/watch?v=ymsHLkB8u3s.

3. "Matt Damon Heats Up History," CBS News, December 11, 2009, https://www.cbsnews.com/news/matt-damon-heats-up-history/; Anonymous, Dennis Lewis, and Charles Caro, "Matt Damon: Biography," IMBD, no date, https://www.imdb.com/name/nm0000354/bio?ref_=nm_ov_bio_sm; Davis D. Joyce, *Howard Zinn: A Radical American Vision* (New York: Prometheus Books, 2003), 238.

4. Howard Zinn (adapted by Rebecca Stefoff), *A Young People's History of the United States* (New York: Seven Stories Press, 2009), ix-x.

5. John M. Dunn, *The Vietnam War: A History of U.S. Involvement* (San Diego: Lucent Books, 2001); John M. Dunn, *The Relocation of the North American Indian,* (San Diego; Lucent Books, 1995); John M. Dunn, *The Civil Rights Movement,* (San Diego: Lucent Books, 1998).

6. Stanley Kurtz, "How Zinn Gets In: Road to a National Curriculum," *National Review*, August 17, 2015, https://www.nationalreview.com/corner/how-zinn-gets-road-national-curriculum-stanley-kurtz/.

7. These include *Teaching with Voices of A People's History of the United States; a teacher's edition of A People's History of the United States; and A People's History for the Classroom,* with updated editions coming out periodically—not to mention online resources.

8. "New History Instructor Engages Students with Role-Play Exercises," The Ranger, October 8, 2018. http://theranger.org/2018/10/08/ new-history-instructor-engages-students-with-role-play-exercises/.

9. "Howard Zinn: The Historian Liberals Love," College Insurrection, December 28, 2012, http://collegeinsurrection.com/2012/12/ howard-zinn-the-historian-liberals-love/.

10. W. Jeffrey Ludwig, "We Must Fight for Family Values," *American Thinker,* September 2, 2018, https://www.americanthinker.com/ articles/2018/09/we_must_fight_for_family_values.html; Jeffrey Ludwig email to the author, September 7, 2018.

11. Emily Rentz email to the author, October 5, 2018.

12. Sam Wineburg, "Undue Certainty: Where Howard Zinn's *A People's History* Falls Short," *American Educator,* Winter 2012–13, 27–34, https:// www.aft.org/sites/default/files/periodicals/Wineburg.pdf.

13. Peter Charles Hoffer, *Past Imperfect: Facts, Fictions, Fraud—American History from Bancroft and Parkman to Ambrose, Bellesiles, Ellis, and Goodwin* (New York: Public Affairs, 2004), 14–43. The Ambrose and Goodwin cases are discussed at length in chapter 6, pages 172–207, the Joseph Ellis case in chapter 7, pages 173–229, and Michael Bellesiles in chapter 5, pages 14–71. See also Patricia Cohen, "Scholar Emerges from Doghouse," *New York Times,* August 3, 2010, https://www.nytimes. com/2010/08/04/books/04bellisles.html.

14. "David Irving," Wikipedia, https://en.wikipedia.org/wiki/David_ Irving; Richard J. Evans, *Lying About Hitler: History, Holocaust, and the David Irving Trial* (New York: Basic Books, 2001), 4–6.

15. "Doris Kearns Goodwin Leaves Pulitzer Prize Board," *Wall Street Journal,* May 31, 2002, https://archive.is/NGCMG.

16. Hoffer, *Past Imperfect,* 217.

17. Ibid., 155, 162, 166–67. For a more accurate and devastating account of how blatantly Bellesiles distorted the truth and Cramer's pivotal role in exposing him, see Larry Schweikart, *48 Liberal Lies about American History* (New York: Penguin, 2009), 119–24.

18. Jen Matteis, "Michael Bellesiles: Bartender, Writer, History Buff," The Day, September 19, 2012, http://www.theday.com/article/20120917/ NWS10/309209649.

19. Joyce, *Howard Zinn*, 238; Martin Duberman, *Howard Zinn: A Life on the Left* (New York: New Press, 2012), 309.

20. James Green, "Howard Zinn's History," *Chronicle of Higher Education*, May 23, 2003, B13–B14.

21. Ibid.

22. Gilbert Sewall, "The Howard Zinn Show," *Academic Questions,* May 5, 2012, 209–17.

23. David Detmer, "History Distorted: Sam Wineburg's Critique of Howard Zinn," HowardZinn.org, September 21, 2018, https://www. howardzinn.org/history-distorted-sam-wineburgs-critique/.

24. Author interview of Eugene Genovese, September 1, 2010, Atlanta, Georgia.

25. William Blum, "Shunning Howard Zinn's History," February 6, 2010, Howard Zinn.org. https://www.howardzinn.org/shunning-howard-zinns-history/.

26. Michael Kammen, "How the Other Half Lived," *Washington Post*, March 23, 1980, https://www.washingtonpost.com/archive/ entertainment/books/1980/03/23/how-the-other-half-lived/ ce505900-12fd-427d-a689-90edf3836309/?utm_term=.0dffeb33f831.

27. Eric Foner email to the author, August 8, 2018.

28. Eric Foner, "Majority Report," *New York Times,* March 2, 1980, BR3.

29. Rebecca E. Klatch, *A Generation Divided: The New Left, the New Right, and the 1960s* (Los Angeles: The University of California Press, 1999), 194.

30. Michael Kazin, "Howard Zinn's History Lessons," *Dissent*, Spring 2004, https://www.dissentmagazine.org/article/howard-zinns-history-lessons.

31. Wineburg, "Undue Certainty."

32. Oscar Handlin, "Arawaks" (review of *A People's History of the United States* by Howard Zinn), *American Scholar* 49:4 (Autumn 1980): 546, 548, 550, https://d3aencwbm6zmht.cloudfront.net/asset/97521/A_ Handlin_1980.pdf.

33. Daniel Flynn, "Howard Zinn's Biased History," reprinted from Front Page Magazine in History News Network, June 9, 2003, http:// historynewsnetwork.org/article/1493.

34. David Austin Walsh, "David Barton's *The Jefferson Lies* Voted the Least Credible History in Print," History News Network, July 16, 2012, http://historynewsnetwork.org/article/147149. Barton's book was then

published by World Net Daily Press with superficial corrections. John Fea, "Still Misleading America about Thomas Jefferson," History News Network, February 7, 2016, https://historynewsnetwork.org/article/ 161878. Historian Robert Tracy McKenzie, Holmes Professor of Faith and Learning at Wheaton College, nicely explains why Barton's book is a disservice to both scholarship and Christian faith. See "What's Really at Stake in the 'Christian America' Debate, Faith and History," February 27, 2014, https://faithandamericanhistory.wordpress.com/2014/02/27/ whats-really-at-stake-in-the-christian-america-debate/.

35. Jennifer Schuessler, "TBR: Inside the List," *New York Times*, February 14, 2010, A22; Howard Zinn, *You Can't Be Neutral on a Moving Train*, (Boston: Beacon Press, 1994), 2.

36. David Greenberg, "Agit-Prof: Howard Zinn's Influential Mutilations of American History," *The New Republic*, March 19, 2003.

37. Jennifer Schuessler, "TBR: Inside the List."

38. Gil Kaufman, "Howard Zinn, 'People's' Historian, Dead at 87: Leftist Activist Was Admired by Bruce Springsteen, Matt Damon, Ben Affleck, and Others," MTV News, January 28, 2010, http://www.mtv.com/ news/1630657/howard-zinn-peoples-historian-dead-at-87/.

39. "Obituaries and Tributes," HowardZinn.org, http://howardzinn.org/ about/obituaries-and-tributes/.

40. Schuessler, "TBR: Inside the List."

41. "Even the Rain," iTunes Movie Trailers, 2011, https://trailers.apple.com/ trailers/independent/eventherain/. "Film *Even the Rain/Tambien La Lluvia* Dedicated to Howard Zinn," February 5, 2011, Howard Zinn. org, https://www.howardzinn.org/film-dedicated-to-howard-zinn/.

42. Chris McCoy, "Music Video Monday: Alex Greene and the Rolling Head Orchestra," Memphis Flyer, October 8, 2018, https://www. memphisflyer.com/FilmTVEtcBlog/archives/2018/10/08/ music-video-monday-alex-greene-and-the-rolling-head-orchestra.

43. "Riz Ahmed to Star in 'Englistan,' BBC Series about Three Generations of an Immigrant Family," Scroll.in, May 1, 2018, https://scroll.in/ reel/877472/riz-ahmed-to-star-in-englistan-bbc-series-about-three- generations-of-an-immigrant-family.

44. "The People Speak," Brooklyn Academy of Music, March 21, 2017, https://www.bam.org/talks/2017/the-people-speak.

45. Loren Hunt, "Maybe He's Right: Bob Weick, Currently Playing Karl Marx," Philebrity, January 25, 1017, http://www.philebrity.com/blog/2017/1/25/maybe-hes-right-bob-weick-currently-playing-karl-marx.

46. "Karl Marx Comes to Kings Arms Salford," *Salford Star*, May 26, 2018, http://www.salfordstar.com/article.asp?id=4528; Henrik Eger, "Touring Marx in Soho in Britain and the US: Interview with Bob Weick, Celebrating Marx's 200th Birthday, Part 2," *Phindie*, June 6, 2018, http://phindie.com/touring-marx-in-soho-in-britain-and-the-us-interview-with-bob-weick-celebrating-marxs-200th-birthday-part-2/; Henrik Eger, "Dramatizing Revolution: Howard Zinn's 'Marx in Soho,'" *Progressive*, May 5, 2018, http://progressive.org/dispatches/Dramatizing-Revolution-Howard-Zinns-Marx-in-Soho-180505/.

47. "April 29–May 1: Grrrl Brigade, Decorator Showcase, S.F. Dance Film Festival, Dia de los Libros, Harp Concert, Earplay, Ty Segall, Magic Lantern 3-D Show," *San Francisco Examiner*, April 28, 2018, http://www.sfexaminer.com/april-29-may-1-grrrl-brigade-decorator-showcase-s-f-dance-film-festival-dia-de-los-libros-harp-concert-earplay-ty-segall/.

48. Brendan Kiley, "The Truth Is Out There: Monolinguist Mike Daisey on Lies, History and Howard Zinn at Seattle Rep," October 29, 2018, https://www.seattletimes.com/entertainment/theater/the-truth-is-out-there-monologuist-mike-daisey-on-lies-history-and-howard-zinn-at-seattle-rep/.

49. "Voices of a People's History," City Parks Foundation, August 28, 2018, https://cityparksfoundation.org/events/voices-of-a-peoples-history/?date=20180828; Andrea Park, "Viggo Mortensen Urges Americans to Look to History to Understand Current Political Climate," CBS, August 28, 2018, https://www.cbsnews.com/news/viggo-mortensen-urges-americans-to-look-to-history-to-understand-current-political-climate/.

50. Alexia Nader, "The Occupy Wall Street Library," *New Yorker*, September 29, 2011, https://www.newyorker.com/books/page-turner/the-occupy-wall-street-library; Emily Shugerman, "'Frustration, Anger, Helplessness': Virginia Pipeline Protesters on What Drove Them to Live in the Trees: *The Independent* Spoke with Protesters about Why They're Staging Tree Sits along the Proposed Pipeline Route," *Independent*, May 5, 2018, https://www.independent.co.uk/news/

world/americas/tree-sit-mountain-valley-pipeline-west-virginia-red-terry-franklin-county-protest-a8337311.html.

51. Alex Reimer, "Martellus Bennett Tweets Out Scathing Criticism of Columbus Day," Radio.Com, October 8, 2018, https://weei.radio.com/blogs/alex-reimer/martellus-bennett-twitter-former-patriots-tight-end-writes-scathing-criticism.

52. Mike Finger, "Turning Back Time, Gay Gets Spurs Moving," *San Antonio Express-News*, October 18, 2018, https://www.expressnews.com/spurs-nation/article/Turning-back-time-Gay-gets-Spurs-moving-13316420.php.

53. Sarah Giddings, "Making People's History in Arizona: Educators Rise Up: We Had No Other Choice but to Demonstrate Our Basic Civil Liberties in Pursuit of Real, Transformative Change—by Walking Out of Our Classrooms Together and into the Capitol on the Historic Day of April 26, 2018," Common Dreams, April 30, 2018, https://www.commondreams.org/views/2018/04/30/making-peoples-history-arizona-educators-rise.

54. Sean P. Means, "Utah Students Rap and Sing Their Way onto the 'Hamilton' Stage: About 2,000 High School Students from around the State Heard Advice from the Show's Cast, Then Got to See the Tony-Winning Musical," *Salt Lake Tribune*, May 4, 2018, https://www.sltrib.com/artsliving/arts/2018/05/04/utah-students-take-their-shot-rapping-and-singing-about-history-on-the-hamilton-stage/.

55. "Call for Proposals! #zinn2018: 5th Annual Howard Zinn Book Fair," December 2, 2018, San Francisco, https://howardzinnbookfair.com/; Melanie West and Joan Bender, "A People's Book Fair," *Socialist Worker,* November 15, 2017, https://socialistworker.org/2017/11/15/a-peoples-book-fair.

56. Lisa Butterworth, "The Books High School Students Should Be Reading, according to USC Professors: Sure, Everyone Reads *To Kill a Mockingbird*, but Faculty Members from USC's Department of English Have Updated Suggestions for Today's Teens," USC News (University of Southern California), August 8, 2018, https://news.usc.edu/146764/the-books-high-school-students-should-be-reading-according-to-usc-professors/.

57. "Events Calendar: Howard Zinn's Play, 'Marx in Soho,'" February 13, 2018, Grand Valley State University, http://www.gvsu.edu/events/howard-zinns-play-marx-in-soho/.

58. "Economics Department Presents Performance of Howard Zinn's 'Marx in Soho,'" Carleton, September 27, 2013, https://apps.carleton.edu/media_relations/press_releases/?story_id=1048664.

59. "All-School Seminar Day 2017," New Trier High School, no date, http://www.newtrier.k12.il.us/seminarday/.

60. Howard Zinn, "Quotable Quote," Goodreads, no date, https://www.goodreads.com/quotes/163932-civil-disobedience-is-not-our-problem-our-problem-is-civil.

61. David Detmer, *Zinnophobia: The Battle over History in Education, Politics, and Scholarship* (Hampshire, UK: Zero Books, 2018).

62. Sam Allard, "High Note: Greta Gerwig's *Lady Bird* Soars," *San Antonio Current*, November 15, 2017, https://www.sacurrent.com/sanantonio/high-note-greta-gerwigs-lady-bird-soars/Content?oid=7249558.

63. Wineburg, "Undue Certainty."

64. "Bashing Howard Zinn: A Critical Look at One of the Critics," Zinn Education Project, November 18, 2013, https://www.zinnedproject.org/news/bashing-howard-zinn-a-critical-look-at-one-of-the-critics/.

65. "San Francisco Unified School District Hosts People's History Workshop for All District Librarians," Zinn Education Project, September 13, 2018, https://www.zinnedproject.org/news/san-francisco-unified-school-district-workshop; "Workshops," Zinn Education Project; Request Form: Zinn Education Project Workshop, no date, https://zinned.wufoo.com/forms/request-form-zinn-education-project-workshop/.

66. Paul Bowers, "Reconstruction Era Comes to Life in New Initiative for SC History Classes," *Post and Courier*, October 19, 2018, https://www.postandcourier.com/news/reconstruction-era-comes-to-life-in-new-initiative-for-sc/article_f7ffcf04-d231-11e8-9f57-cb23942ffdc2.html; Paul Bowers, "Proposed S.C. Social Studies Standards Don't Mention MLK, Rosa Parks or John C. Calhoun," *Post and Courier*, February 2, 2018, https://www.postandcourier.com/news/proposed-s-c-social-studies-standards-don-t-mention-mlk/article_8492b92c-075d-11e8-bfaa-0fa934b57487.html.

67. Adam Sanchez, "When Black Lives Mattered: Why Teach Reconstruction," September 19, 2017, https://www.zinnedproject.org/

if-we-knew-our-history/when-black-lives-mattered/. "Teach Reconstruction Campaign," https://www.zinnedproject.org/campaigns/teach-reconstruction/.

68. "Abolish Columbus Day Campaign," Zinn Education Project, https://www.zinnedproject.org/campaigns/abolish-columbus-day; "Teaching Materials," Zinn Education Project, https://www.zinnedproject.org/materials; Perry Stein, "Rush Limbaugh Attacks the Bookstore at Busboys and Poets," *Washington City Paper*, June 17, 2014, https://www.washingtoncitypaper.com/news/city-desk/blog/13068736/rush-limbaugh-attacks-the-bookstore-at-busboys-and-poets; Susan Berry, "Zinn Education Project Launches Campaign to 'Kick Koch Brothers Out of Our Schools," Breitbart, December 15, 2014, http://www.breitbart.com/Texas/2014/12/15/ZINN-Education-Project-Launches-Anti-Koch-Campaign/.

69. Wineburg, "Undue Certainty."

70. Will Bunch, "Howard Zinn Book in Philly Schools? Yes, Please!", *Philadelphia Inquirer*, October 24, 2103, http://www.philly.com/philly/blogs/attytood/Howard-Zinn-book-in-Philly-schools-Yes-please.html.

71. "A Discussion with Howard Zinn," in *A People's History of the United States* (New York: HarperCollins, 2003), 3.

72. Ivan I. Kurilla and Victoria I. Zhuraleva, "Teaching U.S. History in Russia: Issues, Challenges, and Prospects," *Journal of American History*, 96:4, (March 2010), 1138–44.

73. Ahmed Akhtar, "A Power Governments Cannot Suppress by Howard Zinn, a Companion Guide to Present-Day Life in America," *Daily Princetonian*, February 20, 2017, http://www.dailyprincetonian.com/blog/intersections/2017/02/zinn-book-review; Zoe Ervolino, "Cornel West's History," *Yale Herald*, February 16, 2018, https://yaleherald.com/cornel-wests-history-1446f43627c7.

74. Rochelle Riley, "Parkland Shooting Should Have Spurred More Political Disobedience," *Detroit Daily News*, February 25, 2018, https://www.freep.com/story/news/columnists/rochelle-riley/2018/02/25/riley-parkland-shooting-political-disobedience/365506002/.

75. Associated Press, "Camille Cosby's Statement: 'Lynch Mobs' Led to Conviction," *Philadelphia Tribune*, May 4, 2018, http://www.

phillytrib.com/news/camille-cosby-s-statement-lynch-mobs-led-to-convictions/article_886edb04-430b-5742-aaf6-ea908ed86a79.html.

76. James Kloppenberg, *Reading Obama: Dreams, Hopes and the American Political Tradition* (Princeton: Princeton University Press, 2011), 27.

77. Peter Wood, "Defending a Debased Version of the Liberal Arts," National Association of Scholars, June 7, 2018, https://www.nas.org/articles/pushing_american_history_as_a_long_tale_of_oppression.

78. "Pearls of Wisdom," *The Rush Limbaugh Show*, December 20, 2016, https://www.rushlimbaugh.com/daily/2016/12/20/pearls_of_wisdom-137/.

79. "Indiana Schools Host People's History Workshops," Zinn Education Project, April 19, 2018, https://www.zinnedproject.org/news/indiana-schools-host-peoples-history-workshops/.

80. Bill Bigelow "Arkansas' Howard Zinn Witch-Hunt Fizzles," Zinn Education Project, April 4, 2017, https://www.zinnedproject.org/news/arkansas-howard-zinn-witch-hunt-fizzles/.

81. Howard Zinn, *A People's History of the United States* (New York: HarperCollins, 2003), 10.

82. Bruce Kuklick, "The People? Yes.," *The Nation*, May 24, 1980, 634–36.

83. "Books—Authors," *New York Times*, January 1, 1959, 29.

84. Sam Roberts, "Carl N. Degler, 93, A Scholarly Voice of the Oppressed," *New York Times*, January 14, 2015, 22.

85. Charles A. Barker, review of *Out of Our Past: The Forces that Shaped Modern America* by Carl N. Degler, *The American Historical Review*, Vol. 65, No. 1, (October 1959), 131–32.

86. Vincent P. Carosso, review of *Out of Our Past: The Forces That Shaped Modern America* by Carl N. Degler, *The Business History Review*, Vol. 33, No. 4 (Winter, 1959), 582–583.

87. "Oscar Handlin," Wikipedia. https://en.wikipedia.org/wiki/Oscar_Handlin; Stephan Thernstrom, "In Memoriam, Oscar Handlin (1915–2011)," *Perspectives on History*, January 2012; https://www.historians.org/publications-and-directories/perspectives-on-history/january-2012/in-memoriam-oscar-handlin.

88. Oscar Handlin, *Truth in History* (Cambridge, Massachusetts: Cambridge University Press, 1979), 82–83.

89. Green, "Howard Zinn's History," B13–B14.

90. Zinn, *A People's History*, 683.

91. Ibid., 684.

92. Ibid.

93. Howard Zinn, "Arawaks," *The American Scholar*, Vol. 50, No. 3 (Summer 1981), 431–32.

94. Richard J. Evans, *Lying About Hitler: History, Holocaust, and the David Irving Trial* (Basic Books: New York, 2001), 69–70, 95.

95. Hoffer, *Past Imperfect*, 135–36.

96. "Statement on Standards of Professional Conduct (Updated 2018)," American Historical Association, 2018, https://www.historians.org/jobs-and-professional-development/statements-standards-and-guidelines-of-the-discipline/statement-on-standards-of-professional-conduct.

97. Hoffer, *Past Imperfect*, 135.

Chapter One: Columbus Bad, Indians Good

1.   Howard Zinn, *You Can't Be Neutral on a Moving Train* (Boston: Beacon Press, 1994), 2.

2.   Jennifer C. Braceras, "The Intellectual Roots of the War against Columbus," *National Review*, October 9, 2017, https://www.nationalreview.com/2017/10/christopher-columbus-day-left-marxists-anti-capitalist-ku-klux-klan-anti-catholic/.

3.   Leslie Eastman, "How Badly Were Christopher Columbus Statues Vandalized This Year?", *Legal Insurrection*, October 10, 2017, https://legalinsurrection.com/2017/10/how-badly-were-christopher-columbus-statues-vandalized-this-year/?utm_source=feedburner&utm_medium=feed&utm_campaign=Feed%3A+LegalInsurrection+%28Le%C2%B7gal+In%C2%B7sur%C2%B7rec%C2%B7tion%29.

4.   Tamar Lapin and Natalie Musumeci, "Christopher Columbus Statue defaced in Central Park," *New York Post*, September 12, 2017, https://nypost.com/2017/09/12/christopher-columbus-statue-defaced-in-central-park/.

5.   Mariya Manzhos, "Winchester Students, Citing Atrocities Ask Schools to Rename Columbus Day," Wicked Local Winchester, November 24, 2017, https://winchester.wickedlocal.com/news/20171124/winchester-students-citing-atrocities-ask-schools-to-rename-columbus-day.

6.   Holly Yan, "Across the US, More Cities Ditch Columbus Day to Honor Those Who Really Discovered America," CNN, October 8, 2018, https://www.cnn.com/2018/10/08/us/columbus-day-vs-indigenous-peoples-day/index.html.

7.   Kristin Lamb, "For First Time, Columbus Will Not Honor Columbus Day, Its Namesake Holiday," *USA Today,* October 7, 2018, https://www.usatoday.com/story/news/2018/10/07/columbus-ohio-not-observe-columbus-day/1560105002/; Colin Kalmbacher, "Columbus, Ohio Will No Longer Celebrate Columbus Day," Law & Crime, October 8, 2018, https://lawandcrime.com/politics/columbus-ohio-will-no-longer-celebrate-columbus-day/.

8.   Nicholas Lovino, "San Francisco Replaces Columbus Day with Indigenous Peoples' Day," *Courthouse News Service*, January 23, 2018, https://www.courthousenews.com/sf-replaces-columbus-day-with-indigenous-peoples-day/.

9.   Jessica Kramer, "What Do Americans Really Think About Columbus Day?" The Daily Caller, October 8, 2018, https://dailycaller.com/2018/10/08/americans-really-think-columbus-day/.

10.   James Green, "Howard Zinn's History," *Chronicle of Higher Education*, May 23, 2003, B13–14.

11.   Howard Zinn, *A People's History of the United States,* revised and updated edition (New York: Harper Collins, 1995), 613–16.

12.   Ibid., 616.

13.   Howard Zinn, "The Future of History," July 27 and 28, 1998, in Howard Zinn, *The Future of History: Interviews with David Barsamian* (Monroe, ME: Common Courage Press, 1999), 136.

14.   Howard Zinn, *A People's History of the United States* (New York: HarperCollins, 2003), 1. All references to *A People's History of the United States* below are to the 2003 edition unless otherwise noted.

15.   Zinn, "The Future of History," 135.

16.   Ibid., 136.

17.   Davis D. Joyce, *Howard Zinn: A Radical American Vision* (Amherst, New York: Prometheus Books, 2003), 173.

18.   Zinn, *A People's History,* 2.

19.   Hans Koning, *Columbus: His Enterprise: Exploding the Myth,* (New York: Monthly Review Press, 1991), 17. Originally published in 1976.

20. Zinn, *A People's History*, 3.
21. Koning, *Columbus: His Enterprise*, 54–55.
22. Sam Dillon, "Schools Growing Harsher in Scrutiny of Columbus," *New York Times*, October 12, 1992.
23. James Ferguson, "Hans Koning," *Guardian*, June 5, 2007.
24. Ibid.
25. Douglas Martin, "Hans Koning, 85, Prolific Left-Leaning Writer, Is Dead," *New York Times*, April 18, 2007, C12.
26. Hans Koning, "Don't Celebrate 1492—Mourn It," *New York Times*, August 14, 1990.
27. Hans Koning, "Rewriting Our History," *Monthly Review*, vol. 44, no. 3, July–August 1992.
28. Koning, *Columbus: His Enterprise*, 12.
29. Ibid., 11, 22, 24, 27–28, and 32.
30. Harvey Morris, "Profile: Christopher Columbus: A Good Thing, Even: Harvey Morris Berates Those Who Lay All the Ills of the West at One Man's Feet," *Independent*, October 11, 1992, https://www.independent.co.uk/voices/profile-christopher-columbus-a-good-thing-even-harvey-morris-berates-those-who-lay-all-the-ills-of-1556723.html.
31. P. Gray and C. Booth, "The Trouble with Columbus," *Time*, October 7, 1991, 52.
32. Felipe Fernández-Armesto, "In Defense of Columbus: The Trouble with Eden," *Economist*, December 21, 1991, 73.
33. William D. Phillips Jr. and Carla Rahn Phillips, *The Worlds of Christopher Columbus* (New York: Cambridge University Press, 1992, 11.
34. Andrew G. Bostom, "Ignored History: Columbus Sought to End Islamic Tyranny," PJ Media, October 8, 2018, https://pjmedia.com/homeland-security/ignored-history-columbus-sought-to-end-islamic-tyranny/.
35. Phillips and Phillips, *The Worlds of Christopher Columbus*, 17, 159.
36. Robert H. Fuson, trans., *The Log of Christopher Columbus* (Camden, Maine: International Marine, 1987), 76.
37. Cecil Jane, trans., *The Journal of Christopher Columbus* (New York: Bramhall House, 1960), 22–24.
38. Fuson, trans., *The Log of Christopher Columbus*, 31–32.
39. Jane, trans., *The Journal of Christopher Columbus*, 24, 28.

40. Zinn, *A People's History*, 1–4.

41. Koning, *Columbus: His Enterprise*, 51.

42. Ibid., 35.

43. Carol Delaney, "Columbus's Ultimate Goal: Jerusalem," *Comparative Studies in Society and History*, Vol. 48, No. 2 (April 2006), 260–92.

44. Phillips and Philips, *The Worlds of Christopher Columbus*, 38.

45. Delaney, "Columbus's Ultimate Goal."

46. Edward Countryman, letter to Howard Zinn, February 24, 1989, Howard Zinn Papers, Tamiment Library, New York University.

47. Howard Zinn to Edward Countryman, February 28, 1989, Howard Zinn Papers, Tamiment Library, New York University.

48. Zinn, *A People's History*, p. 63.

49. Edward Countryman to Howard Zinn, February 24, 1989, Howard Zinn Papers, Tamiment Library, New York University.

50. Zinn, *A People's History*, 5–6.

51. Ibid., 3.

52. Koning, *Columbus: His Enterprise*, 58.

53. Zinn, *A People's History*, 4.

54. William F. Keegan, "Destruction of the Taino," *Archaeology* (January/February 1992), 51–56.

55. Zinn, *A People's History*, 5.

56. L. A. Vigneras, foreword, *The Journals of Christopher Columbus*, trans. Cecil Jane (New York: Crown, 1989), xiv.

57. Zinn, *A People's History*, 5.

58. Andrée Collard, introduction to Bartolomé de Las Casas, *History of the Indies*, trans. Andrée Collard (New York: Harper & Row, 1971), xi, note 2.

59. Ibid., ix–x.

60. Ibid., xiii.

61. Las Casas, *History of the Indies*, 154; quoted by Zinn, 7.

62. Zinn, *A People's History*, 7.

63. Ibid.

64. Phillips and Phillips, *The Worlds of Christopher Columbus*, 254.

65. Collard, introduction to *History of the Indies*, xiv.

66. Ibid., xv.

67. Las Casas, *History of the Indies*, 34–35.

68. Collard, introduction to *History of the Indies*, xviii–xix.

69. Laurence Bergreen, *Columbus: The Four Voyages* (New York: Viking, 2011), 365.

70. Collard, introduction to *History of the Indies*, p.xii.

71. Zinn, *A People's History*, 9, 11.

72. Ibid., 5.

73. Las Casas, *History of the Indies*, 63.

74. Ibid., 64–65.

75. Ibid., 77–82.

76. Collard, introduction to *History of the Indies*, xvii.

77. Zinn, *A People's History*, 1.

78. Ibid., 7.

79. Koning, *Columbus: His Enterprise*, 88.

80. Zinn, *A People's History*, 7–8.

81. Bergreen, *Columbus: The Four Voyages*, 373.

82. Samuel Eliot Morison, "Texts and Translations of the Journal of Columbus's First Voyage," the *Hispanic American Historical Review*, Vol. 19, No. 3 (August 1939), 235–61.

83. Zinn, *A People's History*, 10.

84. Ibid., 10, 8.

85. Ibid., 8.

86. Ibid., 1.

87. Samuel Eliot Morison, *Christopher Columbus, Mariner* (Boston: Little, Brown and Company, 1942, 1955), 51.

88. Ibid., 66.

89. Ibid., 100.

90. Ibid.

91. Ibid., 112.

92. Ibid, 124–25.

93. Samuel Eliot Morison, *The European Discovery of America: The Southern Voyages A.D. 1492–1616* (New York: Oxford University Press, 1974), 81.

94. Morison, *Christopher Columbus, Mariner*, 131.

95. Ibid., 172–73.

96. Ray Raphael, "Thomas A. Bailey: Dead and Forgotten by His Publisher?" History News Network, April 26, 2015, http://historynewsnetwork.org/article/159214.

97. Thomas A. Bailey, *The American Pageant,* 2nd ed. (Boston: D.C. Heath and Company, 1961), 7, 9–10.

98. Curtis P. Nettels, *The Roots of American Civilization: A History of American Colonial Life,* second edition (New York: Appleton-Century-Crofts, 1963), 34.

99. Peter Charles Hoffer, *Past Imperfect: Facts, Fictions, Fraud—American History from Bancroft and Parkman to Ambrose, Bellesiles, Ellis, and Goodwin* (New York: Public Affairs, 2004), 45.

100. Samuel Eliot Morison and Henry Steele Commager, *The Growth of the American Republic,* volume one, 5th ed. (New York: Oxford University Press, 1962), 24.

101. Zinn, *A People's History,* 9.

102. Ibid.

103. Ibid, 10.

104. Ibid, 8.

105. Ibid, 9.

106. Author interview of Eugene Genovese, September 1, 2010, Atlanta, Georgia.

107. Leah Shafer and Bari Walsh, "The Columbus Day Problem," Usable Knowledge, Harvard Graduate School of Education, October 5, 2017, https://www.independent.co.uk/voices/profile-christopher-columbus-a-good-thing-even-harvey-morris-berates-those-who-lay-all-the-ills-of-1556723.html.

Chapter Two: The Life of Zinn

1. Howard Zinn, *You Can't Be Neutral on a Moving Train* (Boston: Beacon Press, 1994), 1–2.

2. Martin Duberman, *Howard Zinn: A Life on the Left* (New York: The New Press, 2012), 277.

3. Howard Zinn, *A People's History of the United States* (New York: HarperCollins, 2003), 643–44.

4. Ibid., 633–34.

5. "About," Before Columbus Foundation, no date, http://www.beforecolumbusfoundation.com/about/.

6.   Zinn, *You Can't Be Neutral*, 2.

7.   Ibid.

8.   Zinn, *A People's History*, 9.

9.   Zinn, *You Can't Be Neutral*, 2.

10. Zinn, *A People's History*, 59.

11. Ibid., 73.

12. Ibid., 96.

13. Ibid., 99.

14. Zinn, *You Can't Be Neutral*, 3.

15. Ibid., 4.

16. Ibid., 6–7.

17. "New Faculty Appointments Are Announced," *Atlanta Daily World*, September 15, 1956, p. 1, col. 5.

18. Duberman, *Howard Zinn*, 22.

19. Howard Zinn, FBI files, Part 1, pp. 4, 5, 11, 50, 54, 80, and 109, https://vault.fbi.gov/Howard%20Zinn%20.

20. Duberman, *Howard Zinn*, 23–24.

21. Zinn, *You Can't Be Neutral*, 171–72.

22. Ibid., 172–73.

23. "Red Agitators Dispersed," *New York Times*, October 2, 1938, 41.

24. Zinn, *You Can't Be Neutral*, 175.

25. Maurice Isserman, "When New York City Was the Capital of American Communism," *New York Times*, October 20, 2017. https://www.nytimes.com/2017/10/20/opinion/new-york-american-communism.html?_r=0.

26. Robert Cohen, *Howard Zinn's Southern Diary: Sit-ins, Civil Rights, and Black Women's Student Activism* (Athens, Georgia: University of Georgia Press, 2018), 243–44, note 64.

27. John Earl Haynes, *Red Scare or Red Menace?* (Chicago: Ivan R. Dee, 1996), 197.

28. John Barron, *Operation Solo: The FBI's Man in the Kremlin* (Washington, DC: Regnery Publishing, 1996), 31.

29. Ronald Radosh, "Aside from That, He Was Also a Red," *Weekly Standard*, August 16, 2010, http://www.weeklystandard.com/aside-from-that-he-was-also-a-red/article/489471.

30. Duberman, *Howard Zinn*, 26–27.

31. Zygmund Dobbs, *Red Intrigue and Race Turmoil* (New York: Alliance, Inc., c. 1958), 73.

32. Maurice Isserman, *If I Had a Hammer: The Death of the Old Left and the Birth of the New Left* (New York: Basic Books, 1987), 29–33, 186–187.

33. Davis D. Joyce, *Howard Zinn: A Radical Vision* (Amherst, New York: Prometheus Books, 2003), 48.

34. Karen Vanlandingham, "In Pursuit of a Changing Dream: Spelman College Students and the Civil Rights Movement, 1955–1962," master's thesis, 1985, Emory University, 45–46.

35. Ibid.

36. Howard Zinn, "Finishing School for Pickets," *Nation*, August 6, 1960.

37. Howard Zinn, *You Can't Be Neutral*, 38.

38. Vanlandingham, "In Pursuit of a Changing Dream," 50.

39. Joyce, *Howard Zinn*, 41–48.

40. Vanlandingham, "In Pursuit of a Changing Dream," 61.

41. Ibid., 57.

42. Ibid., 65, 71, and 58.

43. Albert E. Manley, *A Legacy Continues: The Manley Years at Spelman College, 1953–1976*, (Lanham, MD: University Press of America, 1995), 174.

44. Ibid.

45. Zinn, *You Can't Be Neutral*, 37.

46. Ibid, 40.

47. Ibid., 41–42.

48. Marian Wright Edelman, "Spelman College: A Safe Haven for a Young Black Woman," *Journal of Blacks in Higher Education*, No. 27 (spring, 2000), 118–23.

49. FBI file on Howard Zinn, page 108, part 1, https://vault.fbi.gov/Howard%20Zinn%20.

50. "Feels U.N. Should Accept Red China," *Atlanta Daily World*, February 15, 1962, 1.

51. Cohen, *Howard Zinn's Southern Diary*, 239, note 10.

52. "20 Chicagoans Attend SNCC Meeting in Atlanta," *Daily Defender*, April 7, 1964, 4.

53. Zinn, *You Can't Be Neutral*, 43.

54. Duberman, *Howard Zinn*, 79–83.

55. Ibid., 85.

56. Howard Zinn, "Biographical Data," Howard Zinn Papers, Tamiment Library, New York University.

57. Duberman, *Howard Zinn*, 85.

58. Ibid., 87–89.

59. Ibid., 87.

60. Zinn, *You Can't Be Neutral*, 27.

61. Duberman, *Howard Zinn*, 89–90.

62. Ibid., 91–92.

63. David Greenberg, "Agit-Prof, Howard Zinn's Mutilations of American History," *The New Republic*, March 19, 2013.

64. Duberman, *Howard Zinn*, 188–89.

65. Cohen, *Howard Zinn's Southern Diary*, 73, 74.

66. Zinn, *You Can't Be Neutral*, 184–85; William Holtzman, "Howard Zinn, My Courageous Friend," Teaching a People's History: Zinn Education Project, August 17, 2012, https://www.zinnedproject.org/news/howard-zinn-my-courageous-friend/.

67. Zinn, *You Can't Be Neutral*, 185–92.

68. Alice Walker, "Saying Goodbye to My Friend Howard Zinn," *Boston Globe*, January 31, 2010, http://archive.boston.com/ae/books/articles/2010/01/31/alice_walker_says_goodbye_to_her_friend_howard_zinn/.

69. Zinn, *You Can't Be Neutral*, 119.

70. Holtzman, "Howard Zinn."

71. Author interview of Emily Rentz, October 5, 2018.

72. Zinn, *You Can't Be Neutral*, 198.

73. Ibid., 141, 148–49.

74. Ibid., 141.

75. Peter Wood, email to the author, February 23, 2018.

76. Joyce, *Howard Zinn*, 86–87.

77. Wood, email to the author.

78. Zinn, *You Can't Be Neutral*, 7–8.

79. Joyce, *Howard Zinn*, 83–85.

80. Ibid.

81. Ibid.

82. Robert Cohen, "Mentor to the Movement: Howard Zinn, SNCC, and the Spelman College Freedom Struggle," in *Howard Zinn's Southern Diary*, 17.

83. Joyce, *Howard Zinn*, 82–83.

84. Zinn, *You Can't Be Neutral*, 199–200.

85. Paul Kengor, "Hollywood's Blacklisted Communist: The Truth About Trumbo," *Human Events*, November 6, 2015, http://humanevents. com/2015/11/06/the-truth-about-trumbo/.

86. Paul Kengor, "Arthur Miller—Communist," *American Spectator*, October 16, 2015, https://spectator. org/64379_arthur-miller-communist/.

87. Zinn, *You Can't Be Neutral*, 121.

88. Ibid., 126–27.

89. Sydney Gruson, "Dispute in Laos on Travel," *New York Times*, February 17, 1968, 7.

90. "Pentagon Papers," National Archives, https://www.archives.gov/ research/pentagon-papers.

91. Duberman, *Howard Zinn*, 175–78.

92. Zinn, *You Can't Be Neutral*, 159–61.

93. Ibid., 206.

94. David Zirin, "You Have to Go Beyond Capitalism [interview of Howard Zinn]," *International Socialist Review*, issue 66, https:// isreview.org/issue/66/you-have-go-beyond-capitalism.

95. Joyce, *Howard Zinn*, 151.

96. George Bush, "Proclamation 6484—Columbus Day 1992," the American Presidency Project, http://presidency.proxied.lsit.ucsb.edu/ ws/?pid=47411.

97. William J. Clinton, "Proclamation 6608—Columbus Day, 1993," the American Presidency Project, http://www.presidency.ucsb.edu/ws/ index.php?pid=62444.

98. Julia Fair, "How Donald Trump's Columbus Day Proclamation Compares to Previous Presidents," *USA Today*, October 9, 2017, https://www.usatoday.com/story/news/politics/onpolitics/2017/10/09/ president-trumps-columbus-day-proclamation-excludes-native-americans/746436001/.

Chapter Three: Howard Zinn's "Usable Indian"

1. Howard Zinn, *A People's History of the United States* (New York: HarperCollins, 2003), 11; Victor Davis Hanson, *Carnage and Culture: Landmark Battles in the Rise of Western Power* (New York: Doubleday, 2001), 194–95.

2. Zinn, *A People's History*, 11.

3. Albert Marrin, *Aztecs and Spaniards: Cortes and the Conquest of Mexico* (New York: Atheneum, 1986), 88, 94; Hanson, *Carnage and Culture*, 212.

4. Marrin, *Aztecs and Spaniards*, 151.

5. Hanson, *Carnage*, 211–12.

6. Zinn, *A People's History*, 12.

7. Ibid.

8. Gary B. Nash, *Red, White, and Black: The Peoples of Early North America*, (Englewood Cliffs, New Jersey: Pearson, 1974), 32.

9. Zinn, *A People's History*, 12.

10. Ibid., 12–13.

11. Ibid., 12; Edmund S. Morgan, *American Slavery, American Freedom: The Ordeal of Colonial Virginia* (New York: W.W. Norton, 1975), 73–74.

12. Larry Gragg, "Powhatan Wars" in *American Indian History*, vol. 2, ed. Carole E. Barrett (Pasadena, California: Salem Press, 2003), 424–26.

13. Bert M. Mutersbaugh, "Metacom's War" in *American Indian History*, vol. 1, ed. Carole E. Barrett (Pasadena, California: Salem Press, 2003), 365 vol. 2, ed. Carole E. Barrett 70.

14. Zinn, *A People's History*, 14.

15. Thomas E. Woods Jr., *The Politically Incorrect Guide to American History* (Washington, D.C.: Regnery, 2004), 7–9.

16. Alden T. Vaughan, *New England Frontier: Puritans and Indians 1620–1675*, 3rd ed. (Norman, Oklahoma: University of Oklahoma Press, 1995,), xiii–xiv, xix.

17. Zinn, *A People's History*, 14.

18. Suzanne Riffle Boyce, "Tuscarora War," in *American Indian History*, vol. 2, ed. Carole A. Barrett (Pasadena, California: Salem Press, 2003), 566–69.

19. Harold D. Tallant, "Yamasee War," in *American Indian History*, vol. 2, ed. Carole A. Barrett (Pasadena, California: Salem Press, 2003), 608–9.

20. C. George Fry, "Pequot War" in *American Indian History*, vol. 2, ed. by Carol Barrett (Pasadena, California: Salem Press, 2003), 409–12.

21. Zinn, *A People's History,* 14–15.
22. "Captain John Underhill's History of the Pequot War," *News from America,* London, 1638, Massachusetts Historical Society, 7–8.
23. Ibid., 12.
24. Ibid., 15.
25. Ibid., 15, 26.
26. Shannon E. Duffy, "The Pequot War: 1636-1638," *The Routledge Handbook of American Military and Diplomatic History, the Colonial Period to 1877,* ed. Antonio S. Thompson and Christos G. Frentzos (New York: Routledge, 2015) 26–32.
27. Zinn, *A People's History,* 15.
28. Francis Jennings, *The Invasion of America: Indians, Colonialism, and the Cant of Conquest* (Chapel Hill, North Carolina: The University of North Carolina Press, 1975), ix.
29. Oscar Handlin, *Truth in History* (Cambridge: Harvard University Press, 1979), 397–98.
30. Zinn, *A People's History,* 14–16; Duffy, "The Pequot War."
31. Zinn, *A People's History,* 16.
32. Richard R. Johnson, "The Search for a Usable Indian: An Aspect of the Defense of Colonial New England," *Journal of American History*, Vol. 64, No. 3, (December 1977), 623–51.
33. Ibid.
34. Ibid.
35. Zinn, *A People's History,* 16–17.
36. Ibid., 17.
37. Ibid., 17–18.
38. Ibid., 18.
39. Ibid.
40. Ibid., 20.
41. Handlin, *Truth in History,* 398.
42. Zinn, *A People's History,* 20; Edna Kenton, ed., *The Jesuit Relations and Allied Documents* (New York: The Vanguard Press, 1954), 219–24; Nash, *Red, White, and Black,* 20.
43. Zinn, *A People's History,* 20.
44. Nash, *Red, White, and Black,* 20.
45. Zinn, *A People's History,* 20.

46. Nash, *Red, White, and Black*, 21.

47. Ibid.

48. Zinn, *A People's History*, 20.

49. Morgan, *American Slavery*, 52.

50. Zinn, *A People's History*, 20.

51. Nash, *Red, White, and Black*, 21.

52. Zinn, *A People's History*, 20.

53. Ibid., 21; Nash, *Red, White, and Black*, 23.

54. Zinn, *A People's History*, 21.

55. Nash, *Red, White, and Black*, 25.

56. Ibid., 93–94.

57. Zinn, *A People's History*, 20.

58. Ibid., 21.

59. Ibid.

60. Karim M. Tiro, "Iroquois Ways of War and Peace," in Cadwallader Colden, *The History of the Five Indian Nations Depending on the Province of New-York in America* (Ithaca: Cornell University Press, 2017), xviii–xxviii.

61. Abraham D. Lavender, "Indian Slave Trade," *American Indian History,* vol. 1, ed. Carol A. Barrett (Pasadena, California: Salem Press: 2003), 220–24.

62. Francis Parkman, *The Parkman Reader: From the Works of Francis Parkman,* sel. and ed. Samuel Eliot Morison (Boston: Little, Brown and Company, 1955), 33.

63. Ibid., 36.

64. Carole A. Barrett, "World Wars" in *American Indian History,* vol. 2, ed. Carol A. Barrett (Pasadena, California: Salem Press: 2003), 593–98.

65. Michael V. Namorato, "Code Talkers," in *American Indian History*, vol. 1, ed. Carol A. Barrett (Pasadena, California: Salem Press: 2003), 105–8; Benny Johnson, "Navajo Code Talker Breaks Silence After Trump Pocahontas Comment," The Daily Caller, November 28, 2017, http://dailycaller.com/2017/11/28/navajo-code-talker-breaks-silence-after-trump-pocahontas-comment-what-he-says-wow/.

66. William Brandon, *The Last Americans: The Indian in American Culture* (New York: McGraw-Hill, 1974), 6–7.

67. Peter Wood, email to author, October 30, 2018.

68. Brandon, *The Last Americans*, 6–7.
69. Tristram Hunt, Introduction in Friedrich Engels, *The Origin of the Family, Private Property and the State*, (London: Penguin Classics, 2010), 3.
70. Ibid., 5–7.
71. Ibid., 11.
72. Zinn, *A People's History*, 103.
73. Ibid., 504.
74. Ibid., 103.
75. Ibid., 103–4.
76. Hunt, Introduction, 17–18.
77. William Z. Foster, *Outline Political History of the Americas* (New York: International Publishers, 1951), 40, 31.
78. Ibid., 30–31.
79. Larry Schweikart, *48 Liberal Lies About American History* (New York: Penguin, 2008), 81.
80. John Thornton, *Africa and Africans in the Making of the Atlantic World, 1400–1680* (Cambridge: Cambridge University Press, 1992), 85–86; Elisabeth Anthony Dexter, *Colonial Women of Affairs: A Study of Women in Business and the Professions in America before 1776* (Boston: Houghton Miflin Company, 1924).

Chapter Four: America the Racist

1. Fred Siegel, "History and Politics: A Common Fate," *Academic Questions*, (December 1991), 32–36.
2. Arna Bontemps, "Dark Odyssey," (review of *They Came in Chains* by J. Saunders Redding) *Saturday Review*, September 2, 1950, 16.
3. Howard Zinn, *A People's History of the United States* (New York: HarperCollins, 2003), 23.
4. Ibid., 29.
5. Robert Paquette to the author, March 3, 2018.
6. P.C. Emmer, *The Dutch Slave Trade: 1500–1800* (New York: Berghan Books, 2006), 39–40.
7. Zinn, *A People's History*, 27.
8. Ibid., 27–28.
9. Robert Paquette email to author, February 23, 2018.

10. Zinn, *A People's History*, 28.
11. Ibid., 38.
12. Ibid., 198.
13. Robert L. Paquette and Mark M. Smith, "Introduction: Slavery in the Americas" in *The Oxford Handbook of Slavery in the Americas*. ed. Robert L. Paquette and Mark M. Smith (New York: Oxford University Press, 2010), 3–17.
14. Bernard Lewis, *Race and Slavery in the Middle East: An Historical Enquiry* (New York: Oxford University Press, 1990), 3.
15. Ibid.
16. Allan Gallay, "Indian Slavery" in *The Oxford Handbook of Slavery in the Americas,* ed. Robert L. Paquette and Mark M. Smith (New York: Oxford University Press, 2010), 312–35.
17. Paquette and Smith, "Introduction: Slavery in the Americas" in *The Oxford Handbook of Slavery in the Americas,* ed. Robert L. Paquette and Mark M. Smith (New York: Oxford University Press, 2010), 3–17.
18. Lewis, *Race and Slavery in the Middle East*, 99.
19. Zinn, *A People's History*, 24.
20. Zinn, *A People's History*, 30–31.
21. Robert William Fogel, *Without Consent or Contract: The Rise and Fall of American Slavery* (New York: W.W. Norton, 1989), 17.
22. William G. Clarence-Smith and David Eltis, "White Servitude" in *The Cambridge World History of Slavery, Volume 3, AD 1420–AD 1804,* vol. 3, ed. David Eltis and Stanley L. Engerman (New York: Cambridge University Press, 2011), 132.
23. Lewis, *Race and Slavery in the Middle East,* 92, 94.
24. Ibid., 97.
25. Ibid., 78.
26. Ibid., 12.
27. Ibid., 77.
28. Thomas Sowell, *Ethnic America: A History*, (New York: Basic Books, 1981), 185.
29. Lewis, *Race and Slavery in the Middle East*, 73.
30. Ibid., 76.
31. Ibid., 78–79.
32. Zinn, *A People's History*, 28.

33. Lewis, *Race and Slavery in the Middle East*, 51.

34. John Thornton, *Africa and Africans in the Making of the Atlantic World, 1400–1680* (Cambridge: Cambridge University Press, 1992), 76.

35. Ibid., 87–88; Robert Paquette to the author, March 3, 2018.

36. Thomas Sowell, *Ethnic America*, 186.

37. Thornton, *Africa and Africans* 175, 183–84.

38. Ibid., 175, 183–84; Paquette and Smith, "Introduction: Slavery in the Americas," *The Oxford Handbook of Slavery in the Americas* (Oxford: Oxford University Press, 2010), 15, note 13.

39. Zinn, *A People's History*, 180.

40. Ibid.

41. Frederick Douglass, *Narrative of the Life of Frederick Douglass*, 1845 edition, in *The Norton Anthology of African American Literature*, 352.

42. Ibid. 337–40, 350–352.

43. Ibid. 362–69.

44. Lorena S. Walsh, "Slavery in the North American Mainland Colonies," in *The Cambridge World History of Slavery, Volume 3*, 407–430.

45. Edgar J. McManus, *A History of Negro Slavery in New York* (Syracuse University Press, 2001), ix–x, 11–12, 47–48.

46. Walsh, "Slavery in the North American Mainland Colonies" in *The Cambridge World History of Slavery, Volume 3*, 407-430.

47. McManus, *A History of Negro Slavery in New York*, 157–58.

48. Ibid., 152.

49. Zinn, *A People's History*, 72.

50. McManus, *A History of Negro Slavery*,168–69.

51. Abdi Latif Dahir, "Africa is now the world's epicenter of modern-day slavery," Quartz Africa, July 23, 2018. https://qz.com/africa/1333946/global-slavery-index-africa-has-the-highest-rate-of-modern-day-slavery-in-the-world/.

52. Seif Kousmate, "The Unspeakable Truth about Slavery in Mauritania," *Guardian*, June 8, 2018, https://www.theguardian.com/global-development/2018/jun/08/the-unspeakable-truth-about-slavery-in-mauritania.

53. Zinn, *A People's History*, 172.

54. Ibid, 173.

55. Ibid., 172.

56. Fogel, *Without Consent or Contract*, 140.

57. Zinn, *A People's History*, 172.

58. Ibid. 172–73.

59. Larry Schweikart and Michael Allen, *A Patriot's History of the United States: From Columbus's Great Discovery to the War on Terror* (New York: Penguin Books, 2004), 259.

60. Zinn, *A People's History*, 182–83.

61. Schweikart and Allen, *A Patriot's History*, 264.

62. Frederick Douglass, "What to the Slave Is the Fourth of July?" Teaching American History.org, http://teachingamericanhistory.org/library/document/what-to-the-slave-is-the-fourth-of-july/; "What to the Slave Is the Fourth of July?" Conservapedia, https://www.conservapedia.com/What_to_the_Slave_is_the_Fourth_of_July%3F.

63. Zinn, *A People's History*, 187.

64. Ibid. 186.

65. Thomas E. Woods Jr., *The Politically Incorrect Guide to American History* (Washington, D.C.: Regnery, 2004), 58–59.

66. Zinn, *A People's History*, 171.

67. Ibid., 188–89.

68. Samuel Eliot Morison and Henry Steele Commager, *The Growth of the American Republic*, 5th ed. (New York: Oxford University Press, 1962), 667–68.

69. Alexander H. Stephens, "Cornerstone" Speech, March 21, 1861. https://teachingamericanhistory.org/library/document/cornerstone-speech/.

70. Zinn, *A People's History*, 189.

71. James M. McPherson, *Tried by War: Abraham Lincoln as Commander in Chief* (New York: Penguin, 2008) 20–21.

72. Zinn, *A People's History*, 191–92.

73. James Oakes, *Freedom National: The Destruction of Slavery in the United States, 1861–1865* (New York: Norton, 2013), 343.

74. McPherson, *Tried by War*, 107–8.

75. Ibid., 127–28.

76. Zinn, *A People's History*, 188–89.

77. James McPherson, *Tried by War*, 107.

78. Zinn, *A People's History*, 191–92.

79. James McPherson, *Tried by War*, 129–30.

80. Debra Sheffer, "Abraham Lincoln: Diplomacy and Emancipation" in *The Routledge Handbook of American Military and Diplomatic History, the Colonial Period to 1877* (New York: Routledge, 2015), 307–8.

81. Zinn, *A People's History*, 187.

82. Oakes, *Freedom National*, xviii.

83. Frederick Douglass, "What the Black Man Wants," Teaching American History.org. http://teachingamericanhistory.org/library/document/what-the-black-man-wants/.

84. Zinn, *A People's History*, 171.

85. Robert Paquette, "Mitch Daniels v. Howard Zinn, Part 2," See Thru Edu, August 25, 2013, seethruedu.com/updatesmitch-daniels-v-howard-zinn-part-2/.

86. Abraham Lincoln, Gettysburg Address, November 19, 1863, Teaching American History, http://teachingamericanhistory.org/library/document/gettysburg-address/. Accessed October 12, 2018.

Chapter Five: Casting a Pall on the Finest Hour

1. Howard Zinn, *A People's History of the United States* (New York: HarperCollins, 2003), 407–8.

2. Ibid., 417.

3. Thomas A. Bailey, *The American Pageant*, second edition (Boston: D.C. Heath and Company, 1961), 863.

4. Franklin D. Roosevelt, Second Fireside Chat, May 7, 1933, the American Presidency Project, http://www.presidency.ucsb.edu/ws/index.php?pid=14636.

5. Robert Dallek, *Franklin D. Roosevelt: A Political Life* (New York: Viking, 2017), 160.

6. Larry Schweikart and Michael Allen, *A Patriot's History of the United States: From Columbus's Great Discovery to the War on Terror* (New York: Penguin Books, 2004), 587.

7. Victor Davis Hanson, *The Second World Wars: How the First Global Conflict Was Fought and Won* (Basic Books, 2017), 62–63.

8. Zinn, *A People's History*, 407; William Henry Chamberlin, *America's Second Crusade* (Henry Regnery, 1950), republished Liberty Fund Books, no date), 185. In this book, published five years after the war, Chamberlin states that "a people's war" was the "fashionable" term.

9. Zinn, *A People's History*, 407–8.

10. Melvyn Leffler, *A Preponderance of Power: National Security, the Truman Administration, and the Cold War* (Stanford: Stanford University Press, 1992), 15.

11. Zinn, *A People's History*, 409.

12. George S. Schuyler (1895–1977), the famous black anticommunist columnist for the *Pittsburgh Courier*, often bitterly commented on the discrimination against blacks even as Hitler's crimes were being denounced. Schuyler was chairman of Negroes Against War, a founding member of the New York State Conservative Party, and then a member of the John Birch Society.

13. Richard Bernstein, "Doubts Mar Film of Black Army Unit," *New York Times*, March 1, 1993, B1.

14. "Black Soldiers Honored," *New York Times*, April 21, 1978, A15.

15. Joe Wilson Jr., *The 761st "Black Panther" Tank Battalion in World War II* (Jefferson, NC: McFarland & Company, 1999), 192.

16. Zinn, *A People's History*, 409.

17. Ibid., 408.

18. Ibid., 408–9.

19. Ibid., 409.

20. Ibid., 410.

21. Ibid., 410–11.

22. Thomas A. Bailey, *Presidential Saints and Sinners* (New York: The Free Press, 1981), 219–20.

23. Schweikart and Allen, *A Patriot's History*, 582–83, 596.

24. Zinn, *A People's History*, 411.

25. "Radhabinod Pal," Wikipedia, https://en.wikipedia.org/wiki/Radhabinod_Pal, citing Norimitsu Onishi, "Decades After War Trials, Japan Still Honors a Dissenting Judge," *New York Times*, August 31, 2007 and Timothy Brook, "The Tokyo Judgment and the Rape of Nanking," *Journal of Asian Studies*, August 2001.

26. Richard H. Minear, *Victors' Justice: The Tokyo War Crimes Trial* (Princeton, New Jersey: Princeton University Press, 1971), 152.

27. Hanson, *The Second World Wars*, 48.

28. Fredrik Logevall, *Embers of War: The Fall of an Empire and the Making of America's Vietnam* (New York: Random House, 2012), 42.

29. Schweikart and Allen, *A Patriot's History*, 592–93.

30. Zinn, *A People's History*, 411.

31. Bailey, *The American Pageant*, 877.

32. Ibid.

33. "Parley at the White House," *New York Times*, November 26, 1941, 8.

34. "Stimson Assails Telling War Plan," *New York Times*, December 6, 1941, 3.

35. Zinn, *A People's History*, 415.

36. Henry L. Feingold, *The Politics of Rescue: The Roosevelt Administration and the Holocaust, 1938–1945* (New Brunswick, New Jersey, 1970), 131, 135, 175, 258–59, 280, 285–86, 303–4; Sol Stern, "Franklin Roosevelt Betrayed Europe's Jews, Leading American Historians and Rabbis Covered for FDR's Mistake," Tablet, January 30, 2020.

37. Dallek, *Franklin D. Roosevelt*, 626.

38. Zinn, *A People's History*, 415.

39. Ibid., 29.

40. Ibid., 416.

41. Schweikart and Allen, *A Patriot's History*, 608.

42. Allison Michelle Maher, "The Internment of Japanese-Canadians: A Policy Founded on Racism, Not on National Security," *Concord Review* 2: 4 (1990), 139–54. I would like to thank *Concord Review* editor Will Fitzhugh for bringing this paper to my attention.

43. Ken Masugi, "Lessons from the WW II Japanese Relocation," *Law and Liberty*, May 8, 2013, http://www.libertylawsite.org/2013/05/08/lessons-from-the-ww-ii-japanese-relocation/; Richard B. Frank, "Zero Hour on Niihau," *World War II*, July 2009, republished at http://www.historynet.com/zero-hour-on-nihau.htm.

44. Masugi, "Lessons from the WW II Japanese Relocation."

45. Ken Masugi email to author, August 24, 2018.

46. Charles W. Sasser, *Patton's Panthers* (New York: Simon & Schuster, 2004), 333–34.

47. Schweikart and Allen, *A Patriot's History*, 609.

48. Zinn, *A People's History*, 416.

49. Lawrence E. Davies, "West Coast Moves to Oust Japanese," *New York Times*, January 29, 1942, 12.

50. Lawrence E. Davies, "Japanese Seized in Raid on Coast," *New York Times*, February 3, 1942, 14.

51. Lawrence E. Davies, "California Aliens Face Changed Way," *New York Times*, February 4, 1942, 7.

52. Lawrence E. Davies, "20 Aliens on Coast Seized with Arms," *New York Times*, February 11, 1942, 12.

53. Lawrence E. Davies, "West Coast Widens Martial Law Call," *New York Times*, February 12, 1942, 10.

54. Lawrence E. Davies, "Japanese Officers Held in California," *New York Times*, February 18, 1942, 10.

55. "800 West Coast Japanese Go to Enemy Camps As Army Maps Widened 'Prohibited' Zones," *New York Times*, February 24, 1942, 11.

56. Lawrence E. Davies, "Shifting of Aliens Nearing on Coast," *New York Times*, February 28, 1942, 8.

57. Brian Masaru Hayashi, *Democratizing the Enemy: The Japanese American Internment* (Princeton: Princeton University Press, 2004), 86.

58. Carey McWilliams, "Moving the West Coast Japanese," *Harper's Magazine*, September 1942, 359–69.

59. Masugi, "Lessons from the WW II Japanese Relocation."

60. Quester Entertainment, "Japanese Relocation: Government Film (1942)—3613," YouTube, June 25, 2013, https://www.youtube.com/watch?v=esVege1S0OE.

61. "Japanese Decries Mass Evacuation," *New York Times*, June 19, 1942, 8.

62. "Asks Draft of Japanese," *New York Times*, July 17, 1943, 6.

63. "Captive Exchange Halted by Japan," *New York Times*, December 14, 1943, 5.

64. "Praises Prisoner Camps," *New York Times*, April 5, 1944, 10.

65. Zinn, *A People's History*, 416–17.

66. Robert Dallek, *Franklin D. Roosevelt*, 281–82.

67. Schweikart and Allen, *A Patriot's History of the United States*, 602, 597–99.

68. Lynne Olson, *Those Angry Days: Roosevelt, Lindbergh, and America's Fight Over World War II, 1939–1941* (New York: Random House, 2014), 427.

69. David W. Moore, "Support for War on Terrorism Rivals Support for WWII," Gallup, October 3, 2001,

70. Schweikart and Allen, *A Patriot's History*, 602.

71. Hanson, *The Second World Wars*, 451, 449.

72. Zinn, *A People's History*, 417.

73. W. Ellison Chalmers, "Voluntarism and Compulsion in Dispute Settlement," in *Problems and Policies of Dispute Settlement and Wage Stabilization During World War II*, Bulletin No. 1009 (United States Department of Labor, 1950), 26–71; Immanuel Ness, Benjamin Day, and Aaron Brenner, *The Encyclopedia of Strikes* (New York: Routledge, 2009), 216.

74. Joshua Freeman, "Delivering the Goods: Industrial Unionism during World War II" in *The Labor History Reader* ed. Daniel J. Leab (Urbana: University of Illinois Press, 1985), 383–406; Burton W. Folsom Jr. and Anita Folsom, *FDR Goes to War* (New York: Simon & Schuster, 2011), 67.

75. Zinn, *A People's History*, 419.

76. Ibid.

77. Sam Wineburg, "Undue Certainty: Where Howard Zinn's *A People's History* Falls Short," *American Educator,* Winter 2012–13, https://www.aft.org/sites/default/files/periodicals/Wineburg.pdf; P. L. Prattis, "The Horizon," *Pittsburgh Courier*, April 19, 1941, 6; A. Philip Randolph, "England's Fight Our Cause," *Pittsburgh Courier*, February 8, 1941, 13; Harry MacKinley Williams, "When Black Is Right: The Life and Writings of George S. Schuyler" (Ph.D. diss. Brown University, 1988), 331–32.

78. Wineburg, "Undue Certainty."

79. Lawrence S. Wittner, *Rebels Against the War: The American Peace Movement, 1941–1960* (New York: Columbia University Press, 1969), 46–47.

80. Zinn, *A People's History*, 421.

81. Wineburg, "Undue Certainty."

82. Ibid.

83. Walter Laqueur, "Springtime for Hitler," review of David Irving, *Hitler's War* (The Viking Press) and Peter Hoffman, *The History of the German Resistance, New York Times*, April 3, 1977, 253; John Lukacs, "Caveat Lector," *National Review*, August 19, 1977, 946–47.

84. Hanson, *The Second World Wars*, 3.

85. Ibid., 38–39.

86. Ibid., 40–41.

87. Zinn, *A People's History*, 423.

88. *Reporting World War II: Part II* (New York: Library of America, 1995), 893–94; Bailey, *The American Pageant*, 900.

89. Zinn, *A People's History*, 423.

90. Sadao Asada, "The Shock of the Atomic Bomb and Japan's Decision to Surrender: A Reconsideration," *Pacific Historical Review* 67: 4 (November 1998), 477–512.

91. Zinn, *A People's History*, 424.

92. Ibid.

93. Ibid., 425.

Chapter Six: Writing the Red Menace Out of History

1. Howard Zinn, *A People's History of the United States* (New York: HarperCollins, 2003), 425.

2. Howard Jones, *"A New Kind of War": America's Global Strategy and the Truman Doctrine in Greece* (New York: Oxford University Press, 1989), 7.

3. Zinn, *A People's History*, 425.

4. John Lewis Gaddis, *The Cold War: A New History* (New York: Penguin, 2005) 35, 56.

5. Anne Applebaum, *Iron Curtain: The Crushing of Eastern Europe, 1944–1956* (New York: Doubleday, 2012), 239, 238.

6. Gaddis, *The Cold War*, 36.

7. Zinn, *A People's History*, 427.

8. "Our Critique [of chapter 37 of David M. Kennedy, Lizabeth Cohen, and Thomas A. Bailey, *The American Pageant* 12th ed. (Houghton Mifflin, 2001)]" the Education and Research Institute, no date, https://www.trueamericanhistory.us/pageant/toc/chapter-37-page-858/.

9. Gaddis, *The Cold War*, 37–39.

10. Ibid., 42.

11. Ibid., 110–12.

12. Melvyn P. Leffler, *A Preponderance of Power: National Security, the Truman Administration, and the Cold War* (Stanford: Stanford University Press, 1992), 11.

13. Jones, *"A New Kind of War,"* 11.

14. Ibid. 12–13.

15. Gaddis, *The Cold War,* 162.

16. Zinn, *A People's History,* 425–27.

17. John Earl Haynes and Harvey Klehr, *Venona: Decoding Soviet Espionage in America* (New Haven: Yale University Press, 1999), 52–54.

18. Jones, *"A New Kind of War",* 17–18.

19. Ibid., 5–6.

20. Ibid., 4.

21. Ibid., 63.

22. Ibid., 66.

23. Ibid., 121.

24. Zinn, *A People's History,* 429–30.

25. Gaddis, *The Cold War,* 40–42.

26. John E. Haynes, *Red Scare or Red Menace? American Communism and Anticommunism in the Cold War,* American Ways Series (Ivan R. Dee, 1995), 63.

27. Zinn, *A People's History,* 427–28.

28. Benedict J. Kerkvliet, *The Huk Rebellion: A Study of Peasant Revolt in the Philippines* (Berkeley: University of California Press, 1977), 18.

29. Ibid., 218–19.

30. Ibid., 224–25.

31. Robert Aura Smith, *Philippine Freedom* (New York: Columbia University Press, 1958), 142–43.

32. Zinn, *A People's History,* 430.

33. John Earl Haynes, *Red Scare,* 51, 72–73.

34. Christopher Andrew and Vasili Mitrokhin, *The Sword and the Shield: The Mitrokhin Archive and the Secret History of the KGB* (New York: Basic Books, 1999), 164.

35. John Earl Haynes, *Red Scare,* 147–48.

36. Ibid.

37. Howard Zinn, *A People's History,* 430-431.

38. M. Stanton Evans, *Blacklisted by History: The Untold Story of Senator Joe McCarthy and His Fight against America's Enemies* (New York: Random House, 2007), 469, 471; John Earl Haynes and Harvey Klehr, *In Denial: Historians, Communism & Espionage* (San Francisco:

Encounter Books, 2003), 38; "Philip Foner," Discover the Networks, https://www.discoverthenetworks.org/individuals/philip-foner/.

39. William Henry Chamberlin, *America's Second Crusade* (Henry Regnery), 257–59.

40. William Buckley Jr. and L. Brent Bozell, *McCarthy and His Enemies* (Chicago: Henry Regnery, 1954), 273; Evans, *Blacklisted by History*, 39; John Earl Haynes, Harvey Klehr, and Alexander Vassiliev, *Spies: The Rise and Fall of the KGB in America* (Yale University Press, 2009), 271-278.

41. M. Stanton Evans, *Blacklisted*, 633, 252, 358; Haynes, Klehr and Vessiliev, *Spies*, 296–305.

42. Haynes, Klehr, and Vassiliev, *Spies,* 296–305.

43. Ibid., 317–20.

44. Ibid., 195.

45. Haynes and Klehr, *Venona,* 17.

46. Buckley and Bozell, *McCarthy*, 388–92.

47. Haynes, *Red Scare*, 14.

48. Chamberlin, *America's Second Crusade*, 260–1.

49. Evans, *Blacklisted*, 106, 415–20, 424.

50. Haynes, *Red Scare*, 150–2.

51. William F. Buckley and the editors of *National Review, The Committee and Its Critics: A Calm Review of the House Committee on Un-American Activities* (New York: G.P. Putnam's Sons, 1962), 212.

52. Zinn, *A People's History,* 436, 432.

53. Ibid., 435.

54. Buckley, *The Committee and Its Critics*, 17–19, 212.

55. Zinn, *A People's History,* 431.

56. David Horowitz, *Radical Son: A Generational Odyssey* (New York: Simon and Schuster, 1997). 66–69.

57. Haynes, *Red Scare*, 199–200.

58. Zinn, *A People's History,* 432.

59. Ibid.

60. Haynes, *Red Scare*, 168–69.

61. Haynes and Klehr, *Venona,* 7, 9–11.

62. Haynes, Klehr, and Vessiliev, *Spies*, 262–65.

63. Haynes and Klehr, *Venona*, 90-92.

64. Allen Weinstein, *Perjury: The Hiss-Chambers Case* (New York: Alfred A. Knopf, 1978), 64-65, 328-331.

65. Haynes, Klehr, and Vassiliev, *Spies*, 31.

66. Ronald Radosh and Joyce Milton, *The Rosenberg File: A Search for the Truth* (New York: Holt, Rinehart & Winston, 1983), x–xi

67. Ibid., xii–xiii.

68. Zinn, *A People's History*, 433–35.

69. Ibid., 434.

70. Ronald Radosh, "Case Closed: The Rosenbergs Were Soviet Spies," *Los Angeles Times*, September 17, 2008, https://www.latimes.com/la-oe-radosh17-2008sep17-story.html.

71. Sam Roberts, "A Spy Confesses, and Still Some Weep for the Rosenbergs," *New York Times*, September 20, 2008.

72. Zinn, *A People's History*, 437.

73. Ibid., 435.

74. Karl Marx, "The Victory of the Counter-Revolution in Vienna," *Neue Rheinische Zeitung* 136 (November 1848), trans. by the Marx-Engels Institute, https://www.marxists.org/archive/marx/works/1848/11/06.htm.

75. Vladimir Lenin, "Lessons of the Commune," *Zagranichnaya Gazeta* 2 (March 23, 1908), trans. Bernard Isaacs, *Collected Works*, Vol. 13, p. 478, https://www.marxists.org/archive/lenin/works/1908/mar/23.htm.

76. Samuel H. Beer, ed., *The Communist Manifesto* by Karl Marx and Friedrich Engels (Harvard University Press, 1955), 42–43, 46.

77. Zinn, *A People's History*, 437.

78. Gaddis, *The Cold War*, 150.

79. Zinn, *A People's History*, 438.

80. William Z. Foster, *Outline Political History of the Americas* (New York: International Publishers, 1951), 487.

81. Zinn, *A People's History*, 438–39.

82. Ibid., 439–41.

83. Gaddis, *The Cold War*, 168.

84. Zinn, Ibid., 441.

Chapter Seven: Black Mascots for a Red Revolution

1. Howard Zinn, *A People's History of the United States* (New York: HarperCollins, 2003), 443.
2. Ibid., 444.
3. Nathan Irvin Huggins, *Harlem Renaissance* (New York: Oxford University Press, 1971), 219.
4. Zinn, *A People's History*, 444.
5. Gerard Early, *My Soul's High Song: The Collected Writings of Countee Cullen, Voice of the Harlem Renaissance* (New York: Doubleday, 1991), 20–21, 23, 48–49.
6. Zinn, *A People's History*, 446.
7. Theodore Draper, *American Communism and Soviet Russia* (New York: The Viking Press, 1960), 320–22.
8. Zinn, *A People's History*, 447.
9. Kevern Verney and Lee Sartain, *Long Is the Way and Hard: One Hundred Years of the NAACP* (Fayetteville: The University of Arkansas Press, 2009), xx.
10. Zinn, *A People's History*, 398.
11. Manning Marable and Leith Mullings, *Let Nobody Turn Us Around: Voices of Resistance, Reform, and Renewal, An African American Anthology* (New York: Rowman & Littlefield, 2000), 313–14.
12. Ibid., 308–13.
13. George Schuyler, *Black and Conservative* (New Rochelle, New York: Arlington House, 1966), 220.
14. Earl Ofari Hutchinson, *Blacks and Reds: Race and Class in Conflict, 1919–1990* (East Lansing: Michigan State University Press, 1995), 68–69.
15. Edward A. Hatfield, "Angelo Herndon Case," *New Georgia Encyclopedia*, August 14, 2009, http://www.georgiaencyclopedia.org/articles/history-archaeology/angelo-herndon-case.
16. Zinn, *A People's History*, 448.
17. Daniel W. Aldridge III, "A Militant Liberalism: Anti-Communism and the African American Intelligentsia, 1939–1955, Conference Paper for the 2004 American Historical Association, December 2003, http://www.hartford-hwp.com/archives/45a/689.html.
18. Robert Shogan, *Harry Truman and the Struggle for Racial Justice* (Lawrence, Kansas: University Press of Kansas, 2013), 126–27.

19. Wilson Record, *The Negro and the Communist Party* (Chapel Hill: North Carolina University Press, 1951), 282–83.

20. Aldridge, "A Militant Liberalism."

21. Record, *The Negro and the Communist Party*, 282–83.

22. Aldridge, "A Militant Liberalism."

23. Ibid.

24. David Horowitz, *Radical Son: A Generational Odyssey* (New York: Simon & Schuster, 1997), 53.

25. FBI file on Howard Zinn, page 11, part 1, https://vault.fbi.gov/ Howard%20Zinn%20.

26. James Rorty, "The Lessons of the Peekskill Riots: What Happened and Why," *Commentary*, October 1, 1950. https://www.commentary magazine.com/articles/the-lessons-of-the-peekskill-riotswhat-happened-and-why/.

27. Harvey Klehr, John Earl Haynes, and Kyrill M. Anderson, *The Soviet World of American Communism* (New Haven: Yale University Press, 1998), 221.

28. Ibid., 218–27.

29. Glenda Elizabeth Gilmore, *Defying Dixie: The Radical Roots of Civil Rights, 1919–1950* (New York: W.W. Norton, 2008), 154.

30. Homer Smith, *Black Man in Red Russia* (Chicago: Johnson Publishing Company, 1964), 78, 80.

31. Horowitz, *Radical Son*, 73–74.

32. Aldridge, "A Militant Liberalism."

33. Zinn, *A People's History*, 458, 464.

34. Ibid., 404.

35. Ibid., 448.

36. William J. Collins, "Race, Roosevelt, and Wartime Production: Fair Employment in World War II Labor Markets," *American Economic Review* 91: 1 (March 2001), 272–86.

37. "Race Leaders to Fight for Army Bills," *Pittsburgh Courier*, April 10, 1938, 24.

38. Jervis Anderson, *A. Philip Randolph: A Biographical Portrait* (New York: Harcourt Brace Jovanovich, 1972), 274–80.

39. Ibid.

40. Simon Hall, "The NAACP and the Challenges of 1960s Radicalism," in Verney and Sartain, *Long Is the Way and Hard*, 75–85.

41. "Howard Zinn," SNCC Digital Gateway, https://snccdigital.org/people/howard-zinn/; Howard Zinn, *You Can't Be Neutral on a Moving Train* (Boston: Beacon Press, 1994), 51.

42. Martin Duberman, *Howard Zinn: A Life on the Left* (New York: The New Press, 2012), 53; "20 Chicagoans Attend SNCC Meet in Atlanta," *Daily Defender*, April 7, 1964, 4.

43. Roy Wilkins to J. Edgar Hoover, April 1, 1957; J. Edgar Hoover to Roy Wilkins, April 5, 1957; Roy Wilkins to NAACP Youth Council and College Chapters, May 21, 1957; Independent Service on the Vienna Youth Festival committee to Herb Wright, Director, Youth Division, NAACP, December 15, 1958; Herbert Wright to NAACP Youth and College Officers, May 6, 1959, NAACP Papers, Library of Congress, III: E53; Richard Gid Powers, *Not without Honor: The History of American Anticommunism* (New York: The Free Press, 1995), 308.

44. Powers, *Not without Honor*, 297–98.

45. Howard Zinn, "Finishing School for Pickets," *The Nation*, August 6, 1960.

46. Howard Zinn, *SNCC: The New Abolitionists*, (Cambridge, Massachusetts: South End Press, 2002), 233, 235.

47. Ibid., 271–72.

48. Marian Wright Edelman, "Spelman College: A Safe Haven for a Young Black Woman," *Journal of Blacks in Higher Education* 27 (spring 2000), 118–23.

49. FBI file on Howard Zinn, Part 1, p. 107–13, 120–2, https://vault.fbi.gov/Howard%20Zinn%20.

50. Author interview with Harvey Klehr, December 21, 2017, Atlanta, Georgia; according to Klehr, Wilkinson was a member of the Communist Party.

51. Dorothy Marshall to John Lewis, December 12, 1963, SNCC Papers, Martin Luther King Center, Archives, Atlanta, Georgia, Box 23.

52. Frank Wilkinson to John Lewis, James Forman, and Robert Moses, May 22, 1964, SNCC Papers, Martin Luther King Center Archives, Atlanta, Georgia, Box 23.

53. Roy Wilkins to Edward King, September 1, 1961, NAACP Papers, Library of Congress, III: A212.

54. Roy Wilkins to Barbee William Durham, November 3, 1961, NAACP Papers, Library of Congress, III: A199.

55. Howard Zinn, *SNCC*, 29.

56. Robert Cohen, *Howard Zinn's Southern Diary: Sit-Ins, Civil Rights, and Black Women's Student Activism* (University of Georgia Press, 2018), 99–100, 103.

57. Zinn, *A People's History*, 348–49, 382.

58. William Z. Foster, *The History of the Communist Party of the United States* (International Publishers, 1951), 286.

59. Central Committee, Communist Party, U.S.A., "Workers, Negroes Unite! Stop the 'Legal' Lynching of Nine Negro Boys in Alabama!" *Daily Worker*, and "8 Negro Workers Sentenced to Die by Lynching," reprinted in Philip Foner and Herbert Shapiro, eds., *American Communism and Black Americans: A Documentary History, 1930–1934* (Philadelphia: Temple University Press, 1991), 252–255.

60. "Nine Alabama Men Saved from Lynchers," *Chicago Defender*, April 4, 1931, 1.

61. "10,000 Hear Boy Rapists Sentenced," *Pittsburgh Courier*, April 18, 1931, 4; "Eight Boys Sentenced to Chair in Alabama," *Chicago Defender*, April 18, 1931, 11; "Sentence of Octet to Electric Chair in One Day is Nation's Record," *Afro-American*, April 18, 1931, 4.

62. "N.A.A.C.P. Defends 9 Ala. Youths, To Appeal Case," *Afro-American*, May 2, 1931, 7; George D. Tyler, "Reds Tie Up Harlem Cops; Parade in Protest Against Ala. Outrage," *Afro-American*, May 2, 1931, 7.

63. "I.L.D. Says It Represents All Eight Alabama Boys," *Afro-American*, May 16, 1931, 7.

64. "Darrow May Defend Ala. Boys," *Pittsburgh Courier*, May 16, 1931, 1.

65. "Lawyers Busy in Scottsboro," *Pittsburgh Courier*, May 23, 1931, 1.

66. "Negro Pastors Assail Labor Defense Body," *New York Times*, May 24, 1931, N6.

67. "Reds Threaten DePriest," *Chicago Defender*, June 20, 1931, 1.

68. George B. Murphy, Jr. "Pickens Heckled by Communist Leaders in New York and Boston," *Afro-American*, July 4, 1931, 1.

69. "'Red' Speakers Heckled NAACP Pa. Conference," *Afro-American*, July 11, 1931, 16.

70. "Blames 'Black Laws' in Scottsboro Case," *New York Times*, July 4, 1931, 19.

71. "Fight for Doomed Negroes," *New York Times*, July 1, 1931, 9.

72. "The Week," *The New Republic*, July 29, 193, 270–1.

73. Walter White, "The Negro and the Communists," *Harper's Magazine*, December 1931, reprinted in Philip S. Foner and Herbert Shapiro, eds., *American Communism and Black Americans: A Documentary History, 1930–1934* (Philadelphia: Temple University Press, 1991), 285–86.

74. James Goodman, *Stories of Scottsboro* (New York: Random House, 1994), 394.

75. Ibid., 202.

76. Ibid., 203–4.

77. George Schuyler, Views and Reviews, *Pittsburgh Courier*, August 15, 1931, 10.

78. George Schuyler, Views and Reviews, *Pittsburgh Courier*, August 29, 1931.

79. George Schuyler, Views and Reviews, *Pittsburgh Courier*, May 6, 1933.

80. George Schuyler, *Black and Conservative*, 218–19.

81. "Another Communist 'Victory,'" *Pittsburgh Courier*, June 23, 1934, 10.

82. Zinn, *A People's History*, 448.

83. Ibid., 448–49.

84. Ibid., 449-450.

85. Howard Zinn, "A Fate Worse Than Integration," *Harper's Monthly* 219: 1311 (August 1959), 53–56.

86. Howard Zinn, "A Case of Quiet Social Change," *Crisis* 66: 8 (October 1959), 471–76.

87. Zinn, *A People's History*, 450.

88. Walter G. Hooke to Howard Zinn, July 21, 1995, Howard Zinn Papers, Tammament Library, New York University, Box 10.

89. Zinn, *A People's History*, 451.

90. Trezzvant W. Anderson, "How Has Dramatic Bus Boycott Affected Negroes?" *Pittsburgh Courier*, November 9, 1957, B1.

91. Zinn, *A People's History*, 465.

92. Ibid., 454.

93. Ibid., 455.

94. Ibid., 456–57.

95. Ibid., 457.

96. Lauren Feeney, "Two Versions of John Lewis' Speech," Bill Moyers & Company, July 24, 2013, http://billmoyers.com/content/two-versions-of-john-lewis-speech/.

97. Gene Roberts, "The Story of Snick: From 'Freedom High' to 'Black Power,'" *New York Times Magazine*, September 25, 1966, 27.

98. David Lawrence, "Root of the Riots: Provocative Speeches," *Rochester Democrat and Chronicle*, August 1, 1967, 10A.

99. Michael Javen Fortner, *Black Silent Majority: The Rockefeller Drug Laws and the Politics of Punishment* (Cambridge, Massachusetts: Harvard University Press, 2015), 165–66.

100. Ibid., 184–85.

101. Zinn, *A People's History*, 458.

102. Ibid., 454.

103. Cohen, *Howard Zinn's Southern Diary*, 143.

104. Zinn, *A People's History*, 464.

105. Howard Zinn, "Conclusion: Fighting Back," in *Justice in Everyday Life: The Way It Really Works* (New York: William Morrow & Company, 1974), 355.

106. Howard Zinn, "The New Radicalism," originally published as "Marxism and the New Left," in *The New Left* (Boston: Porter Sargent, 1969), republished in *The Zinn Reader* (New York: Seven Stories Press, 1997), 620–32.

107. Zinn, *A People's History*, 458.

108. Schuyler, *Black and Conservative*, 345.

109. Zinn, *A People's History* 459.

110. Ibid., 460.

111. George Schuyler, "Anatomy of Black Insurrection," typescript, August 18, 1965, George Schuyler Papers, Special Collections Research Center, Syracuse University Libraries.

112. *Report of the National Advisory Commission on Civil Disorders* (New York: The New York Times Company, 1968), 251.

113. Zinn, *A People's History*, 460–1.

114. Manning Marable, *Malcolm X: A Life of Reinvention* (New York: Viking, 2011), 432–36.

115. Zinn, *A People's History*, 461.

116. Elizabeth Harrington, "Park Service Cancels Funding for Project 'Honoring Legacy' of Black Panther Party," *Washington Free Beacon*, October 24, 2017, http://freebeacon.com/issues/park-service-cancels-funding-project-honoring-legacy-black-panther-party/.

117. Michael Moynihan, "Whitewashing the Black Panthers," The Daily Beast, July 15, 2015.

118. David Horowitz, *The Black Book of the American Left* (New York: Encounter Books, 2013), 27, 44–55.

119. Zinn, *A People's History*, 461.

120. Ibid., 463.

121. Ibid., 462.

122. George Schuyler, Jay Parker, Myrna Bain, Thomas Matthews, "The Right Wing Negro," Pacifica Radio, WBAI, March 26, 1967, moderated and produced by Charles Childs and Charles Hobson.

123. Fortner, *Black Silent Majority*, 80–1.

124. Zinn, *A People's History*, 464–65.

125. Ibid., 468.

126. Ibid., 518.

Chapter Eight: Ho, Ho, Ho Chi Minh! Howard Zinn and the Commies Win!

1.   Howard Zinn, *A People's History of the United States* (New York: HarperCollins, 2003), 469.

2.   Anne Applebaum, *Iron Curtain: The Crushing of Eastern Europe, 1944–1956* (New York: Doubleday, 2012), 436; John Lewis Gaddis, *The Cold War: A History* (New York: Penguin Press, 2005), 33. Gaddis states that it had "never been established" whether Jan Masaryk "jumped or was pushed."

3.   Zinn, *A People's History*, 429–30.

4.   Ibid., 469.

5.   Ibid., 470.

6.   Fredrik Logevall, *Embers of War: The Fall of an Empire and the Making of America's Vietnam* (New York: Random House, 2012), 10–14.

7.   Ibid., 16–17.

8.   Stephen J. Morris, "The Bad War," *Weekly Standard*, October 13, 2017, http://www.weeklystandard.com/the-bad-war/article/2010065; It should be noted that Fredrik Logevall, who, unlike Zinn, does fully

acknowledge Ho Chi Minh's dedication to international communism and Stalinism, sees, however, no contradiction between Ho's "emphasis on patriotism and national unity, and the internationalism of the Comintern," because "the Comintern did not deny colonized peoples the right to celebrate their past or to try to throw off their oppressors." Logevall, *Embers of War*, 36.

9. Ron Radosh, "The Vietnam War Documentary: How Burns and Novick Fail to Portray Ho Chi Minh Accurately," PJ Media, October 10, 2017. https://pjmedia.com/ronradosh/2017/10/10/vietnam-war-documentary-burns-novick-fail-portray-ho-chi-minh-accurately/.

10. Logevall, *Embers of War*, 18–19.

11. Morris, "The Bad War."

12. Logevall, *Embers of War*, 19.

13. Ibid., 34–43.

14. Ibid., 48–49.

15. Ibid., 53–58.

16. Ibid., 78.

17. Milton J. Bates, et al., eds., *Reporting Vietnam Part Two: American Journalism 1969–1975* (New York: The Library of America, 1998), 772.

18. Logevall, *Embers of War*, 79–81.

19. Bates, et al., eds., *Reporting Vietnam*, 772.

20. Mark Moyar, *Triumph Forsaken: The Vietnam War, 1954–1965* (New York: Cambridge University Press, 2006), 16–19.

21. Logevall, *Embers*, 82-85, 100-101; R. Harris Smith, *OSS: The Secret History of America's First Intelligence Agency* (Los Angeles: University of California Press, 1972), 334.

22. Logevall, *Embers of War*, 104.

23. Moyar, *Triumph Forsaken*, 17.

24. Ibid., 1–2.

25. Logevall, *Embers of War*, 102.

26. Howard Zinn, *Vietnam: The Logic of Withdrawal* (Boston: Beacon Press, 1967), 81, 101.

27. "Ho Sees Vietnam Aided," *New York Times*, August 24, 1949, 15; "Aid by China's Reds to Vietminh Bared," *New York Times*, August 13, 1950, 1; "Vietminh Getting Arms, French Say," *New York Times*, December 19, 1954, 7.

28. Bates, et al., eds., *Reporting Vietnam*, 774-45.

29. Jonathan Leaf, *The Politically Incorrect Guide to the Sixties* (Washington, D.C.: Regnery, 2009), 186.

30. Zinn, *Vietnam*, 89, 101.

31. Lewis Sorley, *A Better War: The Unexamined Victories and Final Tragedy of America's Last Years in Vietnam* (New York: Harcourt Brace & Company, 1999), 275.

32. Zinn, *A People's History*, 471.

33. Ibid.

34. Dwight D. Eisenhower, The President's News Conference, April 7, 1954, http://www.presidency.ucsb.edu/ws/?pid=10202.

35. "250,000 Vietnamese Flee Reds, Far Exceeding Expected Exodus," *New York Times*, September 18, 1954, 1; Nguyen Duc Thanh, "To Aid the Vietnamese," letters to the *Times*, October 10, 1954, E10; "479,000 Quit North Vietnam," *New York Times*, November 7, 1954, 14.

36. Milton J. Bates, et al., eds., *Reporting Vietnam Part One: American Journalism 1959–1969* (New York: The Library of America, 1998), 780.

37. Norman Podhoretz, *Why We Were in Vietnam* (New York: Simon & Schuster, 1982), 55.

38. Zinn, *A People's History*, 472.

39. Ibid.

40. Oscar Handlin, "Arawaks" (review of *A People's History of the United States* by Howard Zinn), *American Scholar* 49: 4 (autumn 1980), 546, 548, 550.

41. Howard Zinn and Oscar Handlin, "Arawaks," *American Scholar*, 50: 3 (summer 1981), 431–32.

42. Podhoretz, *Why We Were in Vietnam*, 41.

43. Moyar, *Triumph Forsaken*, 30–31.

44. Logevall, *Embers of War*, 612–13.

45. Podhoretz, *Why We Were in Vietnam*, 42.

46. Zinn, *A People's History*, 472.

47. Ibid.

48. Moyar, *Triumph Forsaken*, 64–66.

49. Ibid., 231–32.

50. Podhoretz, *Why We Were in Vietnam*, 198.

51. James L. Tyson, "Land Reform in Vietnam: A Progress Report," *Asian Affairs: An American Review* 1: 1(1973), 32–41.

52. Moyar, *Triumph Forsaken*, xiv–xv.

53. Morris, "The Bad War."

54. Logevall, *Embers of War*, 107.

55. Ibid., 172.

56. Morris, "The Bad War."

57. Moyar, *Triumph Forsaken*, xiv.

58. Zinn, *A People's History*, 473.

59. Ibid.

60. Douglas Pike, *Viet Cong: The Organization and Techniques of the National Liberation Front of South Vietnam* (Cambridge, Massachusetts: Cambridge University Press, 1967), viii, 110.

61. Ibid., 110.

62. Zinn, *A People's History*, 473.

63. Pike, *Viet Cong*, 111.

64. Ibid., 120–22.

65. Ibid., 111.

66. Ibid., 130.

67. Ibid., 247.

68. Ibid., 248.

69. Ibid., xi–xii.

70. Mary Susannah Robbins, *Against the War: Writings by Activists* (New York: Rowman and Littlefield, 1999), 4–37.

71. Zinn, *A People's History*, 474.

72. Moyar, *Triumph Forsaken*, xvi.

73. Ibid., 216–17. See note 53 on page 216 and notes 54–55 on page 217.

74. Podhoretz, *Why We Were in Vietnam*, 203.

75. Moyar, *Triumph Forsaken*, 254–56.

76. Zinn, *A People's History*, 471.

77. Ibid.

78. "Statement of Policy by the National Security Council on United States Objectives and Courses of Action with Respect to Southeast Asia," Office of the Historian, Department of State, https://history.state.gov/historicaldocuments/frus1952-54v12p1/d36.

79. Zinn, *A People's History*, 472.

80. *The Pentagon Papers*, the Senator Gravel Edition, ed. by Howard Zinn and Noam Chomsky, vol. 1 (Beacon Press: Boston, 1971), 85.

81. Ibid.

82. Zinn, *A People's History*, 475.

83. U. Alexis Johnson, "The United States and Southeast Asia," Address Made Before the Economic Club of Detroit, April 8, 1963, Department of State Bulletin, April 29, 1963, 636. Reprinted in *The Pentagon Papers*, vol. 2, 817–18.

84. Zinn, *A People's History*, 475.

85. Lyndon B. Johnson, "Radio and Television Report to the American People Following Renewed Aggression in the Gulf of Tonkin," American Presidency Project, August 4, 1964, http://www.presidency. ucsb.edu/ws/?pid=26418.

86. Podhoretz, *Why We Were in Vietnam*, 71.

87. Moyar, *Triumph Forsaken*, 321.

88. Ibid., 322. See note 61.

89. Zinn, *A People's History*, 479.

90. Podhoretz, *Why We Were in Vietnam*, 187–88.

91. Ibid., 118–19.

92. Ibid., 184.

93. Zinn, *A People's History*, 480.

94. Handlin, "Arawaks."

95. Zinn and Handlin, "Arawaks.".

96. Morris, "The Bad War."

97. Ibid.; Sorley, *A Better War*, 14.

98. Larry Schweikart and Michael Allen, *A Patriot's History of the United States: From Columbus's Great Discovery to the War on Terror* (New York: Penguin, 2004), 694; Morris, "The Bad War".

99. Podhoretz, *Why We Were in Vietnam*, 116–17, 125.

100. Morris, "The Bad War"; Schweikart and Allen, *A Patriot's History*, 694–95.

101. Zinn, *A People's History*, 478.

102. Andrew R. Finlayson, "A Retrospective on Counterinsurgency Operations," Central Intelligence Agency, https://www.cia.gov/library/ center-for-the-study-of-intelligence/csi-publications/csi-studies/studies/ vol51no2/a-retrospective-on-counterinsurgency-operations.html#top.

103. Morris, "The Bad War."

104. Sorley, *A Better War*, 217–18.

105. Leaf, *The Politically Incorrect Guide to the Sixties*, 186.
106. William E. Colby, *Lost Victory: A Firsthand Account of America's Sixteen-Year Involvement in Vietnam* (New York: Contemporary Books, 1989), 320–25.
107. Robert Peter Hager, "Teaching Students about the Vietnam War: The Case for Balance," *Democracy and Security*, Vol. 13, No. 4, 304–35.
108. Leaf, *The Politically Incorrect Guide to the Sixties*, 186.
109. Ibid., 188.
110. Schweikart and Allen, *A Patriot's History*, 689–91.
111. Sorley, *A Better War*, 287–89.
112. Zinn, *A People's History*, 469.
113. Ibid., 485, 483.
114. Ibid., 486.
115. Ibid. 488–89.
116. "Around the Nation," *New York Times*, June 21, 1979, 14; Saundra Saperstein, "Viet Protester Surrenders," *Washington Post*, June 21, 1979; "Carl Schoettler, "Death of an Idealist, Proud Catonsville Nine Member Remembered," *Baltimore Sun*, July 14, 1995.
117. Zinn, *A People's History*, 490.
118. Ibid., 490–92.
119. Ibid., 490.
120. Leaf, *The Politically Incorrect Guide to the Sixties*, 16–17.
121. Zinn, *A People's History*, 492–93.
122. Michael S. Foley, *Confronting the War Machine: Draft Resistance During the Vietnam War* (Chapel Hill: The University of North Carolina Press, 2003), 96, 100.
123. Zinn, *A People's History*, 494–95.
124. Ibid., 495.
125. Swift Vets and POWs for Truth, "Swift Veterans Letter to John Kerry," May 4, 2004, http://www.swiftvets.com/article. php?story=20040629220813790.
126. Howard Zinn, letter to Alice Walker, April 19, 1966 or 1967, Alice Walker Papers, Stuart A. Rose Manuscript, Archives, and Rare Book Library, Emory University.
127. Zinn, *A People's History*, 497–98.

128. Philip Caputo, "Running Again—the Last Retreat," in Milton J. Bates, et al., eds., *Reporting Vietnam Part Two: American Journalism 1969–1975* (New York: The Library of America, 1998), 527–30.

129. Colby, *Lost Victory*, 6.

130. Leaf, *The Politically Incorrect Guide to the Sixties*, 183.

131. Morris, "The Bad War."

132. Sorley, *A Better War*, 383.

133. Zinn, *A People's History*, 498.

134. Mark Moyar, "A Warped Mirror," *City Journal*, October 20, 2017, https://www.city-journal.org/html/warped-mirror-15531.html.

135. Zinn, *A People's History*, 501.

136. *Sir! No Sir!* Zinn Education Project, https://www.zinnedproject.org/materials/sir-no-sir/; *The Most Dangerous Man in America*, Zinn Education Project; Howard Zinn, adapted by Rebecca Stefoff, *A Young People's History of the United States* (New York: Seven Stories Press, 2009), 304.

137. John M. Dunn, *The Vietnam War: A History of U.S. Involvement* (San Diego: Lucent Books, 2001), 15.

Chapter Nine: Howard Zinn, the Founders, and Us

1. Howard Zinn, *A People's History of the United States* (New York: HarperCollins, 2003), 77.

2. Ibid., 79.

3. Ibid., 83.

4. Ibid., 77.

5. Ibid., 81.

6. Ibid., 84.

7. Ibid., 80.

8. Ibid., 84.

9. Samuel H. Beer, ed. *The Communist Manifesto* by Karl Marx and Friedrich Engels (Harvard University Press, 1955), 26, 31.

10. Stanley Lebergott, *The Americans: An Economic Record* (New York: Norton & Company, 1984), 26–27.

11. Ibid.

12. Ibid., 11.

13. Ibid., 30.

14. Ibid., 45–46.

15. Ibid., 54.

16. Zinn, *A People's History*, 90.

17. Ibid., 90–91.

18. Ibid., 98–99.

19. Forrest McDonald, *Recovering the Past: A Historian's Memoir* (Lawrence: The University of Kansas Press, 2004), 68–74.

20. Beer, ed., *The Communist Manifesto*, ix.

21. Ibid., 5.

22. Andrew G. Gardner, "How Did Washington Make His Millions?" *CW Journal*, winter 2013, http://www.history.org/Foundation/journal/winter13/washington.cfm.

23. David McCullough, *1776* (New York: Simon & Schuster, 2005), 47, 48.

24. Lebergott, 54–55.

25. Gordon Wood, *The American Revolution: A History* (New York: Random House, 2002), 59.

26. Ibid.

27. Ibid., 23, 28, 37–38, 31–32.

28. Ibid., 51.

29. Ibid., 61.

30. Jason Willick, "Polarization Is an Old American Story," *Wall Street Journal*, February 2, 2018, https://www.wsj.com/articles/polarization-is-an-old-american-story-1517613751.

31. Howard Zinn, interviewed by Robert Birnbaum, "Howard Zinn on *A People's History of American Empire*," *Identity Theory*, October 1, 2008.

32. Wood, *The American Revolution*, 93.

33. Zinn, *A People's History*, 96.

34. Beer, ed., *The Communist Manifesto*, 29, 32.

35. Ibid., xxv.

36. William Z. Foster, *Outline Political History of the Americas* (International Publishers, 1951), 130; like Zinn, Foster selectively quotes and spins from Morison and Commager's textbook.

37. Howard Zinn, "The Uses of Scholarship," originally published as "The Case for Radical Change," in *Saturday Review*, October 18, 1969, republished in *On History* (New York: Seven Stories Press, 2001), 177–88.

38. Beer, ed., *The Communist Manifesto,* 46.
39. John Hinderaker, "Mitch Daniels, Hero (with Comment from Steve)," Powerline, July 17, 2013, https://www.powerlineblog.com/archives/2013/07/mitch-daniels-hero.php.
40. "An Open Letter to Mitch Daniels from 90 Purdue Professors," Academe Blog, July 23, 2013, https://academeblog.org/2013/07/23/an-open-letter-to-mitch-daniels-from-90-purdue-professors/.
41. Sam Wineburg, "Undue Certainty: Where Howard Zinn's *A People's History* Falls Short," *American Educator* Winter 2012/2013, 27–34.
42. Jennifer Schuessler, "Historians Defend Howard Zinn against a Former Governor's Critique," *New York Times*, July 29, 2013, https://artsbeat.blogs.nytimes.com/2013/07/29/historians-defend-howard-zinn-against-a-former-governors-critique/?_r=1.
43. Michael Kazin, "Howard Zinn's History Lessons," *Dissent*, Spring 2004, https://www.dissentmagazine.org/article/howard-zinns-history-lessons.
44. Michael Kazin, "What Mitch Daniels Doesn't Know about History," Academe Blog, July 18, 2017, https://academeblog.org/2013/07/18/what-mitch-daniels-doesnt-know-about-history/.
45. Robert Paquette, "Mitch Daniels Unmasks Howard Zinn's Propagandizing," See Thru Edu. August 5, 2013, http://www.seethruedu.com/updatesmitch-daniels-unmasks-howard-zinns-propagandizing/.
46. "AHA Releases Statement," Perspectives on History, July 19, 2013, https://www.historians.org/publications-and-directories/perspectives-on-history/summer-2013/aha-releases-statement; "OAH Responds to Recent Concerns of Academic Freedom," July 25, 2013, http://www.oah.org/programs/news/oah-responds-to-recent-concerns-of-academic-freedom/.
47. Indiana Academe: Newsletter of the Indiana Conference of the American Association of University Professors, http://www.inaaup.org/newsletters/AAUP_NewsletterF13.pdf.
48. "Howard Zinn 'Read In' at Purdue Draws a Crowd," *USA Today*, November 6, 2013, http://www.usatoday.com/story/news/nation/2013/11/06/howard-zinn-read-in-mitch-daniels/3460615/.

49. Max Brantley, "Bill Introduced to Ban Howard Zinn Books from Arkansas Public Schools," *Arkansas Times*, March 2, 2017, http://www.arktimes.com/ArkansasBlog/archives/2017/03/02/bill-introduced-to-ban-howard-zinn-books-from-arkansas-public-schools.

50. "Hundreds of Arkansas Teachers Request Howard Zinn's *A People's History*, Zinn Education Project, March 16, 2017, https://www.zinnedproject.org/news/arkansas-teachers-want-teach-peoples-history/.

51. Oscar Handlin, *Truth in History* (Cambridge, Massachusetts: Harvard University Press, 1979), 4–5.

52. Author interview of Eugene Genovese, September 1, 2010, Atlanta, Georgia.

53. David Greenberg, "Agit-Prof: Howard Zinn's Influential Mutilations of American History," *The New Republic*, March 19, 3013, https://newrepublic.com/article/112574/howard-zinns-influential-mutilations-american-history.

54. Bill Bigelow, "The People vs. Columbus, et al.," *A People's History for the Classroom* (the Zinn Education Project, 2008), 21–23.

INDEX

A

abolitionists, 49, 92, 109–110. *See also* abolitionist movement

abolitionist movement, 92. *See also* abolitionists

Accuracy in Academia, xxv

ACLU, 53, 127, 155

ACORN, 59

Advanced Placement (AP) exams, xix, xxxii

Affleck, Ben, xxii

African Americans, xxxv, 116, 132–33, 167, 169–70, 173, 177, 179, 182, 186–88, 191, 194, 197

Age of Discovery, 63

agriculture, 7, 76, 86, 90–91

Allen, Michael, xii, 119–20, 228, 231

Allies, the, xviii, 114–15, 129, 132–34, 153, 207

Ambrose, Stephen, xx–xxii, 261

American Association of University Professors (AAUP), 48–50, 253

American Educator, xxiv, 254

American founding, 242, 251

American Historical Association (AHA), xxi, xxxvii–xxxviii

American Historical Review, 23, 49

American history, ii, xi–xiv, xxii, xxiv, xxvii, xxxi, 4, 10, 27, 29–30, 34, 36, 53, 56, 61, 73, 86, 89, 114, 129, 148, 170, 196, 250, 253, 261

American Labor Party (ALP), 39, 42

American Revolution, 5, 15, 35, 91, 99, 241, 249, 257. *See also* Revolutionary War

American Textbook Council, xxii

anarchism, 56

anti-Communism, 157, 174

Antifa, 1

anti-Semitism, 116, 121

Arawaks, xiii, xxxii, 4, 6–7, 10, 12, 17, 21, 24–25, 29, 33, 61, 63, 69–70, 250. *See also* Taino

Arnove, Anthony, xxvii, 256

Asada, Sadao, 137–38

Atlanta University, 45–46, 50

Auschwitz, 64, 127, 134–35

Axis powers, 129

Aztecs, 63–64

B

Bailey, Thomas, 27, 114, 118, 120

Baker, Ella, 47, 179

Barton, David, xxv, 256

Beard, Charles, 245–47, 251

Bellesiles, Michael, xx–xxii, xxxvii

Bennett, Martellus, xxvii

Bentley, Elizabeth, 151

Berle, Adolf, 159–60